Warping and Morphing
of Graphical Objects

The Morgan Kaufmann Series in Computer Graphics and Geometric Modeling
Series Editor, Brian A. Barsky

Warping and Morphing of Graphical Objects
Jonas Gomes, Lucia Darsa, Bruno Costa, Luiz Velho

Jim Blinn's Corner: Dirty Pixels
Jim Blinn

Rendering with Radiance: The Art and Science of Lighting Visualization
Greg Ward Larson and Rob Shakespeare

Introduction to Implicit Surfaces
Edited by Jules Bloomenthal

Wavelets for Computer Graphics: Theory and Applications
Eric J. Stollnitz, Tony D. DeRose, and David H. Salesin

Jim Blinn's Corner: A Trip Down the Graphics Pipeline
Jim Blinn

Interactive Curves and Surfaces: A Multimedia Tutorial on CAGD
Alyn Rockwood and Peter Chambers

Principles of Digital Image Synthesis
Andrew S. Glassner

Radiosity & Global Illumination
François X. Sillion and Claude Puech

Knotty: A B-Spline Visualization Program
Jonathan Yen

User Interface Management Systems: Models and Algorithms
Dan R. Olsen, Jr.

Making Them Move: Mechanics, Control, and Animation of Articulated Figures
Edited by Norman I. Badler, Brian A. Barsky, and David Zeltzer

Geometric and Solid Modeling: An Introduction
Christoph M. Hoffmann

An Introduction to Splines for Use in Computer Graphics and Geometric Modeling
Richard H. Bartels, John C. Beatty, and Brian A. Barsky

Warping and Morphing of Graphical Objects

Jonas Gomes
Lucia Darsa
Bruno Costa
Luiz Velho

Morgan Kaufmann Publishers, Inc.
San Francisco, California

Senior Editor   Diane D. Cerra
Director of Production & Manufacturing   Yonie Overton
Assistant Production Manager   Julie Pabst
Production Editor   Edward Wade
Cover Design   Ross Carron Design
Text Design, Illustration, and Composition   Windfall Software
Copyeditor   Gary Morris
Proofreader   Ken DellaPenta
Indexer   Bruce Tracy
Printer   Courier Corporation

Designations used by companies to distinguish their products are often claimed as trademarks or registered trademarks. In all instances where Morgan Kaufmann Publishers, Inc. is aware of a claim, the product names appear in initial capital or all capital letters. Readers, however, should contact the appropriate companies for more complete information regarding trademarks and registration.

Morgan Kaufmann Publishers, Inc.
Editorial and Sales Office
340 Pine Street, Sixth Floor
San Francisco, CA 94104-3205
USA
Telephone   415/392-2665
Facsimile   415/982-2665
Email   *mkp@mkp.com*
WWW   *http://www.mkp.com*
Order toll free   800/745-7323

Library of Congress Cataloging-in-Publication Data

Warping and morphing of graphical objects / Jonas Gomes . . . [et al.].
   p.   cm.
   Includes bibliographical references and index.
   ISBN 1-55860-464-2
   1. Computer graphics.   2. Morphing (Computer animation)
   I. Gomes, Jonas.
   T385.W376   1999
   006.6'96--DC21   98-36677
                                                                          CIP

The idea of a duality such as air and water can be expressed in a picture by starting from a plane-filling design of birds and fish; the birds are "water" for the fish, and the fish are "air" for the birds. Heaven and Hell can be symbolized by an interplay of angels and devils. There are many other possible pairs of dynamic subjects—at least in theory, for in most cases, their realization meets with insuperable difficulties.

—M. C. Escher

Contents

19 Warping and Morphing of Surfaces   371

20 Warping and Morphing of Volumetric Objects   401

21 The Morphos System   429

Figure Credits

The following figures are reprinted, by permission, from the ACM: 1.1, 1.10, 1.12, 1.18, 1.19, 2.9, 4.37, 4.4, 4.5, 4.23, 4.26, 5.1, 5.2, 5.3, 6.7, 8.2, 8.3, 9.5, 12.7, 12.11, 14.24, 14.29, 14.30, 16.11, 16.24, 17.22, 19.16, 20.4, 20.15, 20.18, and 20.19. © Association for Computing Machinery, Inc.

Figure 1.2 reprinted, by permission, from Encyclopedia Brittanica Educational Corporation.

Figure 4.2 reprinted, by permission, from Harmony Books.

Figures 1.4, 1.5, 17.25, and 17.26 are reprinted, by permission, from Cambridge University Press.

Figure 1.6 reprinted, by permission, from Hastings House.

Figure 1.7 reprinted from *Limite: Filme de Mario Peixoto*, Saulo Pereira de Mello, INELIVRO/FUNARTE-MEC, Rio de Janeiro, Brasil, ©1979 FUNARTE-MEC.

Figure 1.8 © 1941 MGM-UA.

The following figures are reprinted, by permission, from the IEEE: 1.13, 1.17, 3.35, 3.36, 17.20, 20.16. © IEEE.

The following figures are reprinted, by permission, from Springer-Verlag: 3.5, 9.7, 10.7, 10.8, 13.7, and 17.38.

Figures 3.32 and 3.33 are reprinted, by permission, from Academic Press.

Figures 4.7, 19.25, and 19.26 are reprinted, by permission, from CHCCS. © Canadian Human-Computer Communications Society.

Figures 7.1, 7.2, 10.11, and 13.1 are reprinted, by permission, from Paul Heckbert.

Figures 13.8 and 20.8 are reprinted, by permission, from Siome K. Goldstein.

Figure 16.7 reprinted, by permission, from Adam Piro.

Figure 18.8 reprinted, by permission, from Tom Brigham. © 1983 Tom Brigham/NYIT-CGL.

Figures 12.10, 19.18, 19.21, 19.22, and 21.10 are reprinted, by permission, from Sergio E.M.L. Pinheiro.

Figures 19.23 and 19.24 are reprinted, by permission, from Elsevier Science Publishers.

Preface

Warping and morphing are the core of fundamental operations in computer graphics. The camera transformation is a projective warping; some important interactive modeling techniques are achieved with the use of warping and morphing; also, computer animation is essentially a sequence of warped and morphed objects. Warping of plane curves constitutes an important tool for 2D cartoon animation and also finds several applications in the area of digital publishing; surface and solid warping is a basic tool in geometric and solid modeling, as well as in 3D animation; warping and morphing of images and volumetric objects are widely used in different applications, ranging from the area of medical images to the special-effects arena in the entertainment industry.

Because warping and morphing are intrinsic to the foundations of computer graphics, they will always be trendy. They will evolve, as the field develops, incorporating the latest advances from research and making possible innovative applications. As an example of this fact, we mention the newest research area of image-based rendering. The techniques from this area employ results that have been developed for warping and morphing. For this reason, we considered it timely and appropriate to include a chapter on this subject in the book.

From this perspective, writing a book about warping and morphing is an ambitious endeavor. In fact, studying the different aspects of warping and morphing entails a journey deep into the realm of computer graphics. We have tried to accomplish this task by carefully using an integrated approach:

- The plethora of different elements that can be warped or morphed are encompassed in the concept of a *graphical object*.
- The rich environment of different warping and morphing techniques is unified using the concept of *transformation of graphical objects*.

Thus, graphical objects and transformations play the two major roles in the book. In our analysis of these subjects, we tried to reconcile the conceptual and computational aspects of their use in a warping and morphing environment.

We have been working on this book for the last four years. While writing it, we developed a system architecture for warping and morphing. This architecture has been implemented in *Morphos*, a complete morphing system included with full source code exclusively in the companion CD-ROM. A description of the system and its architecture is also included as a chapter of the book. This approach enabled us to avoid the inclusion of pseudocode: the book contains a conceptual description of the different warping and morphing algorithms, as well as the computational techniques involved. The implementation details are in the CD-ROM as part of the C++ source code and the documentation therein. This separation is a good compromise to satisfy readers more interested in concepts as well as those more concerned with implementation issues.

Very preliminary versions of this book have appeared as course notes for two courses in SIGGRAPH '95 and '97. Also, the authors have taught courses based on the material covered by the book in the Brazilian Mathematical Colloquium, held in Rio de Janeiro in 1995, and in the Brazilian Symposium on Computer Graphics and Image Processing, held in São Carlos in 1996. We have also used parts of the book on seminars and short courses at IMPA, Rio de Janeiro. Certainly the book, or parts of it, can be used as a graduate- or advanced undergraduate-level textbook for a graphics course on warping and morphing.

We would like to acknowledge the collaboration of Thad Beier, John Berton, and George Wolberg, who joined us as speakers in the two SIG-GRAPH courses. We are grateful to the many reviewers who gave us very useful feedback about the book's contents—those from the different scientific meetings where we have taught courses on warping and morphing, and those who reviewed a preliminary version of the book for Morgan Kaufmann.

Brian Barsky was of great help in publishing the book with Morgan Kaufmann. Conversations with Mike Morgan, and the working meetings with Diane Cerra, were quite pleasant and stimulating. Special thanks to Edward Wade, production editor at Morgan Kaufmann, whose efforts and cooperation were very important in bringing the book to its final form. We wish to thank our fellow coworkers at the Computer Graphics Lab at IMPA for helping us build a productive research environment. Some of us would also like to thank our current employers, Microsoft and Equator, for their encouragement while we put the finishing touches on the book. Finally, we would like to thank our families for their support and patience with our sometimes frantic schedules.

We would like this book to be an acknowledgement of the work of the many investigators who contributed to the development of the area of warping and morphing.

PART

I Basic Concepts

This first part of the book gives a broad overview of the warping and morphing of graphical objects. We cover both conceptual and practical aspects of this subject, providing several examples.

The material covered here is of great help in understanding the other parts of the book. This part could be used separately in a short course on warping and morphing of graphical objects, or as part of a regular undergraduate computer graphics course.

1

Introduction

THIS BOOK INVESTIGATES WARPING AND MORPHING in computer graphics. The subject has received a lot of attention in recent years from both academia and the industry. On the academic side, research work has addressed most of the basic problems quite effectively. On the industry side, applications software has been developed, incorporating warping and morphing techniques successfully in various areas.

Warping and morphing are important graphical operations, with applications in many areas, that are used to transform graphical objects. Warping deforms a single object. Morphing interpolates between two objects. These transformations can be applied to the various types of graphical objects, such as 2D drawings, images, surfaces, and volumes.

Today, we can say that the field has reached a state of maturity and is ready for a broad conceptualization, the development of which is one of the goals of the book. We hope that our effort will help consolidate the understanding of the current state of the area and provide a solid basis for further research.

The conceptual framework in this book presents a unifying view of warping and morphing based on the notions of graphical objects and their transformations. These notions make possible a uniform treatment of the basic problems. In addition, the problem of specification and computation of warping and morphing transformations is examined, and several practical examples are given. Finally, warping and morphing techniques are described, and their applicability to different types of graphical objects is discussed.

1.1   Metamorphosis

The word *metamorphosis* has its origins in the Greek *metamorphoun*.[1] The common meaning of the word is *a change in form or nature* [Webster, 1989]. In this section we will give several examples of metamorphosis.

1.1.1   Changes in the Physical World

Objects in the real world undergo constant changes. This dynamic is inherent in Nature. Living beings are born, grow, and die. Their bodies change as the result of complex genetic mechanisms.

Growth processes generate internal forces that make organisms develop. As a consequence, their shape and appearance are modified. The transformations induced by these mechanisms are very complex. Simple forms gradually evolve into highly intricate configurations. They start as amorphous blobs of matter and reach a definite form with the creation of distinctive parts and traits.

A typical example is a plant: a single seed grows into a complete tree, with stems, leaves, and so on. Figure 1.1 shows some stages of a synthesized simulation of the evolution of a plant.

The sequence of illustrations in Figure 1.2 shows a metamorphosis from an aquatic tadpole to a terrestrial adult frog.

Inanimate things may also have their shape or appearance changed under the action of external forces. These forces include environmental phenomena, such as wind, rain, and lightning, as well as other processes, such as mechanical impact, combustion reactions, and so on. Figure 1.3 shows the deformation of a tube that was bent over another tube.

Depending on the material properties of the object, some deformations may be permanent and others temporary. This classifies deformations as *elastic* and *inelastic*.

An important characteristic of the shape transformations discussed above is that, with very few exceptions, they are *continuous* deformations. However, we should point out that noncontinuous deformations are also present in Nature. Several examples could be given, such as material fracture, explosions, and so on.

---

1. Meta (involving change) and morphoun (form).

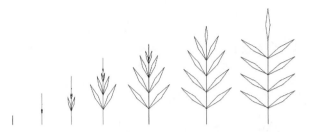

Figure 1.1 Plant growing [from Prusinkiewicz et al., 1993].

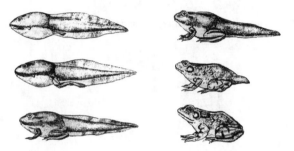

Figure 1.2 Frog metamorphosis [from *Encyclopedia Brittanica*, 1973].

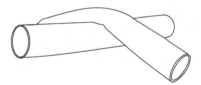

Figure 1.3 Deformation of a tube.

1.1.2 Analysis of Shapes

The theory of transformations can be used in the comparison of related forms and in the study of shape evolution.

A powerful method to analyze the correlation between shapes of the same class is to consider the transformations required to deform one shape into the other. In this way, it is possible to classify the members of a given family based on a few parameters, such as the amount of deformation from a base shape.

Figure 1.4 shows leaves of different types and indicates the transformation that relates them. Transformations can also be used to study the evolution

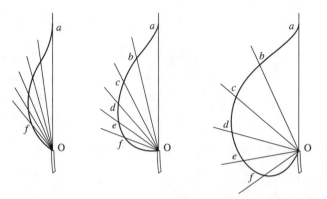

Figure 1.4   Shapes of the same class under a transformation [from Thompson, 1961].

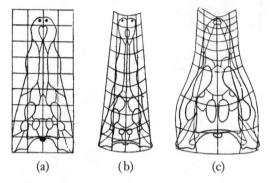

(a)   (b)   (c)

Figure 1.5   Three stages of the evolution of the crocodile: contemporary (a), and two from earlier periods (b) and (c) [from Thompson, 1961].

of forms. For example, as a species develops, it goes through a succession of transitional forms in a metamorphosis process.

Figure 1.5 shows three stages of the evolution of the crocodile. Figure 1.5(a) compares the skull of a contemporary crocodile with those of two other crocodiles from earlier historical periods, as shown in Figures 1.5(b) and 1.5(c).

1.1.3 Images and Illusion

Images are pictorial representations over a 2D support. They can depict bidimensional shapes, such as in a drawing, or even the projection of 3D objects, such as in a photograph. In both cases, images give the illusion of being the actual objects that they represent.

Figure 1.6 Image distortion using an analog device [Smith, 1974].

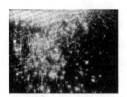

Figure 1.7 Cross-dissolve from the film *Limite*.

When a sequence of images is exhibited in rapid succession, it produces the illusion of movement, which is called *animation*. This is the basic principle of film and television.

Photographic images can be distorted in many ways through the use of optical devices and projections. Video images can also be distorted using electronic analog devices. If an increasing amount of distortion is applied to a base image, it is possible to generate animated sequences that produce the impression of continuous deformation.

Figure 1.6 shows the distortion of an image using an analog electronic device.

Two images can be combined by mixing color information. In this process, first the images are superimposed and then their color values are blended. When the proportions of the mixture between images A and B change continuously from 100% of A and 0% of B to 0% of A and 100% of B, then a smooth transition from A to B is achieved. This visual effect is known as *cross-dissolve*. It is an expressive resource that has been incorporated in the language of film with different purposes, including indicating a transition or a metamorphosis. When the images represent very different objects, the cross-dissolve indicates the passage of time or space. This is illustrated by the sequence in Figure 1.7, showing a cross-dissolve effect from the film *Limite* by the Brazilian filmmaker Mario Peixoto.

Figure 1.8 Transmutation scene from the film *Dr. Jekyll and Mr. Hyde.*

When the objects represented are similar, the cross-dissolve usually indicates a transformation between them. This technique has been used for decades by the film and video industry to attain metamorphosis effects between two objects with related shapes, represented by two different images. The effect is illustrated in Figure 1.8, which shows a transmutation sequence from the famous 1941 version of *Dr. Jekyll and Mr. Hyde.*

1.2 Uses of Shape Transformations

Shape transformations have many uses in applications that deal with animation, modeling, and analysis of forms.

1.2.1 Animation

The fact that shape transformations are continuous makes them ideally suited to applications dealing with time-varying phenomena.

We can define a continuous shape deformation and make the parameter of the transformation dependent on a time variable. A simple example is an animation that incorporates stretch and squash using nonuniform scaling [Lasseter, 1987]. Figure 1.9 shows a few frames of the animation of a ball bouncing on the ground enhanced by a stretch-and-squash effect.

Another way to use shape transformations for animation is to interpolate the shape of two objects. This technique is common in traditional animation. It consists first of creating a sequence of *key-frames* depicting the main events of a scene. These key-frames contain important transition elements of the motion and convey the action that is taking place in the scene. Afterwards, the intermediate frames, or the *in-betweens*, are generated by interpolating

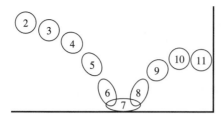

Figure 1.9   Stretch and squash in bouncing ball.

Figure 1.10   Key-framing using shape interpolation [from Sederberg et al., 1992].

the key-frames. In a computer animation system, the intermediate frames can be computed using shape transformation techniques. For this, it is necessary to specify the initial and final shapes and a correspondence between them.

In Figure 1.10 an animated sequence of a cantering horse is shown. The first and last frames are given, and the intermediate frames are computed using shape interpolation.

1.2.2 Shape Modeling

Shape transformations can be used in various ways for modeling purposes. In fact, deformations constitute the basis of powerful operators that modify the shape of objects. A pioneering example of the use of deformations as a shape-modeling operator appeared in [Barr, 1984]. In this work, the nonlinear transformations of *taper*, *bend*, and *twist* are discussed, and rather complex objects are modeled by the deformation of simple primitive objects. Figure 1.11 shows the action of the operators taper, twist, and bend on a cube.

Figure 1.12 shows a rather complex chair constructed from simple geometric primitives using the bend operator.

Figure 1.11   A cube deformed by taper, twist, and bend.

Figure 1.12   A chair constructed using deformation of basic shapes [from Barr, 1984].

Families of Shapes

Shape interpolation makes it possible to create a continuous family of shapes with desired features. If a set of shapes with distinct formal characteristics are defined, we can generate a shape that blends these characteristics in any proportion using interpolation.

Figure 1.13 shows an example of a family of shapes generated by interpolating two bottles with different styles.

Another example of the use of interpolation to construct a family of shapes is the *multiple master* font technology developed by Adobe Systems for digital typography. In this case, a new font design is created by interpolating an existing master font. This is illustrated in Figure 1.14. The word *Morphing* written in the second and third lines uses a font obtained from the font of the first line (Tekton) by interpolating the parameters of *width* and *weight*.

1.2.3   Geometric Correction

Suppose we have an image capture device such as a video camera or a scanner. We can use image transformations to correct geometric distortions that might occur in the image capture process. We use a pattern image, such as the one

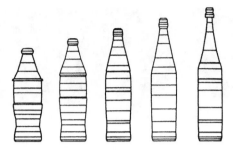

Figure 1.13   Shape family of bottles [from Chen and Parent, 1989].

Morphing

Morphing

Morphing

Figure 1.14   Generation of new fonts by deformation.

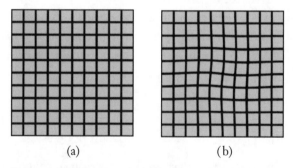

(a)   (b)

Figure 1.15   Geometric calibration of an image capture system: pattern image (a) and distorted pattern (b).

shown in Figure 1.15(a), and we obtain the captured image with the distorted pattern as in Figure 1.15(b). Now we apply a deformation T to the distorted image in order to obtain an image similar to the original pattern image. This transformation T can be applied to any captured image to correct for the distortions.

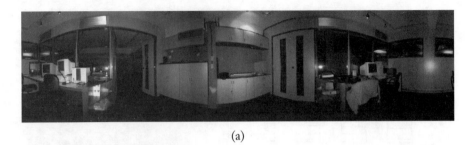

(a)

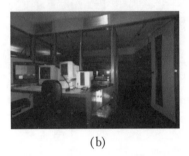

(b)

Figure 1.16 Warping of a panoramic image. The full panoramic image (a) and part of the image warped (b).

This geometric calibration process can be used to correct images captured with fish-eye lenses, microscopes, and so on.

Geometric corrections of captured images are used extensively in image-based rendering and vision-modeling systems. In a *virtual panorama system*, such as Apple Quicktime VR, we have to warp the image in order to map it correctly onto the enclosing panorama surface. This is illustrated in Figure 1.16.

1.2.4 Fitting and Matching

Transformations can be used for analysis and correction of shapes. In particular, they may be employed in solving the problem of shape recognition. In this type of application, the goal is to match a given shape to a template. One way to do that is by computing the amount of deformation necessary to align some features of the shape with each element from a set of templates. The best match is the one that requires the least amount of deformation.

Figure 1.17 shows a template, a set of shapes, and the correspondence between the template and each shape under a deformation.

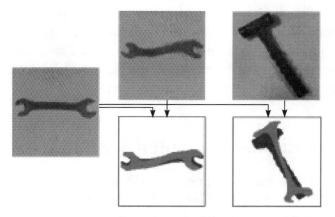

Figure 1.17   Shape recognition using deformations [from Sclaroff and Pentland, 1994].

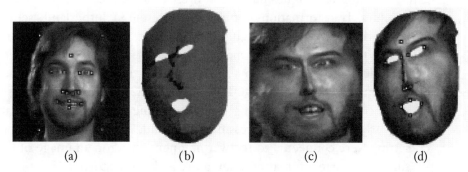

(a)   (b)   (c)   (d)

Figure 1.18   Texture registration: original face (a), 3D mask (b), deformed face (c), and textured mask (d) [from Litwinowicz and Miller, 1994]. See also color plate 1.18.

Shape interpolation may be employed to fit the shape of one object to another. In this way, it is possible to establish a connection between two related objects, making their attributes mutually compatible. One example of shape fitting is the registration of a satellite photograph to a corresponding elevation data set. The image must be distorted to be in perfect alignment with the surface, so that it can be used as a texture map for the terrain model.

Figures 1.18(a) and (b) show, respectively, the image of a face and a geometric model of a mask. In Figure 1.18(c) we warp the face image so that the face features (eyes, mouth, and so on) match those of the mask. In Figure 1.18(d) the distorted face is texture-mapped onto the surface mask.

In the area of medical images, registration is widely used as a means to search and compare images. Warping techniques are used in order to obtain nonrigid registration between some template image and a given image, called the *study image*. For more information about this topic, the reader should consult [Bajcsy and Kovacic, 1989] or [Christensen, 1994].

1.3 Metamorphosis and Computer Graphics

The previous sections clearly demonstrate the widespread use of warping and morphing, as well as the multitude of potential applications of these techniques. In the computer graphics literature, metamorphosis has appeared bearing different names. The most common are *shape blending, shape averaging, shape interpolation*, and *shape evolution*.

Warping techniques have been present since the early days of computer graphics. Transformations of objects are present in Sutherland's seminal work [Sutherland, 1963]. Bézier and Coons patches [Bézier, 1978; Coons, 1974] enable the construction of models that are easily deformable. The area of procedural modeling presents a very fertile setting for object metamorphosis. Early manifestations include [Kawaguchi, 1982] (see Figure 1.19).

The use of image warping to correct camera distortions also dates from the early days of image processing [Rosenfeld, 1969]. The applications in this setting were connected to the warping performed on an image of the earth's surface to correct for surface curvature and lens distortion.

Texture mapping, introduced by Ed Catmull [Catmull, 1974] is in fact the first manifestation of image warping in computer graphics. Later on, in [Catmull and Smith, 1980], Ed Catmull and Alvy Ray Smith discussed the problem of texture mapping and image warping for several interesting transformations, including projective transformations.

Fast and clever implementation of projective warping enabled an implementation in hardware to be used for special effects in the video and television industry (AMPEX ADO). Later, similar results were developed to obtain, in real time, a texture mapping of an image onto an arbitrary shape (Quantel Mirage).

The pioneering work in computer graphics in the use of metamorphosis transformations was done by Tom Brigham at NYIT in the late '70s. The interest of the graphics community in metamorphosis techniques exploded with the impact caused by the use of morphing transformations to produce

Figure 1.19   Procedural modeling [from Kawaguchi, 1982].

metamorphosis in the 1988 movie *Willow* and in Michael Jackson's video clip *Black or White*, produced by Pacific Data Images in 1990.

1.4 Conceptual Framework

Until recently, the research on shape deformation and metamorphosis has taken a pragmatic approach that led to a somewhat artificial classification of techniques according to object types. Moreover, a diverse treatment has been given to the transformations for different objects: images, drawings, surfaces, and volumes. The techniques available in the literature were developed for objects of a certain dimension represented in a particular way. As a consequence, they may reflect a narrow conceptual vision of the problem.

In the examples given previously, we see different types of objects being transformed:

- 3D-shape deformation on the cube in Figure 1.11
- drawing deformation of the horses in Figure 1.10
- image deformation in Figure 1.18
- color interpolation in Figure 1.7
- shape metamorphosis in the sequence of bottles in Figure 1.13

The above problems seem to be very distinct; how can we obtain a unified view of them? This book attempts to demonstrate that all these problems share a common conceptualization that will be generalized for abstract *n*-dimensional graphical objects, regardless of their representation. This integrated view will show that, despite a few inherent idiosyncrasies, some of the existing techniques and solutions to most of these problems can be extended to the others, revealing new connections between them.

The framework is based on two unifying concepts: *graphical objects* and *transformations* of graphical objects.

The concept of a graphical object allows us to establish an abstraction that encompasses all types of graphical entities. The concept of transformation allows us to study in a uniform way the different classes of operators that modify the geometry and the properties of graphical objects.

It is our purpose to define precisely the concept of a graphical object and devise means to construct and represent them on the computer. Analogously, we need to define transformations between graphical objects and devise techniques to specify and represent them on the computer. To do so we will introduce some abstraction paradigms that simplify the study of graphical objects and their transformations.

1.5   Paradigm of the Universes

In order to develop a conceptualization to study the problems of warping and morphing of graphical objects, we will employ the paradigm of the four universes. This paradigm is a methodology for studying problems in computational applied mathematics. It was first introduced by Ari Requicha [Requicha, 1980] in the context of geometric modeling and subsequently extended for different areas of computer graphics in [Gomes and Velho, 1995].

1.5.1   Understanding an Area

Problems in computer graphics, such as warping and morphing, are conveniently modeled, and solved, using methods from different areas of mathematics. The diversified nature of the involved models calls for some unifying paradigm that enables us to address the problems at the appropriate level of abstraction.

These abstraction levels isolate conceptual characteristics intrinsically attached to the different objects and phenomena. This allows us to search for the right mathematical tools to tackle problems in each level. Once we know these tools, more specific problems can be posed, probably associated to lower abstraction levels.

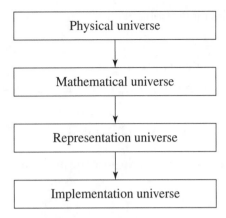

Figure 1.20 Levels of abstraction.

1.5.2 Levels of Abstraction

Real-world objects are associated to an abstraction level called the *physical universe*. The mathematical objects describing elements of the real world belong to the abstraction level called the *mathematical universe*, denoted by M. The elements of M are represented in the computer using a finite symbolic description that is associated to a third abstraction level called the *representation universe*, denoted by R. Finally, the symbolic descriptions in R are implemented in a computational system by mapping the finite descriptions from the representation universe into specific data structures from another abstraction level, the *implementation universe*.

Figure 1.20 shows a diagram illustrating the conceptual framework, with these four abstraction levels.

These four levels of abstraction encapsulate common properties of the objects being studied and allow a global, conceptual view of the methods and techniques involved.

1.5.3 Conceptual Problems

Once the correct abstraction levels are established for an area, it is possible to have a global, conceptual view of the important problems of the area. They can be understood and formulated without taking into account technical details of the specific mathematical models used. The hierarchy of abstractions makes it possible to search, in a systematic way, for proper mathematical tools to pose and solve specific problems. The main problems that can be posed using the universes paradigm are

1. defining the elements of the mathematical universe M;
2. defining operations on the elements of the mathematical universe M;
3. constructing representation schemes for the elements of M; and
4. devising appropriate data structures and implementation techniques.

In order to use the above paradigm to properly pose the problem of warping and morphing, we will need to

- define precisely a graphical object in the mathematical universe;
- define the operations of morphing and warping of graphical objects;
- devise representation schemes for the specification of graphical objects and their transformations; and
- devise an implementation framework in order to allow a numerical computation of graphical objects transformations.

1.6 Structure of the Book

The structure of the book reflects the conceptual approach described in the previous section, covering the following topics:

- graphical objects: their specification, representation, and implementation
- transformations of graphical objects: their representation, specification, and implementation
- warping and morphing of graphical objects
- warping and morphing of common graphical objects such as images, surfaces, drawings, and volumes.

The book is divided in four parts. Part I introduces the basic concepts and gives an overview of the area of warping and morphing. Part II discusses details about graphical objects, description, representation, and reconstruction. Part III details transformations of graphical objects, their description (specification), representation, and computation. Part IV uses the materials from Parts II and III to study, in depth, warping and morphing of specific classes of graphical objects: curves, surfaces, images, and volume data.

1.7 Comments and References

A classical book concerning shape, forms, and their evolution is [Thompson, 1961]. This is a very informative and well-illustrated book. A more recent work, [Koenderink, 1990], also has very interesting and rich discussions about shape.

For more details on the four levels of abstraction paradigm, the reader should consult [Gomes and Velho, 1995].

References

Bajcsy, R., and S. Kovacic. 1989. Multiresolution Elastic Matching. *Computer Vision, Graphics and Image Processing*, **46**, 1–21.

Barr, A. H. 1984. Global and Local Deformations of Solid Primitives. *Computer Graphics (SIGGRAPH '84 Proceedings)*, **18**, 21–30.

Bézier, P. 1978. General Distortion of an Ensemble of Biparametric Patches. *Computer Aided Design*, **10**(2), 116–120.

Catmull, E. 1974. *A Subdivision Algorithm for the Display of Curves and Surfaces*. Ph.D. Thesis. University of Utah.

Catmull, Edwin, and Alvy Ray Smith. 1980. 3D-Transformations of Images in Scanline Order. *Computer Graphics (SIGGRAPH '80 Proceedings)*, **14**(3), 279–285.

Chen, Shenchang Eric, and Richard E. Parent. 1989. Shape Averaging and Its Applications to Industrial Design. *IEEE Computer Graphics and Applications*, **9**(1), 47–54.

Christensen, G. E. 1994. *Deformable Shape Models for Anatomy*. Ph.D. Thesis. Washington University.

Coons, S. 1974. Surface Patches and B-Spline Curves. In Barnhill, R., and R. Riesenfeld (eds.), *Computer Aided Geometric Design*. San Diego: Academic Press.

Encyclopedia Brittanica. 1973. Chicago: Encyclopedia Brittanica Educational Corporation. Vol. 15, p. 259.

Gomes, Jonas, and Luiz Velho. 1995. Abstraction Paradigms for Computer Graphics. *The Visual Computer*, **11**, 227–239.

Kawaguchi, Yoichiro. 1982. A Morphological Study of the Form of Nature. *Computer Graphics (SIGGRAPH '82 Proceedings)*, **16**(3), 223–232.

Koenderink, Jan J. 1990. *Solid Shape*. Cambridge, MA: MIT Press.

Lasseter, John. 1987. Principles of Traditional Animation Applied to 3D Computer Animation. *Computer Graphics (SIGGRAPH '87 Proceedings)*, **21**(4), 35–44.

Litwinowicz, Peter, and Gavin Miller. 1994. Efficient Techniques for Interactive Texture Placement. *Computer Graphics (SIGGRAPH '94 Proceedings)*, 119–122.

Prusinkiewicz, Przemyslaw, Mark S. Hammel, and Eric Mjolsness. 1993. Animation of Plant Development. *Computer Graphics (SIGGRAPH '93 Proceedings)*, **27**(Aug.), 351–360.

Requicha, A. A. G. 1980. Representation for Rigid Solids: Theory, Methods, and Systems. *ACM Computing Surveys*, **12**(Dec.), 437–464.

Rosenfeld, A. 1969. *Picture Processing by Computer*. New York: Academic Press.

Sclaroff, S., and A. Pentland. 1994. Object Recognition and Categorization Using Modal Matching. *Proceedings of 2nd IEEE CAD-Based Vision Workshop*, 258–265.

Sederberg, Thomas W., Peishing Gao, Guojin Wang, and Hong Mu. 1992. 2D Shape Blending: An Intrinsic Solution to the Vertex Path Problem. *Computer Graphics (SIGGRAPH '93 Proceedings)*, **27**, 15–18.

Smith, M. 1974. Computers and the Art of Animation. In Halas, John (ed.), *Computer Animation*. New York: Hastings House, 149–155.

Sutherland, Ivan E. 1963. Sketchpad: A Man-Machine Graphical Communication System. In *SJCC*. New York: Crown Publishers, Inc., Spartan Books.

Thompson, D. W. 1961. *On Growth and Form*. New York: Cambridge University Press.

Webster. 1989. *Webster's Encyclopedic Unabridged Dictionary of the English Language*. New York: Random House.

2
Graphical Objects

AT THE END OF THE PREVIOUS CHAPTER we discussed the use of adequate abstraction paradigms for computer graphics. These abstraction levels allow us to pose the different problems of this area. In this book we are concerned with the problem of object metamorphosis. Therefore, we need a clear concept of the notion of *object* in order to define precisely what we mean by metamorphosis, and also to develop different metamorphosis techniques.

In computer graphics, a multitude of different elements constitute the mathematical universe, such as points, curves, surfaces, fractals, images, 3D images, vector graphics, raster graphics, and so on. These different objects are manipulated on the computer using similar techniques. However, the relationship between these techniques is hindered because there is no unifying concept that encompasses the different objects, their representation, and implementation on the computer.

The objective of this chapter is to present the concept of a *graphical object* in such a way as to include, in a unified manner, the many elements we will use to apply the metamorphosis operations.

The concept of a graphical object, and its different representations, enables us to relate seemingly different algorithms and techniques that exist in the computer graphics literature. Besides the impact on the development of new algorithms and on the understanding of existing ones, this concept also has a great influence on systems design and development.

2.1 The Concept of a Graphical Object

Intuitively, a graphical object consists of any of the entities processed in a computer graphics system: points, curves, surfaces, fractals, vector graphics, images, 3D images, and so on. Inspired by the objects from the physical world, a graphical object should have a shape and attributes such as type of material, color, and so on. A simple definition, broad enough to encompass all of the above objects, is given below.

Definition   A *graphical object* $\mathcal{O}$ of the euclidean space $\mathbb{R}^n$ consists of a subset $U \subset \mathbb{R}^n$ and a function $f \colon U \to \mathbb{R}^p$.

The set U defines the *shape* or the *geometric support* of the object. The function f defines the attributes of the graphical object, and for this reason it is called the *attribute function* of the object. In general we use the notation $\mathcal{O}(U, f)$ when we need to emphasize both the shape U and the attribute function f of the graphical object $\mathcal{O}$. The *dimension* of the graphical object is defined to be the dimension of the shape U.

The shape U defines the geometry and the topology of the object, and the function f defines the different properties (or attributes) of the object, such as color, texture, scalar fields, vector fields, and so on. Each of the distinct attributes is defined by a function $f_j \colon U \to \mathbb{R}^{p_j}$, $j = 1, \ldots, k$, such that $p_1 + p_2 + \cdots + p_k = p$, and the attribute function f,

$$f \colon U \to \mathbb{R}^{p_1} \oplus \cdots \oplus \mathbb{R}^{p_k} = \mathbb{R}^p,$$

has coordinates $f = (f_1, \ldots, f_k)$.

This means that in what follows, it makes no difference whether the attributes are considered as separate functions or not.

2.1.1 Shape Geometry and Topology

It is very common to impose certain topological or geometrical restrictions when defining a shape. These restrictions are used to guarantee some properties of the object's topology and geometry that are of great importance in the solution of specific problems. A good example is the use of shapes that are characterized as *manifolds*. A manifold of dimension n is obtained by gluing together deformed pieces of the euclidean space $\mathbb{R}^n$. Locally it is essentially a stretched and squashed piece of the euclidean space, but globally the topology can assume very complicated types. The gluing process defines different geometries of the manifolds.

2.1.2 Point Membership Classification

The shape of an object $\mathcal{O} = \mathcal{O}(U, f)$ is completely defined by its *characteristic function*, $\chi_\mathcal{O}$, defined by

$$\chi_\mathcal{O} = \begin{cases} 1 & p \in U; \\ 0 & p \notin U. \end{cases}$$

The characteristic function allows us to characterize the shape: it distinguishes points that belong to the shape, for which $\chi_\mathcal{O} = 1$, from points that do not belong to it, where $\chi_\mathcal{O} = 0$. For this reason, this function is well known in the geometric modeling literature by the name of *point membership classification* function. Robust methods to compute this function play an important part in the process of shape description and representation.

From a computational point of view, an object is well described when its point membership classification function is precisely defined; that is, its shape is characterized by a function: $p \in U$ if and only if $\chi_\mathcal{O} = 1$. For computer graphics purposes, the characteristic function should also be computable, and there must be an algorithm that allows the evaluation of $\chi_\mathcal{O}$. Certainly we have to define precisely the meaning of the word *computable*. The interested reader should consult [Blum, 1991].

2.2 Examples of Graphical Objects

In our customary use of objects, the most emphasis is put on the object's shape rather than its attributes (an exception occurs when the object is an image). From a geometric point of view, objects can be classified according to the dimension of their shape and the dimension of the euclidean space in which they are embedded.

2.2.1 Curves

Curves could be defined generically as 1D graphical objects. When a curve γ is contained in the plane, it is called a *plane curve*; otherwise, it is called a *spatial curve*. A plane curve homeomorphic to a circle is called a *Jordan curve* (see Figure 2.1).

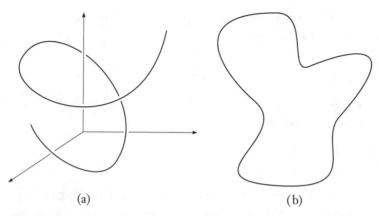

Figure 2.1   Space curve (a) and Jordan curve (b).

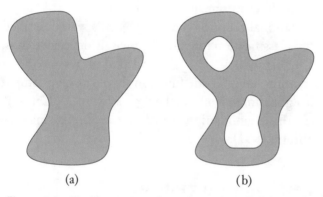

Figure 2.2   Simply connected region (a) and doubly connected region (b).

2.2.2 Planar Regions

A Jordan curve subdivides the plane into two connected components, one of which is bounded. The bounded component defines a simply connected region of the plane. A finite family of Jordan curves of the plane defines a planar region. The number of curves define the topological connectivity of the region. In Figure 2.2 we show examples of a simply connected and a doubly connected planar region.

Planar regions constitute examples of graphical objects of dimension 2 on the plane. In general, the attribute function is a constant function that specifies

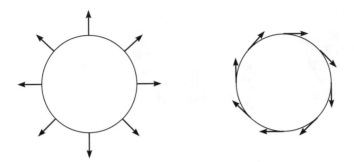

Figure 2.3 Circles with normal and tangent unit vector fields.

the color of the region. Planar regions are usually called *2D solids* in the area of geometric and solid modeling.

Drawings are constituted by some finite collection of curves on the plane. It is very common in a drawing that these curves limit some regions of the plane with which we associate some attributes, such as color.

2.2.3 Objects and Vector Fields

If $\gamma\colon (a, b) \to \mathbb{R}^2$ is defined by parametric equations $\gamma(t) = (x(t), y(t))$, the vector $T(t) = \gamma'(t) = (x'(t), y'(t))$ is tangent to γ and is called the *velocity* vector of the curve. The vector field $n(t) = (y'(t), -x'(t))$ is orthogonal to the velocity vector field. It is a normal vector field to the curve γ. Figure 2.3 shows the drawing of a unit circle $\gamma(t) = (\cos t, \sin t)$, along with its velocity and the corresponding normal vector field.

Normal and tangent vector fields are very important attributes of graphical objects, for example, in shading computations. Also, vector fields defined on some graphical objects are necessary for simulation purposes. As an example, the wind movement on the surface of the earth can be represented by a vector field defined on the surface of a sphere.

2.2.4 Surfaces and Solids

Generically, we can say that a surface is a 2D graphical object (therefore planar regions are particular examples of surfaces). Surfaces are very useful to define regions of the space, called *3D solids*. In fact, the statements concerning Jordan curves and planar regions extend to the 3D space: *a closed and bounded surface homeomorphic to the sphere subdivides the space into two regions, one bounded*

Figure 2.4 Three-dimensional solids bounded by surfaces.

Figure 2.5 Distinct graphical objects with the same shape.

and the other unbounded. The bounded regions define *3D solids* as illustrated in Figure 2.4. Three-dimensional solids of very complex topology can be constructed using the combination of set operations and warping.

2.2.5 Images

An image is a function $f \colon U \subset \mathbb{R}^2 \to \mathbb{R}^n$. The shape of the image is the set U. In general, U is a rectangle of the plane. The function f is the attribute function of the image. To each point $p \in U$, $f(p)$ defines the attributes of p. The most common attribute for an image is color, but there are several other attributes useful in some applications, such as opacity, scene depth, and so on.

Given two distinct images, as shown in Figure 2.5, the shape is the same: a rectangular region of the plane. The difference between these two graphical objects resides in the attribute function, which is responsible for the grayscale intensities that define the woman's face and the cheetah.

The shape of an image is also called *image support*. A very common situation occurs when there exists a subset V of the image support U such that

Figure 2.6 Binary image.

$$f(p) = \begin{cases} 1 & \text{if } p \in V; \\ 0 & \text{if } p \in U - V. \end{cases}$$

In this case the image is called a *binary image* (see Figure 2.6).

In a binary image the attribute function f can be considered the characteristic function of the subset V of the plane. Thus, from the point of view of graphical objects, a binary image describes subsets of the plane (in general these subsets constitute planar regions). An arbitrary image could be considered as describing a 2D solid with texture attributes.

In a *grayscale* image the color attribute represents only luminance values of the pixels (black, white, and intermediate gray values). Thus, the image function assumes 1D values $f: U \subset \mathbb{R}^2 \to \mathbb{R}$. The image can also be represented by the graph $\{(x, y, f(x, y) ; (x, y) \in U\}$ of its attribute function (see Figure 2.7). This graph is a surface embedded into the 3D space; therefore it is another graphical object. Notice that in this description of the image, attribute information is changed into shape information.

It should be observed that the graph of a real-valued function also provides a good description for the geometry of a terrain model. That is, the same mathematical concept (a real-valued function of two variables) describes different objects from the physical universe. Nevertheless, it should be remarked that the graph of the function f describes the terrain shape, while for an image the graph is just a geometric representation of the luminance attributes.

Segmented Image

As mentioned before, besides color we have several other attributes for an image: opacity, depth, and so on. Sometimes we need to distinguish regions

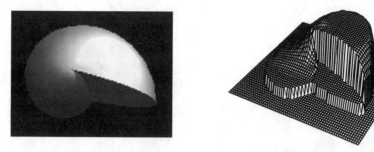

Figure 2.7 A grayscale image and the graph of its attribute function.

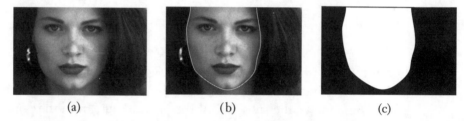

(a)   (b)   (c)

Figure 2.8 Graphical object with different attributes: woman's face (a), face boundary (b), and segmentation (c).

of the image with different attributes. This is achieved by defining a partition of the image domain based on some properties of the attribute function. A common partition consists in determining regions of the image domain where some of the attributes are constant.

In Figure 2.8(a) we show the image of a woman's face. In Figure 2.8(b) we show the same image with a curve delimiting the face "boundary." The partition of the image by this curve consists of two sets $F = \{$face points$\}$ and $\tilde{F} = \{$non-face points$\}$. This defines a new attribute of the image: a function that assumes value 1 at the set F and 0 at the set $\tilde{F}$. The image with this attribute is called a *segmented image* as shown in Figure 2.8(c).

2.2.6 Animation

In general, the word *animation* is used associated to some finite sequence of images $f_1, f_2, \ldots, f_n$. When this sequence is exhibited with some time frequency, the eye performs a temporal integration between them, and we perceive motion.

From the point of view of a graphical object, an animation of a graphical object $\mathcal{O} = (U, f)$, $U \subset \mathbb{R}^n$, is a function $F: \mathcal{O} \times [a, b] \to \mathcal{G}$, where $\mathcal{G}$ is some space of graphical objects. For each $t \in \mathbb{R}$ this map defines an object $F_t(\mathcal{O}) = F(\mathcal{O}, t) \subset \mathcal{G}$. The finite sequence that we usually call an animation is in fact a time sampling of the function F, using some partition $a = t_1 < t_2 < \cdots < t_n = b$ of the time interval $[a, b]$. Notice that the animation can be interpreted as a change of the graphical object $\mathcal{O}$ as the time passes. This is the essence of the metamorphosis of a graphical object. This relationship between metamorphosis of graphical objects and animation will be discussed in more detail in the chapters that follow.

If the graphical object is not embedded in the 2D plane, it has to be projected to transform the animation into an image animation that can be displayed on a monitor screen or recorded on tape, for instance.

2.2.7 Particle Systems

A *particle system* [Reeves, 1983] consists of a finite family U_i, $i = 1, \ldots, n$, of subsets of the space. Each U_i, called a *particle*, has different attributes, such as color, weight, velocity, acceleration, external forces, opacity, and duration in time.

Particle systems have been used to model a wide variety of natural phenomena in computer graphics, such as fire, rain, and so on. Figure 2.9 shows one frame of a waterfall animation using particle systems.

2.2.8 Audio

Audio is the physical phenomenon characterized by an oscillatory change of pressure. It propagates as longitudinal waves in a solid, liquid, or gaseous medium, which are perceived as sounds when they reach the human ear. Audio signals are an integral part of most graphics-centric applications, such as virtual environments, simulations, games, and multimedia.

Mathematically, an audio wave is represented by a real-valued function of one variable $f: [a, b] \subset \mathbb{R} \to \mathbb{R}$, which measures the air pressure variation along the time. As in the case of grayscale images, this function can be represented by its graph $G(f) = \{(t, f(t)) \, ; \, t \in [a, b]\}$. This is illustrated in Figure 2.10, which shows the graph of the sound of a gunshot.

Figure 2.9   Waterfall using a physically based particle system [from Sims, 1990].

Figure 2.10   Graph representation of an audio signal.

2.3 Comments and References

In this chapter we introduced the concept of a graphical object, which will enable us to study the problem of warping and morphing in a unified way. This concept encompasses all of the entities manipulated in a computer graphics system. From this point of view we could say that computer graphics consists in the study of methods and techniques to describe, represent, and manipulate graphical objects in the computer.

Among the graphical objects, audio, images, and animation assume a great significance because they are connected with the most important channels we use to perceive the world around us: sound perception, visual perception, and motion perception.

For obvious reason, the description, representation, and reproduction of these objects have a very strong perceptual component.

The concept of a graphical object used in this chapter was introduced in [Gomes et al., 1996]. A similar concept had appeared before in the book [Fiume, 1989] for the particular case where the only attribute is color.

References

Blum, Lenore. 1991. *Lectures on a Theory of Computation over the Reals*. Rio de Janeiro: Instituto de Matemática Pura e Aplicada (IMPA).

Fiume, E. 1989. *The Mathematical Structure of Raster Graphics*. Boston: Academic Press.

Gomes, Jonas, Bruno Costa, Lucia Darsa, and Luiz Velho. 1996. Graphical Objects. *The Visual Computer*, **12**, 269–282.

Reeves, W. R. 1983. Particle Systems: A Technique for Modeling a Class of Fuzzy Objects. *Computer Graphics (SIGGRAPH '83 Proceedings)*, **17**(3), 359–376.

Sims, Karl. 1990. Particle Animation and Rendering Using Data Parallel Computation. *Computer Graphics (SIGGRAPH '90 Proceedings)*, **24**, 405–413.

3

Transformation
of Graphical Objects

IN THIS CHAPTER WE WILL INTRODUCE the concepts of transformations of the space and transformations of graphical objects. These concepts will allow us to study the problem of warping and morphing in the next chapter.

The discussion in this chapter is directed mostly to graphical objects and transformations in the mathematical universe, according to the abstraction paradigms discussed in Chapter 1. This more abstract treatment provides the framework for a general discussion that is independent of the representational and computational details. Therefore, it is applicable to all kinds of graphical objects.

Transformations between graphical objects constitute a basic operation in computing with graphics. The main operations in essentially all areas of graphics processing involve some form of transformation between graphical objects. Figure 3.1 is a classical diagram depicting the relationships between the main areas of graphics computation.

This diagram shows two classes of graphical objects, and the main areas of graphics as processes of transformation between them. Apart from distracting details, the main idea behind this diagram is to show the distinction of the transformations between graphical objects of different and same dimensionality.

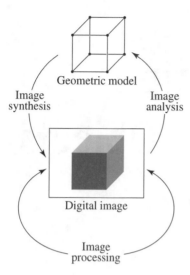

Figure 3.1   Main areas of graphics computation.

3.1 Transformations of the Space

Transformations of the euclidean space is the key concept to study warping and morphing of graphical objects. Consider a subset $U \subset \mathbb{R}^m$ of the euclidean space; a transformation of U is a function $T: U \to \mathbb{R}^n$. The set U is called the *domain* of the transformation, and $T(U)$ is called the *image* of T. A transformation is also called a *mapping* in the literature. When $U = \mathbb{R}^n$, we say that T is a *space transformation* or *global transformation*. A transformation $T: U \to \mathbb{R}^n$ defined only on points of U is called an *intrinsic transformation*. A global transformation affects all points of the ambient space. These concepts are illustrated in Figure 3.2: (a) shows two objects of the plane; in (b) we have a global transformation of the plane that deforms both objects; in (c) we apply an intrinsic transformation to object B only.

A good compromise between a global and an intrinsic transformation is a *local transformation*. This is a transformation T with compact support in a neighborhood of each point. That is, when we apply the transformation at a point p, only points in a neighborhood of p are affected.

3.1.1 Transformations and Change of Coordinates

Consider a transformation $f: U \subset \mathbb{R}^m \to \mathbb{R}^m$. Let $P = (x_1, \ldots, x_m) \in \mathbb{R}^m$, and $f(P) = (y_1, \ldots, y_m) \in \mathbb{R}^m$. Therefore,

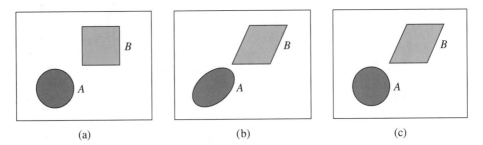

Figure 3.2 Graphical objects (a), global transformation (b), and intrinsic transformation of object B (c).

$$y_1 = f_1(x_1, \ldots, x_m);$$
$$y_2 = f_2(x_1, \ldots, x_m);$$
$$\vdots$$
$$y_m = f_m(x_1, \ldots, x_m).$$

The real-valued functions $f_i \colon \mathbb{R}^m \to \mathbb{R}$, $i = 1, \ldots, m$, are called the *coordinates* of the transformation f. An important point should be noted: we can interpret the transformation f in two different ways. First, f "moves" the point P to the point $f(P)$, and second, f changes the coordinates $(x_1, \ldots, x_m)$ of the space to the coordinates $(y_1, \ldots, y_m)$.

Both interpretations are useful, and in fact, as we will see later on, they have a great influence in the techniques used to compute deformations.

For the second interpretation we are assuming that f is a bijective mapping, so that there is a perfect matching between both coordinates. The interpretation as a coordinate change gives a mathematical model that allows effective specification as well as efficient computation. Coordinates provide a handle that indicates where deformations should be applied and a framework for numerical implementation.

Example 3.1 Figure 3.3(a) shows a square. Figure 3.3(b) is a transformation of the square that consists of a 45° counterclockwise rotation and a translation by the vector $(4, 2)$. In Figure 3.3(c) we show that this transformation can be interpreted as a change of the coordinate system (x_1, x_2) of the original square, to the coordinate system (y_1, y_2).

The transformation is given by

$$T(x_1, x_2) = R_{45^\circ}(x_1, x_2) + (4, 2).$$

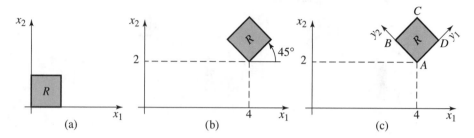

Figure 3.3   Change of coordinates: square (a), rotation (b), and change of coordinates (c).

The two coordinate systems (y_1, y_2) and (x_1, x_2) are related by the equation

$$(y_1, y_2) = R_{45°}(x_1, x_2) + (4, 2),$$

or, equivalently,

$$(y_1, y_2) = R_{45°}^{-1}((x_1, x_2) - (4, 2)).$$

Note that the transformation that changes from the coordinate system (x_1, x_2) to the system (y_1, y_2) is the inverse of the transformation that moves the objects.

3.2 Transforming Graphical Objects

Consider two graphical objects $\mathcal{O}_1 = (U_1, f_1)$ and $\mathcal{O}_2 = (U_2, f_2)$, with attribute functions $f_i: U_i \to \mathbb{R}^m$. A transformation between $\mathcal{O}_1$ and $\mathcal{O}_2$ must take into account both the shape and attributes. The shape transformation is defined by some spatial transformation $T: U_1 \to U_2$. The concept of a transformation between two graphical objects is illustrated in Figure 3.4.

The transformation of the attributes deserves some attention. We have two options to compute the attributes of the transformed object $\mathcal{O}_2 = T(\mathcal{O}_1)$. The first is to compute the attributes from information about the transformed object; the second is to transform the attributes from the original object.

If the attribute function f_2 depends on the shape geometry or topology, it is possible to recompute them at each point of the transformed object. As an example, the object normal vectors are shape dependent and could be computed from geometry information (note that the normal vectors influence

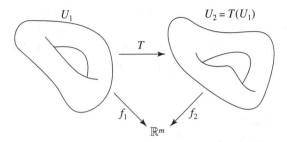

Figure 3.4 Transformation between two graphical objects.

the computation of the attributes of shading).[1] On the other hand, the material type of an object, or the color of each point, could be computed applying the transformation on the color of the points of the original object.

When using the transformation to compute the attributes, we have (see Figure 3.4)

$$f_2(T(p)) = f_1(p). \tag{3.1}$$

This equation says that the attribute of the object $\mathcal{O}_2$ at the point $T(p)$ is equal to the attribute of the object $\mathcal{O}_1$ at the point p. This is represented by the commutative diagram below:

$$U \xrightarrow{T} V = T(U)$$
$$f_1 \searrow \quad \downarrow f_2$$
$$\mathbb{R}^m$$

There are two different strategies to compute the values of the attribute function f_2 of the object $\mathcal{O}_2$:

- **Forward mapping.** In this technique, for each point $p \in U_1$, we compute $T(p) \in U_2$ and define $f_2(T(p)) = f_1(p)$, so that Equation (3.1) is satisfied. That is, we search all points of the shape U_1 and compute the attribute values at the corresponding image points.

---

1. The computation of the transformed normal can be accomplished using vector algebra; see [Barr, 1984].

- **Inverse mapping.** In the inverse mapping technique, for each point $q \in U_2$, we find a point $p \in U_1$ such that $T(p) = q$, and define $f_2(q) = f_1(p)$, so that Equation (3.1) is satisfied. That is, we search all points on the shape U_2 and compute their attributes based on the attributes of the corresponding points in the shape U_1.

We should remark that there are problems in the attribute computation both in the forward and in the inverse methods. In fact we have the following:

- The direct approach fails if $T(U_1)$ does not cover U_2. Also, we have to make some choice if T is not injective, that is, $T(p_i) = T(p_j)$, $p_i \neq p_j$.
- In the inverse method, we also have to make a choice when the inverse image $T^{-1}(q)$ has more than one element for some point $q \in U_2$. Also, for some applications the use of the inverse mapping computation strategy demands the computation of the inverse transformation T^{-1}, which is not an easy task.

Certainly, most of the above problems are completely solved if we demand the shape transformation T to be bijective. This may seem a very strong demand, but, as we will see, in some of the warping and morphing applications it is a natural assumption.

3.2.1   Discretization and Resampling

Demanding bijectivity of the graphical object transformation solves the problem of computing the attribute function of the transformed object in the continuous domain. This problem reappears when we discretize both the graphical object and the transformation in the representation universe.

This happens because when we discretize a bijective transformation $T: U_1 \to U_2$, we may obtain a nonbijective transformation in the discrete domain. This is illustrated by the bijective transformation $h: [0, 8] \to [0, 8]$, whose graph is shown in Figure 3.5.

By observing the figure, we see that although h is bijective in the continuous domain, in the discrete domain we have $h(5) = h(6) = 6$.

The above example shows that we should avoid working with transformations of graphical objects on the discrete domain. Therefore, we must be ready to use reconstruction techniques that should be applied to both graphical objects and their transformations. This topic will be extensively discussed later on.

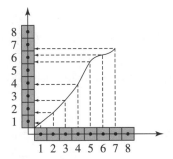

Figure 3.5 Bijective transformation on discrete domain [from Gomes and Velho, 1997].

Figure 3.6 Transformation of an image.

Example 3.2 (Image Transformation)   Figure 3.6 shows a transformation of an image. The rectangle defining the image shape is mapped onto an arbitrary shape, and the color attributes are transformed accordingly.

Example 3.3 (Tangent Vector Field)   Consider a surface $S \subset \mathbb{R}^3$ with a vector field $v: S \to \mathbb{R}^3$ defined on it (the vector field is an attribute of the surface). If $f: S \to \mathbb{R}^3$ maps the surface S onto a surface M, the vector field v is transformed to a vector field w on $M = f(S)$, using the derivative:

$$w(f(p)) = f'(p) \cdot v.$$

This is a forward method for computing the vector field of the transformed surface M.

Example 3.4 (Normal Vector Field)   Consider a surface $S \subset \mathbb{R}^3$ and let $N: S \to \mathbb{R}^3$ be a normal vector field to S (N is an attribute of S). That is, for each $p \in S$, $N(p)$ is a vector perpendicular to the tangent plane of the surface at the point p. If the transformation $f: S \to \mathbb{R}^3$ maps the surface S into a surface $M = f(S)$, the normal vector field N is transformed by

$$N(f(p)) = \det J (J^{-1})^T N(p) \tag{3.2}$$

where J is the matrix of the derivative f' (Jacobian matrix of f), det is the determinant, and the exponent T is the transpose operation. In fact, the determinant factor can be omitted. We just apply the transformation

$$N(f(p)) = (J^{-1})^T N(p),$$

and normalize the resulting normal vector. Proof of the result can be found in [Barr, 1984].

Notice that if f is linear, we have $J = f' = f$. Moreover, if f is an isometry,

$$(J^{-1})^T = J = f.$$

That is, the same transformation used to warp the shape is used to warp the normal vector field.

3.3 Classes of Transformation

It is very useful to classify transformations based on their common properties of (classes). In this section and in the following ones, we will study several classes of transformation that are very useful in the techniques of warping and morphing of graphical objects.

3.3.1 Homeomorphisms and Diffeomorphisms

In topology we are interested in classifying shapes according to their *topological properties*. Intuitively, two objects A and B have the same topology if there is a bijective mapping $h: A \to B$ that is continuous, and if the inverse mapping $h^{-1}: B \to A$ is also continuous. A transformation with these properties is called a *homeomorphism*. Intuitively, a homeomorphism deforms the object A into the object B without tearing.

When we demand from a homeomorphism h that it has differentiability class C^k, $k \geq 1$, and also its inverse has differentiability C^k, it is called a *diffeomorphism*. Diffeomorphisms are important when the objects we deal with are differentiable and we need to preserve the differential properties.

3.3.2 Isometries, Expansions, and Contractions

In general, a transformation changes the relation between the points of the space. By studying the way a transformation T affects the distance between

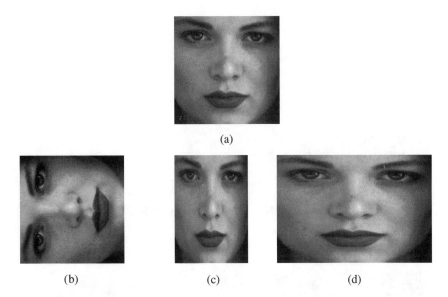

Figure 3.7 Isometry (b), contraction (c), and expansion transformations (d) of the image in (a).

points of the space, we are able to devise three distinct classes of transformation: *isometry*, *expansion*, and *contraction*.

An isometry T preserves the distance between points, that is,

$$\|T(X) - T(Y)\| = \|X - Y\|.$$

An expansion increases the distance between the points of the domain, that is,

$$\|T(X) - T(Y)\| \geq C\|X - Y\|,$$

where, $C > 1$. A contraction decreases the distance between points, that is,

$$\|T(X) - T(Y)\| \leq C\|X - Y\|,$$

with $C < 1$. These classes of transformations are illustrated in Figure 3.7: (b) shows an isometric transformation (a rotation) of (a); (c) shows a contraction, and (d) shows an expansion.

In general, a transformation changes its behavior from region to region of its domain. This is exemplified by the mapping $f : [0, \infty) \to \mathbb{R}$, defined by $f(t) = t^2$, which contracts on the interval $[0, 1/2]$ and expands on the interval $[1/2, \infty)$ (see Figure 3.8(a)). We should observe that the inverse mapping $g(x) = \sqrt{x}$, whose graph is shown in Figure 3.8(b), performs in exactly the

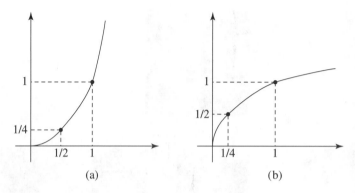

Figure 3.8   Contracting map (a) and expanding map (b).

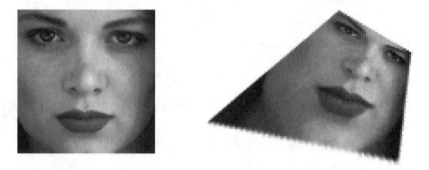

Figure 3.9   Transformation with contraction and expansion.

opposite way: it expands on the interval $[0, 1/2]$ and contracts on the interval $[1/2, \infty)$.

The transformation T of the image shown in Figure 3.9 is a two-dimensional example of a transformation that contracts in some parts of its domain (the top of the image) and expands on other parts (the bottom of the image). On the center of the image (near the nose), the transformation behaves approximately as an isometry.

3.3.3   A Word about the Computation of Transformations

How do we obtain transformations of arbitrary graphical objects $f: U \subset \mathbb{R}^m \to \mathbb{R}^n$? An easy way to do this consists in defining global transformations

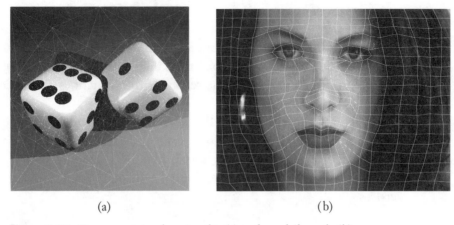

(a)   (b)

Figure 3.10 Representation by triangles (a) and quadrilaterals (b).

of the space $\mathbb{R}^m$. This fact first appeared in the computer graphics literature in [Barr, 1984].

Nevertheless, global transformations are very difficult to control in trying to obtain specific transformations of graphical objects. A good strategy to construct local transformations is to obtain a representation of the object by subdividing it into smaller "pieces," defining the transformation between each of the pieces, and gluing them together to obtain the transformation of the whole object. The rationale behind this method is that in the small pieces the whole transformation can be approximated by simple ones (e.g., linear transformations), and the computation becomes easier.

Triangles and quadrilaterals have been widely used in computer graphics as the building blocks to represent graphical objects. Figure 3.10(a) shows a triangulated image, and Figure 3.10(b) shows a quadrilateral mesh subdivision of an image. From this point of view, techniques to compute transformations between triangles or from one quadrilateral to another turn out to be very important.

We will study several classes of transformation in the rest of this chapter. In each case we will discuss techniques to compute them. Along the way, we will frequently be looking at the problem of triangle and quadrilateral transformation. Keep in mind that we are interested in transformations defined at all points of the graphical objects because we must be able to compute the object attributes at any point. Also, for reasons discussed earlier, invertible transformations are much more flexible to use. Finally, it is important to observe that there are two different, but equivalent and equally useful, ways to interpret a transformation T from a triangle (or quadrilateral) U to another triangle (or quadrilateral) V. The first is that T defines a parameterization of V on the parameter space U; the second is that T defines a local coordinate system on V.

In most of the cases we will study, T is completely determined from the knowledge of its values on the vertices of U. Therefore, T provides an interpolation technique to reconstruct functions sampled at the vertices of U. In fact, we are solving the problem of scattered data interpolation for the vertices.

3.4 Linear Transformations

The vector space structure of the euclidean space $\mathbb{R}^n$ allows us to introduce the very special class of *linear transformations*. A transformation $L \colon \mathbb{R}^n \to \mathbb{R}^n$ is *linear* if

$$L(u + v) = L(u) + L(v), \quad \forall u, v \in \mathbb{R}^n; \tag{3.3}$$

$$L(\lambda v) = \lambda L(v), \quad \forall \lambda \in \mathbb{R}, v \in \mathbb{R}^n. \tag{3.4}$$

The above properties mean that a linear transformation preserves the basic operations of the vector space. From (3.4) it follows, taking $\lambda = 0$, that a linear transformation does not move the origin. Also, it transforms subspaces into subspaces (in particular, lines and planes are transformed into lines or planes). Another important property is the preservation of the parallelism between linear elements of the space.

A linear transformation T is completely defined by its values $T(v_i)$, $i = 1, \ldots, n$, on a basis $\{v_1, v_2, \ldots, v_n\}$ of $\mathbb{R}^n$. In fact, for any $v \in \mathbb{R}^n$, we have

$$v = \sum_{i=1}^{n} x_i v_i \quad \Rightarrow \quad T(v) = \sum_{i=1}^{n} x_i T(v_i).$$

If $\{w_1, \ldots, w_n\}$ is another basis, then

$$T(v_j) = \sum_{i=1}^{n} a_{ij} w_i.$$

Therefore, the transformation T is determined by the matrix (a_{ij}) of order n.

Conversely, it is easy to show that any matrix (a_{ij}) defines a transformation T of $\mathbb{R}^n$ by

$$T(x_1, \ldots, x_n) = \begin{pmatrix} a_{11} & a_{12} & \cdots & a_{1n} \\ a_{21} & a_{22} & \cdots & a_{2n} \\ \vdots & \vdots & \ddots & \vdots \\ a_{n1} & a_{n2} & \cdots & a_{nn} \end{pmatrix} \begin{pmatrix} x_1 \\ x_2 \\ \vdots \\ x_n \end{pmatrix}.$$

Example 3.5 (Rotations) The rotation R_θ of an angle θ around the origin of the euclidean plane is defined by

$$R_\theta(x, y) = \begin{pmatrix} \cos\theta & -\sin\theta \\ \sin\theta & \cos\theta \end{pmatrix} \begin{pmatrix} x \\ y \end{pmatrix}.$$

3.5 Affine Transformations

A transformation $f: \mathbb{R}^n \to \mathbb{R}^n$ is *affine* if

$$f((1 - t)P + tQ) = (1 - t)f(P) + tf(Q), \tag{3.5}$$

for $P, Q \in \mathbb{R}^n$, and $t \in \mathbb{R}$. Geometrically, this means that the transformation preserves collinearity and preserves linear interpolation on each line; that is, it maintains the ratio of segments on each line.

Theorem 1 Introducing coordinates on the space, every affine transformation is the composition of a linear transformation and a translation.

Indeed, suppose we have a coordinate system of the space with origin 0, and define, for any $u \in \mathbb{R}^n$, $T(u) = f(u) - f(0)$. T is a linear transformation. In fact, for any $\lambda \in \mathbb{R}$, we have

$$T(\lambda u) = f(\lambda u) - f(0) = f(\lambda u + (1 - \lambda)0) - f(0)$$
$$= \lambda f(u) + (1 - \lambda)f(0) - f(0) = \lambda f(u) - \lambda f(0)$$
$$= \lambda(f(u) - f(0)) = \lambda T(u).$$

On the other hand,

$$T(u + v) = T(2 \cdot \frac{u + v}{2})) = 2 \cdot T(\frac{u + v}{2})$$

$$= 2f(\frac{u + v}{2}) - 2f(0) = 2 \cdot \frac{1}{2}f(u) + 2 \cdot \frac{1}{2}f(v) - 2f(0)$$

$$= f(u) - f(0) + f(v) - f(0) = T(u) + T(v)$$

Therefore, we have $f(u) = T(u) + f(0)$, and the theorem is proved.

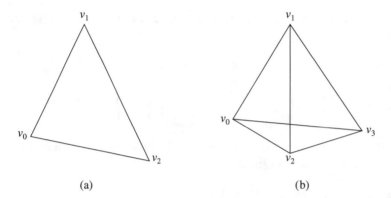

Figure 3.11 Two-dimensional affine frame (a) and three-dimensional affine frame (b).

We have seen that a linear transformation of the space is characterized by its values on a basis of the space. How can we characterize an affine mapping? An *affine frame* of the space $\mathbb{R}^n$ is a set of $n + 1$ vectors $\mathfrak{F} = \{v_0, v_1, \ldots, v_n\}$ such that the set $\{v_1 - v_0, v_2 - v_0, \ldots, v_n - v_0\}$ is a basis.

Example 3.6 (Affine Frames) Two distinct points constitute an affine frame of the line $\mathbb{R}$; three noncollinear points constitute a frame of the plane $\mathbb{R}^2$. These points define a triangle of the plane as shown in Figure 3.11(a). Four noncoplanar points of the space $\mathbb{R}^3$ constitute an *affine frame*. These points define a tetrahedra of the space as shown in Figure 3.11(b).

3.5.1 Barycentric coordinates

In this section we will see that an affine frame enables us to introduce coordinates on the affine space. Consider the frame $\mathfrak{F}$, and a vector $X \in \mathbb{R}^n$. From the definition of a frame, there exist constants $\lambda_j \in \mathbb{R}$ such that

$$X - v_0 = \sum_{j=1}^{n} \lambda_j (v_j - v_0).$$

Hence,

$$X = v_0 + \sum_{j=1}^{n} \lambda_j (v_j - v_0) = \left(1 - \sum_{j=1}^{n} \lambda_j\right) v_0 + \sum_{j=1}^{n} \lambda_j v_j.$$

Taking $\lambda_0 = 1 - \sum_{j=1}^{n} \lambda_j$, we conclude that, for any point $X \in \mathbb{R}^n$, we have

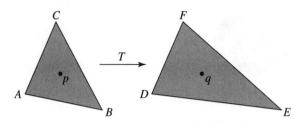

Figure 3.12 Affine transformation between two triangles.

$$X = \lambda_0 v_0 + \lambda_1 v_1 + \cdots + \lambda_n v_n = \sum_{j=0}^{n} \lambda_j v_j, \tag{3.6}$$

with $\sum_{j=0}^{n} \lambda_j = 1$. We should remark that the λ_j's are uniquely determined by the vector X. They are called *barycentric coordinates* of X. Now we state the main result:

Theorem 2 An affine transformation is completely characterized by its values on an affine frame.

Indeed, for any $X \in \mathbb{R}^n$, inspired by (3.6), we define

$$T(X) = \sum_{j=0}^{n} \lambda_j T(v_j).$$

It is easy to verify that T is affine and is uniquely defined.

Example 3.7 (Affine Transformation on Triangles) Consider the particular case of computing the affine transformation between two triangles ABC and DEF (see Figure 3.12).

First, we define T at the vertices by $T(A) = D$, $T(B) = E$, and $T(C) = F$. Now we extend T to any point of the triangle, using barycentric coordinates. A point p of the triangle ABC has barycentric coordinates $(\lambda_1, \lambda_2, \lambda_3)$, that is,

$$p = \lambda_1 A + \lambda_2 B + \lambda_3 C,$$

where $\lambda_i \geq 0$ and $\lambda_1 + \lambda_2 + \lambda_3 = 1$. The transformation of $q = T(p)$ is obtained by

$$\begin{aligned} q = T(p) &= T(\lambda_1 A + \lambda_2 B + \lambda_3 C) \\ &= \lambda_1 T(A) + \lambda_2 T(B) + \lambda_3 T(C) \\ &= \lambda_1 D + \lambda_2 E + \lambda_3 F. \end{aligned}$$

Figure 3.13   Piecewise affine interpolation.

Example 3.8 (Piecewise Affine Transformation)   It is possible to define a transformation on a quadrilateral by gluing together affine transformations. Suppose we know the values of a transformation $T(A)$, $T(B)$, $T(C)$, $T(D)$ on the vertices of a quadrilateral $ABCD$. We subdivide the quadrilateral into two triangles and use affine interpolation in each triangle. The transformation obtained is continuous, but there is a discontinuity in the first derivative. Figure 3.13 shows an example of this interpolation technique. Notice that line segments that cross the sectioning diagonal of the quadrilateral appear broken after the transformation.

It is also possible to represent an affine transformation by a matrix. This will follow from the results in Section 3.7.

3.6 Bilinear Interpolation

The study of affine transformations enabled us to obtain techniques to interpolate a transformation known on the vertices of a triangle. We also used the result to obtain a piecewise affine transformation between two quadrilaterals. In this case, the resulting transformation presented problems of discontinuity in the first derivative, which caused the bending of line segments. We will return to the problem in this section: *Consider the unit square* $[0, 1]^2 = [0, 1] \times [0, 1]$ *and four points* A, B, C *and* D *on the plane* $\mathbb{R}^2$*. We know the values of a transformation on the vertices of the square to be*

$$T(0, 0) = A, \quad T(1, 0) = B, \quad T(1, 1) = C, \quad T(0, 1) = D. \tag{3.7}$$

Interpolate the transformation to the whole square.

We will describe a polynomial transformation of the second degree that gives a solution to the problem. Note that this is a problem of *scattered data interpolation*, with only four points. We should find a transformation $T\colon \mathbb{R}^2 \to \mathbb{R}^2$ satisfying (3.7). We have

$$T(u, v) = (T_1(u, v), T_2(u, v)), \qquad (u, v) \in [0, 1]^2, \tag{3.8}$$

where $T_1, T_2: [0, 1]^2 \to \mathbb{R}$ are real-valued functions. Suppose that

$$A = (a_1, a_2), \quad B = (b_1, b_2), \quad C = (c_1, c_2), \quad D = (d_1, d_2). \tag{3.9}$$

We must obtain T_1 and T_2 such that

$$\begin{aligned}
T_1(0, 0) &= a_1 \\
T_1(1, 0) &= b_1 \\
T_1(1, 1) &= c_1 \\
T_1(0, 1) &= d_1 \\
T_2(0, 0) &= a_2 \\
T_2(1, 0) &= b_2 \\
T_2(1, 1) &= c_2 \\
T_2(0, 1) &= d_2.
\end{aligned} \tag{3.10}$$

We will adopt a very simple strategy to obtain T_1 and T_2. We define a real-valued quadratic function $L: \mathbb{R}^2 \to \mathbb{R}$ by taking the tensor product of two affine functions L_1 and L_2 of one variable. That is,

$$L(u, v) = L_1(u) \cdot L_2(v) = (mu + n)(pv + q). \tag{3.11}$$

L is defined by a second-degree equation of the form

$$L(u, v) = auv + bu + cv + d.$$

It is called a *bilinear function*. The transformation in (3.8), where each coordinate function T_i is a bilinear function, is called a *bilinear transformation*. The technique of using a bilinear transformation to solve our four-points problem is called *bilinear interpolation*.

We remark that a bilinear function is defined by four parameters: a, b, c, and d. Therefore we need eight parameters to define a bilinear transformation (four for each component function). Note that this is exactly the number of equations we have in (3.10).

Before doing the computations to obtain the bilinear transformation T satisfying (3.10), we will give a geometric interpretation of the bilinear transformation. Besides giving a good insight into the problem, this geometric interpretation is useful in the computations.

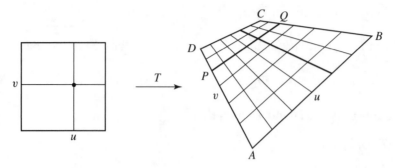

Figure 3.14   Bilinear interpolation scheme.

3.6.1   A Geometric Interpretation

Since the bilinear function in (3.11) is the tensor product of two affine functions, geometrically its value on an arbitrary point (u, v) of the unit square can be obtained by performing two linear interpolations. As illustrated in Figure 3.14, first we interpolate on the edges AD and BC, obtaining the points P and Q:

$$P = (1 - v)A + vD$$
$$Q = (1 - v)B + vC$$

Next, we interpolate the segment PQ using the parameter u:

$$T(u, v) = (1 - u)P + uQ.$$

The final transformation is

$$T(u, v) = (1 - u)[(1 - v)A + vD] + u[(1 - v)B + vC]$$
$$= (1 - u)(1 - v)A + (1 - u)vD + u(1 - v)B + uvC.$$

This can be written in matrix notation:

$$T(u, v) = (\,1 - u \quad u\,) \begin{pmatrix} A & D \\ B & C \end{pmatrix} \begin{pmatrix} 1 - v \\ v \end{pmatrix}.$$

This geometric interpretation guarantees the existence of a unique solution to the linear system (3.10).

3.6.2   Computing the Bilinear Transformation

In this section we will compute the coefficients of the bilinear transformation T, solving the system (3.10). We have $T = (T_1, T_2)$, with

$$T_1(u, v) = auv + bu + cv + d$$
$$T_2(u, v) = euv + fu + gv + h. \tag{3.12}$$

Substituting the above expressions of $T_1(u, v)$ and $T_2(u, v)$ in (3.10), we obtain

$$d = a_1$$
$$h = a_2$$
$$b + d = b_1$$
$$f + h = b_2$$
$$a + b + c + d = c_1$$
$$e + f + g + h = c_2$$
$$c + d = d_1$$
$$g + h = d_2$$

This system is easily solved symbolically. We obtain

$$a = c_1 - b_1 + a_1 - d_1$$
$$b = b_1 - a_1$$
$$c = d_1 - a_1$$
$$d = a_1$$
$$e = c_2 - b_2 + a_2 - d_2$$
$$f = b_2 - a_2$$
$$g = d_2 - a_2$$
$$h = a_2.$$

This allows us to directly determine the bilinear transformation from the four corners of a quadrilateral, by plugging in these values in Equation (3.12).

Some Properties and Examples

The following properties of the bilinear interpolation are easily obtained from the definition and from the geometric interpretation:

- Horizontal and vertical lines of the (u, v) plane segments are transformed into lines.
- Other lines of the (u, v) plane are transformed into curves of second degree (parabolas).
- A uniform subdivision of the edges of the unit square is mapped onto a uniform subdivision of the edges of the quadrilateral.

Figure 3.15   Bilinear interpolation.

Figure 3.15 shows the transformation of an image with a chessboard pattern onto a plane quadrilateral using bilinear interpolation. The above properties can be checked on the transformed image.

3.6.3   The Inverse of a Bilinear Transformation

We have pointed out that invertibility of a transformation is important when computing warping and morphing operations. It enables us to use the inverse method to compute the attributes of the transformed object. Thus it is a natural problem to investigate the invertibility of the bilinear transformation. We will divide this study into two parts: geometric interpretation and computation of the inverse. We will start with the computation of the inverse. These computations will follow [Heckbert, 1989].

We denote the coordinates in the image plane by (x, y), and the coordinates of the domain by (u, v). Thus, we have

$$x = T_1(u, v) = auv + bu + cv + d$$
$$y = T_2(u, v) = euv + fu + gv + h \tag{3.13}$$

Solving for v in the first equation of (3.13), we obtain

$$v = \frac{x - bu - d}{au + c}.$$

Substituting this value in the second equation of (3.13) gives

$$(au + c)(fu + h - y) - (eu + g)(bu + d - x) = 0. \tag{3.14}$$

Now, solving for u in the second equation of (3.13), and substituting in the first equation, we obtain

$$(av + b)(gv + h - y) - (ev + f)(cv + d - x) = 0. \tag{3.15}$$

Equations (3.14) and (3.15) can be written as

$$Au^2 + Bu + C = 0$$
$$Dv^2 + Ev + F = 0, \qquad (3.16)$$

where

$$A = af - be, \quad B = ex - ay + ah - de + cf - bg, \quad C = gx - cy + ch - dg$$
$$D = ag - ce, \quad E = ex - ay + ah - de - cf + bg, \quad F = fx - by + bh - df.$$

The first equation in (3.16) gives two solutions:

$$u = \frac{-B \pm \sqrt{B^2 - 4AC}}{2A},$$
$$v = \frac{x - bu - d}{au + c}. \qquad (3.17)$$

Similarly, the second equation in (3.16) gives two solutions:

$$v = \frac{-E \pm \sqrt{E^2 - 4DF}}{2D},$$
$$u = \frac{y - gv - h}{ev + f}. \qquad (3.18)$$

The computations above are quite straightforward. What do they say? Two conclusions are easily drawn:

- No values of (u, v) can be computed for values of (x, y) where $B^2 - 4AC < 0$, or $E^2 - 4DF < 0$.

- When the computation of the (u, v) coordinates is possible, we have four values for each (x, y): two solutions from Equation (3.17) and two from Equation (3.18) (on the points where $B^2 - 4AC = 0$, or $E^2 - 4DF = 0$, we have only two solutions).

In particular, it follows that the inverse mapping does not exist. But this is not the whole story. We are interested in computing the inverse mapping only on the transformed quadrilateral. The inverse on the quadrilateral always exists, and it is uniquely determined from the above equations. In order to understand this we will look at the geometry of the bilinear transformation.

The equations $B^2 - 4AC = 0$ and $E^2 - 4DF = 0$ implicitly define the same curve of the (x, y) plane: a parabola. This parabola is plotted in Figure 3.16. The points where the inverse is not defined are the points in the convex region of the plane defined by the parabola (shaded region).

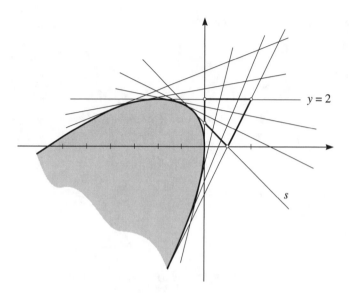

Figure 3.16   Image of the bilinear transformation.

The inverse is only defined on the concave region, including the parabola. In order to understand the behavior of the inverse transformation in this region, we take the family of all lines $u = u_0$, u_0 constant (vertical lines on the (u, v) domain). We know that these lines are transformed into lines. The parabola is the envoltory of the transformed lines, as illustrated in Figure 3.16. [The example in this figure was computed for $A = (1, 0)$, $B = (2, 2)$, $C = (0, 2)$ and $D = (0, 1)$.] Also note the foldover of the lines that characterizes the existence of two solutions. But it is clear from the figure (and can be proved analytically) that for points inside the quadrilateral, when we compute the two points of the inverse, using Equation (3.17), only one of them belongs to the unit square of the domain.

Now we should observe that Equation (3.18) does not give any new solution. Geometrically, the family of horizontal lines $v = v_0$, v_0 constant, of the (u, v) domain, is transformed into exactly the same family of lines tangent to the parabola.

3.6.4   Transformation Between Arbitrary Quadrilaterals

Now that we have studied the inverse of the bilinear transformation and have written the equations to compute it, it is possible to obtain a transformation

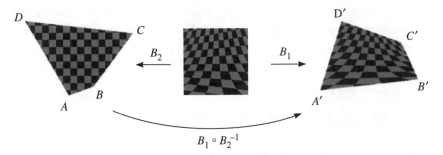

Figure 3.17 Transformation between two arbitrary plane quadrilaterals.

between two arbitrary quadrilaterals $ABCD$ and $A'B'C'D'$ in the following steps:

1. Compute the bilinear transformation $B_1 \colon [0, 1]^2 \to A'B'C'D'$.

2. Compute the bilinear transformation $B_2 \colon [0, 1]^2 \to ABCD$.

3. Take the composite transformation $B_1 \circ B_2^{-1} \colon ABCD \to A'B'C'D'$. It gives the transformation we are looking for.

This process is illustrated in Figure 3.17.

We should remark that the transformation $B_1 \circ B_2^{-1}$ is not a bilinear transformation, because the inverse of a bilinear transformation is not a bilinear itself. Nevertheless, the transformation has a distinguished property: it takes two families of transversal line segments from the source quadrilateral into another family of transversal line segments of the target quadrilateral.

3.6.5 Extensions to Higher Dimensions

The bilinear transformation extends easily to n-dimensional space. In the case of $n = 3$, we have a trilinear function of three variables defined as a tensor product of three one-dimensional affine functions:

$$L(u, v, w) = L_1(u)L_2(v)L_3(w)$$
$$= auvw + buv + cuw + dvw + eu + fv + gw + h.$$

A trilinear transformation $T \colon \mathbb{R}^3 \to \mathbb{R}^3$ has three trilinear functions as coordinates:

$$T(u, v, w) = (T_1(u, v, w)T_2(u, v, w), T_3(u, v, w)).$$

Therefore, it is determined by 24 parameters.

We conclude that we need eight points of the space to completely define a trilinear transformation; that is, a trilinear transformation defines a transformation between two cubical domains of the space. This is useful in obtaining transformations of graphical objects described by volumetric data.

3.7 Projective Space and Transformations

Plane projections constitute the starting point as a motivation to study projective transformations. Consider two planes Π_1 and Π_2 of the three-dimensional space $\mathbb{R}^3$. A transformation $F\colon \Pi_1 \to \Pi_2$ is affine if

$$F((1-t)P + tQ) = (1-t)F(P) + tF(Q).$$

To define a *parallel projection* from Π_1 to Π_2, we consider a line r that intersects both planes. For each point $p \in \Pi_1$, we take the line s that contains p and is parallel to r, and define the projection $F(p)$, of p onto Π_2, as the point where s intersects Π_2 (see Figure 3.18).

It is a good and simple exercise to show that a parallel projection is an affine transformation. We will now describe the relationship between projective transformations and conic projections. Consider two planes Π_1 and Π_2, and a fixed point O that does not belong to either of the planes. For each $P \in \Pi_1$ the conic projection of P with origin at O is the point of $F(P) \in \Pi_2$ where the line, $O + t\overrightarrow{OP}$, $t \in \mathbb{R}$, through the points O and P intersects Π_2 (see Figure 3.19). The point O is called the *center of the projection*.

We should remark that any point of the projection line $O + t\overrightarrow{OP}$, $t \in \mathbb{R}$, through O and P projects onto the point Q. Thus, from the point of view of conic projection, any point $P \in \Pi_1$ can be identified with the line OP. Any point of the line could be chosen as a representative of P. We must eliminate the point O itself as a representation because it belongs to all of the lines. This remark gives the motivation to introduce the following definition:

Definition (Projective Plane)   The projective plane with origin O is the set of all lines of the space passing through O, excluding the point O. Thus, each line is a point of the projective space. The projective plane will be denoted by $\mathbb{R}P^2(O)$.

Sometimes it is convenient to distinguish between the affine point P and the projective point defined by the line through OP. When this happens we will use the notation $[P]$ to represent the projective point. The reader should

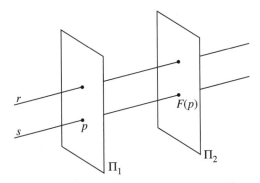

Figure 3.18 Parallel projection between two planes.

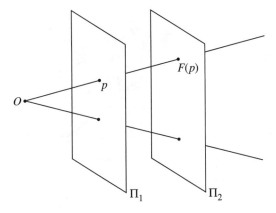

Figure 3.19 Conic projection between two planes.

notice that since the origin O is fixed, we have a vector space structure on the three-dimensional space; therefore, the equality $[P_1] = [P_2]$ means that there exists a $\lambda \neq 0$ such that $P_1 = \lambda P_2$. Geometrically, P_1 and P_2 are on the same line through the origin O.

There are points of the projective plane $\mathbb{R}P^2(O)$ that have no projection onto the affine plane Π_2. These are the points represented by lines parallel to the plane Π_1 (see Figure 3.20). These points are called *ideal points*. The other points of the projective plane, that is, points that project onto Π_2, are called *regular points*. By forgetting our "euclidean view" of the conic projection from the affine plane Π_1 to Π_2, we should notice that there is no intrinsic difference

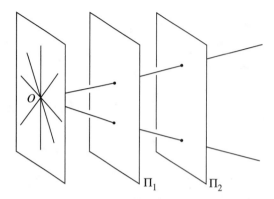

Figure 3.20   Ideal points of the projective plane.

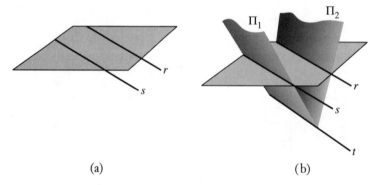

(a)   (b)

Figure 3.21   Ideal points (a) and parallel lines (b).

between the ideal and the regular points of the projective plane: any point is
represented by some straight line through O (excluding O itself).

3.7.1 Ideal Points and Parallelism

What is the geometric meaning of the ideal points in the projective plane?
To answer this question, consider the plane Π shown in Figure 3.21(a), with
two parallel lines r and s. By choosing a point $O \notin \Pi$ and transforming Π into
a projective plane, as shown in Figure 3.21(b), we see that these two lines,
represented for our euclidean eyes by planes Π_1 and Π_2, intersect at the ideal
point represented by the line t through O. The conclusion is simple: there
are no parallel lines in the projective plane. Parallel lines in the affine plane
intersect at ideal points of the projective plane.

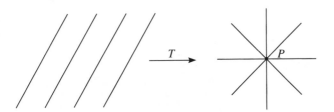

Figure 3.22 Ideal point is mapped onto the point P.

3.7.2 Projective Transformations

Consider the projective plane $\mathbb{R}P^2(O)$. A *projective transformation* is a nonsingular affine transformation of the space that keeps the point O fixed (note that this is well defined because nonsingular affine mappings transform lines into lines). Similarly, a projective transformation $\mathbb{R}P^2(O_1)$ to $\mathbb{R}P^2(O_2)$ is an affine transformation F of the space, such that $F(O_1) = O_2$. It should be clear that a projective transformation is defined up to multiplication by some nonzero scalar, that is, $T = \lambda T$, $\lambda \neq 0$.

Example 3.9 (Projective Transformations and Parallelism) Each family of parallel lines of the euclidean plane intersects at the same ideal point of the projective plane. When a projective transformation maps this ideal point to a regular point, it is destroying the parallelism from the euclidean point of view. This is illustrated in Figure 3.22.

The point P, the image of the ideal point, is called a *vanishing point* of the direction defined by the parallel lines.

3.7.3 Homogeneous Coordinates

In order to do computations with projective transformations, we must introduce coordinates on the projective plane and obtain representations of the transformations on these coordinates. The natural coordinates of the projective plane are *homogeneous coordinates* that will be introduced in this section.

Consider a projective plane $\mathbb{R}P^2(O)$ and define an orthogonal coordinate system (x, y, z) on the three-dimensional space satisfying two conditions: the origin of the coordinate system is the point O, and the line at infinity of the projective plane is represented by the plane $z = 0$ (xy-plane). This is illustrated in Figure 3.23(a).

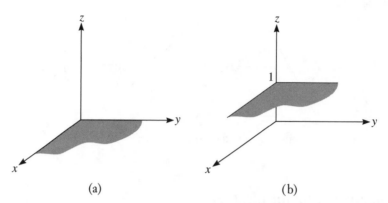

(a)   (b)

Figure 3.23   Homogeneous coordinates: line at infinity (a) and regular points (b).

A point $[P]$ of the projective plane $\mathbb{R}P^2(O)$ is represented by a line through the origin O (the origin excluded). The euclidean coordinates (x, y, z) of P are the projective coordinates of the projective point $[P]$. Any point λP on the line could be used as a representative of the projective point $[P]$. This means that the projective coordinates of the point are defined up to a multiplication by some nonnull real number:

$$(x, y, z) = \lambda(x, y, z), \quad \lambda \neq 0.$$

For this reason these coordinates are called *homogeneous coordinates*.

The projective points are divided into two classes: *ideal points*, which have homogeneous coordinates $(x, y, 0)$, $x, y \in \mathbb{R}$; and *regular points*, which have homogeneous coordinates (x, y, z), $x, y, z \in \mathbb{R}$, $z \neq 0$.

By multiplying the coordinates (x, y, z) of a regular point by $1/z$, we obtain the coordinates $(x/z, y/z, 1)$. Geometrically, this means that any regular point has a representative on the plane $z = 1$, as shown in Figure 3.23(b). Thus this plane represents a "copy" of the affine plane inside the projective plane.

Projective Transformations and Homogeneous Coordinates

In homogeneous coordinates, a projective transformation is defined by a nonsingular linear transformation of $\mathbb{R}^3$. Therefore, it's represented by some 3×3 matrix

$$\begin{pmatrix} a & b & t_1 \\ c & d & t_2 \\ p_1 & p_2 & s \end{pmatrix},$$

that is uniquely defined, up to a multiplication by some nonzero real number.

Note that the above matrix is divided into four blocks

$$\begin{pmatrix} A & T \\ P & S \end{pmatrix},$$

where

$$A = \begin{pmatrix} a & b \\ c & d \end{pmatrix}, \quad P = (\, p_1 \quad p_2\,), \quad T = \begin{pmatrix} t_1 \\ t_2 \end{pmatrix}, \quad \text{and} \quad S = (s).$$

This block subdivision helps us understand the geometry of the projective transformations. In fact, we have

$$\begin{pmatrix} a & b & 0 \\ c & d & 0 \\ 0 & 0 & 1 \end{pmatrix} \cdot \begin{pmatrix} x \\ y \\ 1 \end{pmatrix} = (ax + by, cx + dy, 1).$$

This shows that the block A represents a linear transformation of the euclidean plane $z = 1$. From

$$\begin{pmatrix} a & b & t_1 \\ c & d & t_2 \\ 0 & 0 & 1 \end{pmatrix} \cdot \begin{pmatrix} x \\ y \\ 1 \end{pmatrix} = (ax + by + t_1, cx + dy + t_2, 1),$$

we conclude that the block T is responsible for translations of the euclidean plane $z = 1$ (with translation vector (t_1, t_2)). In sum, the block matrix (AT) represents affine transformations of the plane $z = 1$. The reader should verify that the block $S = (s)$, $s \neq 0$, represents a scaling transformation of the plane $z = 1$ by the factor $1/s$.

In order to analyze the block $P = (\, p_1 \quad p_2\,)$, the reader should verify that

$$\begin{pmatrix} 1 & 0 & 0 \\ 0 & 1 & 0 \\ p_1 & p_2 & 1 \end{pmatrix} \cdot \begin{pmatrix} x \\ y \\ z \end{pmatrix} = (x, y, p_1 x + p_2 y + z).$$

Since $p_1 \cdot p_2 \neq 0$, the equation $p_1 x + p_2 y + z = 0$ has nonnull solutions both for $z = 0$ and for $z \neq 0$. Geometrically, this means that the projective transformation maps ideal points (i.e., points with coordinate $z = 0$) to regular points, and vice versa. In fact, it is easy to verify that when $p_1 \neq 0$, the ideal point corresponding to the direction of the x-axis is transformed into some regular point. Also, when $p_2 \neq 0$, the ideal point corresponding to the direction of the y-axis is mapped into a regular point. Thus, for $p_1 \cdot p_2 \neq 0$, the transformation has two vanishing points associated to the x and y directions. Figure 3.24 illustrates the transformation of a rectangle using a projective transformation with two vanishing points.

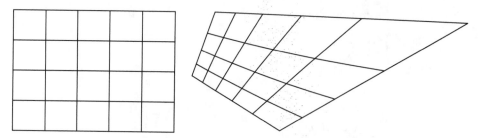

Figure 3.24   Projective transformation with two vanishing points.

Projective Transformation on Affine Coordinates

Consider a projective transformation defined, in homogeneous coordinates, by the matrix

$$\begin{pmatrix} a & b & c \\ d & e & f \\ g & h & i \end{pmatrix}.$$

If $z = (x, y, 1)$ is a regular point, we have

$$T(x, y, 1) = \begin{pmatrix} a & b & c \\ d & e & f \\ g & h & i \end{pmatrix} \cdot \begin{pmatrix} x \\ y \\ 1 \end{pmatrix} = (ax + by + c, dx + ey + f, gx + hy + i).$$

If $gx + hy + i \neq 0$ (i.e., the image of $(x, y, 1)$ is not an ideal point), we have

$$T(x, y, 1) = T(x, y) = \left(\frac{ax + by + c}{gx + hy + i}, \frac{dx + ey + f}{gx + hy + i} \right). \tag{3.19}$$

This is the expression of the projective transformation T on affine coordinates.

The Inverse of a Projective Transformation

A projective transformation is a nonsingular linear map; therefore it is invertible, and the inverse mapping is also a projective transformation. If M is the matrix of a transformation T, in homogeneous coordinates, the inverse is defined by the matrix

$$M^{-1} = \frac{1}{\det(M)} \text{Adj}(M),$$

where det is the determinant of the matrix and Adj is the adjoint matrix. Since projective transformations are defined up to multiplication by some real number, we can discard the multiplication by $1/\det(A)$, and the matrix of the inverse transformation is given by $M^{-1} = \text{Adj}(M)$. If

$$M = \begin{pmatrix} a & b & c \\ d & e & f \\ g & h & i \end{pmatrix},$$

we have

$$M^{-1} = \text{Adj}(M) = \begin{pmatrix} ei - fh & fg - di & dh - ge \\ ch - bi & ai - cg & bg - ah \\ bf - ce & cd - af & ae - bd \end{pmatrix}.$$

This is very useful and saves time when computing the inverse transformation.

3.7.4 Projective Frames and the Fundamental Theorem

We have seen that an affine frame of the plane (three noncollinear points) suffices to define a nondegenerate affine transformation. We could pose a similar question here: How many points are necessary to define a projective transformation? The answer is simple: *four points, such that any three of them are noncollinear*. This result is known in the literature as the *fundamental theorem of plane projective geometry*. The simplest and most elegant way to prove the theorem is by introducing the concept of a projective frame.

A *projective frame* of the projective plane is a set of four points $\{P_0, P_1, P_2, P_3\}$ such that there exists a basis $\{v_1, v_2, v_3\}$ of the three-dimensional space satisfying

- $[P_1] = [v_1]$;
- $[P_2] = [v_2]$;
- $[P_3] = [v_3]$; and
- $[P_0] = [v_1 + v_2 + v_3]$.

The basis $\{v_1, v_2, v_3\}$ is called a *generating basis* for the projective frame (see Figure 3.25).

Theorem 3 If $\{\overline{w}_1, \overline{w}_2, \overline{w}_3\}$ is another generating basis of the projective frame $\{P_0, P_1, P_2, P_3\}$, then $w_i = \lambda v_i$ for some nonnull real number λ.

Indeed, from the definition of the generating basis, we have $w_i = \lambda_i \overline{w}_i$, $i = 1, 2, 3$, and $w_1 + w_2 + w_3 = \lambda P_0 = \lambda(\overline{w}_1 + \overline{w}_2 + \overline{w}_3)$. Hence,

$$\lambda_1 \overline{w}_1 + \lambda_2 \overline{w}_2 + \lambda_3 \overline{w}_3 = \lambda(\overline{w}_1 + \overline{w}_2 + \overline{w}_3).$$

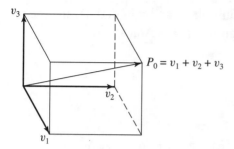

Figure 3.25   A projective frame.

Since the vectors $\overline{w}_i$, $i = 1, 2, 3$, form a basis of the euclidean space, we must have $\lambda_i = \lambda$.

Theorem 4   If $\{P_0, P_1, P_2, P_3\}$ is a projective frame and T is a projective transformation such that $T([P_i]) = [P_i]$, then T is a multiple of the identity.

We must prove that there exists some constant λ such that $T = \lambda I$, where I denotes the identity transformation. For this it suffices to show that there is a basis $\{w_1, w_2, w_3\}$ of the euclidean space such that $T(w_i) = \lambda w_i$. From the hypothesis, there are constants c_1, c_2, c_3, such that

$$T(P_i) = c_i P_i. \tag{3.20}$$

Consider a generating basis $\{w_1, w_2, w_3\}$ of the projective frame $\{P_0, P_1, P_2, P_3\}$. Then

$$w_i = \lambda_i P_i, \quad i = 1, 2, 3. \tag{3.21}$$

From (3.20) and (3.21) we have

$$T(w_i) = T(\lambda_i P_i) = \lambda_i T(P_i) = \lambda_i c_i P_i. \tag{3.22}$$

On the other hand, we have

$$T(w_1) + T(w_2) + T(w_3) = T(w_1 + w_2 + w_3) = \lambda T(P_0) = \lambda c_0 P_0. \tag{3.23}$$

Equations (3.22) and (3.23) show that $\{T(w_1), T(w_2), T(w_3)\}$ is a generating basis of the projective frame $\{P_0, P_1, P_2, P_3\}$. Hence, from Theorem 3, we conclude that $T(w_i) = \lambda w_i$.

As a consequence of Theorem 4 we have the following:

Corollary 1 A projective transformation is uniquely defined on a projective frame.

In fact, if f and g are two projective transformations satisfying $f([Pi]) = g([Pi])$, the projective transformation $T = f \circ g^{-1}$ satisfies $T([Pi]) = [Pi]$, hence $f \circ g^{-1} = \lambda I$. From the theorem we have $T = f \circ g^{-1} = \lambda I$, that is, $f = \lambda g$.

The above result enables us to obtain the result we were searching for:

Theorem 5 (Fundamental Theorem of Projective Geometry) A plane projective transformation is completely determined by four points P_0, P_1, P_2, P_3 such that any three of them are noncollinear.

Indeed, the four points define a projective frame, hence the result follows from Corollary 1. In the next section we will see how to compute the projective transformation defined by four points.

3.7.5 Computing Projective Transformations

From the fundamental theorem of plane projective geometry (Theorem 5), a projective transformation is uniquely defined at four points P_0, P_1, P_2, and P_3 such that no three of them are collinear. Geometrically, this means that it is possible to obtain a projective transformation between two arbitrary plane quadrilaterals. In this section we will make the computation of the transformation explicit (see [Heckbert, 1989]).

We will use Equation (3.19) to compute T. Without loss of generality we will suppose that $i = 1$. Suppose that $P_k = (u_k, v_k)$, and

$$T(u_k, v_k) = (x_k, y_k), \quad k = 0, 1, 2, 3.$$

We have

$$x_k = \frac{au_k + bv_k + c}{gu_k + hv_k + 1} \Rightarrow u_k a + v_k b + c - u_k x_k g - v_k x_k h = x_k$$

$$y_k = \frac{du_k + ev_k + f}{gu_k + hv_k + 1} \Rightarrow u_k d + v_k e + f - u_k y_k g - v_k y_k h = y_k.$$

Taking $k = 0, 1, 2, 3$, we obtain the linear system with eight equations:

$$
\begin{pmatrix}
u_0 & v_0 & 1 & 0 & 0 & 0 & -u_0x_0 & -v_0x_0 \\
u_1 & v_1 & 1 & 0 & 0 & 0 & -u_1x_1 & -v_1x_1 \\
u_2 & v_2 & 2 & 0 & 0 & 0 & -u_2x_2 & -v_2x_2 \\
u_3 & v_3 & 3 & 0 & 0 & 0 & -u_3x_3 & -v_3x_3 \\
0 & 0 & 0 & u_0 & v_0 & 1 & -u_0y_0 & -v_0y_0 \\
0 & 0 & 0 & u_1 & v_1 & 1 & -u_1y_1 & -v_1y_1 \\
0 & 0 & 0 & u_2 & v_2 & 2 & -u_2y_2 & -v_2y_2 \\
0 & 0 & 0 & u_3 & v_3 & 3 & -u_3y_3 & -v_3y_3
\end{pmatrix}
\begin{pmatrix}
a \\ b \\ c \\ d \\ e \\ f \\ g \\ h
\end{pmatrix}
=
\begin{pmatrix}
x_0 \\ x_1 \\ x_2 \\ x_3 \\ y_0 \\ y_1 \\ y_2 \\ y_3
\end{pmatrix}.
\tag{3.24}
$$

This system has a unique solution, but solving it is not the most efficient way to compute the projective transformations between two quadrilaterals. We will use the same strategy we used in Section 3.6.4 to compute a bilinear transformation between two arbitrary quadrilaterals: the transformation will be broken into simpler transformations. As in the bilinear case, this is achieved by considering three distinct cases:

- Case 1: Square to quadrilateral projective transformation
- Case 2: Quadrilateral to square projective transformation
- Case 3: Quadrilateral to quadrilateral projective transformation

Case 1: Square to Quadrilateral Projective Transformation

This transformation will be computed by solving the system (3.24) symbolically. In fact, we have

$u_0 = 0, v_0 = 0;$

$u_1 = 1, v_1 = 0;$

$u_2 = 1, v_2 = 1;$

$u_3 = 0, v_3 = 1,$

and the system (3.24) reduces to

$$c = x_0$$
$$a + c - gx_1 = x_1$$
$$a + b + c - gx_2 + hx_2 = x_2$$
$$b + c - hx_3 = x_3$$
$$f = y_0$$
$$d + f - gy_1 = y_1$$
$$d + e + f - gy_2 + hy_2 = y_2$$
$$e + f - hy_3 = y_3$$

We will use the notation

$$\Delta x_1 = x_1 - x_2; \quad \Delta x_2 = x_3 - x_2; \quad \sum x = x_0 - x_1 + x_2 - x_3;$$

$$\Delta y_1 = y_1 - y_2; \quad \Delta y_2 = y_3 - y_2; \quad \sum y = y_0 - y_1 + y_2 - y_3.$$

The solution splits into two subcases:

(a) $\sum x = 0$ and $\sum y = 0$. In this case the transformed quadrilateral is a parallelogram; therefore, the mapping is affine and we have $a = x_1 - x_0$, $b = x_2 - x_1$, $c = x_0$, $d = y_1 - y_0$, $e = y_2 - y_1$, $f = y_0$, and $g = h = 0$.

(b) $\sum x \neq 0$ or $\sum y \neq 0$. In this case the transformation is not affine, and we have

$$g = \det \begin{pmatrix} \sum x & \Delta x_2 \\ \sum y & \Delta y_2 \end{pmatrix} \Big/ \det \begin{pmatrix} \Delta x_1 & \Delta x_2 \\ \Delta y_1 & \Delta y_2 \end{pmatrix}$$

$$h = \det \begin{pmatrix} \Delta x_1 & \sum x \\ \Delta y_1 & \sum y \end{pmatrix} \Big/ \det \begin{pmatrix} \Delta x_1 & \Delta x_2 \\ \Delta y_1 & \Delta y_2 \end{pmatrix}$$

$$a = x_1 - x_0 + g x_1$$
$$b = x_3 - x_0 + h x_3$$
$$c = x_0$$
$$d = y_1 - y_0 + g y_1$$
$$e = y_3 - y_0 + h y_3$$
$$f = y_0$$

Obviously, from the transformation above we obtain the projective transformation from an arbitrary rectangle onto a quadrilateral by using scales and translations.

Case 2: Quadrilateral to Square Projective Transformation

This transformation is obtained by computing the square to quadrilateral transformation as explained above and taking the inverse transformation using the adjoint matrix.

Case 3: Quadrilateral to Quadrilateral Projective Transformation

This transformation is obtained by compositing a transformation from a quadrilateral to the unit square (Case 2 above) with the transformation from the square to a quadrilateral (Case 1 above). This is illustrated in Figure 3.26.

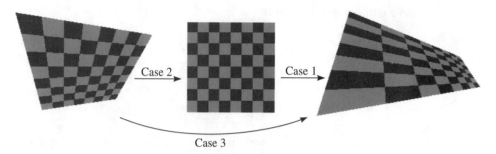

Figure 3.26   Projective interpolation scheme.

Figure 3.27   Projective transformation of a rectangle.

3.7.6   The Projective Space

Everything we did before for the projective plane extends to n dimensions. This enables us to define the n-dimensional projective space and projective transformations of the space.

We will not go over details here. An n-dimensional projective frame has $n + 2$ points, and a projective transformation is completely characterized by the knowledge of the transformation at $n + 2$ points such that any $n + 1$ of them defines an affine frame.

Three-dimensional projective transformations are very useful in the camera transformations in computer graphics. Also, they can be used to obtain warping of graphical objects embedded in the three-dimensional space (surfaces and volumetric data, for instance).

We have seen that there exists a unique projective transformation defined on the four corners of a quadrilateral. This gives a technique to interpolate the values of a transformation defined on the vertices of the quadrilateral. This interpolation method is called *projective interpolation*. The result of the method on a rectangle is shown in Figure 3.27.

Note that a projective interpolation preserves linear elements of the projective space (lines, planes, etc.), but destroys parallelism. Based on the fundamental result that a plane projective transformation is completely determined

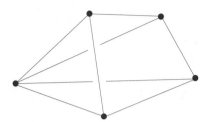

Figure 3.28 Quadrangular pyramid.

on the vertices of a quadrilateral, a rapid intuition could lead us to believe that we can use projective transformations to transform from one cubical region of the three-dimensional space to another.

Nonetheless, it should be noted, as stated above, that the fundamental theorem of projective geometry in the three-dimensional space says that a three-dimensional projective transformation is completely defined on five points of the space that define the vertices of a quadrangular pyramid (see Figure 3.28).

From the point of view of computer graphics, this says that there exists a projective change of coordinates between any two arbitrary camera coordinate systems.

We have seen before that the bilinear interpolation extends to n dimensions; in particular, in 3D space it gives a solution to the problem of scattered data interpolation for eight points (transformation between two cubes). This is one of the advantages of bilinear over projective transformations as related to warping and morphing.

3.8 Coons Patch Transformation

A natural extension to the transformation problem defined by four corner points is to allow the sides to be defined by arbitrary curves. Consider four points p_{00}, p_{10}, p_{01}, and p_{11} in $\mathbb{R}^3$, and four curves $p_{0v}(v)$, $p_{1v}(v)$, $p_{u0}(u)$, and $p_{u1}(u)$, such that (see Figure 3.29)

$$p_{u0}(0) = p_{0v}(0) = p_{00}$$
$$p_{u1}(0) = p_{0v}(1) = p_{01}$$
$$p_{u0}(1) = p_{1v}(0) = p_{10}$$
$$p_{u1}(1) = p_{1v}(1) = p_{11}$$

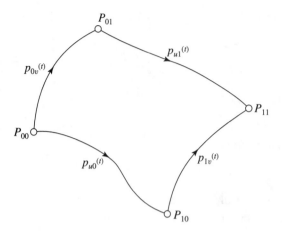

Figure 3.29   Space curves.

We pose the following problem: *Construct a parametric patch* $C: [0, 1] \times [0, 1] \to \mathbb{R}^3$ *such that the curves* $p_{0v}(v)$, $p_{1v}(v)$, $p_{u0}(u)$, *and* $p_{u1}(u)$ *are the boundary of the patch.*

More precisely, the boundary curves of the unit square are mapped onto the curves:

$$C(0, v) = p_{0v}(v); \quad C(1, v) = p_{1v}(v); \quad C(u, 0)$$
$$= p_{u0}(u); \quad C(u, 1) = p_{u1}(u). \tag{3.25}$$

Certainly, the solution to this problem is not unique. Also, it should be observed that if the paths $p_{0v}(v)$, $p_{1v}(v)$, $p_{u0}(u)$, and $p_{u1}(u)$ are line segments, a solution is given by the bilinear transformation shown in Section 3.6 of this chapter. It seems natural to look for a solution that reduces to the bilinear transformation when the curves are line segments.

Alan Coons [Coons, 1974] devised a very simple solution to the problem. It consists of using linear blending of the boundary curves to construct the patch. This boundary blending is attained in four steps:

1. **Vertical Lofting.** First we interpolate the u-curves p_{u0} and p_{u1} by using linear interpolation in v:

$$(1 - v)p_{u0}(u) + vp_{u1}(u).$$

This operation, called a *lofting*, is illustrated in Figure 3.30(a).

2. **Horizontal Lofting.** This step computes a lofting surface using the v-curves p_{0v} and p_{1v}:

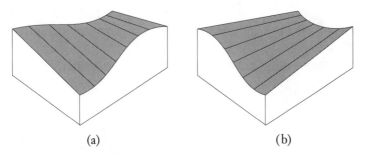

(a)   (b)

Figure 3.30 Lofting: vertical (a) and horizontal (b).

$$(1 - u)p_{0v}(v) + up_{1v}(v).$$

This is illustrated in Figure 3.30(b).

3. **Lofting Summation.** Now we sum the operations of horizontal and vertical lofting, obtaining the patch

$$\widetilde{C}(u, v) = (1 - v)p_{u0}(u) + vp_{u1}(u)$$
$$+ (1 - u)p_{0v}(v) + up_{1v}(v). \tag{3.26}$$

Note that the boundary curve of this patch,

$$\widetilde{C}(0, v) = (1 - v)p_{00} + vp_{01} + p_{0v}(v),$$

consists of the original curve p_{0v} added to a linear interpolation of the end points p_{00} and p_{01}. Similar results are valid for the other boundary curves $\widetilde{C}(1, v)$, $\widetilde{C}(u, 0)$, and $\widetilde{C}(u, 1)$.

4. **Bilinear Subtraction.** It can be observed that by subtracting from $\widetilde{C}(u, v)$ the bilinear transformation $B(u, v)$ defined by the four points p_{00}, p_{01}, p_{10}, and p_{11}, we obtain a patch

$$C(u, v) = \widetilde{C}(u, v) - B(u, v)$$

that satisfies our initial requirements in Equation (3.25). Moreover, it is easy to see that it reduces to the bilinear patch when the boundary curves are line segments. C is called a *Coons patch* (see Figure 3.31).

When the boundary curves $p_{0v}(v)$, $p_{1v}(v)$, $p_{u0}(u)$, and $p_{u1}(u)$ are plane curves, the image of the Coons patch is contained on the plane; therefore, $C(u, v)$ defines a transformation $C: [0, 1] \times [0, 1] \rightarrow \mathbb{R}^2$. The patch describes a plane region bounded by the curves.

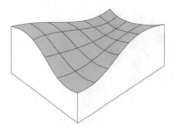

Figure 3.31   Coons patch.

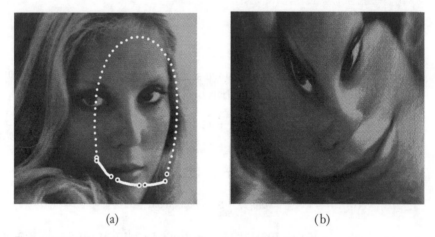

           (a)   (b)

Figure 3.32   Image warping using Coons patch: four boundary curves (a) and warped image (b) [from Heckbert, 1994].

The use of the Coons patch plane transformation for warping images dates back to work done by Lance Williams in the late '70s and has been described in [Heckbert, 1994]. The user specifies the four boundary curves on the image, and the region limited by these curves are warped onto a square of the plane.

This is illustrated in Figure 3.32. In Figure 3.32(a) we show the planar region delimited by the four curves, and in Figure 3.32(b) we show the transformed square region. The computation of the transformation uses an inverse mapping strategy, computing the Coons transformation from the square into the planar region. This avoids the computation of the Coons patch inverse transformation, which is a difficult task.

We should remark that when the curves specified by the user self-intersect, they do not define a planar region. In this case the Coons patch transformation

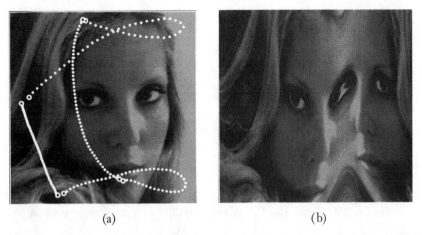

(a)   (b)

Figure 3.33 Four secondary curves (a) and warped image with foldover (b) [from Heckbert, 1994].

is not bijective. Foldover effects can be produced by carefully choosing the curves. An example is shown in Figure 3.33(b), where the region defined by the four boundary curves in Figure 3.33(a) was used.

3.9 Conformal Transformations

A transformation $T \colon \mathbb{R}^n \to \mathbb{R}^n$ is *conformal* if it preserves angles between vectors. That is, for any point $p \in \mathbb{R}^n$, if v_1 and v_2 are vectors at p with an angle θ between them (see Figure 3.34), then the image of these vectors by the derivative df of f,

$$w_1 = df(p).v_1, \quad \text{and} \quad w_2 = df(p).v_2,$$

also has angle θ.

Certainly, isometries are examples of conformal mappings, and this class includes in particular translations and rotations of the space. A scaling transformation $T(P) = \lambda P$, $p \in \mathbb{R}^n$, $\lambda \neq 0$ is an example of a conformal transformation that is not an isometry.

In fact, the class of conformal transformations of the plane $\mathbb{R}^2$ is a very rich one. To see this, consider the plane $\mathbb{R}^2$ as the complex plane with the usual identification of vectors with complex numbers:

$$(x, y) \leftrightarrow x + iy.$$

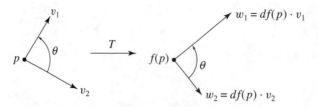

Figure 3.34   Angle preservation mapping.

Thus, a complex function $f: \mathbb{C} \to \mathbb{C}$ induces naturally a transformation of the plane. We have the following classical result: *Any complex analytic function $f: \mathbb{C} \to \mathbb{C}$ of the complex plane, with $f'(z) \neq 0$, defines a conformal transformation of the plane.*

The truth of the above assertion follows from the fact that the derivative df of f at a point $p \in \mathbb{C}$, applied to a vector $v \in \mathbb{C}$, is given by

$$df(p).v = f'(p) \cdot v,$$

where $f'(p)$ is the complex derivative of f (a complex number), and the · on the right means the product of two complex numbers. Therefore, the effect of applying the derivative to the vector v consists in multiplying the vector by some complex number. Now we just have to remember that when we multiply a vector $v \in \mathbb{R}^2$ by some complex number, the vector v is rotated and scaled (this is easy to see by writing the complex number in its polar form $p = |p|e^{\theta(p)}$). Since rotation and scaling preserve angles, we conclude the proof of the assertion.

Figure 3.35 shows the transformation of an image of a rectangular uniform grid by the complex analytic map of the plane defined by

$$f(z) = \frac{z-1}{z+1}, \qquad z \neq -1.$$

The previous example uses a global conformal transformation of the plane. The interesting fact about conformal mappings is the Riemann mapping theorem, which asserts the following: *Given any simply connected region U which is not the whole plane, there exists a complex analytic diffeomorphism from U on the unit disk $D^2 = \{z \in \mathbb{C};\ |z| < 1\}$.* (A plane region is simply connected if it has no holes.) Moreover, the transformation is unique up to orientation, and the choice of the value of the transformation at an arbitrary point of the domain U.

Figure 3.35 Conformal transformation of a uniform rectangular grid [from Frederick and Schwartz, 1990].

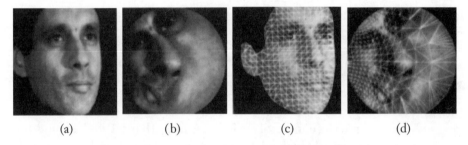

(a) (b) (c) (d)

Figure 3.36 Angle preservation mapping: original image (a), warped image (b), source mesh (c), and target mesh (d) [from Frederick and Schwartz, 1990].

It follows immediately, by composition, that there is a conformal diffeomorphism between two arbitrary simply connected domains of the plain. There are constructive proofs of the Riemann mapping theorem. This enables us to compute, numerically, the conformal diffeomorphism between two simply connected regions.

The use of the Riemann mapping theorem for image warping has been addressed in the literature in [Frederick and Schwartz, 1990] and also in [Fiume et al., 1987]. Figure 3.36(b) shows a conformal transformation from the image of a man's face in Figure 3.36(a). In Figures 3.36(c) and (d) we can see the triangulation used to compute the transformation numerically.

3.10 Families of Transformation

Graphical object metamorphosis consists of a transition between the shape and the attributes of two graphical objects. From the mathematical point of view, this transition is achieved by a continuum of transformations from one object to the other. This notion of a "continuum of transformations" can be mathematically described using a k-parameter family of transformations.

Definition   A k-parameter family of transformations of a subset $U \subset \mathbb{R}^n$ is a map $T: U \times \mathbb{R}^k \to \mathbb{R}^m$. For each vector $v \in \mathbb{R}^k$, we obtain a transformation $T_v: U \to \mathbb{R}^m$ defining the transformed set $T_v(U)$. The space $\mathbb{R}^k$ is called the *parameter space*. It is sometimes convenient to take the parameter space as being a subset of $\mathbb{R}^k$, instead of the whole space.

Example 3.10 (Family of Rotations)   A rotation R of the space $\mathbb{R}^3$ by an angle θ around the z-axis is defined by the matrix

$$R_\theta = \begin{pmatrix} \cos\theta & \sin\theta & 0 \\ -\sin\theta & \cos\theta & 0 \\ 0 & 0 & 1 \end{pmatrix}.$$

If the angle θ is allowed to vary on the set of real numbers, we obtain a one-parameter family of rotations $R: \mathbb{R}^3 \times \mathbb{R} \to \mathbb{R}^3$. For each $\theta \in \mathbb{R}$, we obtain a rotation R_θ of the family.

Example 3.11 (Family of Twists)   A *twist* [Barr, 1984] around the z-axis is a transformation obtained by rotating a point around the z-axis by an angle θ, which varies with the z-coordinate that is $\theta = \theta(z)$. Therefore, points with differing z-coordinates will undergo a different amount of rotation. Geometrically, the twist rotates the point around the z-axis and translates it along the axis.

A twist transformation can be expressed analytically in matrix notation by

$$R(x, y, z) = \begin{pmatrix} \cos\theta(z) & -\sin\theta(z) & 0 \\ \sin\theta(z) & \cos\theta(z) & 0 \\ 0 & 0 & 1 \end{pmatrix} \begin{pmatrix} x \\ y \\ z \end{pmatrix}.$$

If the function θ is the identity function, $\theta(z) = z$, the twist transformation reduces to a rotation.

By allowing the angle θ to vary on the set of real numbers, we obtain a one-parameter family of twists. It is easy to see that under the action of the family of twists, the orbit of a point P out of the z-axis is a helix. Figure 3.37 shows

Figure 3.37 Action of the twist family [from Barr, 1984].

a sequence of twists of a graphical object under the action of a one-parameter family of twists.

3.10.1 Transformation Groups

A *group* is a set G with a binary operation $*: G \times G \to G$ defined between its elements, satisfying

- **Associativity.** For every $a, b, c \in G$, we have $(a * b) * c = a * (b * c)$.
- **Identity element.** There exists an identity $I \in G$, such that $I * g = g * I = g$, for all $g \in G$.
- **Inverse element.** Each element $g \in G$ has an inverse element, denoted by g^{-1}, such that $g * g^{-1} = g^{-1} * g = I$.

If G is a group, a *transformation group* of a set $U \subset \mathbb{R}^n$ is a map $F: G \times U \to U$ satisfying the following properties:

- $F(I, p) = p, \forall p \in U$
- For all $T_1, T_2, \in G$, $F(T_1, T_2(p)) = F(T_1 * T_2, p)$

For each $g \in G$, we obtain a transformation $F_g: U \to U$ defined by $F_g(p) = F(g, p)$. Therefore, a transformation group can be interpreted as a family of transformations of the set U, parameterized by the elements of the group G.

If $p \in U$ is a point, the set

$$\mathcal{O}(p) = \{F_g(p) = F(g, p); \ g \in G\}$$

is called the *orbit* of the point p generated by the transformation group. Intuitively, it describes the trajectory of the point as we vary the parameter of the family.

Example 3.12 (Orthogonal Group)   The orthogonal group $O(2)$ is the group of matrices M_θ,

$$M_\theta = \begin{pmatrix} \cos \theta & \sin \theta \\ -\sin \theta & \cos \theta \end{pmatrix},$$

with the usual operation of matrix multiplication.

This group defines a transformation group of $\mathbb{R}^3$. In fact, for any point $p = (x, y, z)$ of the euclidean space $\mathbb{R}^3$ we define

$$F(M_\theta, p) = \begin{pmatrix} \cos\theta & \sin\theta & 0 \\ -\sin\theta & \cos\theta & 0 \\ 0 & 0 & 1 \end{pmatrix} \begin{pmatrix} x \\ y \\ z \end{pmatrix}.$$

Geometrically, the transformations are rotations of the space around the z-axis. The orbit of a point p on the z-axis is the point itself, and the orbit of a point out of the axis is a circle.

Example 3.13 (Matrix Groups) The above example can be generalized. Consider a group of matrices of order n with the usual operation of product of two matrices. This group defines a transformation group F of the space $\mathbb{R}^n$ by defining

$$F(M, p) = M \cdot p,$$

where the dot indicates the usual product of a matrix by a vector.

As a particular case of this, we have the transformation group of rotations of the space; the transformation group of linear transformations; the transformation group of projective transformations; and the projective group of affine transformations.

The reader should verify that the family of twists introduced in Example 3.11 is a transformation group.

Example 3.14 (Isometry Group) The set of all isometries of a subset $U \subset \mathbb{R}^n$ constitutes a group under the operation of *transformation composition*:

$$(L * T)(v) = L(T(v)), \quad \forall v \in U.$$

This is the *isometry group* of the set U, and it is denoted by $I(U)$.

The isometry group $I(U)$ of the space U defines in a natural way a transformation group $F: U \times I(U) \rightarrow U$, by $F(u, t) = T(u)$. The orthogonal group in Example 3.12 constitutes a one-parameter group of isometries of $\mathbb{R}^3$.

3.10.2 Homotopy

The word *homotopy* has appeared in the literature about morphing (although sometimes the term has been used incorrectly). It is important to familiarize yourself with this important concept.

Consider a space of functions $\mathcal{F} = \{f: U \to V\}$. If f and g are two functions on $\mathcal{F}$, a homotopy between f and g is a continuous transformation,

$$H: U \times [0, 1] \to \mathcal{F},$$

such that $H(u, 0) = f(u)$ and $H(u, 1) = g(u)$. That is, for each $t \in [0, 1]$ we obtain a function $H_t: U \to V \in \mathcal{F}$, defined by $H_t(u) = H(u, t)$. Geometrically, the homotopy defines a path in the space of functions $\mathcal{F}$, connecting the function f to the function g. When f and g are diffeomorphisms and each transformation H_t is also a diffeomorphism, the homotopy is called an *isotopy*.

If U is the shape of a graphical object, the space $\mathcal{F}$ can be interpreted as being the space of attributes of the object. Therefore, a homotopy is a continuous one-parameter family of transformations of the object U, and it performs a metamorphosis between f and g.

3.11 Comments and References

The study of the affine, bilinear, and projective transformations from the warping and morphing point of view has been carefully and nicely described in Paul Heckbert's master's thesis [Heckbert, 1989]. Although a bit old, this technical report is an excellent source with lots of useful information about image filtering, texture mapping, and image warping.

The implementation on the CD-ROM of the Coons patch warping is based on the C code from [Heckbert, 1994]. This article also contains interesting comments about the early days of warping and morphing on NYIT.

The study of conformal warping has been addressed in the literature in [Frederick and Schwartz, 1990] and [Fiume et al., 1987] (see also [Fiume, 1989]). Very complete discussions of the numerical implementation of the Riemann mapping theorem and other issues in computational complex analysis can be found in [Henrici, 1986].

References

Barr, A. H. 1984. Global and Local Deformations of Solid Primitives. *Computer Graphics (SIGGRAPH '84 Proceedings)*, **18**, 21–30.

Coons, S. 1974. Surface Patches and B-Spline Curves. In Barnhill, R., and R. Riesenfeld (eds.), *Computer Aided Geometric Design*. San Diego: Academic Press.

Fiume, E. 1989. *The Mathematical Structure of Raster Graphics*. Boston: Academic Press.

Fiume, E., A. Fournier, and V. Canale. 1987. Conformal Texture Mapping. *Proceedings of Eurographics '87*. Amsterdam: Elsevier Science Publishers, 53–64.

Frederick, Carl, and Eric L. Schwartz. 1990. Conformal Image Warping. *IEEE Computer Graphics and Applications*, **10**(3), 54–61.

Gomes, J., and L. Velho. 1997. *Image Processing for Computer Graphics*. New York: Springer-Verlag.

Heckbert, P. 1989. *Fundamentals of Texture Mapping and Image Warping*. Master's Thesis (Technical Report No. UCB/CSD 89/516). University of California, Berkeley (*www.cs.cmu.edu/˜ph*).

Heckbert, P. 1994. Bilinear Coons Patch Image Warping. In Heckbert, Paul S. (ed.), *Graphics Gems IV*. Boston: Academic Press, 438–446.

Henrici, P. 1986. *Applied and Computational Complex Analysis*. New York: John Wiley.

4

Warping and Morphing

IN THE PREVIOUS CHAPTERS we have studied graphical objects and the transformations between them. Now we are ready to study the operations of warping and morphing of graphical objects.

4.1 Basic Definitions and Examples

Consider a graphical object $\mathcal{O} = (U, f)$, $U \subset \mathbb{R}^m$. A continuous k-parameter family of transformations $F: \mathcal{O} \times \mathbb{R}^k \to \mathbb{R}^n$ is called a *warping* of the graphical object $\mathcal{O}$. Intuitively, a warping is a continuous deformation of a graphical object. For each fixed vector $v \in \mathbb{R}^k$, the graphical object $F_v(\mathcal{O})$ is called an *instantiation* of the warping.

If $\mathcal{O}_1 = (U_1, f_1)$ and $\mathcal{O}_2 = (U_2, f_2)$ are two graphical objects, with $U_1, U_2 \subset \mathbb{R}^m$, a *morphing* or *metamorphosis* between $\mathcal{O}_1$ and $\mathcal{O}_2$ is a k-parameter continuous family of transformations

$$F: \mathcal{O}_1 \times \mathbb{R}^k \to \mathbb{R}^n,$$

such that there are parameter values v_0 and v_1 satisfying $F_{v_0}(\mathcal{O}_1) = \mathcal{O}_1$ and $F_{v_1}(\mathcal{O}_1) = \mathcal{O}_2$. Intuitively, for each parameter $v \in \mathbb{R}^k$ from the parameter space, we obtain a new graphical object $\mathcal{O}_v = F_v(\mathcal{O}_1)$, and this family $\mathcal{O}_v$, $v \in \mathbb{R}^k$, performs the transition from one object to the other, as v varies on the parametric space. Thus, a metamorphosis can be interpreted as a continuous deformation from object O_1 to object O_2. The object O_1 is called the *source* of the metamorphosis, and the object O_2 is called the *target*.

A metamorphosis transformation of a graphical object must change both the shape and the attributes of the object. This is in accordance with the usual meaning of the word in the dictionaries: "a change in form or nature" [Webster, 1989].

4.1.1 Morphing and Animation

When the parameter space has dimension k, we have k degrees of freedom in choosing a metamorphosis between O_1 and O_2. A practical way to select these parameter values consists in defining a curve $c \colon [0, 1] \to \mathbb{R}^k$ on the parameter space satisfying $c(0) = v_0$ and $c(1) = v_1$. In this case, we obtain a one-parameter family of transformations

$$F \circ c \colon O_1 \times [0, 1] \to \mathbb{R}^n.$$

For $t = 0$ we have

$$F \circ c(O_1, 0) = F(O_1, c(0)) = F(O_1, v_0) = O_1,$$

and for $t = 1$ we get

$$F \circ c(O_1, 1) = F(O_1, c(1)) = F(O_1, v_1) = O_2.$$

Thus, as the parameter t varies from 0 to 1, the object O_1 is transformed into the object O_2. By interpreting t as time, we see that the one-parameter family $F \circ c$ defines an animation between the two graphical objects. (Notice that $F \circ c$ can also be interpreted as a homotopy between the objects O_1 and O_2.) The curve c is called an *animation path*. Figure 4.1 illustrates an animation path in a space of three parameters, x, y, and z, from a point A to a point B.

This link between metamorphosis and animation is very important. In brief, we could say that a morphing operation is always materialized as an animation. Obviously the opposite is also true: an animation of some scene can be considered as a morphing between the different graphical objects on the scene (actors, light sources, etc.).

4.1.2 Some Metamorphosis Examples

In this section we will give several examples of warping and morphing using different graphical objects.

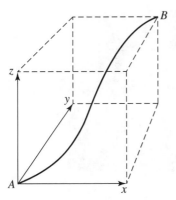

Figure 4.1 An animation path in the space of parameters of a metamorphosis.

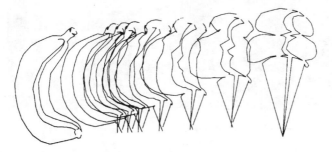

Figure 4.2 Drawing metamorphosis [from Kolomijec, 1976].

Drawing Morphing

Figure 4.2 shows a computer-generated sequence of a morphing transformation between the drawing of a banana and the drawing of an ice-cream cone. This is an example of a drawing morphing, that is, a morphing between two plane curves. Only a change of shape is involved, since each drawing can be considered as not having any attributes.

Image Warping

Figure 4.3 shows a warping transformation of the Mona Lisa. This is an example of an image warping (a 2D graphical object). Notice that intrinsic, local transformations are applied on the image domain and the color attributes are changed accordingly.

Figure 4.3 Image warping.

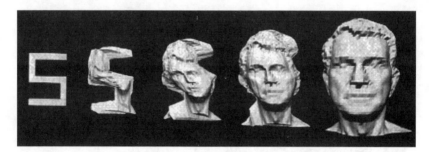

Figure 4.4 Polyhedral surface morphing [from Kent et al., 1992].

Surface Morphing

Figure 4.4 shows frames of a morphing between the number five shape and
a human head. This is an example of a surface morphing, with both objects
described by polygonal surfaces (2D graphical objects of the space). In this
example we have both a change in shape and a change in the shading attributes.
The shading attributes are computed from the geometry of the morphed
object.

Volume Morphing

Figure 4.5 shows four frames of a metamorphosis sequence between a human
skull and the skull of another primate. These skulls are represented by volumetric data. This is an example of a metamorphosis between two solids (3D
graphical objects of the space). As in the previous example, the metamorphosis of the shading is obtained by the volumetric rendering of the transformed
shape.

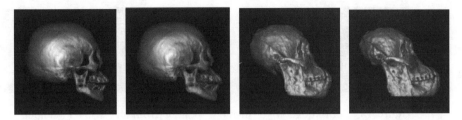

Figure 4.5 Morphing sequence between two solids [from Lerios et al., 1995].

4.2 Metamorphosis and Topology Type

Consider two graphical objects, $\mathcal{O}_1 = (U, f)$ and $\mathcal{O}_2 = (V, g)$, with $U, V \subset \mathbb{R}^n$, and a morphing transformation between them $F: \mathcal{O}_1 \times [0, 1] \to \mathbb{R}^m$. The family F_t computes a continuous deformation from the object $\mathcal{O}_1$ to object $\mathcal{O}_2$, transforming both the shape and the attributes. If the shapes U and V are homeomorphic, it seems natural that the metamorphosis process preserves the topology.

When U and V are not homeomorphic, there must be a change in the topology during the deformation. This change of topology is attained using a topological surgery, as illustrated in Figure 4.6.

In general we do not have a uniqueness in the topological surgery: different surgery may result in the same change in the topology. In general, changing of the topology type is a very delicate and important part of the metamorphosis between nonhomeomorphic objects. Depending on the morphing technique used, the surgery has to be carefully planned and specified.

Figure 4.7 shows a metamorphosis between two objects with different topology. The topology of the source object is changed by introducing two holes. Two topological surgeries occur in the process.

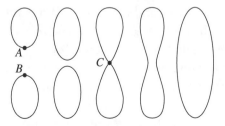

Figure 4.6 Topological surgery.

Figure 4.7   Morphing with change of topology [from DeCarlo and Gallier, 1996].

4.3 Plane and Spatial Warping

In computer graphics, we are interested in the metamorphosis problems for objects of different dimensions. Several applications involve metamorphosis in dimensions 1, 2, and 3, or even higher-dimensional graphical objects:

- One-dimensional metamorphosis could be used to combine different audio signals to obtain some audio effect.
- Plane metamorphosis between 1D objects (drawings) have been widely used by the desktop publishing industry to obtain font warping effects. These techniques are also very important in the cartoon animation industry.
- Plane metamorphosis between two images has been widely used by the video and film industry to create special effects.
- Three-dimensional metamorphosis of solids and surfaces can be used to blend different graphical objects, creating new ones. This process was used extensively in the movie *Mask* and in the deformation of the T1000 character in the movie *Terminator 2: Judgment Day*.

At the end of Section 4.1 we showed examples of metamorphosis between graphical objects of various dimensionality. Nonetheless, these warpings appear as 2D warpings between images. In fact, the metamorphosis between the number five object and the human head, and also the skull metamorphosis, were computed in 3D space. The drawing metamorphosis was obtained by using plane transformations, and the same is true for the Mona Lisa sequence. This raises an important issue to be discussed in this section: the warping and morphing transformations do not necessarily have to take place in the space where the object is embedded.

Objects are visualized by projecting them on the screen using a camera transformation. For real-world images we use a photographic, video, or movie

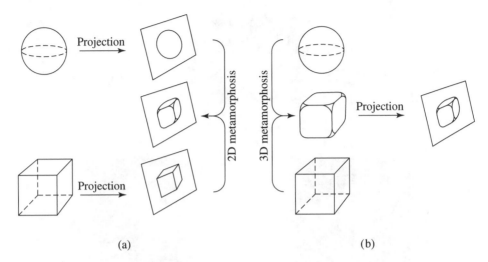

Figure 4.8 Morphing of objects in 3D space: 2D techniques (a) and 3D techniques (b).

camera, and for synthetic models we use a virtual camera. In spite of the fact that we are creating a 2D morphing between 2D objects when we perform an image metamorphosis, we are interested in obtaining a transition between the 3D objects depicted on the image. Therefore, it would be fair to say that image metamorphosis is a $2\frac{1}{2}$-D problem.

When the image is synthesized, we have two options to transform an object that appears on it: we can work on either the object space or the image space. Working on the object space forces us to use 3D transformations; working on the image space means that we should project the objects on the screen and use 2D transformations (see Figure 4.8). Certainly, the methods to compute the 3D morphing are more difficult.

The camera projection reduces a morphing from the 3D space to the plane, decreasing in this way the degrees of freedom we have to attain some particular effects. Also, since projection is a many-to-one mapping, we may lose important features from the 3D environment. Several problems arise related to attributes that are shape dependent (for instance, shading).

Example 4.1 (Warping of a Die) Working on the image space may give acceptable results if, among other restrictions, the objects are seen from a similar point of view with very similar lighting conditions. Figure 4.9 shows warpings of a die performed in 3D and in 2D. Although the deformation is roughly the same, the differences in the transformation of the shadows and highlights are evident. The results of transforming 3D objects in the 2D space

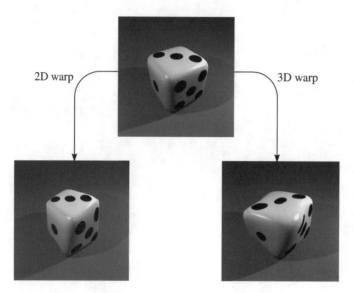

Figure 4.9   Different results transforming in 2D and 3D spaces.

can be confusing, as the visual clues given by shadows and highlights will be wrong.

The reader should observe that projective warps are invariant by the camera projection (because the projection is itself a projective transformation). Therefore, the projective warp of an object can be obtained either before or after projection. In fact, if the photography is taken from a distant camera position, the resulting projection is approximated by an affine transformation. This fact is widely exploited in the area of aerophotogrammetry, where affine warpings are used to attain registration of images taken from different satellite sources.

4.4 Metamorphosis and Interpolation

Consider a morphing $F\colon \mathcal{O}_1 \times \mathbb{R}^k \to \mathcal{O}_2$, from a graphical object $\mathcal{O}_1 = (U_1, f_1)$ to the graphical object $\mathcal{O}_2 = (U_2, f_2)$. By choosing a parameter path $c\colon [0, 1] \to \mathbb{R}^k$ in the parameter space, we obtain an animation $F\colon \mathcal{O}_1 \times [0, 1] \to \mathcal{O}_2$. For each point $p \in U_1$, the restriction $F|\{p\} \times [0, 1]\colon \{p\} \times [0, 1] \to \mathcal{O}_2$ defines a path φ on $\mathbb{R}^n$ that connects p to the point $F(p) \in U_2$. The path φ is called a *morphing path* or an *animation path* associated with the point p.

Thus, the morphing transformation interpolates the points p and $F(p)$, along the path φ. This is very important to remember: a metamorphosis between two graphical objects defines a spatial interpolation between the points on the shape of the objects. Certainly, the same results hold for a complete metamorphosis, including the attributes.

4.4.1 Nonuniform Interpolation

In general, the animation path has the same parameterization for all points of the domain. This makes all points from the source U_1 "travel" to the target V_2 at the same speed. Very interesting results are obtained if we reparameterize the animation path, so that the reparameterization depends on the initial point on object shape U_1. In this way, we have $c: [0, 1] \to \mathbb{R}^k$, $c(t) = c(t(p))$, $p \in U_1$. This adaptive parameterization allows much more flexibility in a transformation and is closely related with the effects of slow-in and slow-out in animation (see Section 4.6).

In this section, we will exploit the above remarks to produce some simple but traditional examples of metamorphosis.

4.4.2 Shape Morphing by Linear Interpolation

A simple linear interpolation scheme can generate useful intermediate graphical objects, especially for some types of graphical object representation.

A *piecewise linear*, or polygonal, graphical object is one composed by linear geometrical elements: vertices, edges, and faces. The faces constitute polygons, which are combined to define the geometry and topology of the object shape. Particular examples of polygonal graphical objects are the polygonal plane curves, polygonal plane regions, and triangulated surfaces of $\mathbb{R}^3$. These objects are illustrated in Figure 4.10(a), (b), and (c), respectively.

A metamorphosis of polygonal graphical objects can be obtained by transforming each of their linear elements maintaining the combinatorial relationship between them. This enables us to devise a very simple metamorphosis technique between two polygonal graphical objects $\mathcal{O}_1$ and $\mathcal{O}_2$.

First, we define a correspondence between the vertices of $\mathcal{O}_1$ and the vertices of $\mathcal{O}_2$: we associate vertices of one object to vertices of the other object in such a way that the linear elements of one object (edges and faces) are associated to linear elements of the other object. This association may cause some problems if we do not have a one-to-one correspondence between the vertices of the two objects. There are two solutions to this problem:

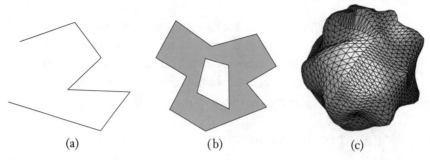

Figure 4.10   Examples of the polygonal graphical objects: plane curves (a), plane regions (b), and triangulated surfaces of $\mathbb{R}^3$ (c).

- Introduce new vertices without changing the shape geometry.
- Associate a vertex in one object to more than one vertex of the other object. (This can be considered as a particular case of the previous rule, where the introduced vertex coincides with an existing one.)

After solving the problem of vertex correspondence, we proceed as follows. If $v_1 \in \mathcal{O}_1$ and $v_2 \in \mathcal{O}_2$ are two corresponding vertices, we define the animation path between them using linear interpolation:

$$\varphi(t) = (1 - t)v_1 + tv_2.$$

In this case, the animation path is called a *vertex path*. Notice that for $t = 0$ we obtain the initial vertex $\varphi(0) = v_0$, and for $t = 1$ we obtain the final vertex $\varphi(1) = v_1$. Because of the vertex correspondence, this interpolation enables us to obtain a metamorphosis from the linear elements of object $\mathcal{O}_1$ to the corresponding linear elements of object $\mathcal{O}_2$, and consequently between the objects $\mathcal{O}_1$ and $\mathcal{O}_2$.

This technique is called *morphing by linear interpolation*. Figure 4.11 shows two examples of linear interpolation morphing between a triangle and a square. In Figure 4.11(a) we associate one triangle vertex to two vertices of the square, and in Figure 4.11(b) we introduce two different additional vertices.

4.4.3   Attributes Morphing by Linear Interpolation

It is possible to obtain a simple metamorphosis transformation between two objects by using linear interpolation of their attribute functions. Indeed, if $A = (U, f)$ and $B = (V, g)$ are graphical objects, the morphing transformation is given by the one-parameter family $\mathcal{O}_\lambda$ of objects, $\lambda \in [0, 1]$, such that

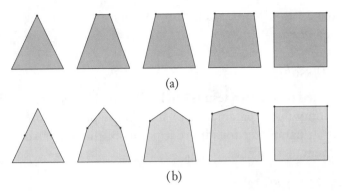

(a)

(b)

Figure 4.11 Metamorphosis by linear interpolation: vertex splitting (a) and vertex insertion (b).

Figure 4.12 Cross-dissolve between two images. See also color plate 4.12.

$$\mathcal{O}_\lambda = (U, (1 - \lambda)f + \lambda g). \tag{4.1}$$

It is easy to verify that $\mathcal{O}_0 = \mathcal{A}$, and $\mathcal{O}_1 = \mathcal{B}$.

For images, this metamorphosis is called a *cross-dissolve* between the two objects. Figure 4.12 shows six instances of a cross-dissolve between the image of a cheetah and the face of a woman. In fact, since the '30s, the cross-dissolve has been used in the movie industry to attain metamorphosis. Nowadays, it has been replaced by more sophisticated morphing techniques that will be studied in detail in Part IV of the book. Also, cross-dissolve is widely used in the audio industry to obtain a transition between two audio signals. In this field, it is called *mixing*.

Nonuniform Dissolve

We have remarked that better results can be obtained by using linear interpolation with a nonuniform parameter. That is, in the present context, we vary the interpolation parameter for different points of the object shape. Instead of using Equation (4.1), we use

$$\mathcal{O}_\lambda = (U, \varphi(\lambda)f + \xi(\lambda)g),$$

where $\varphi, \xi \colon U \times [0, 1] \to \mathbb{R}$ satisfy the conditions

- $\varphi, \xi \geq 0$;
- $\varphi(p, \lambda) + \xi(p, \lambda) = 1$;
- $\varphi(p, 0) = 1$ and $\xi(p, 1) = 0, \forall p \in U$.

This reduces to the previous (uniform) cross-dissolve when $\varphi(p, \lambda) = 1 - \lambda$ and $\xi(p, \lambda) = \lambda$.

4.4.4 Affine, Bilinear, and Projective Interpolation

The metamorphosis by linear interpolation described in Section 4.4.2 enables us to obtain a morphing sequence between the shape of two graphical objects. This is adequate for graphical objects that have no attributes other than their geometry and topology, or for those whose attributes must be recomputed. Also, the attribute linear interpolation scheme is only useful if attributes are defined for all points of the graphical object.

If the attributes of a graphical object are defined just in a subset of its points, and the object has attributes that must undergo the morphing transformation, we must know how to compute the transformation at all points of the object.

For polygonal objects, for instance, some attributes are defined just at the vertices, and the attributes at points in the interior of the faces must be computed. In the previous chapter we described three simple techniques that can be used for this task:

- affine interpolation between triangles
- bilinear interpolation for quadrilateral faces
- projective transformations for quadrilateral faces

Figure 4.13 Affine interpolation.

Figure 4.14 Bilinear interpolation.

Affine Interpolation

Affine interpolation enables us to compute the transformation for the interior points of a triangle when we know the values of the transformations at the vertices. It preserves line segments contained in the triangles. In particular, it can be used to obtain piecewise affine interpolation on triangulated graphical objects. Figure 4.13 shows a metamorphosis from a rectangle with a chessboard pattern into a quadrilateral. Notice how the discontinuity of the first derivative at the inner boundary of the triangles affects the mapping of the chessboard pattern.

Bilinear Interpolation

Bilinear interpolation allows us to compute a transformation from a plane rectangle $[a, b] \times [c, d]$ to an arbitrary quadrilateral (not necessarily planar) when we know the values of the transformation at the vertices. Horizontal and vertical line segments are transformed into line segments of the target quadrilateral. This technique is illustrated in the sequence in Figure 4.14. Notice that with this technique the tiled diagonal segments of the chessboard pattern are transformed into "tiled curves" of second degree.

Figure 4.15 Projective interpolation.

Projective Interpolation

For planar quadrilaterals, projective interpolation can be used to compute a transformation from the rectangle $[a, b] \times [c, d]$ to some planar, nondegenerated quadrilateral in such a way that line segments are always transformed into line segments, as shown in the previous chapter. Figure 4.15 illustrates this technique. For certain applications, this technique can be the most suitable method for the intended metamorphosis of the square.

In the previous chapter we described two other transformations: Coons patch transformation and conformal transformations of the plane. These transformations can be used to define warping and morphing of planar graphical objects.

4.5 Different Views of Warping and Morphing

There are two different ways to interpret a morphing transformation. In the particular case of curves and surfaces, these interpretations lead to interesting morphing techniques. We will describe the models using curves, but they extend to surfaces as well.

4.5.1 Warping and Interface Evolution

A Jordan curve divides the plane into two regions. A warping of the curve can be interpreted as the evolution of the interface between these two regions.

Physical properties related to each region can be used in order to obtain models for tracking the evolution of the interface. This evolution constitutes a warping deformation. A very complete discussion of these techniques, which also contains a comprehensive bibliography, can be found in [Sethian, 1996].

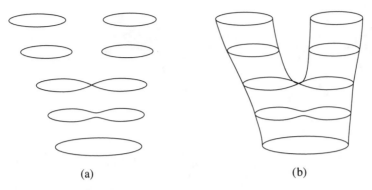

(a)   (b)

Figure 4.16 Morphing as level sets of an implicit function: level sets (a) and implicit surface (b).

4.5.2 Morphing as Level Sets

Consider an implicit function $f: \mathbb{R}^{n+1} \to \mathbb{R}$. For each $t \in \mathbb{R}$, we obtain an n-dimensional graphical object $f^{-1}(t) \subset \mathbb{R}^{n+1}$. As t varies on the interval $[t_0, t_1]$, the family $f^{-1}(t)$ defines a metamorphosis from the implicit object $f^{-1}(t_0)$ to $f^{-1}(t_1)$. This is illustrated in Figure 4.16.

Conversely, if $F: \mathcal{O}_1 \times \mathbb{R}^k \to \mathbb{R}^n$ is a metamorphosis from the object $\mathcal{O}_1$ to the object $\mathcal{O}_2$, with $F(\mathcal{O}_1, v_0) = \mathcal{O}_1$ and $F(\mathcal{O}_1, v_1) = \mathcal{O}_2$, and $c: [0, 1] \to \mathbb{R}^k$ is an animation path satisfying $c(0) = v_0$ and $c(1) = v_1$, the family of objects $\mathcal{O}_t = F(\mathcal{O}_1, c(t)), t \in [0, 1]$ constitutes a graphical object on the space $\mathbb{R}^n \times \mathbb{R} = \mathbb{R}^{n+1}$, such that the objects $\mathcal{O}_t$ are level sets.

Thus the problem of obtaining a morphing transformation is related with the problem of reconstructing a surface from its sections. Viewing morphing as a surface reconstruction process gives very good insight into the problem and its solution. To illustrate this, consider the sequence of morphing by linear interpolation in Figure 4.17(a). A surface associated to this morphing is shown in Figure 4.17(b). The above example clearly shows that from this point of view, the use of morphing by linear interpolation is related to the construction of a piecewise linear, non–self-intersecting cylinder, which has the two curves as a boundary. An interesting fact is that such a cylinder does not always exist (see [Gitlin et al., 1996]). This demonstrates the inadequacy of morphing by linear interpolation. But this is not the end of the story. We will return to this subject in different parts of the book.

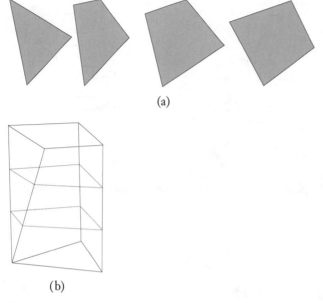

(a)

(b)

Figure 4.17   Metamorphosis by linear interpolation (a) and its reconstructed surface (b).

4.6 Optimal Morphing

Certainly a morphing transformation between two graphical objects is non-unique. In general, there are infinite ways to define an animation path on the parameter space. Figure 4.18 shows six instances of a morphing between the cheetah and the woman's face. Comparing this morphing sequence with the morphing by cross-dissolve shown in Figure 4.12, it is undoubtedly clear that the example shown in Figure 4.18 is much better. Therefore it is pertinent to pose the question of finding the optimal morphing transformation between two graphical objects.

Giving a precise meaning to the word *optimal* here is very difficult, since it is application dependent. In the special-effects industry, the optimal morph is a problem of "gestalt," thus involving perceptual issues. In some technical applications, it is easy to attribute a mathematical meaning to the phrase "optimal morphing." As a matter of fact, some morphing techniques use a variational approach to this problem: they introduce an energy functional and compute the morphing transformation in such a way that it minimizes the functional.

In this section we are interested in devising some properties and guidelines that should be followed in order to obtain good morphing transformations.

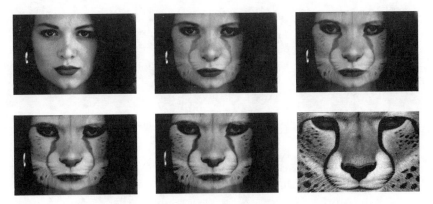

Figure 4.18 Frames from a morphing sequence. See also color plate 4.18.

It is obvious that these principles are intended just as guidance for obtaining more natural and pleasing results; real applications may have restrictions that can limit or even prohibit the use of part of these guidelines.

The reader should observe that since a metamorphosis is materialized as an animation, there is a close relationship between the principles to be discussed here and the well-known generic principles for a good animation, as discussed, for instance, in [Lasseter, 1987].

4.6.1 Some Principles for a Good Morphing

We have selected 10 principles that should guide the user to obtain a good metamorphosis.

1. Attributes transformation
2. Topology preservation
3. Feature preservation
4. Rigidity preservation
5. Smoothness preservation
6. Monotonicity
7. Nonlinearity
8. Use of transformation groups
9. Slow-in and slow-out
10. Avoiding morphing leakage

Each of these principles will be explained below.

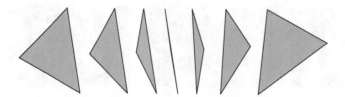

Figure 4.19   Non–topology-preserving transformation.

Attributes Transformation

A graphical object consists of a geometric shape with attributes. The attributes from one object should be transformed accordingly onto the corresponding attributes of the other object. The subject of attribute transformation was discussed in Chapter 3.

Topology Preservation

If the shapes of the graphical objects are homeomorphic, the topology of the source object should be preserved during the transformation. Figure 4.19 shows an example where the topology is not preserved.

Feature Preservation

Distinguished features of one object should be transformed onto distinguished features of the other object. Figure 4.20(a) shows a morphing sequence between two triangles, satisfying the feature preservation principle: vertices are transformed into vertices.

On the other hand, the morphing sequence in Figure 4.20(b) does not preserve features: vertices are not transformed into vertices (in fact, they disappear during the transformation, and new vertices are created).

We should remark that there are geometric and attribute features. If we consider the image with the woman's face (the first image of the morphing sequence in Figure 4.12), we can say that the four corners of the image rectangle are geometric features, while the eyes, nose, and mouth are attribute features.

The feature preservation principle indicates that the use of multiresolution techniques for computing morphing transformations might be of great help. An example is given in the cross-dissolve algorithm described in [Stein and

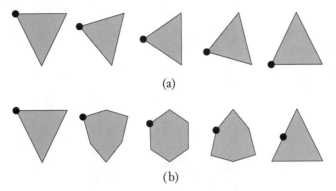

(a)

(b)

Figure 4.20 Feature preservation morphing sequences between two triangles: (a) preserves features and (b) does not.

Hitchner, 1988], which uses a multiresolution representation with pyramids. We will give more information about multiresolution techniques later on.

Rigidity Preservation

The rigidity principle should be observed in various levels. In a general setting, rigidity means that some geometric properties of the object shape should be preserved during the transformation. A very restrictive condition would require the metamorphosis transformation to be a family of isometries of the object shape (distance between points would be preserved). Less restrictive rigidity conditions are obtained by demanding preservation of volume, angles, and convexity.

Certainly, isometries would preserve volume, angles, and convexity. But remember that it is sometimes necessary to deform the object preserving the volume. In this case isometry is a very strong rigidity condition. This example occurs frequently in animation metamorphosis: it is the well-known technique of "stretch and squash" (see [Lasseter, 1987]).

Figure 4.21(a) shows sequences where an isometric metamorphosis should be used and Figure 4.21(b) shows where volume rigidity is preserved but the object does not remain isometric during the transformation.

Convex rigidity should be observed in different levels, for different parts of the object. If a convex subset of a graphical object $\mathcal{O}_1$ must be transformed into a convex subset of the target object $\mathcal{O}_2$, then the morphed subset must remain convex.

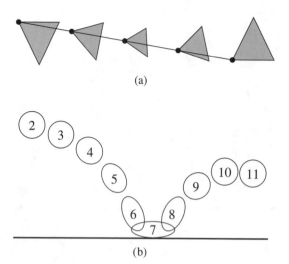

(a)

(b)

Figure 4.21 Nonrigid morphing sequence (a) and morphing with volume (area) rigidity (b).

Figure 4.22 Nonpreservation of convex elements.

In the metamorphosis sequence of Figure 4.22, the object as a whole remains convex, but its edges do not remain convex during the transformation.

Smoothness Preservation

Smooth boundaries should be mapped onto smooth boundaries. This principle is related to the principle of feature preservation because, in general, features are related with some kind of nonsmoothness.

The morphing sequence of Figure 4.23 illustrates the principles of both feature preservation and boundary smoothness.

We should remark that smoothness of the time parameter is also important. The k-parameter family that defines the morphing should be at least continuous.

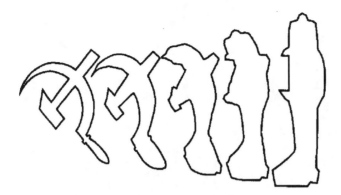

Figure 4.23 Features and smoothness preservation [from Sederberg et al., 1992].

Figure 4.24 Nonmonotonic morphing transformation.

Monotonicity

Volume, areas, or parts of the object should change monotonically. Figure 4.24 shows an example of a nonmonotonic morphing transformation between two congruent triangles.

Nonlinearity

Avoid "linearities" in the morphing transformation (i.e., morphing using linear interpolation, bilinear transformation, uniform cross-dissolve, etc.). Unfortunately, in general this very simple class of metamorphosis techniques is not a good choice unless you have very strong reasons to use it.

A very simple and effective example of the principle is the fact that linear interpolation metamorphosis does not perform well in computing rotational metamorphosis. The rotational morphing sequence between the segment AB and CD of Figure 4.25(a), if performed with linear interpolation of the vertices' positions, results in the poor morphing sequence shown in Figure 4.25(b).

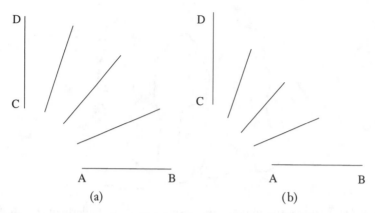

Figure 4.25 A good morphing sequence (a) and a linear interpolation of it (b).

Figure 4.26 A good morphing sequence (a) and a morphing sequence using linear interpolation (b) [from Sederberg et al., 1992].

A concrete example of the above situation is the construction of a morphing sequence of a person with its arm up and the same person with the arm down. This cannot be obtained using linear interpolation, as the two morphing sequences in Figure 4.26 show.

Use of Transformation Groups

This is in fact more of a mathematical hint. Sometimes the shape of the target object is obtained from the shape of the source object using a transformation that belongs to some transformation group of the space. The natural choice for a metamorphosis between them is to use a k-parameter transformation group that contains the transformation.

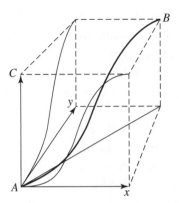

Figure 4.27 A particular choice of parameters for animation morphing.

A good example of this appeared in Figure 4.15: to obtain a perspective metamorphosis of a rectangle, we should use the transformation group of projective mappings.

Slow In and Out

Consider a metamorphosis $F\colon \mathcal{O}_1 \times \mathbb{R}^k \to \mathbb{R}^m$ between a graphical object $\mathcal{O}_1 = F(\mathcal{O}_1, v_1)$ and $\mathcal{O}_2 = F(\mathcal{O}_2, v_2)$. We have seen that this morphing materializes as an animation: we consider the animation path $c\colon [a, b] \to \mathbb{R}^k$ with $c(a) = v_1$ and $c(b) = v_2$, and we obtain an animation of the metamorphosis by taking the one-parameter family of transformations $F \circ c\colon \mathcal{O}_1 \times [a, b] \to \mathbb{R}^m$. In order to obtain pleasing results, the curve c should be defined so as to obtain the effects of slow-in and slow-out, both in shape and attributes transformation (see [Lasseter, 1987]). That is, accelerate in the beginning and decelerate at the end. The example below illustrates this better.

Example 4.2 (Slow In and Out Path) Consider a metamorphosis between two grayscale images. The parameter space has dimension 3: two parameters are used for the pixel coordinates, and one parameter for the grayscale values. We denote the pixel coordinates by (x, y), and the color values by c. Figure 4.27 depicts a path in the parameter space (x, y, c), from a point A to a point B. The picture also shows the projection of the curve onto the planes (x, y), (x, c), and (y, c). From these projections we are able to deduce important information about the metamorphosis animation defined by the curve. In fact, we can observe in this example that the warping of the object shape evolves linearly with the time parameter (projection on the xy-plane), but the grayscale transformation does not (projection on the xc- and yc-planes). It starts and ends slowly and accelerates at the middle, so that the grayscale change is barely noticeable at the beginning or the ending of the animation and it takes place quickly (compared to shape transformation) during the middle of the animation. This particular progression is normally used with few modifications as a practical template that produces perceptually better results.

We should point out that there is a trade-off between the user control over the morphing transformation and the number of parameters: the smaller the number of parameters, the easier it will be to control the animation of the morphing sequence. As the number of parameters increases, we have to work harder to control the animation, but we have greater flexibility in choosing the best result.

Avoiding Morphing Leakage

If we apply a global deformation to some object, it deforms all of the ambient space. We call this phenomenon *morphing leakage*. When we need to apply a metamorphosis to some isolated object on the scene, we must use intrinsic deformations to avoid leakage.

A very common situation occurs when doing image metamorphosis. Sometimes we need to apply the morphing transformation only to some foreground object. An easy method to avoid leakage consists in generating the foreground separated from the background, applying the morphing transformation to the foreground object, and doing image compositing of the morphing sequence with the background. This is illustrated in Figure 4.28: (a) shows the source image; (b) shows the warped image with leakage; (c) shows the warping of the foreground, and (d) shows the warped image without leakage.

4.6.2 A Case Analysis

Now we will return to the two morphing transformations shown in Figures 4.12 and 4.18 between the cheetah and the woman's face. The metamorphosis of Figure 4.18 is better because it uses some of the principles mentioned above:

- Distinguished features are preserved in the metamorphosis. In fact, the eyes, mouth, and nose are mapped accordingly in the metamorphosis process.

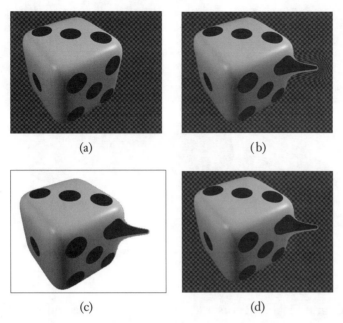

Figure 4.28 Avoiding leakage in image morphing: source image (a), warped image with leakage (b), warping of the foreground (c), and warped image without leakage (d).

■ The metamorphosis of the attributes is not a uniform cross-dissolve. By observing the morphing sequence shown in Figure 4.18, the reader can notice the change of grayscale values in the face and in the hair: it takes much longer for the hair attributes to be surpassed by those from the cheetah.

■ The slow in and out technique is also used in the morphing of the attributes.

In the next section we will explain the strategy to be used in the morphing computation to obtain the above results.

4.7 Morphing = Geometry Alignment + Blending

In order to perform the morphing in accordance with the feature preservation, it is necessary to use intrinsic, local transformations of the shape (e.g., image rectangle) in order to obtain a feature alignment. If $\mathcal{O}_\lambda$, $0 \leq \lambda \leq 1$, is a morphing sequence from the graphical object $\mathcal{O}_1$ to the graphical object $\mathcal{O}_2$, for each λ we obtain a graphical object $\mathcal{O}_\lambda$ with intermediate shape and attributes. We

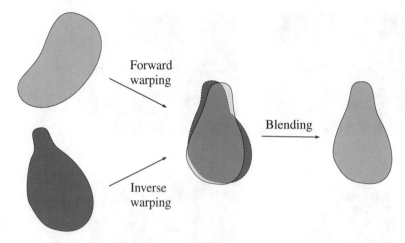

Figure 4.29 Morphing = forward warping + inverse warping + blending.

say that this graphical object is a *blending* of the source and target graphical objects. In fact, we have a weighted blending such that when λ is close to 0 the blended object resembles O_1, and when λ is close to 1 the object shape and attributes approximate those of O_2.

The general strategy to compute the blending is the following (see Figure 4.29):

1. **Forward warping:** Warp the source object O_1.
2. **Inverse warping:** Warp the target object O_2.
3. Blend the two warped objects in 1 and 2.

The forward and inverse warpings bring the source and target objects close together, so that it is easier to devise good techniques to blend them. The forward and inverse warpings must be computed so as to guarantee the property of feature preservation in order to obtain a good morphing transformation. The different choices of the forward and inverse warpings, along with the blending operations, constitute the different morphing techniques. Notice that the blending operation comprises both the geometry and the attributes. Sometimes, instead of blending the attributes, we recompute them from the blended geometry. In brief, the above computations show that during the metamorphosis operation the objects undergo a *geometry alignment*, before

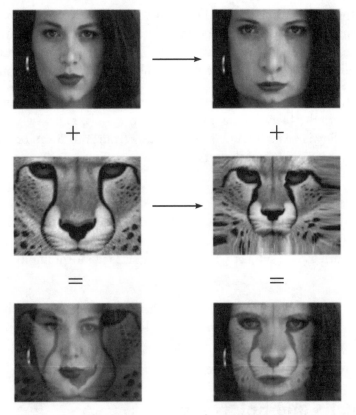

Figure 4.30 Morphing $=$ (warping)^2 + blending. See also color plate 4.30.

computing the geometry and attributes of the intermediate computation. This could be summarized in the equation

$$\text{morphing} = (\text{warping})^2 + \text{blending}.$$

Example 4.3 (Morphing of the Woman and the Cheetah) We will illustrate the above computational strategy with the morphing between the woman and the cheetah (see Figure 4.30). The inputs are the image with the woman's face in the upper-left part, and the image of the cheetah just below it. The first row shows the forward warping of the woman; the second row shows the inverse warping of the cheetah. The image on the right of the third row shows the blending operation. The image on the left shows the blending without the registration operations of forward and inverse warpings. The blending used is a linear interpolation. The morphing, on the right, is much more appealing than a pure cross-dissolve, and effectively represents a new, perceptually feasible object created as a combination of the two inputs.

Example 4.4 (Blending with Union)   The union operation between two sets can be used as the blending operatior. More precisely, given two sets A and B, the blending is given by $A \cup B$. A morphing from A to B can be computed using a weighted scaling of the sets:

$$C_\lambda = (1 - \lambda)A \bigcup \lambda B.$$

We scale down the set A, while at the same time scaling up the set B, and we blend them with the union. Other set operations can be used for blending. We will return to this subject when we study surface morphing in Part IV of the book.

Before finishing, we should remark that since the warped objects are close together, *linear interpolation* is a good option to be considered in the computation of the geometric blending.

4.8 Comments and References

Defining a graphical object warp, or a metamorphosis between two graphical objects in general, involves a lot of work related to description and representation of the graphical objects, and specification and computation of the morphing transformation. Each of these problems will be studied in detail in later chapters.

We have mentioned in Chapter 1 that the metamorphosis transformation is closely related to the problem of "in-between" in animation. The metamorphosis by linear interpolation described in this chapter has been discussed in some early articles. These include [Burtnik and Wein, 1971] for 2D objects (drawings); an early description of the method for polygonal surfaces in [Hong et al., 1988]; and a similar technique described in [Wesley and Uselton, 1989].

Viewing metamorphosis as a problem of level sets reconstruction, as discussed in Section 4.5.2, has been exploited as a morphing technique in [Aubert and Bechmann, 1997].

A brief introduction to projective geometry and projective transformations was given in the previous chapter. For further study we recommend [Berger, 1987]. Another reference, more suited for a computer graphics reader, is [Penna and Patterson, 1986].

References

Aubert, Fabrice, and Dominique Bechmann. 1997. Animation by Deformation of Space-Time Objects. *Computer Graphics Forum (Eurographics '97 Proceedings)*, **16**(3), 57–66.

Berger, M. 1987. *Geometry I*. New York: Springer-Verlag.

Burtnik, N., and M. Wein. 1971. Computer Generated Key-Frame Animation. *SMPTE Journal*, **80**, 149–153.

DeCarlo, Douglas, and Jean Gallier. 1996. Topological Evolution of Surfaces. *Proceedings of Graphics Interface '96*, 194–203.

Gitlin, C., J. O'Rourke, and V. Subramanian. 1996. On Reconstruction of Polyhedra from Slices. *Int. J. Computational Geometry and Applications*, **6**(1), 103–112.

Hong, M. T., N. M. Thalmann, and D. Thalmann. 1988. A General Algorithm for 3D-Shape Interpolation in a Facet-Based Representation. *Proceedings of Graphics Interface '88*, 229–235.

Kent, J. R., W. E. Carlson, and R. E. Parent. 1992. Shape Transformation for Polyhedral Objects. *Computer Graphics (SIGGRAPH '92 Proceedings)*, **26**(2), 47–54.

Kolomijec, William. 1976. The Appeal of Computer Graphics. In *Artist and Computer*. New York: Crown Publishers Inc., Harmony Books.

Lasseter, John. 1987. Principles of Traditional Animation Applied to 3D Computer Animation. *Computer Graphics (SIGGRAPH '87 Proceedings)*, **21**(4), 35–44.

Lerios, Apostolos, Chase D. Garfinkle, and Marc Levoy. 1995. Feature-Based Volume Metamorphosis. *Computer Graphics (SIGGRAPH '95 Proceedings)*, **29**, 449–456.

Penna, Michael A., and Richard R. Patterson. 1986. *Projective Geometry and Its Applications to Computer Graphics*. Englewood Cliffs, NJ: Prentice Hall.

Sederberg, Thomas W., Peishing Gao, Guojin Wang, and Hong Mu. 1992. 2D Shape Blending: An Intrinsic Solution to the Vertex Path Problem. *Computer Graphics (SIGGRAPH '93 Proceedings)*, **27**, 15–18.

Sethian, J. A. 1996. *Level Set Methods: Evolving Interfaces in Geometry, Fluid Mechanics, Computer Vision and Materials Sciences*. New York: Cambridge University Press.

Stein, Charles S., and Lewis E. Hitchner. 1988. The Multiresolution Dissolve. *SMPTE Journal*, (Dec.), 977–984.

Webster. 1989. *Webster's Encyclopedic Unabridged Dictionary of the English Language*. New York: Random House.

Wesley, E. Bethel, and S. P. Uselton. 1989. Shape Distortion in Computer-Assisted Keyframe Animation. In Thalmann, N. M., and D. Thalmann (eds.), *State-of-the-Art in Computer Animation*, 215–224. New York: Springer-Verlag.

5

Domain and Range Morphing

A GRAPHICAL OBJECT is essentially a function $f: U \subset \mathbb{R}^n \to \mathbb{R}^p$, where U is the object shape and f is the attribute function. Therefore, a transformation between graphical objects involves essentially a *functional transformation*, that is, a transformation in a function space. A simple and geometric way to achieve function transformations consists in making separate changes either in the domain U or in the image set $f(U)$ of the function f. This has the effect of changing either the object shape or the attribute values of the object; in the first case, we say that we have a *domain transformation*, for example, the rotation of an image; in the second case, a *range transformation*, an example of which is a change in the color of the pixels of an image.

In the next section we will discuss the problem of computing metamorphosis on the functional space and give some examples.

5.1 Procedural Modeling and Metamorphosis

Consider some family $\{\mathcal{O}_\lambda\}$ of graphical objects (this family could be some space of images, a set of synthetic plants, etc.). Let $\varphi: \mathbb{R}^k \to \{\mathcal{O}_\lambda\}$ be some parameterization of the family $\{\mathcal{O}_\lambda\}$. Thus, graphical objects of the family are described by k parameters $(x_1, \ldots, x_k) \in \mathbb{R}^k$. The family $\{\mathcal{O}_\lambda\}$ with the parameterization is called a *parameterized family of graphical objects*.

Figure 5.1 Plant evolution with algorithmic model [from Prusinkiewicz et al., 1988].

Now, consider a curve $c: [0, 1] \to \mathbb{R}^k$ on the parameter space of some parameterized family. The curve c originates another curve $\varphi \circ c: [0, 1] \to \{\mathcal{O}_\lambda\}$ on the family of graphical objects. As we know, if this new curve is continuous, it can be interpreted as a metamorphosis from the object $\varphi \circ c(0)$ and the object $\varphi \circ c(1)$ of the family. Remember that the path c is called an animation path.

There are several examples in the computer graphics literature where the family $\{\mathcal{O}_\lambda\}$ is defined in a procedural way: there exists an algorithm that describes the graphical objects of the family, and, in general, the animation path c is also defined procedurally. This class of examples in fact constitutes a research area, called *algorithmic* or *procedural modeling* [Ebert et al., 1994].

Example 5.1 (Family of Plants) Several examples of algorithmic modeling have appeared in the literature connected with plant growth. The plant is described by a graph grammar that encodes the rules for the plant evolution. Plant growth is simulated by the repeated application of these rules to an initial seed. Figure 5.1 shows various stages of the plant growth.

In sum, the techniques from the area of algorithmic modeling enable us to create graphical objects and compute metamorphosis between different graphical objects of the family.

A pioneering work in this area, in [Kawaguchi, 1982], was inspired by the fact that the growth of shells was based upon rational principles that

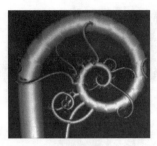

Figure 5.2 Spiral growth [from Kawaguchi, 1982].

can be formulated mathematically. Figure 5.2 shows spirals grown using the formulated model.

Geometric grammars, or *shape grammars*, have been used to produce arbitrarily complex shapes from simple basic shapes. In fact, an important theoretical issue concerns the conjecture that all fractals can be generated by a shape grammar [Smith, 1984a]. In topological grammars, or *graph grammars*, the connectivity of an object is defined, producing a structure that must then be interpreted in a geometry. The models generated by topological grammars are also called *graftals* [Smith, 1984b]. Graftals have been applied to the modeling of biological systems, and formal languages known as L-systems were developed for that purpose [Prusinkiewicz et al., 1988]. There is an extensive literature about the use of procedural modeling for plant growth. Two interesting papers are [de Reffye et al., 1988], which synthesizes plants procedurally, based on botanical information about the plant structure; and [Greene, 1989], which describes a growth model using a volumetric description of the plants.

The idea of interpolating in the parameter space can be taken to extremes where the parameter spaces are very large and describe most of the object information. Karl Sims [Sims, 1991] describes, among other schemes, how to grow synthetic 3D plants using a "genetic" parameter space, an application of morphing very close to natural metamorphosis. Interpolations between plants that share a common genetic structure, or a common parameter space, are done to create evolution sequences. Frames from an interpolation in the genetic space are shown in Figure 5.3.

5.1.1 Function Transformations

Procedural models allow us to give an example that clarifies the difference among domain transformations, range transformations, and more general

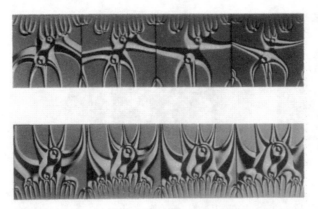

Figure 5.3   Frames from a genetic metamorphosis [from Sims, 1991].

function transformations. The example below shows that working on the function space or making changes in the domain or in the range might give different results.

A 2D procedural texture is an image $f: U \subset \mathbb{R}^2 \to \mathbb{R}^k$, where the attribute function f is computed in a procedural way. As explained above, it depends on a finite number of parameters, and by changing these parameters, we obtain different flavors for the texture attributes. Figure 5.4(a) and (b) show two different wood textures generated procedurally.

Consider the problem of morphing these two wood textures. Range morphing interpolation here means that we should interpolate the computed texture intensities using a cross-dissolve technique. Function interpolation means that we should use a functional interpolation, that is, an interpolation on the space of the functions that defines the procedural textures. In our case this space is parameterized, and we interpolate the parameters that define each of the wood textures. The entirely different results obtained can be seen in the two images in the middle of Figure 5.4. The figure on the top shows the function interpolation, while the figure on the bottom shows the cross-dissolve morphing.

The choice between using a functional, a domain, or a range transformation is dictated by different factors that range from the underlying application to the level of difficulty involved. In our example above, the combination in the parameter space generates much better results, since a new texture function is generated.

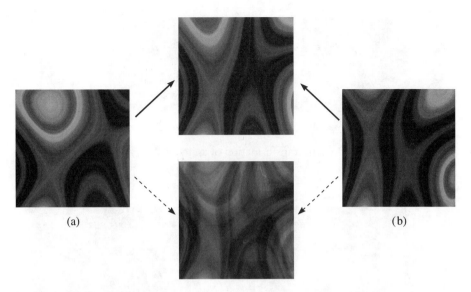

Figure 5.4   Combinations of procedural textures in color space (lower) and in parameter space (upper): source texture (a) and target texture (b). See also color plate 5.4.

5.2 Domain Transformations: Warping

Consider a graphical object with shape $U \subset \mathbb{R}^n$, and attribute function $f : U \to \mathbb{R}^m$. A domain transformation is a mapping $W : U \to U' \subset \mathbb{R}^n$ that produces a change of coordinates in the shape of the object. A domain transformation can be seen as a tool for the creation of new deformed graphical objects, as shown in the diagram below, where the new object is given by $f \circ W^{-1}$:

$$
\begin{array}{ccc}
U & \xrightarrow{\ f\ } & \mathbb{R}^m \\
{\scriptstyle W}\big\downarrow & \nearrow{\scriptstyle f \circ W^{-1}} & \\
U' & &
\end{array}
$$

An example of a domain transformation is shown in Figure 5.5. In this example a shear transformation was applied to the domain of an image.

A more interesting example is shown in Figure 5.6. A tridimensional non-linear warp was applied to the image domain shown in (a) in order to obtain the image in (b).

It is helpful to analyze examples of domain transformations of 1D objects. Such 1D examples will be extensively used in this chapter, as they are simpler

Figure 5.5 Domain transformation of an image.

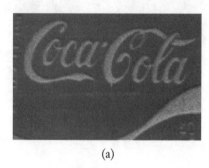
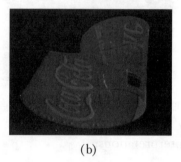

(a)   (b)

Figure 5.6 Texture and warping: original image (a) and image with a tridimensional nonlinear warp applied to it (b).

to analyze and understand, and possess the same basic properties. We can think of them as being the warping of audio or of an image scanline.

Let $f : \mathbb{R} \to \mathbb{R}$ be a graphical object defined by $f(x) = \sin x$. The shape of the object is $\mathbb{R}$, and f is its attribute function. This object has a graphical representation shown in Figure 5.7(a). Consider the domain transformation defined by $W(x) = \sqrt{x}$, $x \geq 0$, and the resulting transformed object g, shown in (b), is obtained as

$$\left. \begin{array}{l} W^{-1}(x) = x^2 \\ g(x) = f \circ W^{-1}(x) \end{array} \right\} \Rightarrow g(x) = f(x^2) = \sin x^2.$$

Note that the domain is contracted for values of x in $(0, \frac{1}{2})$ and expanded in the interval $(\frac{1}{2}, +\infty)$.

5.2.1 Family of Domain Transformations

The deformation of an object, through a transformation of the domain, involves two entities: an input object and a domain transformation. Suppose

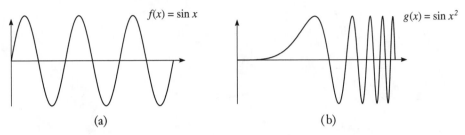

Figure 5.7 Domain transformation: expansion (a) and contraction (b).

now that we use a k-parameter family of domain transformations $W: U \times \mathbb{R}^k \to \mathbb{R}^m$. We would obtain the diagram of transformation

$$U \times \mathbb{R}^k \xrightarrow{\ f\ } \mathbb{R}^m$$
$$W \downarrow \quad \nearrow f \circ W^{-1}$$
$$U'$$

It is interesting to observe that the diagram above allows us different interpretations:

- *Parameterized input object:* The object $f: U \to \mathbb{R}^m$ could be considered as a k-parameter family of objects $f_v: U \to \mathbb{R}^m$, $v \in \mathbb{R}^k$.
- *Parameterized input transformation:* The domain transformation W could be considered as a k-parameter family of transformations $W_v: U \to U'$, $v \in \mathbb{R}^k$.
- *Parameterized input object and transformation:* In this case we split the parameter space $R^k = \mathbb{R}^q \oplus \mathbb{R}^p$, and consider a q-parameter family of objects and a p-parameter family of transformations $f_u: U \to \mathbb{R}^m$, $u \in \mathbb{R}^q$, $W_v: U \to U'$, $v \in \mathbb{R}^p$.

We will discuss each of the above cases in more detail.

Parameterized Input Object

In this case, our interpretation of the diagram results in a k-parameter family of objects that is transformed by the same mapping W of the domain. Intuitively, this means that we have an animation of a graphical object, and for each frame of this animation, its domain is being transformed by the same transformation.

From the above diagram, the original parametric object is given by $f : U \times \mathbb{R}^k \to \mathbb{R}^m$. For each vector v in $\mathbb{R}^k$ there is an object f_v, which is transformed according to

$$g_v : \mathbb{R}^n \to \mathbb{R}^m, \quad g_v = f_v \circ W^{-1}.$$

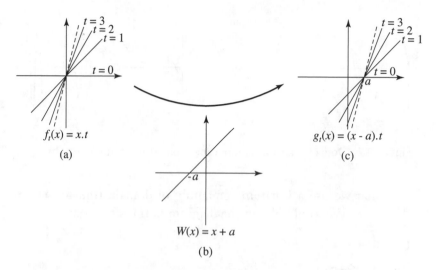

Figure 5.8 Parameterized output object: family of lines (a), translation (b), and translated family of lines (c).

A 1D example is shown in Figure 5.8, where the parameter t is also 1D. In that case, the input object is a one-parameter family of lines of the plane $\mathbb{R}^2$ defined by $f_t(x) = x.t$. The transformation W is a translation given by $W(x) = x + a$. From the composition of f_t and W^{-1}, the transformed object g_t is obtained as

$$\left. \begin{array}{l} W^{-1}(x) = x - a \\ g_t(x) = f_t \circ W^{-1}(x) \end{array} \right\} \Rightarrow g_t(x) = f_t(x - a) = t(x - a),$$

and the result, a translated family of lines, is shown in Figure 5.8(c).

A 2D example is shown in Figure 5.9 for the case of a surface. Here, the function used as input to the transformation is an animation; that is, it has the form $f : U \times \mathbb{R} \to \mathbb{R}^3$ (it is a morphing from a cylinder to a cone). A warping transformation W (rotation of 60°) is then applied to every frame f_t of f to produce a transformed surface g_t.

$$W(x, y) = \begin{pmatrix} \cos \frac{\pi}{3} & -\sin \frac{\pi}{3} \\ \sin \frac{\pi}{3} & \cos \frac{\pi}{3} \end{pmatrix} \begin{pmatrix} x \\ y \end{pmatrix} = \left(\frac{x - y\sqrt{3}}{2}, \frac{x\sqrt{3} + y}{2} \right).$$

The computation of the transformed animation frames will be done by compositing the inverse warping

$$W^{-1}(x, y) = \begin{pmatrix} \cos \frac{\pi}{3} & \sin \frac{\pi}{3} \\ -\sin \frac{\pi}{3} & \cos \frac{\pi}{3} \end{pmatrix} \begin{pmatrix} x \\ y \end{pmatrix} = \left(\frac{x + y\sqrt{3}}{2}, \frac{-x\sqrt{3} + y}{2} \right),$$

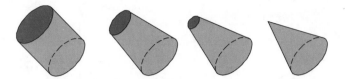

Figure 5.9 Frames of an animation: a fixed rotation of a deformation.

and the input frames, resulting in

$$g_t(x, y) = f_t \circ W^{-1}(x, y) = f_t\left(\frac{x + y\sqrt{3}}{2}, \frac{-x\sqrt{3} + y}{2}\right).$$

An interesting application of transformation of a k-parameter family of graphical objects is found in the correction of distortions in head-mounted displays [Watson and Hodges, 1995]. Here, an inverse warping is used to compensate the distracting distortions caused by the optical systems in head-mounted displays; the deformation is a function of the lenses, and therefore the same warping is applied to every frame of the computer-generated animations.

Parameterized Input Transformation

In this case we have a k-parameter family of transformations $W \colon U \times \mathbb{R}^k \to \mathbb{R}^n$, and one input object $f \colon U \to \mathbb{R}^m$. For each vector v in $\mathbb{R}^k$ there is a transformation $W_v \colon U \to \mathbb{R}^n$, and, consequently,

$$g_v \colon U \to \mathbb{R}^m \quad g_v = f \circ W_v^{-1}.$$

This is illustrated in the example of Figure 5.10, for 1D objects. The input object is simply $f(x) = x$, and the one-parameter family of transformations $W \colon \mathbb{R} \times \mathbb{R} \to \mathbb{R}$ is given by $W_t(x) = x + at$, where a is a fixed real number. The transformed object, shown in (c), is then

$$\left.\begin{array}{l} W_t^{-1}(x) = x - at \\ g_t(x) = f \circ W_t^{-1}(x) \end{array}\right\} \Rightarrow g_t(x) = f(x - at) = x - at.$$

Note that the output function in this case is also a k-parameter family, just as in the previous situation.

A 2D example is shown in Figure 5.11, where an animation is created from a static image of a cylinder, and a parameterized family of transformations.

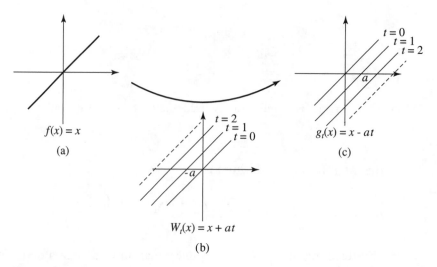

Figure 5.10   Parameterized output object: single line (a), warping family (b), and family of lines (c).

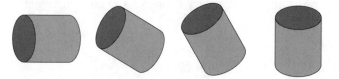

Figure 5.11   Frames of an animation: rotating a surface.

In this example, the transformation is a one-parameter family of rotations, where the parameter is the angle of rotation θ:

$$W_\theta(x, y) = \begin{pmatrix} \cos\theta & -\sin\theta \\ \sin\theta & \cos\theta \end{pmatrix} \begin{pmatrix} x \\ y \end{pmatrix}. \tag{5.1}$$

When each transformation is applied to the domain of an image f, an image g is produced that is a version of f rotated by an angle θ, as follows:

$$W_\theta^{-1}(x, y) = \begin{pmatrix} \cos\theta & \sin\theta \\ -\sin\theta & \cos\theta \end{pmatrix} \begin{pmatrix} x \\ y \end{pmatrix},$$

and therefore

$$g_\theta(x, y) = f(x\cos\theta + y\sin\theta, -x\sin\theta + y\cos\theta).$$

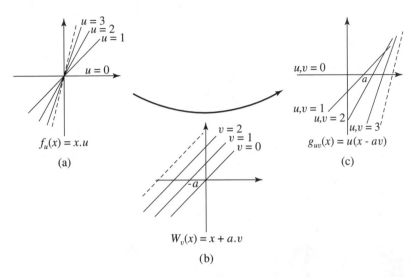

Figure 5.12 A parametric output object: family of lines (a), family of warpings (b), and warped family of lines (c).

As observed before, g_θ can be interpreted as an animation if the angle θ is increased with time.

There are several machines common in the video and television industry that use different flavors of transformations to obtain special effects (e.g., Ampex ADO and Quantel Mirage).

Parameterized Input Object and Transformation

In this last case, both the input object and the transformation constitute a parameterized family; that is, the input graphical object is given by $f : U \times \mathbb{R}^k \to \mathbb{R}^m$, or $f_u : U \to \mathbb{R}^m$, and the transformation is given by $W : U \times \mathbb{R}^l \to U'$, or, as before, $W_v : U \to U'$. The transformed object is therefore a $(k + l)$-parameter family of transformations,

$$g_{uv} : U \to \mathbb{R}^m, \quad g_{uv} = f_u \circ W_v^{-1}.$$

Again, this is easily illustrated using a 1D example, as shown in Figure 5.12. The input one-parameter family of graphical objects is a family of rotating lines defined by $f_u(x) = x.u$, and the one-parameter family of transformations is defined by $W_v(x) = x + a.v$, where a is a constant (this represents a family of translations). Therefore, the output g_{uv} is given by

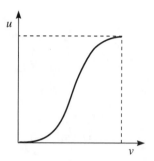

Figure 5.13   Sample path in 2D parameter space.

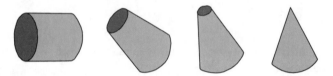

Figure 5.14   Frames of an animation: progressive rotation of a deformation.

$$\left.\begin{array}{l} W_v^{-1}(x) = x - av \\ g_{uv}(x) = f_u \circ W_v^{-1}(x) \end{array}\right\} \Rightarrow g_{uv}(x) = f_u(x - av) = u(x - av).$$

The uv parameter space of the resulting graphical object has dimension 2 (see Figure 5.13). By choosing an animation path in this space, we are able to obtain an animation. The sequence of frames shown in Figure 5.12(c) was obtained using the curve with equation $u = v$. Note how (c) is a natural combination of the "movements" in (a) and (b).

The selection of values for u and v allows precise control over the result of the transformation. In general, a suitable path in the parameter space must be chosen to control how the final animation will appear. Paths with at least C^1 continuity, such as the one shown in Figure 5.13, are used to produce smooth animations. Intuitively, the graph indicates the relationship between the "playback speed" of the input animation (u-axis) and the rate at which the transformation occurs (v-axis).

An experienced animator is able to use such parameterized families of transformations to produce surprising animations where a subject is transformed while moving. A 2D example is shown in Figure 5.14, where a cylinder rotates while it is morphed into a cone.

5.3 Range Transformations

In the previous section we studied object transformations by changing the object shape. An object can also have its attributes transformed to create a new object. The attributes are defined by the values of the attribute function, and for this reason these transformations are called *range transformations*. These transformations do not modify the spatial relationship of the points; they alter just the values of the object attributes.

If the object is defined by $f: U \to \mathbb{R}^m$, and $T: \mathbb{R}^m \to \mathbb{R}^p$ is a transformation, the new graphical object is defined by $T \circ f: U \to \mathbb{R}^p$. This is illustrated by the diagram below:

$$
\begin{array}{ccc}
U & \xrightarrow{\ f\ } & \mathbb{R}^m \\
& {\scriptstyle T \circ f}\searrow & \downarrow {\scriptstyle T} \\
& & \mathbb{R}^p
\end{array}
$$

Recall that a graphical object is defined as a subset U and a collection of its properties f_i as

$$f : U \subseteq \mathbb{R}^n \to \mathbb{R}^{r_1} \times \mathbb{R}^{r_2} \times \cdots \times \mathbb{R}^{r_k}, \quad r_1 + r_2 + \cdots + r_k = m,$$

where $f^j : U \subseteq \mathbb{R}^n \to \mathbb{R}^{r_j}$ are the coordinate functions of the attribute function $f = (f^1, f^2, \ldots, f^k)$.

Therefore, we have

$$T : \mathbb{R}^{r_1} \times \mathbb{R}^{r_2} \times \cdots \times \mathbb{R}^{r_k} \to \mathbb{R}^p,$$

or simply $T : \mathbb{R}^m \to \mathbb{R}^p$, where T has coordinates $T = (T^1, T^2, \ldots, T^k)$.

We might not have uncoupled transformations $T^i: \mathbb{R}^{r_i} \to \mathbb{R}^p$, because the transformation of some of the object attribute values are not, in general, independent of the other object attributes.

The simple 1D example in Figure 5.15 summarizes the above discussion, evidencing the amplitude modification character of range transformations. In this example we take the object $f(x) = \sin x$ and a transformation $T(x) = x/2$; the output $g(x)$, shown in (b), is given by

$$g(x) = T \circ f(x) = \frac{\sin x}{2}.$$

Two-dimensional range transformations are also easy to obtain. Recall that in the simplest case, an image is expressed by a function $f : U \to C$, where the

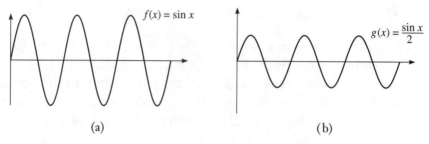

Figure 5.15 Range transformation of an object (b) of the signal in (a).

range C is a color space. Therefore, modifying image attributes amounts to making changes in the image color space. An example is the gamma correction transformation used before displaying an image. Another widely used example is the luminance mapping that allows us to obtain a monochrome image from a color one.

5.3.1 Family of Range Transformations

As in the case of domain transformations, the use of range transformation and k-parameter families should be examined. The combination of parameterized object and transformations results in three distinct situations, analogous to those discussed for domain transformations:

- range transformation of k-parameter families of objects
- k-parameter family of range transformations of one graphical object
- a combination of the above situations

These three situations result in parametric objects that can be represented by families of transformations, as has been done before for domain transformations. We will not go over the details of each case here, because they are analogous to those related to domain transformation. The three cases are summarized by the diagram below:

$$U \times \mathbb{R}^k \xrightarrow{\ f\ } \mathbb{R}^m \times \mathbb{R}^l$$
$$T \circ f \searrow \quad \downarrow T$$
$$\mathbb{R}^p$$

In the first case we have $l = 0$; in the second case we have $k = 0$; and in the last case, both k and l assume nonzero values.

Figure 5.16 Cross-dissolve between two images.

An illustrative example of parameterized range transformation is given by the operation of cross-dissolve between two images. In this case we have two images $f, g \colon U \subset \mathbb{R}^2 \to \mathbb{R}^3$. We define a one-parameter family of transformation $T \colon U \times [0, 1] \to \mathbb{R}^3$ by

$$T(u_1, u_2, t) = T_t(u_1, u_2) = (1 - t)f(u_1, u_2) + tg(u_1, u_2).$$

$T(u_1, u_2, t)$ is a one-parameter family of images such that when the parameter t varies from 0 to 1, the images in the family vary from f to g. In Figure 5.16, we illustrate the operation of cross-dissolving between the face of a woman and a cheetah. It shows an intermediate frame, obtained for the value $t = 1/2$.

5.4 Comments and References

Procedural modeling is closely connected with animation; therefore it is essentially a morphing technique. In fact, most of the computer graphics literature in this topic describes mathematical models for the problem of shape evolution as described in the introductory chapter of the book. One example is the problem of plant growing.

We decided to include a discussion about this topic in a separate chapter, so we could relate it to the problem of splitting a warping transformation into a domain or range warping.

References

de Reffye, Phillippe, Claude Edelin, Jean Francon, Marc Jaeger, and Claude Puech. 1988. Plant Models Faithful to Botanical Structure and Development. *Computer Graphics (SIGGRAPH '88 Proceedings)*, **22**, 151–158.

Ebert, David S., F. Kenton Musgrave, Darwyn Peachey, Ken Perlin, and Steven Worley. 1994. *Texturing and Modeling: A Procedural Approach*. San Diego: Academic Press.

Greene, Ned. 1989. Voxel Space Automata: Modeling with Stochastic Growth Processes in Voxel Space. *Computer Graphics (SIGGRAPH '89 Proceedings)*, **23**, 175–184.

Kawaguchi, Yoichiro. 1982. A Morphological Study of the Form of Nature. *Computer Graphics (SIGGRAPH '82 Proceedings)*, **16**(3), 223–232.

Prusinkiewicz, P., A. Lindenmayer, and J. Hanan. 1988. Developmental Models of Herbaceous Plants for Computer Imagery Purposes. *Computer Graphics (SIGGRAPH '88 Proceedings)*, **22**(4), 141–150.

Sims, Karl. 1991. Artificial Evolution for Computer Graphics. *Computer Graphics (SIGGRAPH '91 Proceedings)*, **25**(4), 319–328.

Smith, Alvy Ray. 1984a. *Graftal Formalism Notes*. Technical memo 4. Pixar, Richmond, CA.

Smith, Alvy Ray. 1984b. Plants, Fractals and Formal Languages. *Computer Graphics (SIGGRAPH '84 Proceedings)*, **18**(3), 1–10.

Watson, Benjamin A., and Larry F. Hodges. 1995. Using Texture Maps to Correct for Optical Distortion in Head-Mounted Displays. In Bryson, Steven, and Steven Feiner (eds.), *Proceedings of IEEE Virtual Reality Annual International Symposium '95*, 172–178.

6

Image Mapping

IMAGE MAPPING TECHNIQUES constitute the pioneering work in the area of image warping. Introduced by Ed Catmull [Catmull, 1974], it has been applied to different areas such as modeling and image synthesis. In the '80s the techniques were introduced into the everyday production of television stations in products such as the Ampex ADO (Ampex Digital Optics) and the Quantel Mirage.

In this chapter we will describe image mappings from the warping point of view. We will use the conceptual framework introduced in the previous chapters. Besides studying a classical topic from this point of view, this chapter constitutes an example of the flexibility of the conceptual framework for warping and morphing.

6.1 Warping and Image Mapping

The problem of image mapping is very simple to pose. In fact, it can be stated intuitively as follows: *Given an image I and a surface $S \subset \mathbb{R}^3$, we want to paint the image onto the surface.*

Supposing that the image is printed on some kind of pelicule, the intuitive idea is to transfer the image to the surface by contact. This process is illustrated in Figure 6.1.

Mathematically, the problem of texture mapping can be posed as follows: The image I is defined by the image function $f: U \subset \mathbb{R}^2 \to \mathbb{R}^3$ (see Figure 6.2).

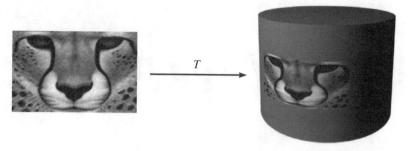

Figure 6.1   Mapping an image onto a surface. See also color plate 6.1.

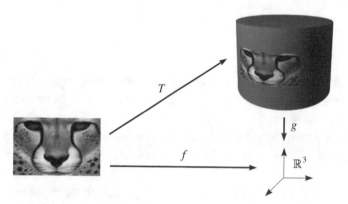

Figure 6.2   Texture mapping and transformations.

The transfer process is done by some transformation $T: U \to S \subset \mathbb{R}^3$ from the image domain U to the surface S. From the transformation T we define the *image mapping* by

$$g(p) = f(T^{-1}(p)),$$

as illustrated in Figure 6.2.

The function g constitutes a new attribute of the surface S. The resulting effect of image mapping is a warp of the image by the transformation T. This image warping technique has several applications. We will discuss some of them later in this chapter.

Depending on the application, we need to impose restrictions on the transformation T. In general we demand that T is a homeomorphism, or at least that it is bijective. For some applications, T must be an isometry or a conformal mapping.

6.2   Image Mapping Techniques

In this section, we will describe three very common techniques for image mapping:

- image mapping by coordinate change
- image mapping using an auxiliary surface
- image mapping by projection

6.2.1   Image Mapping by Coordinate Change

Suppose S is a parametric surface and $j: V \subset \mathbb{R}^2 \to S$ is a parameterization of S (see Figure 6.3). We define change of coordinates $h: U \to V$, from the image domain U to the parametric domain V. The image mapping T is defined by the composition operation $T = j \circ h$, as illustrated in Figure 6.3.

In several applications, we have $V = U$ and h is the identity function. When S is defined by several parametric patches, the parameterization j must be defined carefully so as to map subdomains of the image domain U to different coordinate patches. This is the case when the surface is represented by some triangulation: each triangle defines an affine patch.

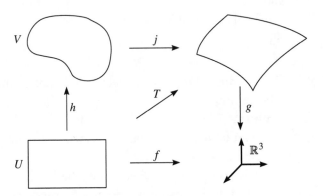

Figure 6.3   Mapping by changing of coordinates.

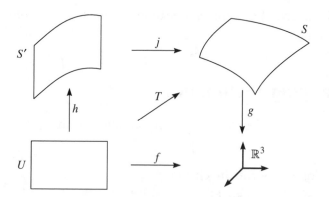

Figure 6.4   An image mapping an auxiliary surface.

6.2.2   Image Mapping Using an Auxiliary Surface

In this method we define an auxiliary surface $S' \subset \mathbb{R}^3$, satisfying two conditions: first, that there exists a transformation $j\colon S' \to S$; second, that there exists a map $h\colon U \to S'$, as illustrated in Figure 6.4. Note that the method described in the previous section can be considered a particular case of this one.

The mapping T of the image onto the surface S is defined by the compositing map $T = j \circ h$. Useful auxiliary surfaces include the cylinder, the sphere, and the cube. These surfaces have global parameterizations that are very easy to compute.

The image mapping technique by change of coordinates is very suited to using image mappings with parametric surfaces. The auxiliary surface technique described above can be used to define image mappings on implicit surfaces. We will describe this in the next example.

Example 6.1 (Image Mapping and Implicit Surfaces)   Consider an implicit surface $S \subset \mathbb{R}^3$, and let S' be an auxiliary implicit surface contained in a neighborhood of S. By blending the gradient vector fields of S and S', we obtain a vector field whose integral curves move from S to S'. These curves will define a diffeomorphism j from the auxiliary surface S' to the implicit surface S. The surface S' can be used as an auxiliary surface to define image mappings on the surface S.

An easy way to effectively compute j has been published in [Zonenschein et al., 1997], based on a "physically inspired" technique: the vector field is

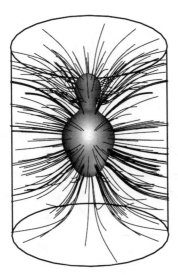

Figure 6.5 Image mapping of an implicit surface using auxiliary surface. See also color plate 6.5.

considered as an attractive force field, and particles are used to map points from the surface S' to the surface S. Figure 6.5 illustrates the use of this technique employing this computational approach: the auxiliary surface is a cylinder, and the implicit surface is a bowling pin modeled as a blob surface. The curves shown represent the trajectories of some of the particles from the cylinder to the implicit surface.

6.2.3 Image Mapping by Projection

In this technique, we consider a parallel projection p from the space $\mathbb{R}^3$ onto the image plane, in such a way that $p(S) \subset U$; that is, the surface S is projected on a subset of the image domain U. This is illustrated in Figure 6.6.

By fixing a projection, the containment condition, $p(S) \subset U$, is easily attained by translating either S or U.

Once we have chosen an apropriate projection, we define a mapping from U to S by associating to each point $x \in U$ the points in the projection line $p^{-1}(x)$ belonging to S. Notice that this correspondence may define a multivalued mapping. Intuitively, this mapping technique corresponds to using some projecting device (e.g., a 35mm slide projector) to project the image onto the surface.

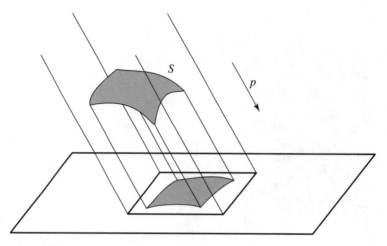

Figure 6.6   Image mapping by projection.

6.3 Some Applications of Image Mapping

In this section, we will describe some applications of image mapping techniques in computer graphics.

6.3.1 Texture Mapping

This is the application that pioneered the use of image mapping techniques. It was introduced by Ed Catmull in [Catmull, 1974].

In this application the warped image g is used to modulate the diffuse component of the energy reflected by the surface. The resulting effect amounts to transferring the image onto the surface. This is illustrated by the image in Figure 6.1. The mapping in this image was obtained using the technique of image mapping by change of coordinates.

Texture mapping is very useful for modeling microgeometry information of the surface: instead of introducing this information on the surface shape, we model it in the illumination model. This is a very effective and cheap technique.

As we have seen, parametric surfaces are very suitable for applying texture mapping using the technique of image mapping by change of coordinates. The technique of image mapping using auxiliary surface can be used to apply textures to implicit surfaces. Figure 6.7 shows the example of a texture applied to an implicit surface using the force field technique described in Example 6.1.

Figure 6.7 Texture mapping onto an implicit surface [from Zonenschein et al., 1997]. See also color plate 6.7.

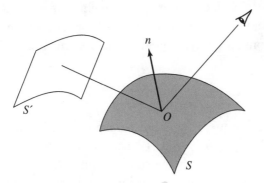

Figure 6.8 Computation of the reflectance vector.

6.3.2 Reflectance Mapping

This is an application that uses an auxiliary surface S' to compute the image mapping. The mapping between the surface S and the auxiliary surface S' is computed by using the reflected vector, from the point of view of an observer (camera position). This is illustrated in Figure 6.8.

The mapped image function is used to produce a texture on the surface. Because of the way the warping transformation is defined, the texture image gives an approximation to the first-order specular reflection produced with ray tracing.

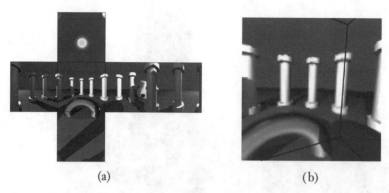

(a)   (b)

Figure 6.9   Unfolded cubic environment mapping (a) and an arbitrary viewpoint (b).

This technique is very easy to implement, and it is computationally much more efficient than shading using ray tracing. Also, for certain applications it is very effective. It was introduced in [Blinn and Newell, 1976]. The technique is also called *environment mapping* in the literature.

Figure 6.9 illustrates the reflectance mapping technique using a cube as the auxiliary surface, where (a) shows the unfolded cube with the image, and (b) shows a rendering from an arbitrary viewpoint, with the seams shown as a reference.

6.3.3 Bump Mapping

In this image mapping technique, the mapped image is used to perturb the normal to the surface. The perturbation is based on the intensities of the warped image. The technique was introduced in [Blinn, 1978].

The tweaking of the normals by the mapped image function has the effect of transferring texture details from the image to the surface, when the shading is computed. This is very well illustrated by the image in Figure 6.10: All of the geometry details of the coin face (number one, date, etc.) were modeled using this technique.

A disadvantage of this technique is that silhouette bumps get lost because they are not part of the geometry. This problem is solved using the mapped image intensities to warp the geometry, as explained in the next section.

6.3.4 Displacement Mapping

In this application of image mapping technique, the mapped image is used to deform the surface geometry, based on the image intensities. This technique was introduced in [Cook, 1984].

Figure 6.10 Coin face generated with bump mapping.

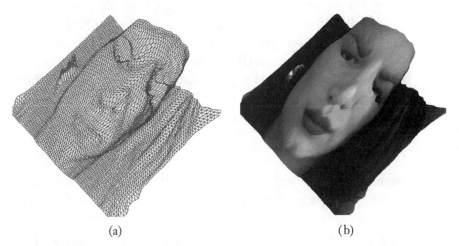

(a)   (b)

Figure 6.11 Displacement mapping with texture: a woman's face is used to warp a planar region (a) and the woman's face is used to put a texture on the "displaced" surface (b).

Contrary to the technique of bump mapping, described in the previous section, the displacement mapping technique computes a warping of the surface geometry. Figure 6.11 is an example of this technique: in (a) we use a woman's face to warp a planar region and in (b) we use the image of the woman's face to put a texture on the "displaced" surface.

In some applications, the simulation of surface rugosity can be attained by using bump mapping. When bump mapping fails (e.g., when we have to expose silhouette edges, the bumps disappear), displacement mapping is recommended. In [Becker and Max, 1993], the reader can find an integrated use of both bump mapping and displacement mapping in a rendering environment.

6.4 Comments and References

This chapter constitutes a brief survey of the classical techique of image mapping, using the conceptual framework of warping introduced in the previous chapters.

Image mapping techniques have been used in very important applications in different areas. They are very important in the area of image-based rendering and modeling (see Chapter 16). In particular, they are used in the construction of virtual panoramas (e.g., Apple Quicktime VR [Chen, 1995]).

Details about the specifications and computations of the techniques described in this chapter can be found in the references mentioned in the text. Nevertheless there is a lot of good material in the literature covering this subject. A very good and well-illustrated survey is [Heckbert, 1986]. Also, [Heckbert, 1989] is an excellent reference for the subject of texture mapping.

Texture mapping using auxiliary surface was introduced in the literature in [Bier and Sloan, 1986], although in [Blinn and Newell, 1976] auxiliary surfaces were naturally used in the reflectance mapping computation.

References

Becker, Barry G., and Nelson L. Max. 1993. Smooth Transitions Between Bump Rendering Algorithms. *Computer Graphics (SIGGRAPH '93 Proceedings)*, **27**, 183–189.

Bier, E., and K. Sloan. 1986. Two Part Texture Mapping. *IEEE Computer Graphics and Applications*, **6**(9), 40–53.

Blinn, James F. 1978. Simulation of Wrinkled Surfaces. *Computer Graphics (SIGGRAPH '78 Proceedings)*, **12**(3), 286–292.

Blinn, James F., and M. E. Newell. 1976. Texture and Reflection in Computer Generated Images. *Communications of the ACM*, **19**(10), 542–547.

Catmull, E. 1974. *A Subdivision Algorithm for the Display of Curves and Surfaces*. Ph.D. Thesis. University of Utah.

Chen, Shenchang Eric. 1995. QuickTime VR—An Image-Based Approach to Virtual Environment Navigation. *Computer Graphics (SIGGRAPH '95 Proceedings)*, 29–38.

Cook, Robert L. 1984. Shade Trees. *Computer Graphics (SIGGRAPH '84 Proceedings)*, **18**, 223–231.

Heckbert, P. 1989. *Fundamentals of Texture Mapping and Image Warping*. Master's Thesis (Technical Report No. UCB/CSD 89/516). University of California, Berkeley (*www.cs.cmu.edu/~ph*).

Heckbert, Paul S. 1986. Survey of Texture Mapping. *IEEE Computer Graphics and Applications*, **6**(11), 56–67.

Zonenschein, Ruben, Jonas Gomes, Luiz Velho, and Luiz Henrique de Figueiredo. 1997. Texturing Implicit Surfaces with Particle Systems. *Computer Graphics (SIGGRAPH '97 Visual Proceedings)*, 172.

PART

II Graphical Objects

In Part I we gave a broad overview of graphical objects, their transformations, and the operations of warping and morphing between them. In the next three parts of the book we will present a detailed study of warping and morphing of graphical objects.

This part will study graphical objects. We will discuss their description, representation, and reconstruction techniques.

7

Introduction to Part II

A GRAPHICAL OBJECT was defined in Part I as a function $f\colon U \subset \mathbb{R}^n \to \mathbb{R}^m$. Thus, it is comprised of two parts: a shape U, also called geometric support; and an attribute function f.

Using the abstraction levels from the four-universes paradigm, the main problems in the study of graphical objects are

1. description of graphical objects

2. representation of graphical objects

3. reconstruction of graphical objects

4. data structures to manipulate graphical objects

We will cover the first three of these topics in this part of the book. Implementation issues concerning graphical objects will be covered in Part IV when we discuss the morphing system *Morphos*, that we have developed (included on the companion CD-ROM).

We have already discussed in Part I the importance of reconstruction techniques in the area of warping and morphing. We will stress this with a simple example. Figure 7.1(b) shows a projective warp of the image in (a). Each of the dots represents a sample of the image. Two problems occur on the transformation:

- **Introduction of high frequencies.** The projective warp applies a contracting deformation on the top-left side of the image, and an expansion on its bottom-right side. The contraction introduces high frequencies on

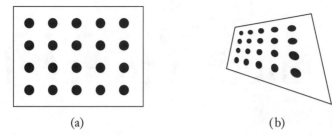

(a)   (b)

Figure 7.1   Projective warp (b) of a discrete image (a) [from Heckbert, 1989].

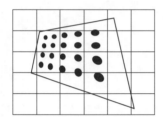

Figure 7.2   Projective warp on the discrete domain [from Heckbert, 1989].

the transformed image. These high frequencies might cause aliasing problems when represented. This is illustrated in Figure 7.2, where the warped image is superposed to the pixel grid.

- **Pixel alignment.** There is no guarantee that when the pixels are transformed they will be aligned with the pixel grid, as illustrated in Figure 7.2.

The two above problems disappear when working on the continuous domain (mathematical universe). Essentially, the interplay between discrete and continuous graphical objects is of the utmost importance for the operations of warping and morphing of graphical objects.

7.1   Computational Pipeline of Graphical Objects

Figure 7.3 summarizes the computational pipeline for dealing with graphical objects. We will briefly describe each of the steps of the diagram.

1. *User interface.* Computer/human interface plays a major role in the manipulation of graphical objects. In fact, robust description techniques must be

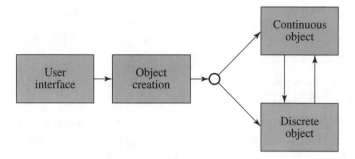

Figure 7.3   Interplay of discrete and continuous graphical objects.

coupled with good graphical interface to provide the ideal setup to create graphical objects.

2. *Object creation*. Description techniques are used to create graphical objects. The finite number of specification elements results in a discrete description of a graphical object. Thus, from the creation process we obtain a representation of the graphical object. Using either symbolic or numerical techniques, from this discrete representation we can reconstruct a continuous graphical object.

3. *Continuous and discrete objects*. As we have already remarked, the interplay between discrete and continuous graphical objects is one of the key factors when dealing with warping and morphing.

All of the above issues (with the exception of user interface) will be discussed in this part of the book. Later on we will briefly discuss user interface issues related to the specification of warping and morphing, in the context of the software on the companion CD-ROM (specifically, the morphing system *Morphos*).

7.2 Comments and References

For a more detailed study of graphical objects, the reader should consult [Gomes et al., 1996]. The four-universes paradigm was briefly discussed in the introductory chapter of Part I. A more detailed discussion is found in [Gomes and Velho, 1995].

References

Gomes, Jonas, and Luiz Velho. 1995. Abstraction Paradigms for Computer Graphics. *The Visual Computer*, **11**, 227–239.

Gomes, Jonas, Bruno Costa, Lucia Darsa, and Luiz Velho. 1996. Graphical Objects. *The Visual Computer*, **12**, 269–282.

Heckbert, P. 1989. *Fundamentals of Texture Mapping and Image Warping*. Master's Thesis (Technical Report No. UCB/CSD 89/516). University of California, Berkeley (*www.cs.cmu.edu/~ph*).

8

Description of Graphical Objects

WHEN DEFINING A GRAPHICAL OBJECT, a subtle but important point concerns the mathematical description of its shape, that is, how the object shape is specified. In general we use functions to describe shapes, a method called *functional shape description*. In this chapter we will look at different ways to describe a shape.

The most convenient way to describe a shape consists in using a functional description, where the shape is described by functions. Therefore, shape description can be reduced to the problem of function description. We have three different basic methods to describe a function: implicit description, parametric description, and algorithmic description.

Keep in mind that the above methods are not mutually exclusive. Some shapes have both parametric and implicit description, some of which can be defined algorithmically. In contraposition with the algorithmic description, the implicit and parametric description are usually called *analytical shape description*.

8.1 Implicit Shape Description

The implicit description of a shape $U \subset \mathbb{R}^m$ is defined by

$$U = \{p \in \mathbb{R}^m; \ f(p) \in A\},$$

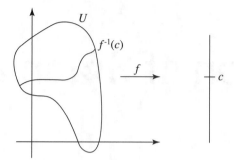

Figure 8.1   Implicit object.

where $f\colon V \to \mathbb{R}^k$ is a function, $U \subset V \subset \mathbb{R}^m$, and A is a subset of $\mathbb{R}^k$. This set is denoted by $f^{-1}(A)$. The most common case occurs when the set A is a unit set $\{c\}$, $c \in \mathbb{R}^k$. In this case, we have

$$U = f^{-1}(c) = \{p \in \mathbb{R}^m;\ f(p) = c\}.$$

This is illustrated in Figure 8.1 for $m = 2$ and $k = 1$.

It should be noted that f is a k-dimensional vector valued function, and therefore has k coordinates $f(p) = (f_1(p), \ldots, f_k(p))$. The equation $f(p) = c$ imposes k-dimensional constraints to the variables of the space $\mathbb{R}^m$. Therefore the shape described has $m - k$ degrees of freedom. In other words, the implicit equation $f(p) = c$ describes an $(m - k)$-dimensional graphical object embedded in $\mathbb{R}^m$. Certainly regularity conditions on the function f are necessary in order to obtain graphical object shapes with good geometric properties. But we will not go into details on this here.

The implicit equation $f(p) = 0$ in fact constitutes a system of k equations in m variables. If $c = (c_1, c_2, \ldots, c_k)$, we have

$$f_1(x_1, \ldots, x_m) = c_1;$$
$$f_2(x_1, \ldots, x_m) = c_2;$$
$$\vdots$$
$$f_k(x_1, \ldots, x_m) = c_k.$$

Most of the problems in the study of graphical objects described using implicit functions can be reduced to the problem of solving the above equation, a very difficult issue.

When the shape of a graphical object $\mathcal{O}$ is described implicitly, we say that $\mathcal{O}$ is an *implicit object*. We should observe that if $f\colon U \to \mathbb{R}^p$ is the attribute function of an implicit object $\mathcal{O}$, defined by an implicit function $g\colon U \to \mathbb{R}^m$, then $\mathcal{O}$ is completely described in a functional form by the function $h\colon U \to \mathbb{R}^{p+m}$, defined by $h = (g, f)$, where g defines the shape and f describes the object attributes.

Implicit objects are very flexible and thus easily manipulated on the computer. They can describe a wide variety of object shapes in computer graphics. This is illustrated by the two classes of implicit objects studied below.

8.1.1 Blobs

The pioneering work showing the potential of implicit models was done by Jim Blinn [Blinn, 1982]. This work was motivated by the need to display molecular structures more accurately. The model is based on electron density maps. We start from a finite number of points that define the *skeleton* of the shape. For each point p_i of the skeleton we define a density function D_i, using a Gaussian, centered at p_i. That is,

$$D_i(\mathbf{x}) = b_i \exp(-a_i r_i^2),$$

where $r_i = \|\mathbf{x} - \mathbf{p}_i\|$ is the euclidean distance from $\mathbf{x}$ to the skeleton point p_i. The parameters a and b are, respectively, the standard deviation and the height of the function.

The implicit function f is defined by the sum

$$f(x) = \sum_{i=1}^{n} D_i(x),$$

where n is the number of points on the skeleton.

A more flexible shape specification is given in terms of the radius ρ of an isolated point skeleton, and the *blobbyness* factor β that controls how the point blends with others. The new equation is

$$D_i(\mathbf{x}) = c \exp(\frac{\beta_i}{\rho_i^2} r_i^2 - \beta_i). \tag{8.1}$$

Since c now is included in the contribution of each term, it can be set to a standard value such as 1. The effect of changing the level surface can be achieved through the blobbyness factor.

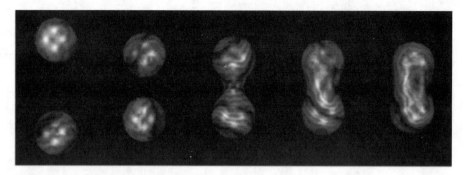

Figure 8.2   Blob model [from Wyvill, 1994].

The implicit function D_i defines an algebraic distance that has spherical symmetry around each point p_i. Therefore, the implicit shape defined by each D_i is a spherical shape. This function can be generalized to allow for arbitrary quadric shape functions if r_i^2 is substituted in the equation by $\mathbf{x} Q_i \mathbf{x}$.

Figure 8.2 shows a textured blobby object generated using a skeleton consisting of two points. Initially, we have two spherical shapes, and as the points get closer together the shape of the implicit object changes because the effect of the density function of each skeleton point overlaps.

8.1.2 Hypertexture

These graphical objects were introduced simultaneously by [Perlin and Hoffert, 1989] and [Kajiya and Kay, 1989]. A hypertexture is defined by a modulation of an implicit shape function

$$H(D, x) = f_n(f_{n-1}(\ldots f_1(D(x)))),$$

where D is the implicit shape function and f_i are density modulation functions.

The equation $H(D, x) = c$ gives an implicit description of a graphical object. The repeated modulation process, with conveniently chosen modulation functions, results in a very effective method to describe objects with a "fuzzy geometry," such as fur and hair. An example of an object generated with a hypertexture object is shown in Figure 8.3.

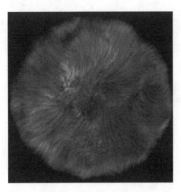

Figure 8.3 Image of a hypertexture object [from Perlin and Hoffert, 1989].

8.2 Parametric Shape Description

In a parametric description, the shape $U \subset \mathbb{R}^k$ of a graphical object is described by defining a coordinate system on U. This coordinate system is defined by a function $\varphi \colon V \subset \mathbb{R}^m \to U$, with $m \leq k$. V is called the *parameter space*. Intuitively, a point $p \in U$ is described by $p = \varphi(v)$, $v \in V$, with m degrees of freedom. Therefore, the graphical object has dimension m.

8.2.1 Parametric Curves and Surfaces

When $m = 1$ in the above definition, we obtain a *parametric curve* in the k-dimensional space. It is defined by a function $\varphi \colon I \subset \mathbb{R} \to \mathbb{R}^k$, where I is some interval of the real line. When $k = 2$, we have a plane curve; and when $k = 3$, we have a spatial curve.

A *parametric surface* in the euclidean space $\mathbb{R}^3$ is defined by a map $\varphi \colon U \subset \mathbb{R}^2 \to \mathbb{R}^3$, from the 2D plane. This is illustrated in Figure 8.4.

Parametric curves and surfaces have their own long chapter in the evolution of shape description techniques in computer graphics. A comprehensive study of this topic with emphasis on Bézier parametrics is found in [Farin, 1988]. Another good source with emphasis on B-splines is [Bartels et al., 1987].

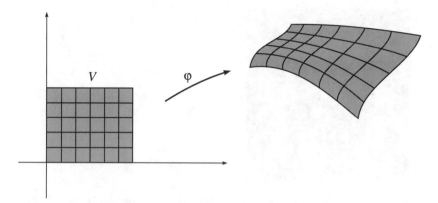

Figure 8.4   Parametric shape description.

8.3 Algorithmic Shape Description

Algorithm function description is the basic ingredient of the area of algorithmic modeling where some of the shapes are very difficult to describe analytically. Fractal shape description is the most prominent example in this arena, but several other shape description techniques exist in the literature. A common technique consists in describing the graphical object by providing information about higher-order derivatives of the shape function that describes the object. Examples of this description are abundant in the literature of physically based modeling. Just to mention one, the shape of shock waves are obtained from the "wave equation," a partial differential equation that describes the wave motion from initial conditions.

Also, we should mention other techniques to describe shapes, such as the "shape from shading" used in computer vision. These techniques of obtaining shape information from images of the object are gaining importance in the area of image-based modeling.

8.4 Piecewise Shape Description

It is not always possible to describe the shape of an object globally using an implicit or parametric form (see [Hoffmann, 1989]). Therefore, when describing a complex object, its shape is, in general, decomposed, and each subshape in the decomposition is described either implicitly or parametrically.

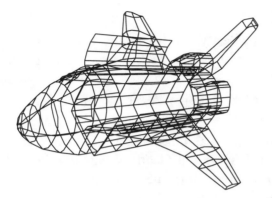

Figure 8.5 Parametric piecewise shape description.

Shape descriptions of this type are called *piecewise descriptions*. Figure 8.5 shows an example of a complex shape that has a parametric piecewise description.

It is possible to use a piecewise implicit, piecewise parametric, or even a hybrid piecewise (implicit/parametric) description.

8.5 Comments and References

We mentioned in the previous chapter that shape description is closely related to user interface: the user specifies a shape using different shape description techniques. We will come back to this topic in the next chapter.

The theoretical study of the mathematics of shape description is covered in the area of differential geometry. For obvious reasons we recommend the classical reference [do Carmo, 1976]. From the topological point of view, the subject of the mathematics of shape description is found in differential topology books. A good introduction is [Milnor, 1965].

Shape description is a very important and widely studied topic in the area of geometric and solid modeling, and it would be impractical to go over details here. For additional information, the reader should consult [Hoffmann, 1989] and the abundant references therein.

A description of some practical applications of implicit objects, including hypertexture and smoke simulation, can be found in [Ebert et al., 1994].

A survey of the use-implicit graphical objects in computer graphics is [Gomes and Velho, 1992]. A reference completely dedicated to implicit graphical objects is [Bloomenthal et al., 1997].

References

Bartels, Richard H., John C. Beatty, and Brian Barsky. 1987. *An Introduction to Splines for Use in Computer Graphics and Geometric Modeling*. San Mateo, CA: Morgan Kaufmann.

Blinn, James F. 1982. A Generalization of Algebraic Surface Drawing. *ACM Transactions on Graphics*, **1**(3), 235–256.

Bloomenthal, Jules, Chandrajit Bajaj, Jim Blinn, Marie-Paule Cani-Gascuel, Alyn Rockwood, Brian Wyvill, and Geoff Wyvill. 1997. *Introduction to Implicit Surfaces*. San Francisco: Morgan Kaufmann.

do Carmo, M. P. 1976. *Differential Geometry of Curves and Surfaces*. Englewood Cliffs, NJ: Prentice Hall.

Ebert, David S., F. Kenton Musgrave, Darwyn Peachey, Ken Perlin, and Steven Worley. 1994. *Texturing and Modeling: A Procedural Approach*. San Diego: Academic Press.

Farin, Gerald. 1988. *Curves and Surfaces for Computer Aided Geometric Design*. San Diego: Academic Press.

Gomes, J., and L. Velho. 1992. *Implicit Objects in Computer Graphics*. Rio de Janeiro, Brazil: Instituto de Matemática Pura e Aplicada (IMPA).

Hoffmann, Chris. 1989. *Geometric and Solid Modeling: An Introduction*. San Mateo, CA: Morgan Kaufmann.

Kajiya, James T., and Timothy L. Kay. 1989. Rendering Fur with Three Dimensional Textures. *Computer Graphics (SIGGRAPH '89 Proceedings)*, **23**(3), 271–280.

Milnor, J. 1965. *Topology from the Differentiable Viewpoint*. Charlottesville, VA: University of Virginia Press.

Perlin, Ken, and E. M. Hoffert. 1989. Hypertexture. *Computer Graphics (SIGGRAPH '89 Proceedings)*, **23**(3), 253–262.

Wyvill, Brian. 1994. *Building and Animating Implicit Surface Models*. In SIGGRAPH '93 Course Notes.

9

Representation of Graphical Objects

WE CAN USE ONLY A FINITE NUMBER of variables and parameters in any computational process. Therefore, in order to manipulate a graphical object in the computer, it is necessary to devise a discretization of the object's shape and its attributes. This operation takes us from the continuous, mathematical universe to the discrete, representation universe.

In this chapter we will study the representation problem for an arbitrary graphical object. Our goal is to obtain a reasonable—and correct—answer to the question: How are different graphical objects mapped into the representation universe?

9.1 Object Representation

Intuitively, an object representation is a relation between the mathematical and the representation universe. It associates to each object a discrete description of its geometry, topology, and attributes. This is necessarily a two-step process: the representation of the object's shape and the representation of the object's attribute function.

When we define a representation O' of some graphical object O, it is very important that we be able to recover the continuous object O from its representation O'. This operation is called *reconstruction*. The mathematical and representation universes are related by the operations of representation and reconstruction, as illustrated in Figure 9.1.

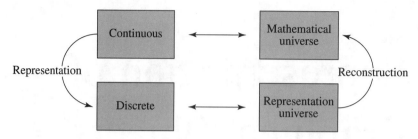

Figure 9.1   Discretization and reconstruction of graphical objects.

In this chapter we will study the representation of graphical objects. The reconstruction operation, also of fundamental importance in computer graphics, will be discussed in detail in the next chapter.

We should remark that we will study object representation from a global point of view. In this way, we will not focus on specific representation techniques for different graphical objects. Our main concern is to present a general framework for object representation. In this framework, we will see, for instance, that the problem of representing an image is essentially the same as that of representing a geometric model; both are graphical objects.

The existence of a classical distinction between image and geometric model representations is related to the fact that images and geometric models have been historically considered as completely disjoint entities, rather than classes of graphical objects. A possible explanation for this fact is that an image has a very well defined and trivial shape (generally, a rectangle in the plane); therefore the discretization process is focused on the attribute function. In geometric modeling the emphasis has been on the object's shape rather than on its attributes. Therefore, objects with complex shapes require more elaborated representation techniques.

It should be clear that by representation of an object we mean a discretization of its shape and its attributes. The shape of an object can be described in many different ways, and its representation is highly influenced by its description. The attributes of a graphical object are defined by a function whose domain is the object's shape. Therefore, its representation reduces to the classical problem of function representation studied in the area of signal processing. These two facts split the study of object representation into two different areas: shape representation and function representation.

We will study each of these viewpoints in the following sections.

9.2 Shape Representation

There are two basic approaches to represent a shape. One approach uses a top-down strategy, where a complex shape is subdivided into a collection of smaller and simpler shapes. The second approach uses a bottom-up strategy: using simple building blocks, along with operations to combine them, we construct complex shapes. These two strategies are called, respectively, *shape representation by decomposition* and *shape representation by construction*.

Certainly there are hybrid strategies where we combine a top-down with a bottom-up approach, but the decomposition and construction approaches constitute the cornerstone of shape representation.

9.2.1 Shape Representation by Construction

This representation is based on the existence of some algebra defined over a collection of subsets of the space. We select a finite number of simple shapes $s_1, s_2, \ldots, s_n$, and from them we obtain more complex shapes by representing them using an arithmetic expression from the algebra

$$S = f(s_1, s_2, \ldots, s_n).$$

The simpler objects are called *primitive graphical objects*, or simply *primitive shapes*. Primitive objects are chosen based on the fact that they should be easy to describe and represent. In the constructive shape representation, complex objects are constructed from simpler objects using shape operators.

A classical example of constructive shape representation is given by the CSG (constructive solid geometry) representation used for solid modeling [Requicha, 1980]. This representation uses the regularized Boolean algebra of sets, with the operations of union, intersection, and complement. This representation is illustrated in Figure 9.2: (a) shows a graphical object, and (b) shows how this object is constructed from the primitive shapes of a square with side of length 1 and a circle of radius 1, both centered at the origin.

The object in Figure 9.2 is obtained by appropriately traversing the tree structure on Figure 9.2(b) and performing the indicated operations according to the following semantics:

- $-$ is the set subtraction operation (left branch minus right branch).
- $\bigcup$ is the usual set union operation.

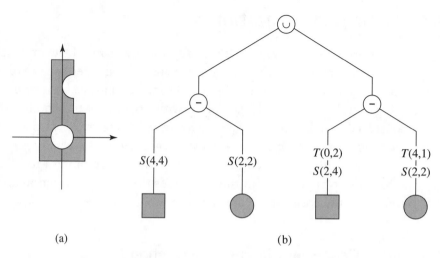

Figure 9.2   Two-dimensional solid (a) and its solid CSG-tree (b).

- $S(s_1, s_2)$ is the scaling transformation of the plane.
- $T(x, y)$ is the translation of the plane by the vector (x, y).

9.2.2   Shape Representation by Decomposition

A *partition* of a shape U is a decomposition

$$U = \bigcup_\lambda U_\lambda \tag{9.1}$$

such that the decomposition sets U_λ are disjoint. That is, $U_{\lambda_1} \cap U_{\lambda_2} = \varnothing$ if $\lambda_1 \neq \lambda_2$. The representation by decomposition computes a partition of the shape, and therefore the shape is represented by each of the partition elements. Two important remarks are in order, however. First, the partition should be finite, and its elements should have a simple geometry and topology. Second, in order to reconstruct the original shape from the partition, we must have a structured partition.

Representation by Simplicial Complexes

A finite *simplicial complex* is a very important partition that satisfies the above requirements. The partition sets are the simplexes, defined as follows: Consider a set $p_0, p_1, \ldots, p_m$ of $m + 1$ points in $\mathbb{R}^n$, such that the m vectors $p_1 - p_0, p_2 - p_0, \ldots,$ and $p_m - p_0$ are linearly independent. A *simplex*

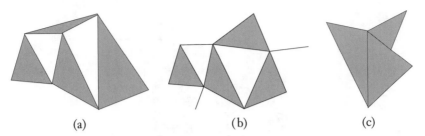

Figure 9.3 Homogeneous simplicial complex (a); nonhomogeneous simplicial complex (b); and non-pseudomanifold (c).

$\sigma = (p_0, p_1, \ldots, p_m)$ is the convex hull of the set. A simplex has a very simple linear geometry, and also a natural system of coordinates. In fact, each point $p \in \sigma$ can be uniquely written as

$$p = \sum_{j=0}^{m} \lambda_j p_j, \quad \lambda_j \geq 0, \quad \sum_{j} \lambda_j = 1.$$

The λ's are called *barycentric coordinates* of the point p. Barycentric coordinates define a natural parameterization of the simplex.

When $m = 1$, the simplex $\sigma = (p_0, p_1)$ is a line segment; when $m = 2$, the simplex $\sigma = (p_0, p_1, p_2)$ is a triangle; and when $m = 3$, the simplex $\sigma = (p_0, p_1, p_2, p_3)$ is a tetrahedron. For a given simplex $\sigma = (p_0, \ldots, p_m)$, the simplexes $(p_{i_1}, \ldots, p_{i_k})$, with $0 \leq k \leq m$, constitute a k-dimensional face. The points p_j constitute the edges of dimension 0, also called *vertices* of the simplex.

A *simplicial complex* is a collection $\sigma_1, \sigma_2, \ldots, \sigma_n$ of simplexes such that two simplexes σ_1 and σ_2 are either disjoint or intersect on a common face. The dimension of the face of highest dimension is called the *dimension of the simplicial complex*. A simplicial complex M of dimension m is called homogeneous when every simplex of M is a face of a simplex of dimension m. This is illustrated in Figure 9.3.

A simplicial complex of dimension n is called a *pseudomanifold* when every face of dimension $n - 1$ is shared by exactly two n-dimensional faces. The 2D simplicial complex shown in Figure 9.3(c) is not a pseudomanifold. Figure 9.4(a) shows an example of a 3D pseudomanifold. When a finite simplicial complex of dimension n is locally homeomorphic to the euclidean space $\mathbb{R}^n$, it is called a *piecewise linear manifold*. An example of a piecewise linear manifold is given by the triangulation of a surface as shown in Figure 9.4(b).

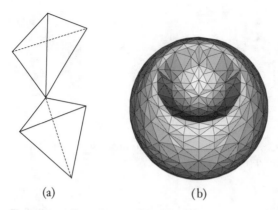

Figure 9.4   Pseudomanifold (a) and triangulation of a surface (b).

The importance of simplicial complexes, and especially of piecewise linear manifolds, as a structured shape decomposition, comes from the fact that an n-dimensional manifold in $\mathbb{R}^m$ is approximated by an n-dimensional piecewise linear manifold. This piecewise linear manifold is used as a representation of the original manifold. A particular case is the representation of surfaces by triangulations and the representation of curves by polygonal curves.

From the point of view of the representation/reconstruction paradigm, the representation by simplicial complexes described above is comprised of three steps:

1. point sampling on the vertices
2. structuring of the samples to obtain the complex
3. reconstruction using linear interpolation in barycentric coordinates

The structuring is necessary to guarantee the correct topology of the shape in the reconstructed object. We will return to this point in the next chapter. Representations of graphical objects using simplicial complexes are known in the literature by the generic name of *piecewise linear representations*.

Representation by Patches

A common shape representation by decomposition consists in subdividing the shape into patches. For surfaces, this amounts to subdividing the surface into a grid of patches, typically four-sided, as shown in Figure 9.5.

When using a patch representation, we must devise techniques to represent and reconstruct each patch. In general the patch is described by a function (either implicitly or parametrically). Thus the problem of patch representa-

Figure 9.5 Patch representation of a surface with associated control grid in white [from Loop and DeRose, 1990].

tion also reduces to that of function representation. A four-sided patch can be represented by the four corner points, by two opposite boundary curves, or by the four boundary curves. For each representation we have a reconstruction technique associated. There exists in the literature a plethora of reconstruction techniques for patches, such as tensor product B-splines, tensor product Bézier, tensor product Nurbs, Lofting, and Coons patches.

The representation by simplicial complexes can be considered as a representation by patches, where the patches are the simplexes and the reconstruction for each patch is given by affine mappings defined on barycentric coordinates.

A graphical object $\mathcal{O} = (U, f)$ is always embedded into some euclidean space $\mathbb{R}^m$, that is, $U \subset \mathbb{R}^m$. When representing the shape U, we have two options: subdivide the shape U or subdivide the ambient space $\mathbb{R}^m$.

The representation of a manifold by simplicial decomposition and also the patch representation constitute examples of the first use, where we have an intrinsic shape subdivision.

Subdivision of the ambient space is necessary when the graphical object has the same dimension of the ambient space. This is the case with images and solids in 2D and 3D space. In the next section we will give an example of a very important representation using spatial subdivision.

Matrix Representation

The oldest example of representation of a graphical object using spatial decomposition is certainly the matrix representation used to obtain a digital

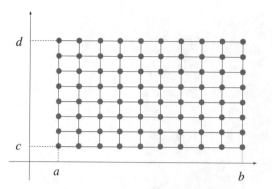

Figure 9.6   Matrix representation of an image.

image from a continuous one. This decomposition has been extended to represent volumes and has influenced the development of other decomposition representation techniques. Matrix representation is a particular case of a representation by patches.

Consider an image $f: [a, b] \times [c, d] \subset \mathbb{R}^2 \to \mathbb{R}^n$. The matrix decomposition is obtained by making a uniform decomposition of the image's shape

$$U = [a, b] \times [c, d] = \{(x, y) \in \mathbb{R}^2; a \leq x \leq b, \text{ and } c \leq y \leq d\}.$$

We define a grid, Δ_U, on U,

$$\Delta_U = \{(x_j, y_k) \in U; x_j = j \cdot \Delta x, \ y_k = k \cdot \Delta y, \ j, k \in \mathbb{Z}, \ \Delta x, \Delta y \in \mathbb{R}\},$$

as illustrated in Figure 9.6.

Each rectangle in the decomposition is completely described by the coordinates (x_j, y_k). The image attribute function is represented (sampled) in each rectangle, and the value obtained is associated with the integer coordinates (j, k). The image $f: U \subset \mathbb{R}^2 \to \mathbb{R}^n$ is conveniently represented by the $m \times n$ matrix $A = (a_{jk}) = (f(x_j, y_k))$. This is the reason for the name *matrix representation*.

The matrix representation can also be used to represent graphical objects other than images. The bidimensional grid defined on the image domain U is easily extended for n-dimensional euclidean space. By conveniently enumerating the grid cells, we define the object's geometry and topology. In each cell, we define the object's attributes by restricting the attribute function to the cell, and representing this restriction using some function representation technique. In Figure 9.7 we show matrix representations of 1D (circle), 2D (disk), and 3D (solid torus) graphical objects.

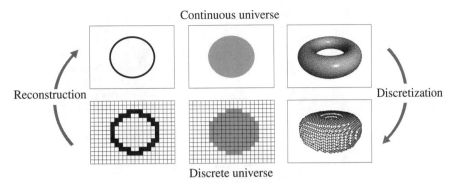

Continuous universe

Reconstruction

Discretization

Discrete universe

Figure 9.7 Matrix representations of different objects [from Gomes and Velho, 1997].

In the area of solid modeling, the matrix representation is called *spatial enumeration*. It is a very popular representation method for volume data (see [Kaufman, 1994]). Sometimes the tridimensional matrix representation is called a 3D-image or a *volume array*.

The process of obtaining a matrix representation from a continuous description of a graphical object is called *rasterization*. The continuous description of a graphical object is usually called a *vector description*. For this reason, in the literature the word *rasterization* appears as the operation that converts from vector to raster graphics.

We should emphasize that the rasterization operation consists of two steps: the first is to discretize the object's shape into the matrix blocks; the second is to compute the object's attributes for each block.

Representation Using Adaptive Decompositions

The matrix representation uses a uniform spatial grid to obtain a decomposition of the object. More efficient decomposition representations use an adaptive subdivision of the object's shape. The adaptiveness criterion in general exploits some properties of the attribute functions of the object. Well-known examples of these representations are the *quadtree*, for bidimensional graphical objects, and the *octree*, for 3D objects. Figure 9.8(a) shows an adaptive decomposition by triangles; Figure 9.8(b) shows a quadtree decomposition. We should point out here the poor choice of the names used for these adaptive representation by decomposition schemes: these names create confusion between the representation method and the subjacent spatial data structures used for implementation purposes.

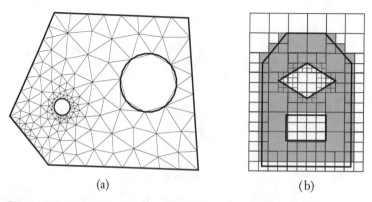

Figure 9.8   Adaptive decompositions: by triangles (a) and by quadtrees (b).

9.3 Function Representation

A graphical object $\mathcal{O} = (U, f)$ has a shape U and an attribute function $f \colon U \to \mathbb{R}^p$. We have already discussed shape representation in the previous section. In this section we will discuss the representation of functions. There are two main strategies to represent a function $f \colon U \to \mathbb{R}^m$: decompose the function domain U and decompose the function equation $f(x)$.

Note that we have a duality in the problem of shape and function representation. In order to represent a shape, we subdivided it so as to obtain simpler shapes (patches) that are described by functions. On the other hand, one of the strategies to represent functions consists in subdividing its domain in order to obtain simpler functions.

9.3.1 Representation by Domain Decomposition

By decomposing the domain U we obtain a partition $U = \bigcup U_\lambda$, and the restriction $f|U_\lambda$ of f to each partition set U_λ is then represented. The rationale is that this restriction is more easily represented than the function f itself. The reconstruction is obtained by gluing together each of the representations.

9.3.2 Representation by Equation Decomposition

Consider some function space Ω; that is, Ω is a vector space whose elements are functions. A representation of a function $f \in \Omega$ is done by decomposing f using some prescribed "dictionary." The dictionary is defined by some family $\{g_\lambda; \lambda \in \Lambda, \ g_\lambda \in \Omega\}$ of functions. For any function f of the space, we write

$$f = \sum_{\lambda \in \Lambda} c_\lambda g_\lambda \tag{9.2}$$

where the sum is supposed to exist. The representation of f is given by the sequence (c_λ), and Equation (9.2) gives the reconstruction.

The correspondence

$$f \mapsto (c_\lambda)_{\lambda \in \Lambda} \tag{9.3}$$

constitutes a representation of the function f using the dictionary $\{g_\lambda\}$. This decomposition is called the *analysis* of the function f, and Equation (9.2), which allows us to reconstruct the function f from its representation, is called the *synthesis*. From the point of view of operator theory, a function representation is an operator $R : \Omega \to S$ from a function space Ω to some space of sequences S, $R(f) = (C_\lambda)_{\lambda \in \Lambda}$.

The mathematical details of function representation can get quite complicated. Some of the problems could include

- giving a clear definition of the space of functions Ω;
- constructing the dictionary $\{g_\lambda\}$;
- studying the problem of synthesis and analysis associated with some prescribed dictionary;
- devising robust techniques to compute the representation sequence; and
- devising good reconstruction techniques.

We will not go over these details here. A precise definition of the space of functions constitutes the realm of functional analysis. Constructing good dictionaries is one of the purposes of the nonelementary theory of functional analysis. Therefore, we will only discuss briefly some representation techniques commonly used in computer graphics. This discussion will lack the mathematical rigor, but it will give the reader the opportunity to realize the beauty and the difficulties of the area of function representation.

From a computational point of view, we need a version of the reconstruction Equation (9.2) with a finite number of terms on the sum. In general we write

$$f_N = \sum_{k=1}^{N} c_k g_k, \tag{9.4}$$

where we impose the condition

$$\|f - f_N\| \to 0 \quad \text{as} \quad N \to \infty, \tag{9.5}$$

for some prescribed norm $\| \cdot \|$ on the space of functions.

In some cases the reconstruction of the function f does not use the same family of functions g_λ from the dictionary. These functions are used to obtain another family $\tilde{g}_\lambda$ and scalars $\tilde{c}_\lambda$ such that

$$f = \sum_\lambda \tilde{c}_\lambda \tilde{g}_\lambda. \tag{9.6}$$

The reconstruction family $\tilde{g}_\lambda$ is called the *dual dictionary*.

9.3.3   Point Sampling

This is the simplest and most frequently used function representation scheme. We choose a sequence

$$(\ldots, t_{-1}, t_0, t_1, t_2, \ldots)$$

of points from the domain of the function f, and the representation is the sequence obtained by evaluating f at the points of (t_i):

$$f \mapsto (\ldots, f(t_{-1}), f(t_0), f(t_1), \ldots).$$

This is illustrated in Figure 9.9. The decomposition dictionary is defined by the family of Dirac delta masses

$$\delta(t - t_k), \quad k \in \mathbb{Z}.$$

In fact, a well-known property of these functions shows that

$$f(t_j) = \int_{\mathbb{R}} f(t)\delta(t - t_j)dt. \tag{9.7}$$

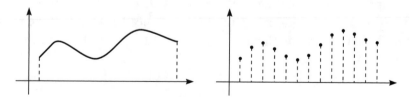

Figure 9.9   Point sampling.

9.3.4 Area Sampling

From the point of view of the general theory of functions, it does not make much sense to evaluate a function at a sequence of points. In fact, if we had defined precisely the concept of a function space, we would have identified functions that differ in sets of measure zero.

Apart from technical considerations, it is easy to convince ourselves that if a function is not continuous, point sampling is prone to severe problems. This is illustrated in Figure 9.10, which shows that samples of $f(t_1)$ and $f(t_2)$ are quite distinct, in spite of the fact that the points t_1 and t_2 are close.

Discontinuities introduce arbitrarily high frequencies in the function, and in this case we need to use more robust representation techniques. A very common representation technique in this case consists in substituting point sampling by some average technique. This accounts for the substitution of the Dirac mass δ in Equation (9.7) by some function that performs a weighted average on each set of the partition.

Average representation techniques are generically known in the computer graphics literature by the name of *area sampling*. Different choices of the dictionary weighting functions originate different area sampling techniques. Area sampling has been used in the generation of synthetic images for a long time. They come with different flavors: analytical sampling, α-buffer, supersampling, and so on. What distinguishes these different area sampling techniques is essentially the computational method used.

In what follows, we will discuss some of the most-used averages for area sampling computation.

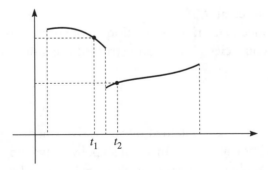

Figure 9.10 Discontinuity and point sampling.

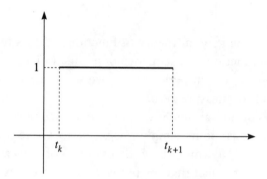

Figure 9.11   Graph of the box function.

Box Average

This is the simplest case. We take a partition $a = t_0 < t_1 < \cdots < t_n = b$ of the interval $[a, b]$ where the function f is defined. The dictionary functions g_k, $k = 0, \ldots, n - 1$, are defined by normalizing the characteristic function $\chi_{[t_k, t_{k+1}]}$ of each partition interval $[t_k, t_{k+1}]$. That is,

$$g_k = \frac{1}{t_{k+1} - t_k} \chi_{[t_k, t_{k+1}]}.$$

The graph of this function is illustrated in Figure 9.11. It is called a *box* function.

In this case, in each interval $[t_k, t_{k+1}]$, the function f is represented by the analytical average

$$\int_{\mathbb{R}} g_k(t) f(t) dt = \frac{1}{t_{k+1} - t_k} \int_{t_k}^{t_{k+1}} f(t) dt$$

of the function f on the interval $[t_k, t_{k+1}]$.

The reader should notice that the above dictionary of characteristic functions introduces high frequencies on the reconstructed function because of the discontinuities.

Triangle Average

Improved average dictionaries are obtained by successive smoothing of the characteristic function dictionary above. In a first step, by convolving the box function g_k with itself, we obtain the *hat function* $h_k = g_k * g_k$, which on the interval $[t_{k-1}, t_{k+1}]$ is given by

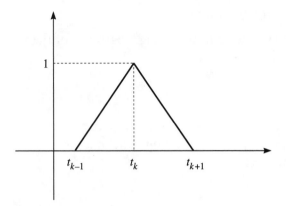

Figure 9.12 Graph of the hat function.

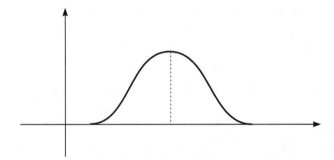

Figure 9.13 Graph of a basic cubic spline function.

$$
h_k(t) = \begin{cases} 0 & t \leq t_{k-1}, \text{ or } t \geq t_{k+1} \\ \frac{t - t_{k-1}}{t_k - t_{k-1}} & t \in [t_{k-1}, t_k] \\ \frac{t_{k+1} - t}{t_{k+1} - t_k} & t \in [t_k, t_{k+1}] \end{cases}
$$

The graph of this function is shown in Figure 9.12.

Higher-Degree Averages

Continuing with the smoothing process will lead us to splines dictionaries of order 2, 3, 4, and so on. Figure 9.13 shows the graph of a basic spline of degree 2, defined by three successive convolutions $s_k = g_k * g_k * g_k$. This family of splines approximate the Gaussian function as the degree grows to infinity.

Supersampling and Area Sampling

This average technique consists in obtaining a partition of the function domain U into a finite number of sets

$$U = \bigcup_i U_i.$$

In order to compute the function average on each partition set U_i, we choose a finite number of points $p_1, p_2, \ldots, p_n$, sample the function f at these points, and take the arithmetic average

$$\frac{1}{n} \sum_{i=1}^{n} f(p_i),$$

as the sample of the function in U_i.

It can be shown that as the number of points increase to infinity, the above average converges to the analytical average of the function on the set U_i, that is,

$$\lim_{n \to \infty} \frac{1}{n} \sum_{i=1}^{n} f(p_i) = \frac{1}{\text{Area}(U_i)} \int_{U_i} f(u)du.$$

For this reason, we consider supersampling an area sampling technique.

9.3.5 Quantization

We discussed in the previous sections the problem of function discretization. We concentrated our discussion in representing the function by simpler functions from a dictionary. It is very important to observe that the representation values must also be discretized in order to obtain a finite representation for the function. The discretization of the representation values is called *quantization*.

9.4 Representation and Level of Detail

In many problems, including the problem of warping and morphing, the level of detail of the object representation plays an important role: a detailed representation might be expensive to compute, while a representation poor in details might not be suitable to solve the problem in question. On the other hand, the level of detail is a very important perceptual cue, and perceptual issues play a key role in devising good morphing techniques.

A good strategy in considering the level of detail in a representation consists in using multiple representations where the level of detail varies between two

Figure 9.14 Different levels of detail of a surface.

distinct representations of the same object. This is illustrated in Figure 9.14, where we show a triangulation of a surface using different meshes, which gives a variable level of detail.

In general, to obtain this multirepresentation, we decompose the space of objects Ω into a sequence of nested subspaces

$$\cdots \Omega_{-2} \subset \Omega_{-1} \subset \Omega_0 \subset \Omega_1 \subset \Omega_2 \subset \cdots,$$

and we define for each j a representation operator $R_j \colon \Omega \to \Omega_j$. As we increase j, we add details to the representation $R_j(f) = f_j$. When we decrease j, we subtract details from the object representation. Two operations generically called *refinement* and *simplification* are defined to enable us to move over the nested sequence of subspaces, in order to increase or decrease the level of details.

Consider $f \in \Omega$ and two consecutive representations

$$R_j(f) = f_j \in \Omega_j, \text{ and}$$

$$R_{j+1}(f) = f_{j+1} \in \Omega_{j+1}.$$

The difference $f_{j+1} - f_j$ is the detail we add to the representation f_j to obtain the representation f_{j+1}. The complement W_j of the space Ω_j in Ω_{j+1} is called the *detail subspace*. The representation should be computed so as to obtain a decomposition of the space Ω as a sum of detail spaces:

$$\Omega = \cdots + W_{-1} + W_0 + W_1 + \cdots.$$

Any function $f \in \Omega_{j+1}$ can be written as

$$f = f_j + w_j.$$

Figure 9.15   Representation of an image on the spaces V_j and W_j.

Using this equation recursively, we have

$$f = f_{j-N} + w_j + w_{j-1} + \cdots + w_{j-N}.$$

That is, f can be written as a sum of a representation f_{j-N}, with a low level of detail, with the details between each consecutive representation space. Figure 9.15 illustrates this decomposition for an image. Here, a low level of detail gives a blurred image with low resolution; the details are represented by the high frequencies on the boundaries of the objects in the image.

What techniques could be used in order to obtain these representations with multiple levels of detail? The above example indicates that the level of detail is related to the high frequencies present in the function. Therefore, a good strategy to obtain the above decompositions consists in moving from the spatial to the frequency domain.

9.4.1 Frequency Domain Representation

There are many different ways to compute the level of detail of a function based on information about its frequencies. The main idea consists in defining operators, called *function transforms*, $F: \Omega \to \Lambda$ such that for each $f \in \Omega$, $F(f) \in \Lambda$ gives information about the frequency contents of f. It is necessary to ask for the invertibility of the transform F so that we can move back and forth from the spatial domain of f to the frequency domain.

There are three main transforms that perform the above operations. These transforms move us from the spatial domain into one of the domains below:

- frequency domain
- frequency-space domain
- scale-space domain

We should observe that the scale-space domain also gives information about the level of details of the function: observing a function at finer scales give us more details than observing on coarse scales.

The *Fourier transform* is responsible for the relationship between the spatial and frequency domains. The *windowed Fourier transform* establishes a correspondence between the spatial domain and the spatial-frequency domain. Finally, the *wavelet transform* has been widely used to establish a correspondence between the spatial and scale-space domains.

We will not go into the details of defining or computing these transforms here. We should mention that of the above three transforms, only the windowed Fourier transform and the wavelet transform are able to compute representations of the function on the space-frequency and space-scale domains. The Fourier transform enables us to obtain frequency information about the function, but does not provide a means to compute a function representation on the frequency domain, unless the function is periodic.

9.4.2 Domain Transforms and Morphing

We have already pointed out that the representation used has a great influence on the computation and the quality of a morphing sequence between two graphical objects.

Some of the above three domains are more convenient to describe and represent a graphical object than representing in the spatial domain. Consider, as an example, a sound with constant frequency. In the time domain, this sound is represented by a sinusoidal-shaped curve, which is not a natural representation from the perceptual point of view. On the time-frequency space (t, f), this sound is represented by some constant function, which is much more plausible with the perception of the sound by the ear.

The above facts give us a cue that these domains could be used in devising good algorithms for morphing computation. There are basically two strategies to exploit the use of variable level of details in the computation of morphing between two graphical objects. The first is to schedule the use of levels of details during the morphing computation in the spatial domain. The second is to compute the morphing directly in one of the domains other than the spatial domain.

A simple example of the first strategy is given in [Stein and Hitchner, 1988], where the level of detail of an image is represented in a pyramidal data structure in order to obtain a multiresolution cross-dissolve between two images.

An example in the second class is shown in [Unuma et al., 1995], where motion warping is attained by doing linear interpolation on the Fourier frequency domain. That is an example where a very simple blending technique, linear interpolation, gives good results when working in another representation domain.

We will return to this topic in the study of warping and morphing techniques in Part IV of the book.

9.5 Blending and Representation Compatibility

We have seen that a fundamental part of a morphing transformation is done by the blending operation between the warped source and target objects.

Blending operations are easier to compute when the objects have the same representation. In the case of piecewise linear representation, easy blending techniques are obtained when the representation of the source and target objects have the same number of faces in each dimension. This means that two polygonal curves should have the same number of vertices, and two triangulated surfaces should have the same number of triangles.

When the two objects have a compatible piecewise representation, and their geometries are close enough, a simple and effective blending technique consists in doing linear interpolation between the corresponding linear elements. This is illustrated in Figure 9.16, where we have added vertices to one of the curves in order to obtain a compatible polygonal description, and we blended the warped curves using linear interpolation.

Techniques to change a piecewise linear representation, so as to obtain the same number of elements as those of another piecewise linear representation,

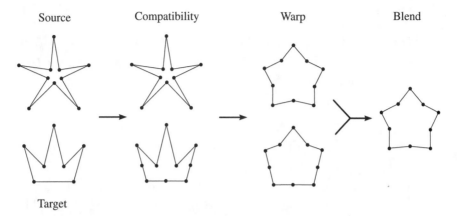

Figure 9.16   Representation compatibility in a morphing between two piecewise linear objects.

are called *combinatorial compatibility* techniques. We will return to this topic in Part IV.

9.6 Comments and References

The geometry and topology of simplicial complexes are studied in the area of simplicial algebraic topology. A good introductory reference is [Munkres, 1984].

For more details about the CSG representation, we recommend [Hoffmann, 1989]. Several other set operators can be used as building block operators. Another example of a constructive operation is the Minkowski sum of sets.

There exists a huge number of good books in the literature covering Fourier transform. We recommend [Weaver, 1989]. A good reference for the windowed Fourier transform and the wavelet transform is the already classic [Daubechies, 1992]. A reference that emphasizes the use of wavelets in computer graphics is [Stollnitz et al., 1996]. This last reference also covers wavelets for objects with a piecewise linear representation.

There is significant work in the area of level of detail representations for piecewise linear objects that are performed on the spatial domain, including [Rossignac and Borrel, 1993; Turk, 1992; Xia and Varshney, 1996; Hoppe, 1996].

References

Daubechies, I. 1992. *Ten Lectures on Wavelets*. Philadelphia: SIAM Books.

Gomes, J., and L. Velho. 1997. *Image Processing for Computer Graphics*. New York: Springer-Verlag.

Hoffmann, Chris. 1989. *Geometric and Solid Modeling: An Introduction*. San Mateo, CA: Morgan Kaufmann.

Hoppe, H. 1996. Progressive Meshes. *Computer Graphics (SIGGRAPH '96 Proceedings)*, 99–108.

Kaufman, Arie. 1994. Voxels as a Computational Representation of Geometry. In *The Computational Representation of Geometry*. SIGGRAPH '94 Course Notes.

Loop, Charles, and Tony DeRose. 1990. Generalized B-Spline Surfaces and Arbitrary Topology. *Computer Graphics (SIGGRAPH '90 Proceedings)*, **24**(4), 347–356.

Munkres, J. M. 1984. *Elements of Algebraic Topology*. Menlo Park, CA: Addison-Wesley.

Requicha, A. A. G. 1980. Representation for Rigid Solids: Theory, Methods, and Systems. *ACM Computing Surveys*, **12**(Dec.), 437–464.

Rossignac, J., and P. Borrel. 1993. Multi-Resolution 3D Approximations for Rendering Complex Scenes. In *Modeling in Computer Graphics*. B. Falcidieno and T. L. Kunii (eds.), New York: Springer-Verlag, 455–465.

Stein, Charles S., and Lewis E. Hitchner. 1988. The Multiresolution Dissolve. *SMPTE Journal*, (Dec.), 977–984.

Stollnitz, E. J., T. D. DeRose, and D. H. Salesin. 1996. *Wavelets for Computer Graphics*. San Francisco: Morgan Kaufmann.

Turk, Greg. 1992. Re-Tiling Polygonal Surfaces. *Computer Graphics (SIGGRAPH '92 Proceedings)*, **26**(2), 55–64.

Unuma, M., K. Anjyo, and R. Takeuchi. 1995. Fourier Principles for Emotion-Based Human Figure Animation. *Computer Graphics (SIGGRAPH '95 Proceedings)*.

Weaver, J. 1989. *Theory of Discrete and Continuous Fourier Transform*. New York: John Wiley and Sons.

Xia, J., and A. Varshney. 1996. Dynamic View-Dependent Simplification for Polygonal Models. *IEEE Visualization '96 Proceedings*. Los Alamitos, CA: IEEE Computer Society Press, 327–334.

10
Reconstruction of Graphical Objects

As we mentioned in Chapter 9, when we define a representation $\mathcal{O}'$ of some graphical object $\mathcal{O}$, it is very important that we be able to recover $\mathcal{O}$ from its representation $\mathcal{O}'$. This operation is called *reconstruction*. The mathematical and representation universes are related by the operations of representation and reconstruction, as illustrated in Figure 10.1. In this chapter we will study the problem of reconstruction of graphical objects.

10.1 Reconstruction and Interpolation

A graphical object $\mathcal{O} = (U, f)$ is defined by its shape U and the attribute function f. In Chapter 9 we have seen that in general the shape is described by functions; therefore the problem of representing and reconstructing a graphical object reduces to the problem of representing and reconstructing functions. In particular, when we represent a graphical object $\mathcal{O}$ by sampling the functions that describe it, a method to reconstruct $\mathcal{O}$ is in fact an interpolation technique to construct $\mathcal{O}$ from its samples.

From the user point of view, the reconstruction operation is of fundamental importance in the user interface and the visualization process. From the interface viewpoint, the user specification of an object generates for the system a representation of the object, making reconstruction necessary in order to get a continuous object. From the visualization point of view, the output graphics device performs a reconstruction of the object in order to be

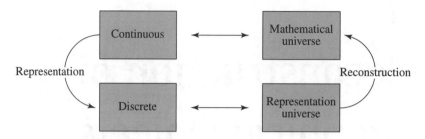

Figure 10.1   Discretization and reconstruction of graphical objects.

visualized. Understanding this reconstruction process is crucial to devising good visualization algorithms.

From the system point of view, robust operations with graphical objects are better implemented using continuous reconstructed objects. Care must be taken in selecting good reconstruction techniques in order to guarantee the correct semantics of the object representation.

Before we go on, keep in mind that in practice we do not have continuous objects in the computer. When we refer to a continuous object, this means that it is possible to sample the object at any point, without restrictions.

10.2   **Representation and Reconstruction**

The representation of a graphical object is complemented by the reconstruction operation. More precisely, we start with a graphical object O and represent it, obtaining another object O_d. In the reconstruction process, we obtain a continuous object O_r. When the original object O coincides with the reconstructed object O_r, $O = O_r$, we say that the reconstruction is *exact*.

When the object shape is very simple (e.g., an image), the problem of representation reduces to the problem of discretization and reconstruction of its attribute function. When the object shape is complex, we have also to cope with shape discretization and reconstruction.

Ideally, both in shape and attribute discretization, we should be able to obtain exact reconstruction from the discrete representation of the object. The experience from image processing shows that this is a very difficult task. If we are not able to perform an exact reconstruction, we must design a reconstruction methodology to recover important properties of the object in the continuous domain. These properties are related to the object shape and its attributes:

- recovering the topology
- recovering the geometry
- recovering the object attributes

Which object characteristics we should recover in the reconstruction process greatly depends on the applications. In general, a good compromise consists in using reconstruction techniques that allow us to recover the topology and obtain a good approximation of the object geometry and some of its attributes. As an example, when we are reconstructing an object that will be observed from a distance far away, we need only an approximation of its geometry. In such cases, even the topology can be simplified without being noticeable.

Representation and reconstruction are the two major problems we face when working with graphical objects. More specifically:

- We must have robust representation schemes. This means that we must devise discretization methods that carry relevant information about the geometry, topology, and attributes of the graphical object.
- We must develop reconstruction techniques in order to obtain the original object from its representation. Since the representation is, in general, not unique, reconstruction techniques are closely related to each particular representation.

Therefore, good solutions for the representation/reconstruction problem have a great dependency on each specific problem. When we discretize and reconstruct images, we usually exploit the relationship between resolution and visual perception. Visual perception is also exploited when we use polygonal decimation to reduce the number of polygons according to the distance that the object is being observed. On the other hand, when the representation is used as input for a milling machine, the reconstruction process must generate the object's shape within tolerance bounds that are acceptable for the manufacturing process.

10.3 Function Reconstruction

In this section we will discuss the problem of function reconstruction. We start with a function f and obtain its representation f_d. When f_d undergoes a reconstruction process, we obtain a function f_r. Ideally, we should look for exact reconstruction, that is, $f_r = f$, but this is very difficult to obtain. In order to understand why, we should point out that the reconstruction process consists in recovering the function from the dictionary elements

$$f_r = \sum_\lambda c_\lambda g_\lambda. \tag{10.1}$$

Several problems may arise that prevent f_r from being equal to f:

- The dictionary might have an infinite number of "basis" functions g_λ. This means that the sum in (10.1) is infinite and must be truncated during computation.
- The dictionary basis functions g_λ might not have compact support. Therefore, they must be restricted to some bounded domain for computations.
- The representation process for obtaining the coefficients c_λ may introduce a loss of information about the function (representation is not exact).

10.3.1   Point Sampling and Reconstruction

A very important and illustrative case occurs when we use representation by point sampling. A partial but relevant answer for the reconstruction from point sampling problem is given by the theorem of Shannon [Shannon, 1949], which we describe below. Consider a function f with finite energy

$$\int_{\mathbb{R}} f^2(t)dt < \infty, \tag{10.2}$$

and such that there exists a constant $K > 0$ satisfying

$$\hat{f}(u) = 0, \quad \text{for} \quad |u| > K \tag{10.3}$$

where $\hat{f}$ is the Fourier transform of the function f. The function is said to be *band limited*.

Finite energy is a very plausible condition from a physical point of view. The condition in Equation (10.2) states that the function does not have arbitrarily high frequencies. In fact, this condition implies that the f derivatives up to a certain order are bounded, meaning that f does not vary too much.

Shannon's theorem states that, under the above conditions, if f is sampled by taking points $1/(2K)$ apart, then the point sampling representation is exact. More precisely, we can recover f from its samples, using the interpolation equation

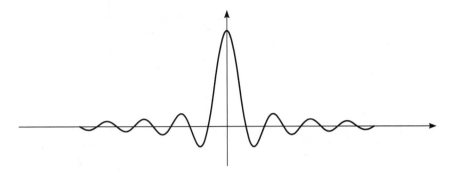

Figure 10.2 Graph of the Shannon basis function.

$$f(t) = \sum_{n=-\infty}^{+\infty} f\left(\frac{n}{2K}\right) \frac{\sin \pi(2Kt - n)}{\pi(2Kt - n)}. \tag{10.4}$$

The sampling interval in Shannon's theorem is $\Delta t = t_{n+1} - t_n = 1/(2\Omega)$. Therefore, the sampling rate is $\sigma = 1/\Delta t = 2\Omega$. This is the minimum number of samples we should take per unit interval if we wish to recover the function f completely from its samples. This sampling rate is called the *Nyquist rate*. Of course, higher sampling rates than Nyquist's can be used to obtain exact reconstruction; this is called *supersampling*.

The graph of a typical dictionary function used in the Shannon theorem,

$$g_n(t) = \mathrm{sinc}\pi(2Kt - n) = \frac{\sin \pi(2Kt - n)}{\pi(2Kt - n)} \tag{10.5}$$

is shown in Figure 10.2. Note that these functions do not have compact support. Therefore, the reconstruction equation (10.4) does not yield an exact reconstruction in practice.

In general, the dictionary functions in the Shannon reconstruction are replaced by simpler functions with compact support, which are simpler to compute. The most-used functions are the box, triangle, and higher-degree splines studied in Chapter 9.

Figure 10.3 illustrates the reconstruction process with these dictionary functions for the 1D case. In (a), where we have a box reconstruction, the resulting function is piecewise constant. In (b), we show a reconstruction with a hat function, and the resulting function is piecewise linear. In (c), we show the reconstruction with basic splines of degree 3. In this case the resulting function is a piecewise cubic polynomial of differentiability class C^2.

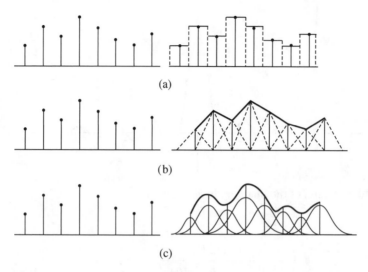

Figure 10.3   Reconstruction with box (a), hat (b), and spline (c) dictionaries.

Notice that as we increase the degree of the reconstruction basis, we obtain smoother reconstructions. Lower-degree filters introduce high frequencies in the reconstructed signal. Higher-degree filters smooth out high frequencies and have the effect of blurring the reconstructed image. When we do not have exact reconstruction, choosing the best reconstruction technique is a compromise between decreasing or increasing the frequencies of the original signal.

10.4 Shape Reconstruction

In Chapter 9 we saw that shape representation by decomposition is widely used in computer graphics. In this representation scheme, the object shape is decomposed, and the decomposition sets are structured in such a way that it is possible to glue the pieces together in order to reconstruct the object. Therefore, reconstruction techniques must be able to reconstruct each piece, and to glue the reconstructed pieces together to obtain the global geometry and topology of the shape.

A simple but illustrative example of shape representation and reconstruction is shown below.

Figure 10.4(a) and (b) show the discretization of a circle using five samples. Structuring here is equivalent to an ordering of the samples. In Figure 10.4(c) we make a linear reconstruction of the circle from its samples, obtaining a

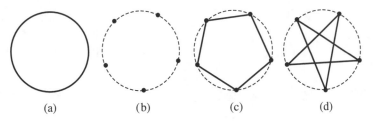

Figure 10.4 Circle representation and reconstruction: discretization of a circle using five samples (a) and (b); linear reconstruction of the circle from samples (c); and linear reconstruction using wrong structuring (d).

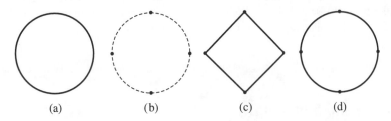

Figure 10.5 Linear and cubical reconstruction: discretization of a circle using four samples (a) and (b); linear reconstruction of the circle from samples (c); and linear reconstruction using Bézier reconstruction (d).

pentagon. In this reconstruction process, we obtain the exact topology and a coarse approximation of the circle's geometry. In Figure 10.4(d), we make a linear reconstruction of the circle from the same samples, using a wrong structuring of the samples.

Figure 10.5(c) shows a linear reconstruction of the circle from four samples. In Figure 10.5(d) we reconstruct the circle from the same samples, using cubical (Bézier) reconstruction. Although topologically both reconstructions give the correct information, the one using Bézier arcs gives a better approximation of the circle geometry.

10.5 Sampling, Reconstruction, and Aliasing

In this section we will discuss briefly a very important problem that occurs when we perform point sampling without taking into account the Nyquist sampling rate.

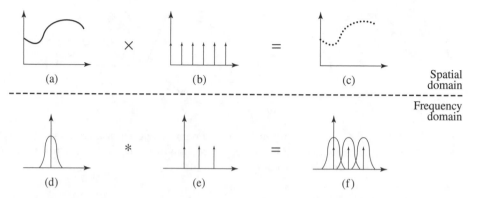

Figure 10.6 Sampling process in spatial and frequency domains: continuous signal (a), impulse train (b), sampled signal (c) Fourier transform of continuous signal (d), Fourier transform of impulse train (e), and Fourier transform of sampled signal (f).

10.5.1 Aliasing and Sampling

Intuitively, the Shannon theorem says that if a function has finite energy and does not have arbitrarily high frequencies, it is possible to obtain an exact point sampling representation by sufficiently increasing the sampling rate. This is illustrated in Figure 10.6, where we use a Fourier transform to represent the function in the frequency domain.

In Figure 10.6(b) we show the impulse train function (comb function), which is a sum of impulse (Dirac) signals spaced according to the sampling rate. The samples of the signal f, shown in Figure 10.6(c), are obtained by multiplying f by the comb function.

It is well known from Fourier analysis that the Fourier transform of a comb function is another comb function with different spacing between two consecutive impulses. Also, multiplication in the spatial domain corresponds to convolution in the frequency domain [Gomes and Velho, 1997]. These results are vital to derive Figures 10.6(e) and (f): the comb function shown in Figure 10.6(e) is the Fourier transform of Figure 10.6(b), just like Figure 10.6(d) is the Fourier transform of Figure 10.6(a), and Figure 10.6(f) is the Fourier transform of Figure 10.6(c). Note that Figure 10.6(f) is also obtainable as a convolution of Figures 10.6(d) and (e). In summary, high frequencies are introduced in the spectrum of the sampled function as translates of the original spectrum. Reconstructing f from the sampled representation amounts to recovering the original spectrum.

      (a)   (b)

Figure 10.7 Aliasing artifacts: original image (a) and window shade distortion caused by aliasing (b) [from Gomes and Velho, 1997].

From the above scenario, we conclude that if the sampling rate is sufficiently high, and the function is band limited, we do not have overlapping in the spectrum of the sampled function. This is shown in Figure 10.6(f). Therefore, it is possible to recover the original spectrum of the function f from the spectrum of the sampled function, using some filtering technique. From the original spectrum, we reconstruct the function f using the inverse Fourier transform. In this process we obtain the reconstruction Equation (10.4).

On the other hand, when the sampling rate is not sufficiently high, the function frequencies overlap in the convolution process as shown in Figure 10.6(f). When this happens, it is impossible to separate the frequencies of the original function from those high frequencies introduced by the sampling process. Therefore, during the reconstruction, high frequencies will be introduced that interfere with the original frequencies, causing a distortion of the reconstructed function. This phenomenon is called *aliasing*.

Figure 10.7 illustrates the distortion caused by aliasing in the sampling process. The image in Figure 10.7(a) was sampled using a sampling rate compatible with the image frequencies. Aliasing artifacts are not noticeable. The image in Figure 10.7(b) was sampled using a low sampling rate, and the aliasing caused a distortion on the window shade.

10.5.2 Aliasing and Reconstruction

The process of sampling and reconstruction is prone to artifacts. Sampling artifacts are known as aliasing, and reconstruction artifacts usually arise because we do not have exact reconstruction.

(a)   (b)

Figure 10.8 Reconstruction with different basis: using the hat basis (a) and using a cubic splines basis (b) [from Gomes and Velho, 1997].

When we sample a function with aliasing, it is *impossible* to have exact reconstruction. When it is sampled without aliasing, exact reconstruction is generally still impossible because of the several reconstruction problems mentioned previously in this chapter. But since the sampling was done according to bounds imposed by the Shannon theorem, we have greater flexibility in choosing reconstruction bases, which seems more adapted to the problem at hand.

Figure 10.8 shows the same image from Figure 10.7(b) reconstructed using two different reconstruction bases. Figure 10.8(a) was reconstructed with the hat basis. Comparing this image with the one in Figure 10.7(b), we observe that the high frequencies have been smoothed out. This is even more noticeable on the image in Figure 10.8(b), which was reconstructed using a basis of cubic splines.

We should point out that the distortions on the windows shade caused by aliasing have not disappeared in Figure 10.8, by using better reconstruction bases. Aliasing distortions can only be avoided, or at least minimized, by taking precautions before sampling. According to the statement of Shannon's theorem, this can be done in two different ways: increasing the sampling rate or smoothing out the image high frequencies.

10.6 Resampling

When applying a morphing to some graphical object, there are several advantages in working on the continuous domain (mathematical universe), rather

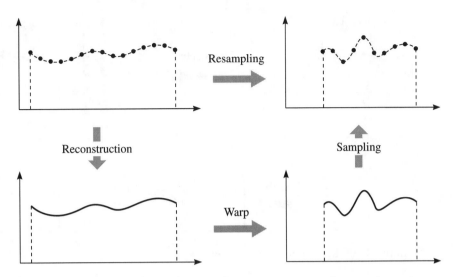

Figure 10.9 Object transformation cycle: reconstruct, transform, and sample.

than on the discrete one (representation universe). Therefore, instead of transforming the discrete representation of the object, we should reconstruct it, apply the transformation to the reconstructed object, and then sample the resulting object. This process, called *resampling*, is illustrated in Figure 10.9 for the 1D case of a function.

In general, the warping operation introduces high frequencies in the transformed object. In order to avoid reconstruction artifacts from aliasing, we should use some low-pass filtering to decrease the high frequencies of the warped object before sampling. Therefore, the resampling operation should be accomplished according to the illustration in Figure 10.10. The filtering operation before sampling the warped object is called *prefiltering*. The importance of resampling for image warping was first addressed in the literature by Paul Heckbert in [Heckbert, 1989].

Although resampling, as introduced above, is a three-step operation (reconstruction, warping, and prefiltering), in practice these operations are computed together as one filtering operation. The filter is called a *resampling filter*. In the next section we will study some properties of the resampling operation.

10.6.1 Resampling Filter

In this section we will follow [Heckbert, 1989] in order to obtain an expression for the resampling filter. This expression will give us insight into the resampling operation.

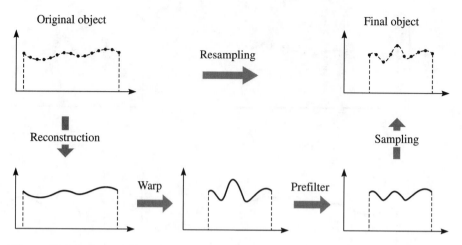

Figure 10.10   Resampling steps.

We will denote the warping map by m, the reconstruction filter by r, and the prefilter by h. We will also suppose that m defines a change of coordinates $x = m(u)$; thus the inverse mapping $u = m^{-1}(x)$ is well defined and differentiable (m is a diffeomorphism).

We will denote by $f_k = f(k)$, $k \in \mathbb{Z}$, the input discrete signal. The reconstructed signal is given by the convolution product

$$f_r(u) = f(k) * r(u) = \sum_k f(k)r(u-k).$$

The warped signal is obtained as a change of coordinates

$$f_{\text{warp}}(x) = f_r(m^{-1}(x)).$$

The prefiltered object $\overline{f}_{\text{warp}}$ is obtained from $f_{\text{warp}}(x)$ by convolving it with the prefilter h:

$$\overline{f}_{\text{warp}}(x) = f_{\text{warp}}(x) * h(x) = \int_{\mathbb{R}^n} f_{\text{warp}}(y)h(x-y)dy.$$

The object $\overline{f}_{\text{warp}}$ is then sampled to obtain the discrete signal in the desired resolution. Putting together the above computations, we have

$$\overline{f}_{\text{warp}}(x) = \int_{\mathbb{R}^n} f_{\text{warp}}(y) h(x - y) \, dy$$

$$= \int_{\mathbb{R}^n} f_r(m^{-1}(y)) h(x - y) \, dy$$

$$= \int_{\mathbb{R}^n} h(x - y) \sum_k f(k) r(m^{-1}(y) - k) \, dy$$

$$= \sum_k f(k) \rho(x, k), \tag{10.6}$$

where

$$\rho_k = \int_{\mathbb{R}^n} h(x - y) r(m^{-1}(y) - k) \, dy. \tag{10.7}$$

Notice that the resampling operation is summarized in the equation

$$\overline{f}_{\text{warp}}(x) = \sum_k f(k) \rho(x, k),$$

where ρ is the *resampling filter*. The expression for the resampling filter in Equation (10.7) is better understood by making a change from the target co-ordinates y to the source coordinates u. This amounts to making a change of variables on the integral in Equation (10.7). Taking $y = m(u)$ in Equation (10.7), we obtain

$$\rho(x, k) = \int_{\mathbb{R}^n} h(x - m(u)) r(u - k) \frac{\partial m}{\partial u} du, \tag{10.8}$$

where $\frac{\partial m}{\partial u}$ is the matrix of the derivative $m' : \mathbb{R}^n \to \mathbb{R}^n$ of the warping transformation (also called the Jacobian matrix).

If the warping m is an affine transformation, the derivative m' is constant; therefore, from Equation (10.8) the resampling filter reduces to a convolution integral. In other words, for affine mappings the resampling filter is linear and spatially invariant. Nonetheless, in general, the resampling filter is spatially variant. The spatial variance nature of the resampling filter is well illustrated in Figure 10.11: the circles are transformed into ellipses of variable eccentricity. For an affine warping, the circles in Figure 10.11(a) would be transformed into ellipses with the same eccentricity.

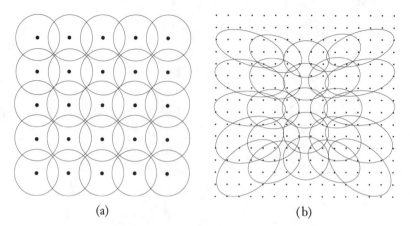

Figure 10.11   Spatially variant filtering: circles on the input image (a) and warped circles after transformation (b) [from Heckbert, 1989].

10.6.2 Postfiltering

When the warping mapping is not affine, resampling is usually a spatially variant filter; thus the implementation is much more difficult and the computation is more expensive. A computationally less expensive solution to reducing aliasing in the warped object consists in sampling the warped object at a higher rate, and filtering the supersampled object before sampling for the final resolution. This operation is called *postfiltering*. We summarize the postfiltering steps below:

1. Reconstruct the object.
2. Warp the reconstructed object.
3. Sample the object at a high resolution.
4. Filter the high-resolution warped object to obtain the discrete object in the final resolution.

It is clear that postfiltering is simpler and computationally less expensive than resampling with prefiltering, as explained in the previous section. Postfiltering gives good results if the sampling frequency in Step 3 above satisfies the Nyquist rate, which is not typically the case.

10.7 **Comments and References**

A very good source to study the problem of resampling for image warping is [Heckbert, 1989]. The discussion of the resampling filter was based on this reference. Also, in this reference the reader will find detailed computations and implementation issues of a family of spatially variant filters called *elliptical Gaussian filters*. These filters perform well as resample filters in image warping.

A very good overview of the existing reconstruction techniques can be found in the second volume of [Glassner, 1995]. In [Gomes and Velho, 1997] the reader will find a chapter dedicated to the problem of aliasing and reconstruction artifacts for images. Another source that addresses the problem of resampling for image warping is [Wolberg, 1990].

References

Glassner, A. 1995. *Principles of Digital Image Synthesis*. San Francisco: Morgan Kaufmann.

Gomes, J., and L. Velho. 1997. *Image Processing for Computer Graphics*. New York: Springer-Verlag.

Heckbert, P. 1989. *Fundamentals of Texture Mapping and Image Warping*. Master's Thesis (Technical Report No. UCB/CSD 89/516). University of California, Berkeley *(www.cs.cmu.edu/˜ph)*.

Shannon, C. E. 1949. *The Mathematical Theory of Communication*. Urbana, IL: University of Illinois Press.

Wolberg, G. 1990. *Digital Image Warping*. Los Alamitos, CA: IEEE Computer Society Press.

PART

III Transformations of Graphical Objects

The fundamental elements in the operations of warping and morphing are the graphical objects and transformations between them. In Part II we studied graphical objects in detail. In this part we will examine the transformations between graphical objects. We will cover their specification, representation, and reconstruction.

11

Introduction to Part III

T HE AREA OF WARPING AND MORPHING has two major players: the graphical objects and the transformations between them. The main problems we are faced with in the study of graphical objects were covered in Part II. These problems were summarized in a diagram that we repeat here in Figure 11.1. We will see the relationship between the graphical object and the transformation computational pipelines.

11.1 Computational Pipeline of Transformations

In this part we will study transformations between graphical objects. According to the abstraction levels we have been using, the major problems we will cover are

- **Specification of transformations.** Techniques to describe transformations are used to specify transformations between two graphical objects. These techniques provide a description of the transformation, which in turn defines the transformation in either the continuous or the representation universe.
- **User interface.** There is a close relationship between the specification of transformations and the user interface: specification techniques should be coupled with appropriate user interfaces.

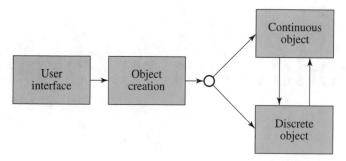

Figure 11.1 Computational pipeline of graphical objects.

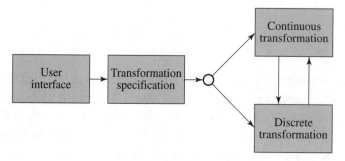

Figure 11.2 Computational pipeline of transformations.

- **Discrete and continuous transformations.** Either a *continuous* or a *discrete transformation* results from the specification of a transformation. Continuous transformations must be discretized to be manipulated on the computer. Discrete transformation must be reconstructed when performing the operations of warping and morphing of graphical objects.

The above problems are well illustrated by the diagram in Figure 11.2.

11.1.1 Spaces of Functions

The similarity between the problems of computing with graphical objects and transformations should be noted. The similarity, apparent in the diagrams of Figures 11.1 and 11.2, reflects the fact that both graphical objects and transformations find their natural habitat in the space of functions. Therefore, when computing with graphical objects and transformations, we are essentially specifying, discretizing, and reconstructing functions.

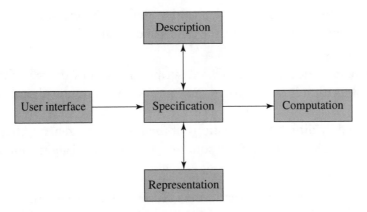

Figure 11.3   Exploded abstraction levels for transformation.

Both the functional aspects of graphical objects and the transformations between them could be covered together, but considering them separately gives a better understanding of their role in the computation of warping and morphing.

11.1.2 Description, Specification, Representation, and Reconstruction

The diagram of Figure 11.2 can be exploded to give a better view of the relation between user interface, specification, representation, and reconstruction of transformations. This is shown in Figure 11.3.

Note that there is a two-way relationship between specification techniques and the techniques for description and representation of the transformation. Reconstruction is the central piece in the computation of the transformations. In fact, this part of the book could have been named "A General Overview of Description, Representation, and Reconstruction Techniques for Transformations." In the other chapters of this part we will revisit each of these problems in order to cover them in more detail.

11.2 Description of Transformations

There are essentially three methods to describe a transformation T:

- **Explicit description.** In this description we supply the value $T(p)$ of the transformation for each point p of the space. This is feasible only if the space has a finite number of points.

- **Analytic description.** This description defines the transformation using analytic equations to describe the values of the transformation at each point of the space.

- **Algorithmic description.** This description specifies the transformation as an algorithm in some virtual machine. A very common algorithmic description of a transformation occurs in mechanics, where a transformation is defined by differential equations of the motion. In general, these equations do not have an analytical solution, and numerical algorithms to solve them are necessary.

Example 11.1 (Parametric Description)   A very common technique to obtain an analytic description of a transformation is by parameterizing the space of transformations.

As an example, rotation of the 3D space around the z-axis is parameterized by the angle of rotation. Therefore, any transformation of this class is described parametrically by

$$R_\theta(x, y, z) = \begin{pmatrix} \cos\theta & \sin\theta & 0 \\ -\sin\theta & \cos\theta & 0 \\ 0 & 0 & 1 \end{pmatrix} \begin{pmatrix} x \\ y \\ z \end{pmatrix}.$$

More generally, the space of rotations of the euclidean space $\mathbb{R}^3$ can be parameterized (at least locally) using Euler angles. Thus, any rotation of the space can be described parametrically using three Euler angles. This description is widely used in commercial 3D animation software. Global parameterizations of the space of rotation are obtained using quaternions [Shoemake, 1985].

11.3 Representation of Transformations

A representation of a transformation consists in obtaining a discretization of it. This discrete description enables us to assign to the transformation some abstract data type in order to implement it on the computer.

We should point out that a representation is generally not unique. Choosing the best representation is greatly influenced both by computational efficiency and by the user interface.

Example 11.2 (Linear, Affine, and Projective Transformations)   Linear transformations of the space $\mathbb{R}^n$ are very easy to represent. In fact, results from linear algebra show that they are represented by a matrix of order n. Therefore, using n^2 numbers, we are able to represent any linear transformation of the space.

Another class of transformations easy to represent are the affine transformations of the space. In fact, they are defined by a combination of a translation and a linear transformation. That is, any affine transformation T can be written in the form

$$T(X) = L(X) + v,$$

where L is a linear map and v is a fixed vector of the space.

Linear and affine transformations are particular cases of n-dimensional projective transformations of the projective space $\mathbb{RP}^n$. These transformations are represented by a matrix of order $n + 1$.

11.3.1 Classification of Transformation Representations

Representing transformations is not easy. We could devise the following classes of representation methods:

- parametric representation
- representation by sampling
- representation by parts
- representation by transformation decomposition
- algorithmic representation

Behind these representation techniques we have the divide-and-conquer strategy. In order to represent a transformation, we must decompose it into simpler ones. This can be attained by either decomposing the transformation itself into a combination of simpler transformations, or by decomposing the space into subpieces where the transformation is simpler to describe.

Parametric Representation

This representation is closely related with the parametric description of the transformation. In fact, when we have a finite dimensional parameterization of the space of transformations in use, we are able to describe a transformation by using a finite number of parameters. These parameters can be used to represent the transformation. We have already mentioned the example of rotations and linear transformations.

Representation by Sampling

Consider a transformation $T: U \to V$ and a finite set of points $p_1, p_2, \ldots, p_n$ of the domain U. The representation of T is obtained by sampling it on these points. A particular and important case is point sampling, where the samples are given by the vectors $T(p_i)$ obtained by evaluating T on the points. Geometrically, $T(p_i) - p_i$ gives the *displacement vector* that moves p_i to its transformed position $T(p_i)$.

Representation by Parts

Consider a transformation $T: U \to V$. The representation of T by parts is obtained as follows: We take a collection $U = \{U_i\}$, $i = 1, \ldots, n$, of subsets of the set U, and we represent the restriction $T_i = T | U_i$ of the transformation T for each subset U_i. Therefore, the transformation T is represented by the collection of pairs $\{(U_i, T_i)\}$.

Notice that the collection $\{U_i\}$, $i = 1, \ldots, n$, of subsets of U does not constitute, necessarily, a partition of the set U. In fact, point sampling is a particular case of representation by parts, where $U_i = \{p_i\}$.

Representation by Transformation Decomposition

This method of representation uses a combination of simple transformations to obtain more complex ones. Different operations can be used in the combination process. Three common operations are the vector operations of addition and product by a scalar, and the operation of transformation compositing:

- *Addition:* $(T_1 + T_2)(v) = T_1(v) + T_2(v)$
- *Product by a scalar:* $(\lambda T_1)(v) = \lambda(T_1(v)), \quad \lambda \in \mathbb{R}$
- *Compositing:* If $T_1: U \to V$ and $T_2: V \to O$, then the composite transformation $T_2 \circ T_1$ is defined by

$$(T_2 \circ T_1)(u) = T_2(T_1(u)).$$

When a transformation T is represented by a compositing sequence

$$T = f_n \circ f_{n-1} \circ \cdots \circ f_2 \circ f_1,$$

each of the transformations f_i is called a *primitive transformation*. The idea behind this representation method is that each primitive transformation is easier to represent or to compute than the original transformation.

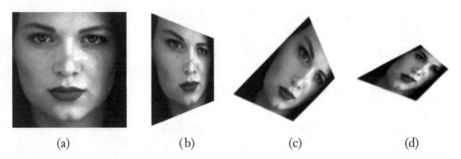

$$\text{(a)} \qquad\qquad \text{(b)} \qquad\qquad \text{(c)} \qquad\qquad \text{(d)}$$

Figure 11.4 Projective warp by successive composition: original image (a), projective warp with vanishing point at the x-axis (b), a rotation of 45 degrees clockwise (c), and projective warp with vanishing point at the y-axis (d).

Example 11.3 (Isometries)   A well-known result from linear algebra says that an isometry of the euclidean space $\mathbb{R}^n$ is the composition of an orthogonal transformation and a translation. A nice decomposition of an orthogonal operator U also comes from linear algebra: the euclidean space decomposes as a sum of three invariant subspaces $\mathbb{R}^n = E_1 \oplus E_2 \oplus E_3$, such that the restriction $U|E_1$ of U to E_1 is the identity operator ($I(v) = v$); $U|E_2 = -I$. The subspace E_3 decomposes as a sum of planes (2D subspaces), and in each plane U is a rotation around the origin.

Example 11.4 (Plane Projective Transformation)   A good example of constructive representation by composition is given by plane projective warps. In fact, a plane projective warp with two arbitrary vanishing points can be computed by defining projective warps with vanishing points over the coordinate axis. By combining these two classes of projective warps with arbitrary rotations of the plane, we are able to obtain projective warpings with arbitrary vanishing points. This is illustrated by the sequence of images in Figure 11.4: we have the original image (a); a projective warp with vanishing point at the x-axis (b); a rotation of 45 degrees in the clockwise direction (c); and another projective warp with vanishing point at the y-axis (d).

Example 11.5 (Twist Transformations)   It should be easy to verify that the twist warping can be represented as a composition of a one-parameter family of rotations around the z-axis and a one-parameter family of translations along the z-axis.

Example 11.6 (Separable Transformations)   A very important case of transformation decomposition occurs when we have a transformation $T\colon \mathbb{R}^n \to \mathbb{R}^n$ of the euclidean space and it has a representation

$$T = T_n \circ T_{n-1} \circ \cdots \circ T_2 \circ T_1,$$

such that each primitive transformation T_i depends only on the i-th coordinate. That is, $T_i(x_1, \ldots, x_i, \ldots, x_n) = T_i(x_i)$. In this case we say that the transformation is *separable*. Separability is a very powerful representation technique from the computational point of view. It originates the multiple-pass technique for warping computation. We will return to this topic in later chapters. The concept of separability should not be confused with a similar one used in image processing related to separable filter kernels. There, the mapping decomposition uses multiplication instead of the compositing operation.

Algorithmic Representation

In this representation the transformation is described by some algorithm in a virtual machine. Instances of the transformation are obtained by executing the algorithm. This transformation representation is widely used in the area of algorithmic modeling.

11.4 Representation and Reconstruction

The discretization in the representation process of a transformation implies some loss of information about the transformation. Therefore, we are faced with the problem of reobtaining the original transformation from its representation. As we have already mentioned in our study of graphical objects, this reconstruction process is very important.

It is generally impossible to compute the original transformation exactly from its representation. When it is possible to recover the original from its representation, we say that the representation is *exact*. A transformation usually does not have an exact representation. The reconstruction process is only able to compute an approximation to the original transformation. We will consider some examples below.

Example 11.7 (Linear, Affine, and Projective Transformations)   As we have said previously, if we know the values of a linear map $T: \mathbb{R}^n \to \mathbb{R}^m$ at n linearly independent vectors $v_1, \ldots, v_n$, then we are able to reconstruct T exactly. In fact, T is the linear transformation whose matrix is constituted by the column vectors $T(v_i)$, $i = 1, \ldots, n$.

An affine transformation of $\mathbb{R}^n$ is uniquely determined by $n + 1$ points $v_0, v_1, \ldots, v_n$ of the space, if the n vectors $v_1 - v_0, v_2 - v_0, \ldots, v_n - v_0$ are linearly independent. As a particular case, an affine mapping of the plane is uniquely determined if we know its values on the vertices of a nondegenerate triangle.

A plane projective transformation of the affine plane $\mathbb{R}^2$ is completely determined by its values at the four vertices of a nondegenerate quadrilateral of the plane. This result extends to $\mathbb{R}^n$.

In what follows, we will examine in more detail the case of representation by parts. The union $U = \cup U_i$ of the subsets U_i generally does not constitute a partition of the space. Therefore, the representation of the transformation loses information about the values of the transformation at other points of the domain.

11.4.1 Representation by Parts and Reconstruction

When we have a representation of a transformation by parts $(\{U_i\}, T|U_i)$, a two-part strategy is used to reconstruct T. First, we define some structuring of the collection U_i of subsets so as to obtain a representation $\widetilde{U}$ of the set U. Second, we extend each transformation T_i to obtain a transformation $\widetilde{T}$ defined on the representation $\widetilde{U}$ of the set U.

In most of the cases, the representation $\widetilde{U}$ only approximates the set U, and also the extended transformation $\widetilde{T}$ only approximates the original transformation T. A simple and important example is given by the reconstruction of a transformation from a representation using point sampling, which we will discuss below.

Point Sampling and Piecewise Linear Reconstruction

Consider a map $T: U \subset \mathbb{R}^n \to \mathbb{R}^n$, and a representation of T by point sampling. That is, we have n points $p_1, \ldots, p_n$ in U and represent T by the values $T(p_i)$.

A simple reconstruction procedure consists in using a simplicial decomposition of the domain U, such that the points p_i are vertices of the simplexes (a common technique is to use a Delaunay triangulation). Now we reconstruct the transformation using linear interpolation in barycentric coordinates. This technique is called *piecewise linear reconstruction*. Certainly, higher-degree polynomials could be used to reconstruct T.

Point Sampling and Mesh Reconstruction

As in the previous section, consider a map $T: U \subset \mathbb{R}^2 \to \mathbb{R}^2$, and a representation of T by point sampling. That is, we obtain n points $p_1, \ldots, p_n$ in U and represent T by the values $T(p_i)$. Now, suppose that the points p_i are structured so as to define a lattice of the domain U. We can use mesh interpolation techniques, such as projective interpolation, bilinear mapping, or even higher-degree polynomial patches to reconstruct T, in each mesh cell, from the mesh vertices.

Point Sampling and Scattered Data

When we represent a transformation T by using point sampling sequence $(p_i, T(p_i))$, the reconstruction of T is part of a well-known problem called *scattered data interpolation*. The piecewise linear reconstruction and the mesh reconstruction discussed above are indeed simple solutions for this generic and very important problem.

11.5 Comments and References

In this introductory chapter we have given an overview of the techniques used to describe, represent, and reconstruct a transformation. We will go over details of these techniques in the chapters to follow.

Representation of plane projective warps by decomposition and the advantages of this decomposition in performing computations first appeared in the literature in [Smith, 1987]. In fact, the paper describes a very general technique for decomposing a generic class of image warpings.

There are several papers about the representation of plane rotations by transformation decomposition [Paeth, 1986; Weiman, 1980; Tanaka et al., 1986].

References

Paeth, Alan W. 1986. A Fast Algorithm for General Raster Rotation. *Proceedings of Graphics Interface '86*, 77–81.

Shoemake, K. 1985. Animating Rotation with Quaternion Curves. *Computer Graphics (SIGGRAPH '85 Proceedings)*, **19**, 245–254.

Smith, Alvy Ray. 1987. Planar 2-Pass Texture Mapping and Warping. *Computer Graphics (SIGGRAPH '87 Proceedings)*, **21**(4), 263–272.

Tanaka, A., M. Kameyama, S. Kazama, and O. Watanabe. 1986. A Rotation Method for Raster Image Using Skew Transformation. *IEEE Conference on Computer Vision and Pattern Recognition Proceedings*, 272–277.

Weiman, Carl F. R. 1980. Continuous Anti-Aliased Rotation and Zoom of Raster Images. *Computer Graphics (SIGGRAPH '80 Proceedings)*, **14**(3), 286–293.

12

Specification of Transformations

GOOD TRANSFORMATION SPECIFICATION TECHNIQUES are very important for warping and morphing. The specification technique has a great influence in the design of the user interface, which enables the user to drive the warping and morphing.

12.1 The Specification Problem

The manipulation of transformations in the computer requires the description of a transformation using some finite representation. Besides the representation problem, we are faced with the specification of the transformation by the user. Some examples will help to clarify the problem.

Linear maps on the space $\mathbb{R}^n$ are completely characterized by knowing their values at n linearly independent vectors; affine mappings need $n + 1$ linearly independent points. Therefore, in order to specify the transformation from the rectangle to the parallelogram in Figure 12.1, the user only needs to specify the image of the points A, B, and C. This is equivalent to specifying the transformation at the oriented line segments $\overrightarrow{BA}$ and $\overrightarrow{BC}$: $T(\overrightarrow{BA}) = \overrightarrow{B'A'}$, and $T(\overrightarrow{BC}) = \overrightarrow{B'C'}$.

Projective mappings of the n-dimensional space need $n + 2$ points to be completely characterized. Therefore, to obtain the projective warping shown in Figure 12.2 the user needs to specify the correspondence between the

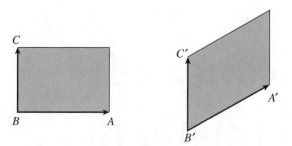

Figure 12.1   Affine warping specification.

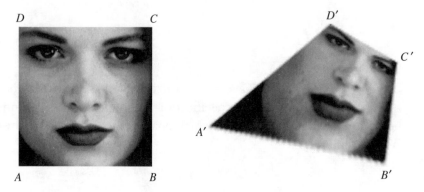

Figure 12.2   Projective warp with two vanishing points.

vertices A, B, C, and D in the original image, and the corresponding vertices A', B', C', and D', to obtain the warped image.

From this finite specification of the affine and projective mappings in the examples above, the computer should be able to reconstruct the transformations so as to compute them at any point of the transformation domain. In this case, this is not a difficult task: from the specifications we obtain the matrix representation of the transformation, which gives an exact, analytic representation of it.

The above examples, although simple, illustrate our goals when dealing with transformation on the computer:

- The user should specify a finite, and hopefully small, number of parameters.

- The computer provides a representation from the user specification.

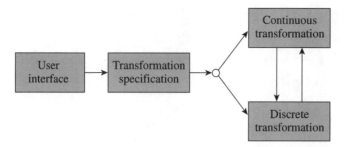

Figure 12.3 User interface, specification, and representation.

- The computer should provide a robust reconstruction from the representation.

This is illustrated by the diagram shown in the introductory chapter of this part, which we reproduce here in Figure 12.3.

12.1.1 Specification Techniques

We have seen that specification is just another facet of the problem of representation and description of transformations. All forms of specification are based on the idea that a transformation can be represented using only a finite number of parameters. From this specification, the computer should be able to reconstruct the transformation and compute it for any point of the warping domain.

Therefore, we should devise techniques that allow us to specify the transformation only at a finite number of elements. There exist different methods for finding the best specification for each problem, and this constitutes a whole area that pervades different fields of mathematics. In fact, most of the problems in computational math consist in finding some function with certain prescribed properties.

Here we are concerned with graphical object metamorphosis. The best-suited function specification for our problem consists in using function extension: we specify the transformation only at some finite set of elements of the domain. From these elements, the function is reconstructed (extended) to the whole domain.

We can classify specifications in three different types:

- parametric specification
- algorithmic specification
- specification by parts

We will discuss each of the above techniques in the following sections.

12.2 Parametric Specification

In this method the user specifies a finite number of parameters. From these parameters we have an analytic description of the transformation. This is a very useful specification technique when we have a parameterization of the space of transformations.

Example 12.1 (Linear and Projective Warps)   The space of linear transformations of the euclidean space $\mathbb{R}^3$ is parameterized by nine parameters (the nine entries in the 3×3 matrix that represents the transformation). Therefore, by specifying nine numbers, the user is able to completely describe a linear map. Certainly, this is not a good specification technique from the point of view of user interface.

A local parameterization of the space of rotations is also given by the Euler angles. Thus, three parameters suffice to specify a rotation of the space. This specification is widely used in commercial animation systems to describe the motion of rigid bodies in the space.

The virtual camera parameters used to specify the camera transformation in a graphics system is a parametric specification of a projective warp of the scene.

12.3 Algorithmic Specification

This is closely related to the algorithmic representation of a transformation. An algorithm is described in some virtual machine, and it is used to compute instances of the transformation when necessary.

12.4 Specification by Parts

This specification technique is directly related to the representation of a transformation by parts described in Chapter 11.

Consider two graphical objects $O_1 = (U, f)$ and $O_2 = (V, g)$, and two finite families $\{U_i\}_{i=1,\ldots,n}$ $\{V_j\}_{j=1,\ldots,m}$ of subsets of U and V, respectively. A specification by parts of a transformation $T: O_1 \to O_2$ consists in a correspondence (U_i, V_j) between the elements of the families and a set of transformations $T_{ij}: U_i \to V_j$. The $\{U_i\}$ are called the source elements, and the $\{V_i\}$ are called the target elements.

One remark is important concerning this technique: In general, we have a one-to-one correspondence between the elements of the two families $\{U_i\}$ and $\{V_j\}$, but this is not necessary. Also, the families $\{U_i\}$ and $\{V_i\}$ do not necessarily constitute a partition of either U or V.

The specification induces a representation of the transformation by the family of triples

$$(U_i, V_j, T_{ij}: U_i \to V_j).$$

From this representation we must provide a reconstruction method that extends the transformations T_{ij} to obtain a transformation T for the whole space. That is, we must obtain a transform $T: U \to V$ such that the restriction $T|U_i$ of T to each set U_i of the family coincides with or approximates the transformation T_{ij} of the specification.

As is the case in every representation by decomposition, a good structuring of the families $\{U_i\}$ and $\{V_i\}$ is necessary in order to obtain the right reconstruction from the specification.

It is possible to devise some subclasses of specification by parts that have been largely used in the literature for obtaining object metamorphosis:

- specification by partition
- mesh specification
- specification by features

We will study each of these methods in the following sections.

12.4.1 Specification by Partition

In a specification by partition, the families $\{U_i\}$ and $\{V_j\}$ of subsets constitute a partition of the object shape, that is,

$$\bigcup U_i = U, \quad \bigcup V_i = V,$$

$$U_i \bigcap U_j = \emptyset \quad V_i \bigcap V_j = \emptyset, \quad \text{if } i \neq j. \tag{12.1}$$

Figure 12.4   Specification by partition.

Moreover, there is a one-to-one correspondence between the elements of $\{U_i\}$ and $\{V_j\}$. Briefly, the object shape and its underlying space are decomposed, and the transformation must be specified for each element of the decomposition. This is illustrated by the image in Figure 12.4, where the decomposition is a triangulation.

Specification by partition has a straight dependence on the structure of the domain decomposition: well-structured decompositions are easy to work with, while arbitrary decompositions are more difficult to represent and to maintain.

In general, we use well-behaved partitions such as triangulations or cellular decompositions. These partitions are generically called *meshes*. Therefore, in the mesh-based approach, two meshes, with equivalent combinatorial topologies, are created and used to specify the transformation at each mesh element. The user is responsible for specifying the transformation between two corresponding meshes to attain the desired results.

There are some particular cases of meshes that are specially relevant. Polygonal or polyhedral meshes, for instance, are a natural choice that can give good results when coupled with robust reconstruction techniques in the computation phase. However, the direct specification of a transformation through manipulation of meshes is a laborious task in 2D, and it is almost impracticable in 3D for morphing applications.

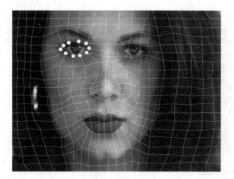 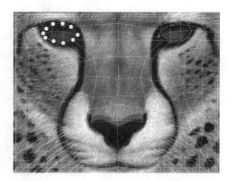

Figure 12.5 Specification by change of coordinates.

Mesh Specification

In Part I of the book we pointed out that there is a close relationship between warping and change of coordinates: a global warping defines a change of coordinates and vice versa. A natural choice is to use a coordinate system to specify the warping.

This specification uses a representation by parts. The coordinate system is represented by some mesh, and the change of coordinates is computed from its values on the mesh representation. The computation techniques greatly depend on the curve representation techniques used in the mesh representation. Figure 12.5 illustrates the specification by change of coordinates.

The use of meshes of spline curves [Smithe, 1990] or surfaces suggests a naturally smooth transformation, and was used in image morphing applications for the first time for the special effects in the 1988 movie *Willow* (see [Wolberg, 1990]).

Although spline meshes permit an extremely efficient computation for sampled implicit objects (discussed in the next chapter), this kind of specification is sometimes restrictive. As noted before, positioning the points of the mesh over the interesting features is a difficult task, and the regularity of the mesh does not necessarily match the "natural" structure of the underlying object. We should point out that because of continuity properties of the warping, the values of the transformation in a mesh greatly influence the results of neighboring meshes.

By definition, specification by partition tries to specify the transformation for the entire object domain. Specification by change of coordinates enables the user to define more precisely what takes place in all parts of the domain.

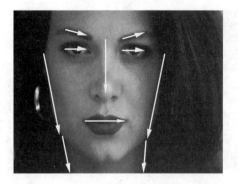

Figure 12.6   Feature specification.

Because of continuity restrictions, however, changes in one set of the partition induce changes in neighboring sets. This forces the user to work on partition domains that do not directly influence the desired results.

12.4.2   Specification by Features

In this specification technique, the source and target elements are used to establish a correspondence between distinguished features of the graphical objects. This specification relies on the property of feature preservation stated in Part I: *a good morphing transformation should preserve features*.

The obvious advantage of feature specification is that the user only needs to specify the transformation at relevant features. In practice, however, users are frequently forced to add secondary features in order to obtain a better control over the warping reconstruction process.

Figure 12.6 illustrates a specification by features, where vectors are conveniently mapped into corresponding vectors of the other graphical object in order to specify the transformation.

In a specification by features, the source and destination sets, S and D, do not define partitions. Some useful conditions are required from the specification to yield reasonable warps. Adjacency relationships in a partition specification, for instance, must be the same in S and D for the warping transformation to be continuous. Also, feature specifications usually satisfy a nonoverlapping condition among them, in order to avoid problems of multiple definition at feature intersections when defining the warping W. Additional constraints to the specification of the features are sometimes imposed when defining some warping techniques.

In feature-based specification, only distinguished features and their transformations are specified by the user. The warp will be computed in such a way as to map each feature of the graphical object to the corresponding transformed state. This corresponds to reconstructing the warping transformation from its specification of just a few selected feature positions.

Point-Based Specification

An important case of feature-based warping is the point-based specification. In this case, each feature is described by a point that belongs to the geometric support of the graphical object. Point-based morphing specification is largely used in commercial image morphing. In some cases, it is possible to reconstruct the warping exactly from a point-based specification. This is the case with affine and projective warpings, as shown in the beginning of this chapter.

When we use points to specify a morphing, pairs of points p_i and p'_i from the source and target objects specify an animation path. When we use points to specify a warping, two pairs of corresponding points p_i and p'_i specify the displacement vector $\overrightarrow{p_i p'_i} = p'_i - p_i$ of the point p_i under the warping transformation.

Higher-Dimensional Features

Point-based specification is a particular case of feature specification where the features have dimension 0. Higher-dimensional features could be used in order to have better local control of the transformation. Figure 12.6 shows an example where 1D features (oriented line segments) have been used.

The pioneering implementation of an image morphing system where the features are described by oriented line segments was done at Pacific Data Images [Beier and Neely, 1992]. The system was used to create the classical morphing sequence in Michael Jackson's video clip *Black or White*.

This oriented segment-based feature system has been extended [Lerios et al., 1995] to implement a morphing system for volumetric objects in 3D space. This extension uses features of various dimensions, including points, vectors, cylinders, and boxes. This is illustrated in Figure 12.7.

Another interesting use of 1D features has been proposed by George Wolberg [Wolberg, 1989]. He addresses the problem of warping an arbitrary-shaped subset of an image that is specified just by two corresponding outlines. A thinning operation is used to determine the mapping for the interior region of the outlines.

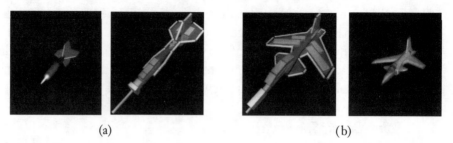

(a)   (b)

Figure 12.7 Two-dimensional feature specification in 3D space: the source object, a dart, with features (a) and the target object, an X-29, with features (b) [from Lerios et al., 1995].

Curve-based features have also been used to describe features of images. In [Lee et al., 1995], snakes are used to fit a curve in the boundary features of images.

Physics-Based Features

In this case, the features have a physical meaning, such as point masses, forces, force fields, velocity, and so on. A more convenient name for this specification technique would be *physically inspired features*, because the physical features are not necessarily related to the real physical systems associated with the objects being transformed.

12.5 Specification and User Interface

The specification of the warping and morphing transformation is closely related to the user interface, as we illustrated before in Figure 12.3. When describing a metamorphosis, we need to specify families of transformations, and in general, the parameter space has an infinite number of parameters. Therefore, we need a very flexible way to specify these parameters.

Consider the simple example of a warping transformation, by a rotation around the origin by an arbitrary angle as shown in Figure 12.8. One way of representing this transformation consists of storing a single parameter that represents the amount of rotation to be performed. From this number we compute the rotation matrix that represents the transformation. Another, more pictorial representation is to store a vector that indicates the rotation.

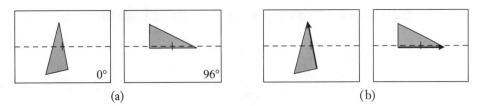

Figure 12.8 Rotation representation by angle (a) and by vector (b).

This form of representation may be more easily used as an interface, because it is possible to manipulate it interactively, providing a natural graphical interface for the user.

The best user specification is closely linked to the underlying application: to achieve certain specific results, as in aligning two graphical objects through rotation, an angle representation would require some guesswork to accomplish the desired result, while a vector representation allows an interactive specification of the desired alignment.

Warping and morphing in practice require a good level of user specification to approach the desired results. The specification of a generic warping can be done in several ways, and the choice of a particular method will influence both the user interface and the computation.

The example of the projective warping described in the beginning of this chapter is not really the common case. Usually, we need to manipulate a huge number of parameters to specify some warping in order to achieve certain prescribed goals. These goals could be of a perceptual nature, or could be related to some other criteria determined by the underlying application.

There are many different techniques to specify a transformation, each of which can be used in dozens of different ways to design a user interface. We will not go into the details of interface widgets for warping and morphing. However, a discussion of the generic principles of user interface design for warping and morphing is appropriate. Three kinds of interface design have been used in existing morphing systems:

- side-by-side interface
- single-window interface
- automatic interface

Figure 12.9   Point-based specification using a side-by-side user interface.

12.5.1   Side-by-Side Interface

This is the most natural interface for morphing. It is in accordance with the fact that in a morphing transformation, we have a source and a target object. The user has at his disposal one window for the source object and another, different window for the target object. In addition, he has interface widgets that allow him to specify the morphing using features, meshes, and so forth. Figure 12.6 showed two typical windows on a side-by-side interface for a feature-based specification. A side-by-side interface is also very effective for specifying a morphing using change of coordinates: The mesh representation of each coordinate system is shown in each window. On the window on the right the mesh has been changed by the user so as to align features in the source and target objects.

Another example of a side-by-side interface is shown in Figure 12.9, where the side-by-side interface is used to specify a morphing between two polygonal curves. Using a point specification: the user chooses points on the source curve on the window on the left and their corresponding points on the target window.

A side-by-side interface can also be used to specify a warping. Although in general we do not have a target object when computing a warping, the side-by-side interface is very useful to specify "guided" warpings.

12.5.2   Single-Window Interface

This interface is mostly used to specify warpings where we do not necessarily have a target object. The object to be warped is displaced in one window,

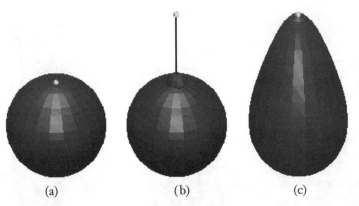

Figure 12.10 Specification of vector displacement using a single-window interface: point to be moved (a), displacement vector (b), and warped surface (c) [from Pinheiro, 1997].

along with interface widgets that allow the user to specify the transformation. As an example, we could use a point specification and let the user specify the displacement vector of each point. This is illustrated in Figure 12.10, which shows three phases of a single-window interface to specify a displacement vector to warp a surface.

12.5.3 Automatic Interface

In an automatic interface, the user provides the source and target objects and the computer computes the morphing between them. Therefore, the computer must be provided with algorithms for automatic specification, representation, and reconstruction of the metamorphosis transformation.

From a conceptual point of view, there is a natural framework that could be used to work in this direction: techniques from computer vision are used for feature detection and pattern matching between the features of the two graphical objects.

For automatic techniques, the correspondence of characteristics is not present in the specification, but is automatically determined by the computation phase instead. It is still necessary, though, to specify other parameters that help control the progress of the transformation. This leads us toward the development of semiautomatic warping techniques.

One approach is to use some preprocessing step to find the relevant features of the objects. The algorithm establishes a correspondence between marked features that can finally be used to compute the transformation. Another possibility is to determine the appropriate mapping directly from the analysis of the

Figure 12.11   Rotoscoped features and resulting animation [from Litwinowicz and Williams, 1994].

objects, without explicitly manipulating features [Sederberg and Greenwood, 1992].

Partial automation can also be obtained by some form of feature digitalization, where the specification is captured from the real world. Rotoscoping of actors with their desired features physically marked (painted on them, for example) is an effective alternative that can reduce specification time dramatically. Figure 12.11 shows a sequence and the controlling features, which were rotoscoped from an actor's face.

Another form of partially automated warping is found in motion capture. Magnetic, optical, or even mechanic sensors are placed at key joints of the subject of the capture, and their motions are automatically recorded. The resulting data can be used to control the animation of a skeleton, which in turn deforms the so-called skin of the 3D object. In another context, morphing is also used to create transitions between motions captured in this way [Rose et al., 1996].

Totally automatic interfaces for morphing have been used for very specific applications. A quite successful example is found on the multiple master font technology developed by Adobe Systems. This system, illustrated in Figure 12.12 and initially discussed in Chapter 1, enables the automatic creation of new fonts by specifying the parameters of font width and weight. A similar technique has been used by Adobe in the product ATM (Adobe Type Manager). In this application, when there is a need for a screen font that is not available, the program creates the font by interpolating parameters from existing loaded fonts.

Morphing

Morphing

Morphing

Figure 12.12 Generation of fonts by automatic warping.

A very interesting automatic specification for warping has been described in [Bregler et al., 1997]. The system accepts an audio signal and uses speech recognition techniques to obtain the correct specification of the warping of the movements of the mouth when talking.

12.6 Comments and References

Several efforts are being made to obtain automatic warping interfaces. These interfaces are very useful in applications where we do not want to force the user to cope with nonnatural or intrusive interface widgets. Examples of these applications include morphs in interactive movies and theme park installations.

References

Beier, Thaddeus, and Shawn Neely. 1992. Feature-Based Image Metamorphosis. *Computer Graphics (SIGGRAPH '92 Proceedings)*, **26**(2), 35–42.

Bregler, Christoph, Michelle Covell, and Malcom Slaney. 1997. Video Rewrite: Driving Visual Speech with Audio. In *Computer Graphics (SIGGRAPH '97 Proceedings)*, 353–360.

Lee, Seung-Yong, Kyung-Yong Chwa, Sung Yong Shin, and George Wolberg. 1995. Image Metamorphosis Using Snakes and Free-Form Deformations. *Computer Graphics (SIGGRAPH '95 Proceedings)*, 439–448.

Lerios, Apostolos, Chase D. Garfinkle, and Marc Levoy. 1995. Feature-Based Volume Metamorphosis. *Computer Graphics (SIGGRAPH '95 Proceedings)*, **29**, 449–456.

Litwinowicz, Peter, and Lance Williams. 1994. Animating Images with Drawings. *Computer Graphics (SIGGRAPH '94 Proceedings)*, **24**, 409–412.

Pinheiro, Sergio E. M. L. 1997. *Interactive Deformations Using Direct Specification*. Master's Thesis. PUC-Rio (in Portuguese).

Rose, Charles, Brian Guenter, Bobby Bodenheimer, and Michael F. Cohen. 1996. Efficient Generation of Motion Transitions using Spacetime Constraints. *Computer Graphics (SIGGRAPH '96 Proceedings)*, 147–154.

Sederberg, Thomas W., and Eugene Greenwood. 1992. A Physically Based Approach to 2-D Shape Blending. *Computer Graphics (SIGGRAPH '92 Proceedings)*, **26**, 25–34.

Smithe, D. B. 1990. *A Two-Pass Mesh Warping Algorithm for Object Transformation and Image Interpolation*. Technical Memo #1030. Industrial Light and Magic.

Wolberg, G. 1990. *Digital Image Warping*. Los Alamitos, CA: IEEE Computer Society Press.

Wolberg, George. 1989. Skeleton-Based Image Warping. *The Visual Computer*, **5**(1/2), 95–108.

13

Computation of Transformations

THERE ARE TWO ASPECTS OF COMPUTING A TRANSFORMATION: computing the attributes and the transformed geometry. The computational methods used are closely related to the specification methods. This correspondence occurs quite naturally through the transformation representation: from a specification the transformation is represented, and the computation of the transformation is related to the representation method used.

13.1 Forward and Inverse Computation

When we have a transformation $T: U \to U'$ of the space, it is possible to interpret it in two different ways.

- T is considered as transforming points of the space U, taking each point p, and moving it to a new position $p' = T(p)$ on the space.
- T can be considered as a change of coordinates of the space U. To each point $p = (x_1, \ldots, x_n)$, T associates new coordinates $p' = (y_1, \ldots, y_n) = T(x_1, \ldots, x_n)$. The coordinates of p in the new system are defined by $T^{-1}(y_1, \ldots, y_n)$.

Considering the above "dual" interpretations for a transformation results in two distinct ways to proceed with its computation: forward and inverse methods.

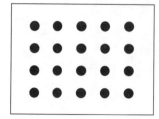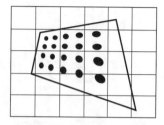

Figure 13.1   Bijectivity and discretization [from Heckbert, 1989].

For continuous objects, the choice of applying a direct or inverse method is immaterial as long as the warping transformation is invertible. For discrete objects, however, these two situations are significantly distinct. In fact, in Parts I and II we stressed the importance of working on the continuous domain (mathematical universe) when dealing with the operations of warping and morphing of graphical objects. When computing with transformations, a new problem arises working on the discrete domain: bijective transformations on the continuous domain are not necessarily bijective on the discrete domain. This is well illustrated by the projective warping of the image in Figure 13.1: in spite of having a bijective transformation, several pixels of the original image (on the left) are mapped onto the same pixel (on the right). This phenomenon is related to the fact that the transformation introduces high frequencies on the transformed graphical object. This has a great influence on the strategy of choosing between a forward or an inverse technique. Also, it is clear from the resampling theory in Part II that the inverse method is well suited for resampling (prefiltering), while the forward method is most suited to postfiltering.

We will exemplify this for image warping. Of course, the discussion below generalizes easily to matrix representations of graphical objects of different dimensions.

13.1.1   Forward Method

Forward mapping processes points in the input with T, determining their mapped position in the output. Since we are working with a discrete object, mapping any set of regular point samples does not necessarily cover all pixels in the output image, leaving holes in it. On the other hand, since the output image is discretized, many point samples may "overlap," being mapped to the

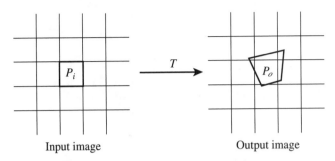

Input image   Output image

Figure 13.2 Forward mapping of an input pixel p_i.

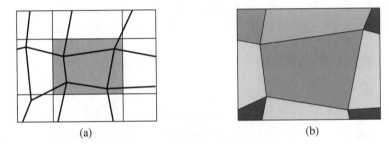

(a)   (b)

Figure 13.3 Reconstruction of regular grid values from an irregular one: regular and transformed grids (a) and values of transformed pixels (b).

same output pixel. Forward mapping may require excessive computation in point sampling unimportant areas, and leave other areas unsampled. Costly computations are required to properly and evenly sample the output image. Taking the pixel geometry as an area instead of a point reduces most of the problems just mentioned (see Figure 13.2). The mapped pixel p_o can be approximated by a quadrilateral, which, after intersecting with the regular output grid, can be used to determine the influence of p_i on the output pixels.

In this technique, the values of the mapping on the regular grid of the output image are computed from its values at the unstructured grid obtained by transforming the regular grid of the input image. This is illustrated in Figure 13.3. In Figure 13.3(a) we show the superposition of the transformed input pixels, and the regular grid of the output pixels. Figure 13.3(b) shows a partition of an output pixel by transformed pixels of the input. By averaging

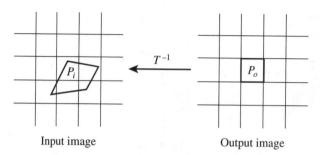

Figure 13.4   Inverse mapping of an output pixel p_o.

the color values we obtain the color of the output pixel. Notice that aliasing artifacts can be minimized by supersampling. This corroborates the statement in the previous section that forward methods are well suited for postfiltering.

13.1.2   Inverse Method

Inverse mapping works on the output image, transforming each point with T^{-1} to determine its originating position in the input image (see Figure 13.4). The coverage of the input image is analogous to that of the output image in forward mapping point sampling; that is, the input image may not be fully covered, samples can overlap in the input and be produced in any order, and so on. In this case, however, overlaps in the input image indicate important areas to be sampled with more accuracy, and holes indicate areas that do not significantly affect the output image. The output image is sampled evenly, and in the order output pixels should be produced. In spite of these properties, artifacts common to all sampling processes can appear. It is not surprising that many implementations of digital image transformations use inverse mapping. Naturally, by considering pixels as approximating quadrilaterals, the influence of the input image pixels can be more precisely computed, as they would if a high number of point samples were used.

In this method, the values of the warping on the unstructured grid are obtained from the grid of the target image by the inverse mapping T^{-1}. The attribute values on the deformed pixel $p_i = T^{-1}(p_0)$ are computed from the image values on the regular grid of the source image. This is illustrated in Figure 13.5. In Figure 13.5(a) we superimpose the regular grid of the source image pixels with the grid of the output image transformed by T^{-1}. The color of the target pixel P_0 is given by the color of the shaded quadrilateral

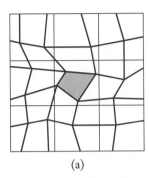 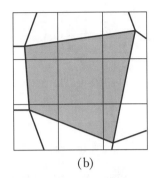

(a)   (b)

Figure 13.5 Reconstruction of irregular grid values from a regular one. Regular and transformed grid (a) and areas of influence of input pixels (b).

in Figure 13.5(b). Notice that this scheme naturally leads to resampling with prefiltering techniques, corroborating what we mentioned before.

13.2 Multiple-Pass Warping

In Example 11.6 of Chapter 11 we introduced the concept of separability of a transformation. A transformation $T\colon \mathbb{R}^n \to \mathbb{R}^n$ of the euclidean space is separable if

$$T = T_n \circ T_{n-1} \circ \cdots \circ T_2 \circ T_1,$$

and each transformation T_i depends only on the i-th coordinate. That is, $T_i(x_1, \ldots, x_i, \ldots, x_n) = T_i(x_i)$. Separability is a very powerful representation technique from the computational point of view when the graphical objects use a matrix representation (e.g., images and volumetric data). When this happens, we reduce the problem of warping computation to the computation of successive 1D warpings. We will exemplify this with a plane transformation.

13.2.1 Two-Pass Plane Warping

In this section we will study the representation of a plane warping by two successive 1D warpings. This is a very effective technique for computing image warpings.

In the case of images, when the warping transformation h is separable, it is possible to compute it by applying separately the horizontal

$$g(x, y) = (g_1(x, y), y)$$

Figure 13.6   Horizontal and vertical warps.

and vertical

$$f(x, y) = (x, f_1(x, y))$$

warps. Therefore, we have a *two-pass warping*. In brief, horizontal lines are invariant by the horizontal warp, and vertical lines are invariant by the vertical warp.

We will perform the computations to find the 1D warps f and g from h. Suppose that h has coordinates h_1 and h_2, that is,

$$h(x, y) = (h_1(x, y), h_2(x, y)). \tag{13.1}$$

We must find f and g in such a way that $h = g \circ f$, f is a vertical warp, and g is a horizontal warp. Since we have a two-step process, we have three coordinate systems: the system (x, y) of the original image; the system (u, v) obtained from (x, y) by the horizontal warp f; and the system (r, s) obtained from the system (u, v) by the vertical warp g. These three systems are illustrated in Figure 13.6.

Therefore, we can write

$$(r, s) = h(x, y) = (h_1(x, y), h_2(x, y)). \tag{13.2}$$

Our purpose is to determine the transformations $f(x, y)$ and $g(u, v)$. Since f is a vertical warp and g is a horizontal warp, we have

$$f(x, y) = (x, f_1(x, y)),$$

and

$$g(u, v) = (g_1(u, v), v). \tag{13.3}$$

Therefore

$$(r, s) = g(u, v) = g(f(x, y)) = g(x, f_1(x, y)) = (g_1(x, f_1(x, y)), f_1(x, y)).$$

Comparing the above equation with Equation (13.2), we obtain

$$f_1(x, y) = h_2(x, y), \tag{13.4}$$

therefore, $f(x, y) = (x, h_2(x, y))$.

Now we will compute $g(u, v)$. We know that

$$g(u, v) = h(x, y) = (h_1(x, y), h_2(x, y)).$$

By comparing this equation with Equation (13.3), and using the fact that $x = u$ (because f is a horizontal warp), we obtain

$$g_1(u, v) = h_1(x, y) = h_1(u, y). \tag{13.5}$$

Therefore, we need to determine a function φ that relates the coordinates y and (u, v), that is, $y = \varphi(u, v)$. We will have

$$g_1(u, v) = h_1(u, \varphi(u, v)), \tag{13.6}$$

that is, $g(u, v) = (h_1(u, \varphi(u, v)), v)$.

The existence of the function φ is granted if g is a one-to-one map. But we should observe that even in this case, we face the problem of computing φ, and in general this is not an easy task. We will give an example when the warping h is a rotation of the plane.

Example 13.1 (Two-Step Rotation) If the warping transformation h is a rotation of the plane by an angle θ, we have

$$h(x, y) = \begin{pmatrix} \cos\theta & -\sin\theta \\ \sin\theta & \cos\theta \end{pmatrix} \begin{pmatrix} x \\ y \end{pmatrix}$$

From this equation we obtain

$$h_1(x, y) = x \cos\theta - y \sin\theta, \tag{13.7}$$

and

$$h_2(x, y) = x \sin\theta + y \cos\theta. \tag{13.8}$$

Using the expression of $h_2(x, y)$ in Equation (13.8), along with Equation (13.4), we obtain

$$f_1(x, y) = x \sin\theta + y \cos\theta,$$

and this determines the transformation f, which accomplishes the vertical warp.

Now we will proceed to obtain the horizontal warp. Using Equation (13.5) with the expression of $h_1(x, y)$, in Equation (13.7), we obtain

$$g_1(u, v) = u \cos\theta - y \sin\theta. \tag{13.9}$$

Figure 13.7   Two-step image rotation [from Gomes and Velho, 1997].

Now we need to compute y as a function of the coordinates u and v (i.e., we need to compute the function φ that appears in Equation (13.6)). We have

$$v = f_1(x, y) = x \sin \theta + y \cos \theta,$$

therefore,

$$y = \frac{v - u \sin \theta}{\cos \theta}, \quad \text{if } \cos \theta \neq 0.$$

Substituting the value of y from above, in Equation (13.9), we obtain the equation

$$g_1(u, v) = u \cos \theta - \frac{v - u \sin \theta}{\cos \theta} \sin \theta, \tag{13.10}$$

which determines the horizontal warp of the decomposition. Note that the horizontal warping is not defined for values $\theta = k\pi + \pi/2$. Moreover, it is clear that when θ approaches one of these values, there is a great distortion of the horizontal warp. For instance, when performing a two-pass 87° rotation in an image, it is advisable to make a 90° rotation—a simple permutation of the pixels—followed by a rotation of 3° in the opposite direction.

Figure 13.7 shows a 30° rotation of an image obtained in two steps: a horizontal followed by a vertical warp.

The reader should notice that when we implement multiple-step warpings, we might face problems of this type with the intermediate 1D warpings. A fairly common case, known as the *bottleneck problem* in the literature, occurs when one of the intermediate transformations is not injective in a discretized domain. In this case, some points collapse.

13.3 Scheduled Computation

A scheduled computation of a transformation $T: U \to V$ is obtained in two steps. First, we must define a collection $U_1, U_2, \ldots, U_m$ of subsets of U, such that

$$\bigcup_i U_i = U.$$

Second, we must compute a transformation $T_i: U_i \to V$ in such a way that, as i increases, T_i approaches the desired transformation T.

Example 13.2 (Adaptive Cross-Dissolve by Scheduling)   An adaptive cross-dissolve between two functions $f(x)$ and $g(x)$ is defined by a one-parameter family

$$f_\lambda(x) = (1 - h(\lambda, x)) f(x) + h(\lambda, x) g(x),$$

where

$$h(0, x) = 0 \quad \text{and} \quad h(1, x) = 1, \quad \forall x.$$

A 1D example of an adaptive cross-dissolve using scheduling can be obtained by taking the function h defined by

$$h(\lambda, x) = \frac{1}{2}x + (2\lambda - \frac{3}{4}),$$

for $x \in [-4\lambda + 1.5, -4\lambda + 3.5]$, with $0 \le \lambda \le 1$.

Figure 13.8 illustrates this scheduled cross-dissolve when f and g are two sinusoidal functions. In Figure 13.8(a) and (c) we show the source function f and the target function g. In Figure 13.8(b) we show three intermediate signals of the morphing, along with the graph of the function h. Note that as λ increases from 0 to 1, bands of the domain of f are incorporated into the cross-dissolving process according to the scheduling defined by the parameter λ progresses.

The use of scheduling is an interesting strategy when we want to compute the transformation taking into account the level of detail in the morphing process. A schedule is used to add increasing levels of detail in the morphing transformation. This strategy has been used in [Hughes, 1992] to compute metamorphosis of volumetric objects on the frequency domain:

1. Apply the Fourier transform to move to the frequency domain.

2. Determine a schedule to compute the morphing on the frequency domain, to add higher frequencies as the schedule progresses.

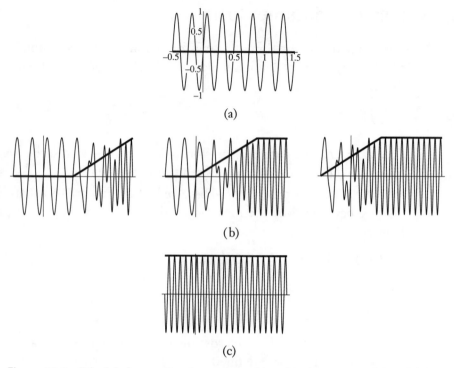

Figure 13.8   Scheduled cross-dissolve: source object (a), three steps of the scheduling (b), and target object (c) [from Goldenstein, 1997].

3. For each intermediate morphed object, compute the inverse Fourier transform to reconstruct the object on the spatial domain.

The above strategy of using scheduling can be extended to work in other domains such as the space-frequency domain or the scale-space domain. The scheduling is constructed based on the frequency bands of the representation. The reconstruction of the interpolated bands yields the final morphed object.

A related approach uses wavelets and scheduled transformations to morph volumetric objects [He et al., 1994]. The volumetric data is decomposed into sets of frequency bands, which are then smoothly interpolated. The main advantage of this approach is to exploit good localization properties on the frequency-scale space. Also, the decomposition and reconstruction processes in this case can be performed in a multiresolution form, which allows control of the level of high-frequency distortion.

13.3.1 Multiresolution Morphing Techniques

Any graphical object can be conceived as being composed from an object with a simple geometric structure, which evolves by the addition of more and more detail.

A multiresolution decomposition of the object is the correct mathematical model to describe the above intuition. The object U is described by a family U_i, $i = 1, 2, 3, \ldots$, and transformations $f_i \colon U_i \to U_{i+1}$, which enable us to pass from one level of detail to the other. Metamorphosis techniques can be computed by exploiting such a decomposition. We obtain a multiresolution decomposition of both objects, compute the metamorphosis transformation between each pair of objects in the multiresolution representation, and combine all of the metamorphosis transformations to obtain the final transformation.

13.4 Comments and References

In this chapter we discussed several strategies that can be undertaken when computing a transformation.

A very good discussion of separable transformations, and techniques for decomposition, can be found in [Smith, 1987].

An example of multiresolution cross-dissolve between images was published in [Stein and Hitchner, 1988], where a pyramidal multiresolution representation is used.

References

Goldenstein, Siome K. 1997. *Sound Metamorphosis*. Master's Thesis. PUC-Rio (in Portuguese).

Gomes, J., and L. Velho. 1997. *Image Processing for Computer Graphics*. New York: Springer-Verlag.

He, Taosong, Sidney Wang, and Arie Kaufman. 1994. Wavelet-Based Volume Morphing. *Proceedings of Visualization '94*, 85–91.

Heckbert, P. 1989. *Fundamentals of Texture Mapping and Image Warping*. Master's Thesis (Technical Report No. UCB/CSD 89/516). University of California, Berkeley *(www.cs.cmu.edu/~ph)*.

Hughes, John F. 1992. Scheduled Fourier Volume Morphing. *Computer Graphics (SIGGRAPH '92 Proceedings)*, **26**(2), 43–46.

Smith, Alvy Ray. 1987. Planar 2-Pass Texture Mapping and Warping. *Computer Graphics (SIGGRAPH '87 Proceedings)*, **21**(4), 263–272.

Stein, Charles S., and Lewis E. Hitchner. 1988. The Multiresolution Dissolve. *SMPTE Journal*, (Dec.), 977–984.

14

Warping and Morphing Techniques

I~N~ C~HAPTER~ 13 ~WE~ ~DISCUSSED~ different strategies to compute a warping or morphing transformation. In this chapter we will continue with the topic of transformation computation, but we will concentrate on the computational reconstruction of the transformation, from the user specification. A warping transformation involves the choice of two key elements: specification method and computation of the warping. The computation involves the strategy to compute the warping, which is related to the reconstruction technique. A combination of a specification method along with a computation technique is called a warping (or morphing) technique.

14.1 Parameter-Based Techniques

This class of techniques is related to the parameter-based specification and representation of a transformation. It encompasses all the warping techniques that are controlled by parameters, such as scale, twisting, and bending. A very early use of this type of technique can be found in [Barr, 1984]. This type of warping can be very efficient, although it is obviously very specific, allowing just a limited number of transformations to be performed in this way. Two simple examples are given below.

14.1.1 Scaling

One of the simplest forms of deforming an object is a change in its scale. A nonuniform scaling of an object is given by $W(x, y, z) = (s_1 x, s_2 y, s_3 z)$, and its Jacobian matrix is

$$J = \begin{pmatrix} s_1 & 0 & 0 \\ 0 & s_2 & 0 \\ 0 & 0 & s_3 \end{pmatrix},$$

so that the warped object normal vectors can be computed analytically using the equation we described in Part I:

$$n' = \det J \; J^{-1^T} n.$$

14.1.2 Twist

Another interesting transformation is to have a twist around a Cartesian axis. This can be defined as a rotation using a variable angle. A twist around the z-axis is computed by

$$W(x, y, z) = (x \cos \theta - y \sin \theta, x \sin \theta + y \cos \theta, z),$$

where $\theta = f(z)$. The Jacobian matrix is

$$J = \begin{pmatrix} \cos \theta & -\sin \theta & -f'(z)(x \sin \theta + y \cos \theta) \\ \sin \theta & \cos \theta & f'(z)(x \cos \theta - y \sin \theta) \\ 0 & 0 & 1 \end{pmatrix}.$$

14.2 Feature–Based Techniques

Feature-based techniques encompass a whole family of warping techniques, with a great variety of different feature geometries. Since the features constitute a subset of the object shape, we are always faced with the problem of extending the warping to the entire shape. This is strongly related to the problem of scattered data interpolation, and in fact shares its solutions for point features.

The user must provide a finite set of features in the shape of the source object, and a corresponding collection on the target object. The warping is defined explicitly by mapping each feature in the source object to its correspondent in the target object. The final warping is defined by extending the definition to the whole shape of the object.

14.2.1 Scattered Data Interpolation Techniques

When we use point-based feature specification, we must deal with the problem of reconstructing the warping transformation from its values on the points. In fact, the reconstruction techniques discussed here are part of the very important problem of *scattered data interpolation* [Schumaker, 1976]: Reconstruct a transformation $T: U \rightarrow V$ when we know the value $T(p_i)$ of T on n points $p_1, \ldots, p_n$ of the domain U. The classical scattered data interpolation problem is posed for functions, but it is easy to show that the above problem reduces easily to the classical problem. Suppose that

$$p_1 = (x_1^1, \ldots, x_m^1);$$
$$p_2 = (x_1^2, \ldots, x_m^2);$$
$$\vdots$$
$$p_n = (x_1^n, \ldots, x_m^n);$$

and

$$T(p_j) = q_j = (y_1^j, \ldots, y_m^j).$$

The transformation T is defined by its coordinate functions $T = (T_1, \ldots, T_m)$, $T_i: \mathbb{R}^m \rightarrow \mathbb{R}$. Therefore, we must have

$$T_i(p_j) = y_i^j, \quad i = 1, \ldots, m; \quad j = 1, \ldots, n.$$

And so for each i we have a classical scattered data interpolation problem [Schumaker, 1976]: *Find the function $T_i: \mathbb{R}^m \rightarrow \mathbb{R}$ such that*

$$T_i(x_1^1, \ldots, x_m^1) = y_i^1;$$
$$T_i(x_1^2, \ldots, x_m^2) = y_i^2;$$
$$\vdots$$
$$T_i(x_1^n, \ldots, x_m^n) = y_i^n.$$

Below, we will study some computational techniques for function reconstruction from a point-based specification, using methods from the area of scattered data interpolation.

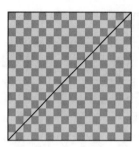 

Figure 14.1   Discontinuity of barycentric coordinate mapping.

Structured Samples

A common methodology to reconstruct a function from its sampled values consists in imposing some structuring on the samples, and using this structuring to devise an interpolation strategy.

When the structuring results in a simplicial complex, interpolation can be attained by using barycentric coordinates in each simplex. The resulting transformation is an affine transformation inside each simplex, and we have continuity on the simplex boundaries. This is illustrated in Figure 14.1. This technique is called *reconstruction by piecewise affine transformation*. Certainly, barycentric coordinates can be used to construct transformation with higher order of continuity using polynomials of higher degrees.

When the samples are on the plane, and are structured so as to define a grid—that is, each element of the structuring consists of a quadrilateral (four points in general position)—we have the obvious option of subdividing the quadrilaterals to obtain a triangulation. Nevertheless, there are several techniques to reconstruct the transformation directly on the quadrilateral.

Some of these techniques were studied in Chapter 3: bilinear interpolation, projective interpolation, and Coons patch. Many other interpolation techniques have been used in the literature, such as spline-based techniques (B-splines, Nurbs, Bézier, etc.). Some of the above techniques easily extend to reconstruct the transformation from samples in the 3D space.

Inverse Distance Weighted Functions

An early example of a simple technique for scattered data interpolation that assumes no structuring on the samples is the use of an inverse distance weighted sum [Shepard, 1968]. The weight at each position p, relative to each point sample p_i, is given by

$$w_i(p) = \frac{1}{\|p - p_i\|^{\mu}}.$$

The exponent μ controls the smoothness of the interpolation. Note that the weights are defined in such a way that as the point p gets further from p_i, the weight decreases.

The weights are used in an average of the values to be interpolated for the x and y coordinates analogously:

$$W_x(p) = \frac{\sum_{i=1}^{n} w_i(p) p_x}{\sum_{i=1}^{n} w_i(p)}.$$

The final warped position is given by $W(p) = (W_x(p), W_y(p))$.

This somewhat simplistic approach is not very suitable for warping transformations, but it is representative of a family of interpolants. Several extensions of this method exist, and some will be described in Section 14.2.2.

Radial Functions

Radial basis functions have been used frequently in the interpolation of scattered data and also for image warping purposes. In these techniques, the warping function is constructed as a linear combination of basis functions dependent on the distance to each point in the warping specification.

One of these techniques, introduced by [Arad and Reisfeld, 1995], primarily uses point specification, but can be modified to handle other types of specification. Although the technique was originally introduced for the 2D case, it is trivially extensible to higher dimensions. We will describe the 2D case of this technique here.

The warping function in this technique is defined in such a way as to allow for the decomposition into rigid and elastic transformations. To that end, the warping function W can be seen as a sum of an affine component A and a radial component R:

$$W(p) = A(p) + R(p)$$
$$A(p) = M_{2 \times 2} p + c$$
$$R(p) = (R_1(p), R_2(p))$$

The affine component is responsible for translations, scales, rotations, and shears, while the radial component is responsible for elastic transformations.

Affine Component. We have seen in Chapter 3 that an affine transformation is completely determined if we know its values on three noncollinear points (it has six degrees of freedom: four for the linear part and two for the translation). On what concerns the user interface, a neat option is to assume that a single point specifies a translation, two points a translation/scaling, and three points a general affine transformation. If no points are specified, the affine component is assumed to be the identity.

Radial Component. To compute the radial, elastic, component, we associate to each point p_i a function g with a radial symmetry. That is,

$$g(p) = g(\|p - p_i\|).$$

This function is called a *radial basis function*. The warping function is globally computed as a weighted sum of radial functions. Suppose there are n points in the specification of the radial component. The components R_1 and R_2 of the radial function R assume the form

$$R_j(p) = \sum_{i=1}^{n} a_i^j g(\|p - p_i\|), \quad j = 1, 2,$$

where a_i^j are coefficients to be computed and g is the radial function. Note that there are $2n$ coefficients to compute, and the specification of the warping gives $2n$ equations (p is a 2D vector):

$$W(p_i) = p_i', \quad i = 1, 2, \dots, n.$$

We first solve the affine component, and then we determine the a_i^j coefficients by solving the following linear system of $2n$ equations:

$$W_1(p_i) = p_{i1}' = A_1(p_i) + \sum_{i=1}^{n} a_i^1 g(\|p - p_i\|)$$

$$W_2(p_i) = p_{i2}' = A_2(p_i) + \sum_{i=1}^{n} a_i^2 g(\|p - p_i\|),$$

where $W = (W_1, W_2)$, and $W(p_i) = (p_{i1}', p_{i2}')$.

The Radial Basis Function. A natural choice is to use a Gaussian function

$$g(t) = e^{-\frac{t^2}{\sigma^2}}$$

as the radial basis function, where the variance σ controls the degree of locality of the transformation. Nevertheless, the Gaussian function is costly to evaluate and has infinite support—every control point influences the whole

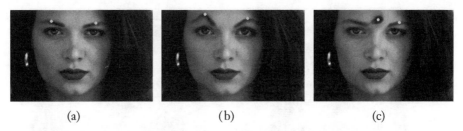

(a)   (b)   (c)

Figure 14.2 Radial functions: original image with points (a), warping using radial basis (b), and foldover (ghost) effect (c). See also color plate 14.2.

transformation. Some approximations to the Gaussian function that have compact support and can be evaluated using lookup tables are shown in [Arad and Reisfeld, 1995].

Figures 14.2(a) and (b) show an example of the locality that can be obtained using this technique. Note that for large displacements of control points, exceeding the locality parameter for that control point, foldover can occur, as indicated by the warping in (c).

The algorithm complexity of this technique is $O(n^3)$ for computing the coefficients, and $O(nN)$ to warp the graphical object, where N is the number of points of the graphical object in question. If the influence of each control point is limited, the run time of applying the warping function can be reduced.

14.2.2 Two-Dimensional Field-Based

This technique is one of the pioneering works on the use of features for warping and morphing of images. It appeared in the literature in [Beier and Neely, 1992], but it had been in use in the production environment of Pacific Data Images for about two years.

The technique uses vectors (1D oriented line segments) as features. For each feature vector v_i, the image vector v_i' under the transformation is specified. The corresponding features are called *source* and *target feature vectors*. This is illustrated in Figure 14.3.

The reconstruction of the transformation for the object shape is done by considering the distance of the points to the segment feature: far points have small influence in the computation, and near points have a greater amount of influence. It is a natural extension to vectors of Shepard's inverse distance weighted interpolant we discussed before. Each feature vector has its own field of influence.

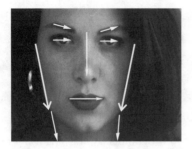

Figure 14.3   Feature correspondence between two images.

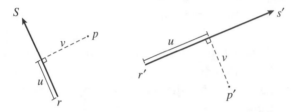

Figure 14.4   Feature-defined coordinate system and mapping.

For each feature vector (see Figure 14.4), we define an orthogonal coordinate system (u, v), where v is the distance perpendicular to the feature and u is the distance along the feature vector. The coordinate u is normalized according to the segment length, but v is an absolute distance, so that by stretching the vector in a direction, the neighborhood of that feature is also stretched along that direction, but not perpendicularly to it. It is possible to define u and v differently, but Beier and Neely conducted experiments that indicated the convenience of such definition in terms of user interface.

Each feature defines a coordinate system. Each of these feature coordinate systems is used to define a local transformation using an inverse distance weighted interpolant. The final warping is obtained as a blending of the local transformation of each feature.

Geometrically, this process is illustrated in Figure 14.5, which shows two features F_1 and F_2, and their images F_1' and F_2'. The local transformation associated to feature F_1 maps the point p to the point p_1', and the local transformation of the feature vector F_2 maps the same point p to the point p_2'. The image of p by the final, global transformation is obtained by blending p_1' and p_2'. The result is a point on the line segment joining p_1' and p_2'.

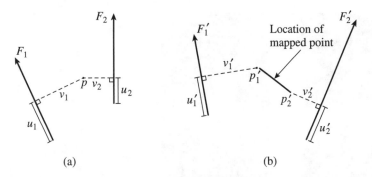

Figure 14.5 Combination of multiple changes of coordinates: source feature (a) and target features (b).

Some details about the computation of the local transformation and the blending operation are given below.

The distance d_i from a point p to the feature F_i, with end points r_i and s_i, is defined as

$$d_i = \begin{cases} |v| & 0 < u < 1 \\ \|p - r_i\| & u \leq 0 \\ \|p - s_i\| & u \geq 1 \end{cases}.$$

The weight of each feature F_i is inversely proportional to the distance d_i:

$$w_i = \left(\frac{l_i^c}{a + d_i} \right)^b, \tag{14.1}$$

where l_i is the length of a feature and a, b, and c are constants used to adjust the weight. The constant a can be seen as the adherence of the feature: for values close to zero, points close to the feature will be mapped exactly as the feature determines; for greater values, points are more loose and free to move even if they are over the feature. The importance of the length of the feature is controlled by c: if it is zero, the length is ignored; otherwise, longer features are more important. The interpretation of b can be seen as the concentration of the strength of the feature: large values make the strength of the feature large near the feature and small away from it, with a very quick decrease; small values make this decay slower, reducing the locality of the feature. Note that different values of constants can be associated to each feature, although it may be more convenient to use a global value of b.

Figure 14.6   Feature-based warping example.

The final warping function is then defined as

$$W(p) = p + \frac{\sum_{i=1}^{n} w_i \Delta p_i}{\sum_{i=1}^{n} w_i}, \qquad \Delta p_i = W_i(p) - p,$$

where $W_i(p)$ is the warped position using a single feature pair.

Note that since the mapping of each point depends on all line segments, the addition of a single line influences the whole deformation. This is illustrated by the example in Figure 14.6: We use three feature vectors, and the specification rotates the uppermost vector to the left. Note how the rotation of the feature vector influences a great part of the image.

A careful choice of the constants a, b, and c in Equation (14.1) can restrict the field of influence of the feature vector, which contributes to localizing the transformation. Also, the weight calculation that must be repeated for each point, relative to each one of the lines, is quite expensive.

As the interpolation is mostly automatic, foldovers might occur. They are avoided, or minimized, by tricky manipulations of the feature vectors on the specification. Figure 14.7 shows an example of a foldover, also called *ghosting* in the literature.

This definition of the coordinate mapping, based on fields of influence around main features of the image, does not depend in any way on the structure or particularities of the graphical object underneath. It is a simple and parameterized form of combination of different transformations, resulting in

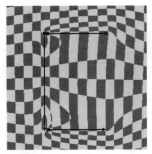

Figure 14.7   Ghosting.

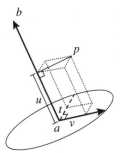

Figure 14.8   3D feature-defined coordinate system.

a global change of coordinates that can be easily used to transform objects in any representation.

14.2.3 Three-Dimensional Field-Based

The extension of the field-based 2D warping technique to 3D space is relatively straightforward. As in the 2D case, important features of the object are marked with oriented line segments, and a different position of each segment defines a deformation of the characteristic. In 3D space, there is an additional degree of freedom that results in an additional segment in the feature-defined coordinate system, as shown in Figure 14.8. The two vectors shown in bold, user specified and constrained to be perpendicular, form an abstraction of a *bone*. A set of such bones, which mark all the relevant features in an object, is called a *skeleton*. This is illustrated in Figure 14.9, where a skeleton is attached to a volumetric model of a lobster.

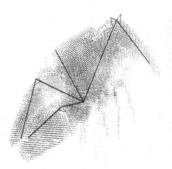

Figure 14.9   Skeleton used to warp a lobster.

To obtain a Cartesian coordinate system, an additional axis is obtained from the cross-product between the two vectors in a bone. Each point can then be projected onto each of these axes to determine its coordinates in this system. The u coordinate is normalized according to the segment length, while v and t are absolute distances. Another natural choice would be the use of cylindrical coordinates.

The global change of coordinates defined by the source and target skeletons is obtained from a combination of the individual changes of coordinates defined by each pair of bones. The combination is a weighted average of the mappings of a point according to each pair of bones, just like the scheme used in the 2D case. The weight of each bone is computed analogously, using the exact same formula, with the distance computation directly extended to 3D.

The resulting technique is expressive and provides user control over the transformation, through the manipulation of the features and the subtle adjustment of the constants. It is also possible to improve the control and locality of this mapping by modifying the weight function.

Since this technique simply defines a coordinate mapping, it is independent of the object representation. For surfaces and implicit volumetric objects, for instance, its application is easy and straightforward. For discrete volumetric objects, on the other hand, besides the required resampling, this is a computationally expensive technique, since it must be applied at least to each voxel.

Figure 14.10 shows an application of this technique to deform an implicitly defined object. The object is a superquadric defined by the function

$$f(x, y, z) = x^6 + y^6 + z^6 - 1,$$

and three feature vectors were used to specify the deformation.

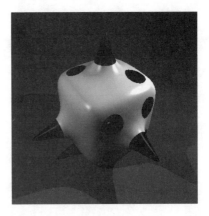

Figure 14.10   Warping of a textured superquadric. See also color plate 14.10.

Some other extensions of the field-based technique to the 3D space have appeared in the literature. In [Lerios et al., 1995], an extension is described where the features have dimension 2: cylinders are used in place of the feature vectors, and other 2D features such as rectangles and boxes are also used.

14.3   Free-Form Techniques

This class of techniques uses specification by coordinate systems. It uses free-form curves (B-splines, Bézier, etc.) to define the coordinate curves. By changing the control points of the free-form curves, we change the coordinate curves, defining a change of coordinates that performs the desired warping.

There are many variations of the computational method used to compute the coordinate change. We will discuss some of them in this section.

14.3.1   Rectilinear and Curvilinear Coordinate Systems

A point O and a basis of vectors $\mathcal{E} = \{e_1, \ldots, e_n\}$ of the euclidean space $\mathbb{R}^n$ define a *coordinate system* $(O, \mathcal{E})$ in $\mathbb{R}^n$. A point $P \in \mathbb{R}^n$ is completely determined by the vector $X = \overrightarrow{OP}$. In this way, we can write

$$X = \sum_{i=1}^{n} x_i e_i.$$

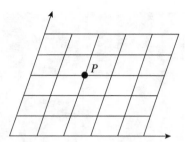

Figure 14.11   Coordinate curves of a rectilinear system.

The n-tuple $(x_1, \ldots, x_n)$ gives the coordinates of P with respect to $(O, \mathcal{E})$. The coordinate systems defined by a basis in the euclidean space are called *rectilinear coordinate systems*. In a rectilinear system $(O, \mathcal{E})$, given a point $P \in \mathbb{R}^n$, the line

$$r_i(t) = P + te_i, \qquad t \in \mathbb{R},$$

is called a *coordinate curve* of the system. The coordinate system is completely determined by its coordinate curves. That is, the coordinates of a point are given by the intersection of the corresponding coordinate curves, as shown in Figure 14.11.

A change of coordinates between two rectilinear coordinate systems of the euclidean space is attained by affine transformations. Consider now a transformation $f : \mathbb{R}^n \to \mathbb{R}^n$, of class C^k, $k \geq 1$, that is bijective and with inverse of class C^k (i.e., a C^k diffeomorphism). The coordinate curves $r_i(t)$ of the euclidean space are transformed by f in curves $\beta_i(t) = f(r_i(t))$, $i = 1, \ldots, n$, as illustrated in Figure 14.12 for the 2D case. Since f is bijective, a point $P \in \mathbb{R}^n$ is completely determined by its coordinates

$$(y_1, \ldots, y_n) = f(x_1, \ldots, x_n).$$

That is, the function f determines a new coordinate system in space. Because lines in the original coordinate system are transformed into arbitrary curves, the coordinate system described by the function f is called a *curvilinear coordinate*. Well-known examples of curvilinear coordinate systems are the polar, cylindrical, and spherical coordinate systems.

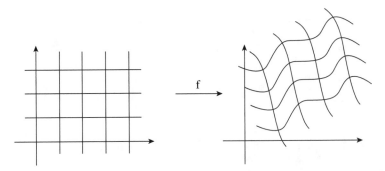

Figure 14.12 Transformation of a rectilinear into a curvilinear coordinate system.

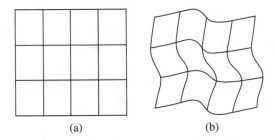

Figure 14.13 Rectilinear (a) and curvilinear (b) lattices.

14.3.2 Representation of Coordinate Systems

A coordinate system is completely determined by its coordinate curves. A representation of a coordinate system is constructed by taking a finite number of coordinate curves for each spatial dimension. Figure 14.13(a) shows the representation of a rectilinear coordinate system, which corresponds to a lattice in the euclidean space. In fact, the rectilinear system is well represented only by the vertices of the lattice.

When we have a curvilinear coordinate system, the coordinate curves used in the representation will be called a *curvilinear lattice*. A curvilinear lattice is shown in Figure 14.13(b). An element of the lattice (a lattice cell) is constructed from the intersection of coordinates in each dimension of the lattice, as shown in Figure 14.14.

Together with the representation of a coordinate system, we must devise a technique to compute the coordinates of an arbitrary point P in space from the coordinate curves of the representation (Figure 14.14). It is generally sufficient

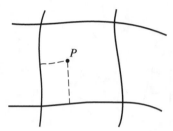

Figure 14.14   Representation and coordinate computation.

to compute the local coordinates of P, that is, the coordinates relative to the lattice element in which the point P is located.

In the case of a rectilinear system, the coordinates of P are determined by the distance of P to the coordinate curves that define the representation, but the reconstruction of coordinates of a point can be very complex, involving interpolation methods. Such methods depend on the representation of the coordinate curves. Some examples will be studied later on.

14.3.3   Warping Using Free-Form Techniques

As discussed earlier, the transformation of a graphical object can be interpreted as a change of coordinate systems. This mapping defines a global deformation of space and, therefore, deforms all the objects embedded in that space.

The process of warping a graphical object using change of coordinates can be attained in four steps (see Figure 14.15):

1. A new coordinate system is specified on the space where the object is embedded. A representation of the coordinate system is used to specify it.

2. The coordinates of the object shape on this new coordinate system are computed.

3. The representation curves of the coordinate system are warped, which causes a deformation of the space.

4. The new object coordinates are changed to Cartesian coordinates in order to reconstruct the warped object.

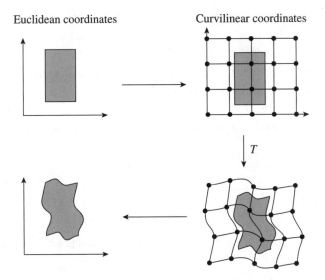

Figure 14.15   Warping by coordinates deformation.

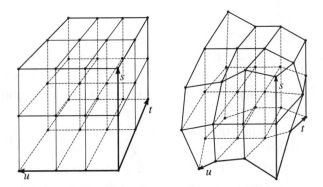

Figure 14.16   Free-form deformation coordinate system.

Bézier Free-Form Coordinates

This was the pioneering technique on the use of free-form coordinate change to compute warpings of the 3D euclidean space, proposed in [Sederberg and Parry, 1986]. The object to be warped is enclosed by a bounding box of the space where we define a coordinate system using Bézier curves. By moving the control points, a deformed coordinate system is defined, as shown in Figure 14.16.

The mapping from the Cartesian system to the deformed one is defined as described above: the new coordinate system (s, t, u) is defined on the bounding box. The coordinate curves of this new system coincide with the coordinate curves of the original Cartesian coordinates system. Therefore, the new system is completely represented by some lattice of n^3 points c_{ijk}, $i, j, k = 0, \ldots, n$. The reconstruction of the coordinates from the lattice representation is done by interpolating with the Bernstein basis polynomials $B_i(t)$ of degree n:

$$B_i^n(t) = \frac{n!}{i!(n-i)!} t^i (1-t)^{n-i}, \quad i = 0, \ldots, n.$$

Thus, the relation between the Cartesian coordinates and the new coordinates (s, t, u) is given by

$$p' = W(s, t, u) = \sum_{i,j,k=0}^{n} c_{i,j,k} B_i^n(u) B_j^n(s) B_k^n(t). \tag{14.2}$$

Notice that initially the coordinate curves of the two systems coincide, but the new coordinates (s, t, u) are normalized to the interval $[0, 1]$.

The warping is specified by moving the lattice points c_{ijk}, in order to obtain new points c'_{ijk}. These new points replace the old ones in Equation (14.2), which is used to compute the new deformed coordinates.

The use of Bernstein polynomials makes this warping transformation global; that is, the modification of a single control point influences the whole domain. To get the effect of a local deformation, it is necessary to position the lattice just over the area of interest, limiting the part of the object that lies inside the lattice. To have precise deformations, it is necessary to position the control points accordingly, which is not very easy. Also, increasing the number of control points to have a more precise transformation increases the degree of the Bernstein polynomials.

As this technique defines a global warping by change of coordinates, it can be easily applied to different object representations. Also, other polynomial bases, such as B-spline basis, can be used instead of Bézier curves. This technique is easily applicable in the 2D case as well, and the modifications are minimal: a bivariate Bernstein polynomial is used instead, with 2D control points.

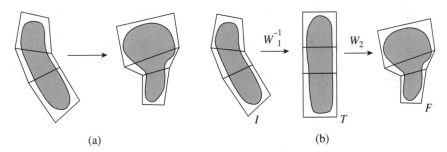

Figure 14.17 Free-form morphing: adapted coordinate system (a) and intermediate coordinate system (b).

14.3.4 Morphing Using Free-Form Technique

Is it possible to use a free-form technique to specify and compute a morphing? To answer this question, we should say that in order to obtain good morphing results, the coordinate system should be adapted to the features of the graphical objects. This means that the coordinate curves used to specify the coordinate system should align with distinguished curves of the object, as illustrated in Figure 14.17(a).

This means that a coordinate change must be computed between two deformed coordinate systems. The Bézier lattice method, for instance, can only compute coordinate changes from a canonical system into a deformed one. Mapping between two arbitrary systems could be attained by using an intermediate Cartesian coordinate system as shown in Figure 14.17(b). The polynomial transformation from the intermediate system T to the final system F is the same as described in the previous section (14.2). But the change of coordinates from the initial system I to the intermediate system T requires the computation of the inverse transform of (14.2). In the case of the Bézier free-form warping, this computation involves finding the roots of a trivariate polynomial with a high degree (which depends on the number of control points in the lattice).

In sum, two problems must be addressed in order to be able to use the change of coordinates technique for morphing. The first is finding a tool to construct lattices of arbitrary topology, and the second is creating a methodology to compute a change of coordinates between lattices of arbitrary topology.

These problems have been addressed in [Coquillart and Jancene, 1991] and [Maccracken and Joy, 1996]. We will return to this discussion in Chapter 19, Warping and Morphing of Surfaces. In the next section we describe another

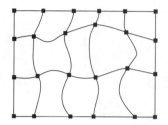 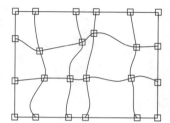

Figure 14.18   Spline meshes.

free-form computation technique that performs reasonably well for image morphing.

14.3.5 Two-Pass Spline Mesh

The two-pass spline mesh warping is a technique that uses a free-form coordinate change to compute the warp. It was developed by Douglas Smithe [Smithe, 1990] at Industrial Light and Magic and was first described in [Wolberg, 1990]. This algorithm was developed specifically for use with digital images by taking advantage of their matrix representation.

The coordinate system is represented by using two regular spline meshes, as illustrated in Figure 14.18, restricted to have rectilinear splines at the edges of the image. The source mesh defines the undeformed coordinate system, and the target describes the deformation of that system.

The computation of the warping is done by separating the transformation into a horizontal and a vertical pass, as described in Chapter 13. The graphical object is first deformed in one direction, and the result of this first pass is fed into the second pass, which then deforms in the other direction. The separation of the transformation makes this technique very efficient, since each pass performs essentially a set of 1D transformations that are simpler than performing the full mapping directly.

An example can be seen in Figure 14.19. The input image on the top left is deformed according to the mesh shown. First, just the horizontal displacements are considered to produce the intermediate image on the top right. Then, this horizontally warped image is used as input to the second pass, where the vertical displacements are considered, yielding the completely deformed image on the bottom right.

The passes are analogous and can be performed in any order. The horizontal pass of this technique follows this algorithm:

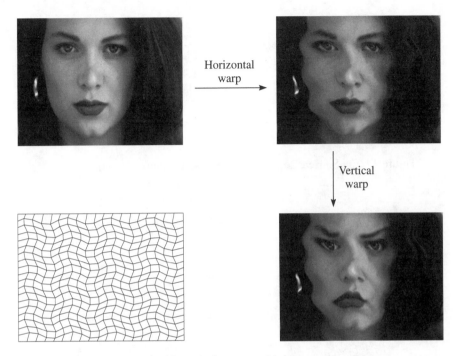

Figure 14.19 Horizontal and vertical passes, with intermediate image.

1. Decompose displacements.
2. Construct vertical splines without the vertical displacements.
3. Intersect scanline with vertical splines.
4. Construct spline for scanline mapping.

In the first phase, just the displacements of the horizontal pass are taken into account. To attain this, an intermediate version containing just the horizontal displacements from the source mesh into the target mesh is created. Figure 14.20 shows a superposition of the source, target, and intermediate meshes control points, with the source shown as black squares, the target as hollow squares, and the control points of the horizontal-only displacements as crosses.

These intermediate control points are used to construct vertical splines, passing through the crosses, containing just horizontal displacements from the source mesh, which are shown as dotted curves in Figure 14.21(a).

Each horizontal scanline is then intersected with the vertical splines in the source and intermediate states, as depicted in Figure 14.21(a)—the diamonds

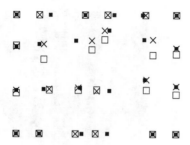

Figure 14.20   Source, target, and intermediate control points.

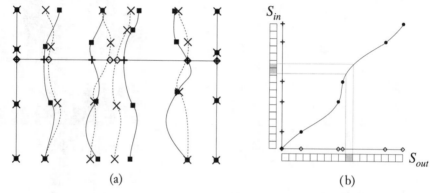

| (a) | (b) |

Figure 14.21   Scanline warping: warping of vertical spline curves (a) and scanline mapping (b).

depict the intersections with the intermediate splines, and the plus signs depict the intersections with the source splines.

Finally, these intersections are used to construct the scanline mapping function, as shown in Figure 14.21(b), by placing intersections with the source splines in one axis and intersections with the intermediate splines in the other. This mapping function relates all pixels of the scanline in the original coordinate system to the pixels in the deformed state. This process is repeated for each scanline to obtain a horizontally deformed image.

Note that turning the mapping into multiple 1D problems is especially attractive for handling sampling and reconstruction problems, as filtering can be very simple and efficient when performed on image strips.

This multipass approach suffers from the *bottleneck problem* (see Chapter 13), where the first pass may not leave enough information for the second

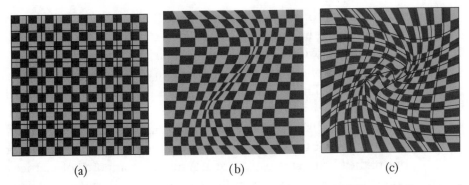

Figure 14.22 Two-pass spline mesh bottleneck problem: original image (a), horizontal pass (b), and final warped image (c).

pass. This problem is illustrated in Figure 14.22: In (a) we show the original image, in (b) the warping resulting from the horizontal pass, and in (c) the final warped image. Notice the small waves that appear in the center of the warped image because of the bottleneck problem.

Although this technique proves to be quite versatile and efficient, the fact that it is based on a mesh specification requires the user to enter too much information while defining the deformation. This is especially true in less important areas of the domain, where a precise control is not needed and some kind of automatic process could be used, as discussed previously.

The spline meshes may be directly created and modified, or indirectly obtained in an attempt to reduce unnecessary user input. It is easy to see that despite its efficiency for digital images, the two-pass spline mesh warping technique is of limited use for other graphical object representations. It is possible to use spline meshes to define coordinate systems and deform drawings, for instance, but the two-pass approach is useless in such cases.

14.3.6 Three-Pass Spline Mesh Warping

This is the natural extension of the technique of the previous section applied to solid objects represented by a uniform array of voxels, which is a very common representation for volumetric models. This warping technique is very useful not only for computing metamorphosis of volumetric data, but also as a tool for modeling volumetric objects through deformation, according to the "lump of clay" modeling paradigm [Sederberg and Parry, 1986]. A major advantage of volumetric models is that there is no special treatment given to objects with different topologies, and therefore, the topology of an object can easily change during the transformation.

The 3D algorithm, three-pass spline surface mesh warping, performs three passes on the volumetric data, each of them computing the deformation in just one direction. The passes of the algorithm are performed sequentially, but the deformation of each scanline in each pass is independent of the other scanlines and, therefore, is suitable for parallelization, as is the 2D algorithm.

Each pass of the algorithm performs the deformation in the direction of one of the Cartesian axes x, y, or z. A mesh is composed of a lattice of control points C_{ijk}, with m points in the x direction, n in the y direction, and p in the z direction, totaling mnp control points, in such a way that each control point can be easily referred to by integer indices. The pass for the x axis is as follows, and the others are performed analogously:

1. An intermediate mesh I is created by considering just the displacements of the control points in the x direction from the original mesh S to the deformed mesh D. In this way, the control points of I will have the same y- and z-coordinates of the corresponding point in S and the x-coordinate of the corresponding point in D.

2. A spline surface S_i is fitted to each set of control points of S with a constant i index, resulting in surfaces that are roughly perpendicular to the x direction. An identical process is performed to obtain the I_i spline surfaces passing through the control points of I.

3. Each voxel strip in the x direction is intersected with the S_i and I_i surfaces, resulting in two sets of collinear intersections.

4. For each voxel strip, the intersections with S_i and I_i are fitted with a spline curve, resulting in a scanline mapping function that is used to map voxels in the source object to their x-direction deformed positions.

The sampling and reconstruction problems are now simpler 1D problems that are handled on a scanline basis, in exactly the same way as the 2D case. This simplification helps make this algorithm a very efficient procedure to warp volumetric data with good-quality results.

An implementation of this algorithm has been used to produce the warp of the lobster shown in Figure 14.23. In fact, this example used a hybrid technique: the specification of the warping was done using the 3D field-based warping described in Section 14.2.3 (see Figure 14.9), and the computation

Figure 14.23   Volumetric lobster, warped to raise its claws.

of the warping was done in three passes using spline meshes just as described above.

In the 2D or 3D case, the specification of the warping using such partition-based techniques is difficult. The use of alternative specifications, such as the one we will discuss in Section 14.4.1, is a much better option. It has the advantage of an easier interface and an efficient implementation for warping volumetric data.

14.3.7   Multilevel Free-Form Deformation

One of the major problems with warping techniques is the generation of non–one-to-one mappings; that is, the warping functions are usually not injective, making the underlying graphical object fold upon itself. This is the foldover problem we have exemplified several times in the book.

In [Lee et al., 1995], a scheme to derive a one-to-one mapping using free-form deformation is devised, in which a hierarchy of control lattices is used. The basis function for the free-form deformation used is a bivariate cubic B-spline tensor product, so that there is local control.

The one-to-one property is achieved through a sequence of applications of the free-form deformation functions in lattices of finer densities. In each application, the maximum displacement for the control points of a given level cannot exceed the threshold for that level. This process is repeated until the control points reach their desired position, that is, the deformation first specified by the user. This formulation for the free-form deformation yields very smooth results, as shown in Figure 14.24.

For comparison purposes, Figure 14.25 shows roughly similar deformations—based on the same specification—using a variation of field-based warping (Section 14.2.2) for point specification, and radial basis functions (Section 14.2.1). Figure 14.25(a) and (b) shows field-based and radial functions applied to images; in (c) and (d), the same warping transformations are applied to spline meshes. Note how the foldovers become evident in the spline meshes.

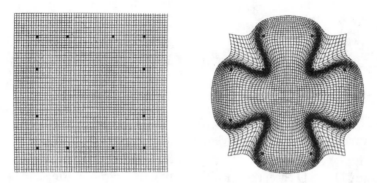

Figure 14.24 Multilevel free-form deformation [from Lee et al., 1995].

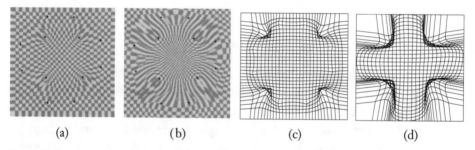

    (a)   (b)   (c)   (d)

Figure 14.25 Foldovers in a warp using different methods: field-based function (a), and radial function (b) applied to image; field-based function (c) and radial function (d) applied to spline mesh.

14.4 Hybrid Techniques

The use of a particular warping technique may induce the use of a type of specification that is not practical to manipulate from the user point of view (e.g., mesh-based interfaces). On the other hand, some specification techniques have very good user interfaces, but are associated with costly reconstruction techniques. In both cases, intermediate specifications can be introduced, yielding hybrid techniques.

In the first case, where the specification technique is inconvenient, an easy-to-use specification can be used and then transformed into the less convenient one, which is fed into the desired warping technique. In the second case, the complex warping function can be applied just to the intermediate specification, which is then fed into a more efficient warping technique.

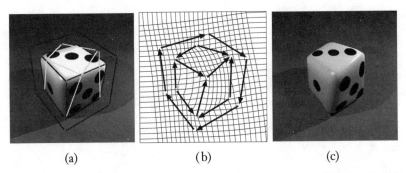

(a)   (b)   (c)

Figure 14.26 Field/mesh warping: features (a), mesh warped by features (b), and image warped by mesh (c).

Although this obviously does not give the same results as applying the original warping function to the graphical object, the approximation can be worth the reduction in execution time. This section shows some uses of this type of combination technique.

14.4.1 Field–Controlled Spline Mesh Warping

This is a technique that combines the efficiency of the two-pass spline mesh algorithm with the ease of use of feature-based specification, and was originally described in [Costa et al., 1992]. After specifying the features of the graphical object with oriented line segments, the algorithm uses these features as constraints to deform a relaxed spline mesh—that can be seen as a lower-resolution graphical object. This deformed mesh is subsequently used as input to the two-pass spline mesh warping algorithm for 2D graphical objects, or the three-pass algorithm for volumetric data. More precisely, the spline control points are moved according to the field of influence—described in Section 14.2.2—of each feature.

An example of this hybrid technique is shown in Figure 14.26. The undeformed image is shown in (a), with the features shown as dark lines in the original state and as lighter lines in the deformed state. Figure 14.26(b) shows the features superimposed on the deformed spline mesh, with the final deformed image shown in (c).

A disadvantage of this approach is that many of the problems of both algorithms are still present, namely, bottleneck and foldover. However, the unpredictable effects of field warping can be detected beforehand by inspecting the

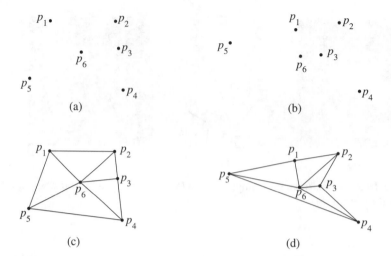

Figure 14.27 Automatic triangulation: source points (a), target points (b), source mesh (c), and target mesh (d).

automatically deformed mesh for any apparent folding. Also, it is possible to control the precision of this approximation by increasing the mesh resolution globally and concentrating control points in the interesting areas.

14.4.2 Automatic Triangulation of Feature Sets

This simple technique uses features to locate distinguishing characteristics of the graphical object and their corresponding warped state. A triangulation is performed based on the features set at any given state, creating a triangle mesh. A Delaunay triangulation [Preparata and Shamos, 1985], for instance, can be used for this purpose if the features are points. It is also possible to use triangulations with restrictions to support line segments as features.

This triangle mesh is then transposed to the other state; that is, the geometry of the second set of points is applied to the same triangle mesh. This scheme yields two triangle meshes with the same combinatorial topology, and techniques described previously (see Section 14.2.1) for warping between two triangle meshes can then be used.

Figure 14.27 shows an example of this technique. In (a) and (b), respectively, the source and target point sets are shown. The triangulation shown in (c) was automatically generated, and then the geometry of the point sets in (b) was applied to the first triangulation to generate (d).

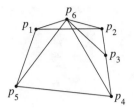

Figure 14.28 Automatic triangulation foldover problem.

Note that automatic triangulation schemes can generate meshes that do not correspond to a partition of the space. If the movement of the points is left unconstrained, meshes such as the one shown in Figure 14.28 can be created.

The triangulation problem has an algorithmic complexity $O(n \log n)$, where n is the number of points in the specification. There are optimal algorithms to obtain a Delaunay triangulation. A Delaunay triangulation has some advantages over other triangulations, such as the maximization of the internal angles of each triangle and avoiding too thin triangles, which are usually problematic and yield increased interpolation artifacts. Nevertheless, the fact that the topology of the triangulation will be transposed to the geometry of the matching point set—resulting in a potentially non-Delaunay triangulation—reduces the advantages of using a Delaunay triangulation in the first place.

The automatic triangulation scheme does not define a warping technique. It solely maps a point-based specification into a triangle mesh specification, making it easier for the user to specify the desired warping. The quality of the warping computation is defined by both the quality of the triangulations generated and the technique used to actually warp the meshes, as described in Section 14.2.1.

14.5 Algorithmic Techniques

There are some warping techniques in the literature that are obtained algorithmically. Some of these techniques are computed algorithmically from simulations related to the physical world. They are generically called *physics-based techniques*. Figure 14.29 shows three frames of a warping sequence that simulates a fracture of a cloth.

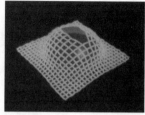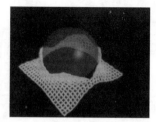

Figure 14.29 Physics simulation of a fracture [from Terzopoulos and Fleischer, 1988].

In the same way that scattered data interpolation plays a fundamental role in feature-based warping techniques, optimization techniques find their natural habitat in the computations of algorithmic warping techniques.

14.5.1 Work Minimization

Sometimes the physics is used only as an inspiration for the warping technique, but the computation itself has no relation to our everyday physics. In this case a better name would be *physically inspired warping techniques*. A very good example of this technique has been used in [Sederberg and Greenwood, 1992] to compute a metamorphosis between two polygonal curves of the plane.

The technique consists in an elaborate heuristic that selects the positions for inserting vertices so that the resulting vertex correspondence produces a morphing that minimizes work, according to an appropriate energy model. The 2D polygonal drawings are considered to be constructed of an ideal metal wire, so that the work for bending and stretching this wire can be computed. The best morphing is considered to be the one that requires the minimum work to transform one shape into another, by bending and stretching the wire.

Given this work metric, the problem is now that of optimizing the positions of the inserted points so that a minimum of work is executed. Obviously, this problem as posed is of a high complexity, but the restriction to insert new vertices only at the position of existing vertices significantly reduces the complexity of the problem. This vertex insertion is equivalent to smartly resampling the graphical object, so as to minimize the work performed during the warp.

An interesting consequence of the minimization of work performed is that matching features in the two drawings tend to be automatically associated. If there is a feature of one object that matches a feature of the other object, and these features are positioned relatively close, the transformation of one

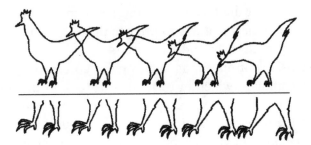

Figure 14.30 Physically inspired morphing [from Sederberg and Greenwood, 1992].

feature into the other requires very little work. In particular, features that do not move do not require any work to be transformed, and therefore do not move during the morphing. This is shown in the example in Figure 14.30, where the feet remain static while the rest is transformed.

For features that are relatively distant, however, the algorithm tends to confuse characteristics, producing unnatural results. In this case, the use of preliminary warpings in order to get an approximate alignment of the two curves would be extremely favorable. These preliminary warpings could be computed with minimum user input, using scattered data interpolation techniques.

As a final remark, the blending between the two warped curves in [Sederberg and Greenwood, 1992] is done by using linear interpolation. A different strategy for blending appeared in [Sederberg et al., 1992]. We will return to this in Chapter 17, Warping and Morphing of Plane Curves.

14.6 Morphing Techniques

This chapter was named "Warping and Morphing Techniques," and up to this point warping reconstruction techniques have dominated the arena. A few words about morphing techniques are in order.

We have emphasized throughout the book that a morphing consists of two warpings and a blending operation. In fact, we have coined the symbolic equation

$$\text{Morphing} = \text{Warping}^2 + \text{Blending}. \tag{14.3}$$

The underlying idea is that the forward and inverse warpings attain a registration of the graphical object features to prepare them to be blended (here we mean a blending of both shape and attributes).

Therefore, discussions of morphing at this point go back to the discussion of blending techniques, which in turn takes us back to the discussion of interpolation techniques. In fact, interpolation techniques have been the main force behind the different warping techniques discussed in this chapter. In sum, from the point of view of warping and morphing computations, Equation (14.3) could be rewritten as

$$\text{Morphing} = (\text{Interpolation})^3.$$

A chapter or section on blending techniques would naturally follow. However, analyzing the different blending techniques used in the literature, we discover that linear interpolation is most commonly used, or variations of it such as adaptive cross-dissolve or the scheduled linear interpolation described in Chapter 13. The rationale behind this ubiquitous nature of linear interpolation for blending is summarized below:

- Linear interpolation yields good results if we use the right domain to interpolate.
- The forward and inverse warps align the object features in such a way that the use of linear interpolation to blend them performs well.
- Linear interpolation is very simple and inexpensive to compute.

Therefore, we decided to disseminate remarks about blending in our tour of the different warping and morphing techniques for specific classes of graphical objects in Part IV.

14.7 Comments and References

A very good survey of 3D space deformation techniques can be found in [Bechmann, 1994]. Free-form deformation techniques have been extended to allow more flexibility: Extended free-form deformation [Coquillart, 1990] extends it to allow coordinate system defined on lattices with arbitrary topology. Rational free-form deformation [Kalra and Thalmann, 1992] allows the insertion of weights at the control points.

Delaunay triangulations are described in [Preparata and Shamos, 1985]. An implementation of an incremental algorithm for Delaunay triangulations can be found in [Lischinski, 1994].

Seeing the warping problem as a problem of scattered data interpolation, where the deformation specified by the features is extended to the entire domain, can be very useful, allowing the years of research in that area to be applied here, as has been done by [Ruprecht and Müller, 1995].

An inverse distance weighted interpolation method, the basis of feature-based image metamorphosis [Beier and Neely, 1992], was presented in [Shepard, 1968] and extended in many opportunities, such as [Franke and Nielson, 1980]. A simple extension for 3D features was done in [Darsa, 1994]. Another work in the same direction that allows for the use of points, vectors, and boxes as feature markers, is described in [Lerios et al., 1995].

Radial basis function techniques have been used to warp images. Thin-plate splines, which are a subset of radial basis functions, were used in [Bookstein, 1989] to minimize a global measure of the warping. Also, [Litwinowicz and Williams, 1994] used thin-plate splines, coupled with a curve-based specification, to produce interesting warping animations using rotoscoped features. Other radial basis functions, such as multiquadrics of the form $g(t) = (t^2 + \sigma^2)^\mu$, suggested by Hardy [Hardy, 1971], can be used instead of Gaussian functions.

References

Arad, N., and D. Reisfeld. 1995. Image Warping Using Few Anchor Points and Radial Functions. *Computer Graphics Forum*, **14**(1), 35–46.

Barr, A. H. 1984. Global and Local Deformation of Solid Primitives. *Computer Graphics (SIGGRAPH '84 Proceedings)*, **18**, 21–30.

Bechmann, Dominique. 1994. Space Deformation Models Survey. *Computers & Graphics*, **18**(4), 571–586.

Beier, Thaddeus, and Shawn Neely. 1992. Feature-Based Image Metamorphosis. *Computer Graphics (SIGGRAPH '92 Proceedings)*, **26**(2), 35–42.

Bookstein, F. L. 1989. Principal Warps: Thin-Plate Splines and the Decomposition of Deformations. *IEEE Transactions of Pattern Analysis and Machine Intelligence*, **11**, 567–585.

Coquillart, S., and P. Jancene. 1991. Animated Free-Form Derformation: An Interactive Animated Technique. *Computer Graphics (SIGGRAPH '91 Proceedings)*, **25**(July), 23–26.

Coquillart, Sabine. 1990. Extended Free-Form Deformations: A Sculpturing Tool for 3D Geometric Modeling. *Computer Graphics (SIGGRAPH '90 Proceedings)*, **24**(Aug.), 187–196.

Costa, B., L. Darsa, and J. Gomes. 1992. Image Metamorphosis. In Gomes, J., and G. Câmara (eds.), *SIBGRAPI '92 Proceedings*, 19–27.

Darsa, L. 1994. *Graphical Objects Metamorphosis*. Master's Thesis. Rio de Janeiro: Computer Science Department. PUC-Rio.

Franke, R., and G. Nielson. 1980. Smooth Interpolation of Large Sets of Scattered Data. *Int'l J. for Numerical Methods in Engineering*, **15**, 1691–1704.

Hardy, R. L. 1971. Multi Quadratic Equations of Topography and Other Irregular Surfaces. *Journal of Geophysical Research*, **76**(8), 1905–1915.

Kalra P., A. Mangili, N. M. Thalmann, and D. Thalmann. 1992. Simulation of Facial Muscle Actions Based on Rational Free-Form Deformation. In *Eurographics '92 (Computer Graphics Forum)*, **2**, 56–69.

Lee, Seung-Yong, Kyung-Yong Chwa, Sung Yong Shin, and George Wolberg. 1995. Image Metamorphosis Using Snakes and Free-Form Deformations. *Computer Graphics (SIGGRAPH '95 Proceedings)*, 439–448.

Lerios, Apostolos, Chase D. Garfinkle, and Marc Levoy. 1995. Feature-Based Volume Metamorphosis. *Computer Graphics (SIGGRAPH '95 Proceedings)*, **29**, 449–456.

Lischinski, Dani. 1994. Incremental Delaunay Triangulation. In Heckbert, Paul S. (ed.), *Graphics Gems IV*. Boston: Academic Press, 47–59.

Litwinowicz, Peter, and Lance Williams. 1994. Animating Images with Drawings. *Computer Graphics (SIGGRAPH '94 Proceedings)*, **24**, 409–412.

Maccracken, Ron, and Kenneth I. Joy. 1996. Free-Form Deformation with Lattices of Arbitrary Topology. *Computer Graphics (SIGGRAPH '96 Proceedings)*, **30**, 181–188.

Preparata, F. P., and M. I. Shamos. 1985. *Computational Geometry: An Introduction*. New York: Springer-Verlag.

Ruprecht, Detlef, and Heinrich Müller. 1995. Image Warping with Scattered Data Interpolation. *IEEE Computer Graphics & Applications*, March, 37–43.

Schumaker, L. L. 1976. Fitting Surfaces to Scattered Data. In Lorentz G. G., C. K. Lui, and L. L. Schumaker (eds.), *Approximation Theory II*. San Diego: Academic Press, 203–268.

Sederberg, T., and S. Parry. 1986. Free-Form Deformation of Solid Geometric Models. *Computer Graphics (SIGGRAPH '86 Proceedings)*, **20**(4), 151–160.

Sederberg, Thomas W., Peishing Gao, Guojin Wang, and Hong Mu. 1992. 2D Shape Blending: An Intrinsic Solution to the Vertex Path Problem. *Computer Graphics (SIGGRAPH '93 Proceedings)*, **27**, 15–18.

Sederberg, Thomas W., and Eugene Greenwood. 1992. A Physically Based Approach to 2-D Shape Blending. *Computer Graphics (SIGGRAPH '92 Proceedings)*, **26**, 25–34.

Shepard, D. 1968. A Two-Dimensional Interpolation Function for Irregularly Spaced Data. *Proc. 23rd National Conference of the ACM*, 517–524.

Smithe, D. B. 1990. *A Two-Pass Mesh Warping Algorithm for Object Transformation and Image Interpolation*. Technical Memo #1030. Industrial Light and Magic.

Terzopoulos, Demetri, and Kurt Fleischer. 1988. Modeling Inelastic Deformation: Viscoelasticity, Plasticity, Fracture. *Computer Graphics (SIGGRAPH '88 Proceedings)*, **22**, 269–278.

Wolberg, G. 1990. *Digital Image Warping*. Los Alamitos, CA: IEEE Computer Society Press.

PART

IV A Tour of Warping and Morphing

In Part II we studied graphical objects, their description, representation, and reconstruction. In Part III we did an equivalent study for transformations between graphical objects. In Part IV we will use the conceptual framework and techniques from these two parts to study warping and morphing of four classes of graphical objects: *plane curves*, *images*, *surfaces*, and *volumetric objects*. Also, we have included a chapter on *image-based rendering*, a very important topic that uses several techniques from the area of warping and morphing. We will also finally address the last level of our four abstraction classes (the four-universes paradigm): implementation. The last chapter of this part brings a complete description of the architecture of the *Morphos* system, which is included on the companion CD-ROM.

15

Introduction to Part IV

In this part of the book we will put together the two major actors in the study of warping and morphing: graphical objects and transformations. We will use the concepts and techniques introduced in Parts II and III to study warping and morphing of graphical objects of different nature and dimensionality.

A chapter will be dedicated to each different type of the four important classes of graphical objects: plane curves, images, surfaces, and solids (volumetric objects). In particular, this part will contain a survey of the literature of warping and morphing from the point of view of the concepts introduced in Parts II and III.

Two other chapters are included in this part: one covering the area of *image-based rendering*, and one describing the architecture of the *Morphos* system, which we have developed for warping and morphing of graphical objects, and included on the companion CD-ROM. This system facilitates the use of different types of graphical object and warping techniques. In fact, several of the techniques described are implemented in the software.

15.1 Classes of Graphical Objects

The four classes of graphical objects we have chosen to cover separately in this part include almost all of the different objects used in computer graphics and its applications.

15.1.1   Plane Curves

These objects are widely used for illustration and drawing purposes. They play an important role in the area of digital publishing, and morphing techniques for them find applications in the cartoon animation industry.

15.1.2   Image

Images were the original motivation for metamorphosis in computer graphics. In fact, the use of metamorphosis as a special-effects tool started in the beginning of this century with image morphing. The interested reader can find more details of this early application in Section 15.4.

Warping and morphing of images find several other applications than in the entertainment industry. One example is the use of warping for nonrigid image registration in the area of medical images.

15.1.3   Surfaces

Surface warping has been used since the beginning of the area of geometric modeling in the '60s. In fact, Bézier control points are an effective way to control an intrinsic warping of a curve or surface. Warping of surfaces has several applications as a modeling tool, and also in the 3D computer animation business. Metamorphosis techniques for surfaces are also very important because they allow us to work with the 3D model instead of the 2D projections of them.

15.1.4   Solids

The relation between solids and surfaces is the same that exists between curves and plane regions. Therefore, when we talk about solids, we include 2D solids as well. Certainly a solid is a very important object in the area of computer-aided design and manufacturing. Solids with a nonconstant density function (the 3D analog of an image) are widely used in the area of medical images, where they are called 3D images. Warping and morphing of these objects is a very important tool for analysis in this area.

15.2   Warping and Morphing of Sound

The four classes of graphical objects mentioned in the previous section exclude a very important object: sound. From the point of view of the concepts

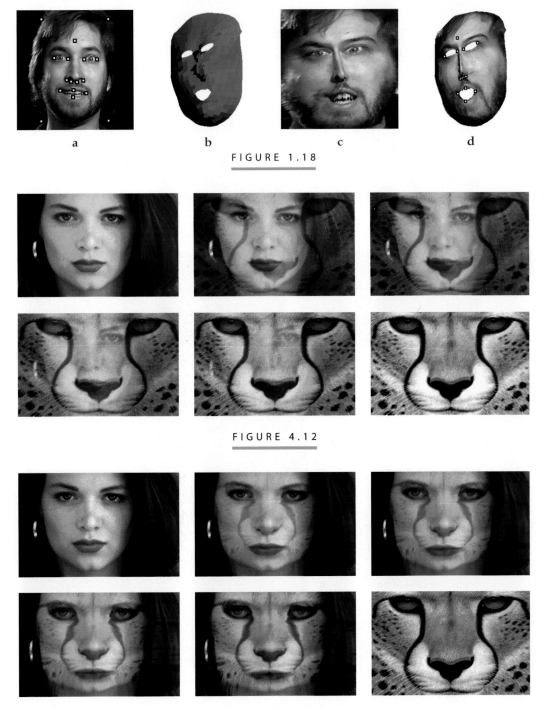

COLOR PLATES

a   b   c   d

FIGURE 1.18

FIGURE 4.12

FIGURE 4.18

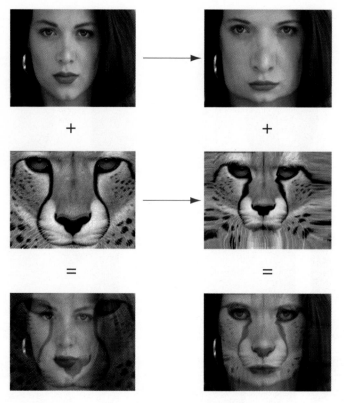

FIGURE 4.30

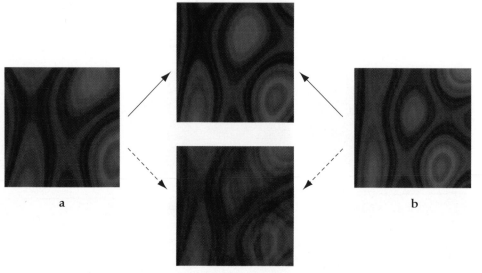

a

b

FIGURE 5.4

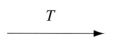

FIGURE 6.1

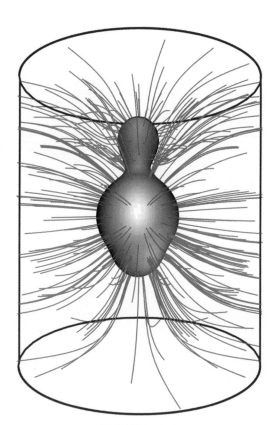

FIGURE 6.5

FIGURE 6.7

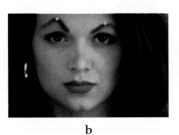

a　　　　　　　　b　　　　　　　　c

FIGURE 14.2

FIGURE 14.10

FIGURE 16.7

a   b

FIGURE 16.11

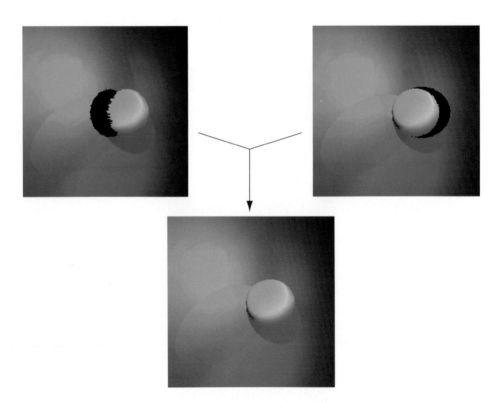

FIGURE 16.17

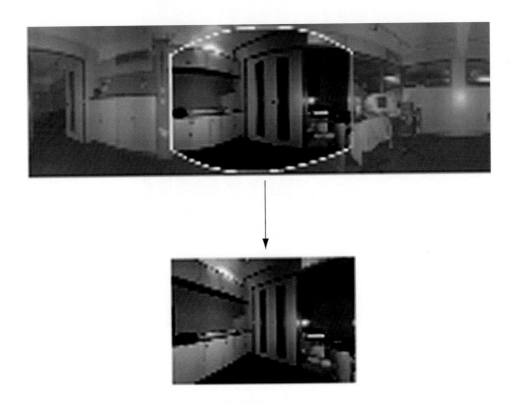

FIGURE 16.20

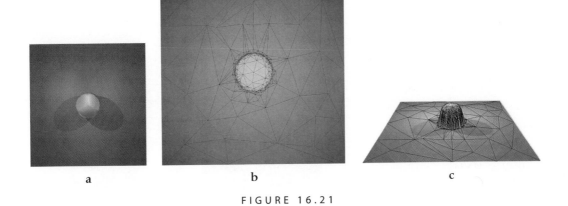

a   b   c

FIGURE 16.21

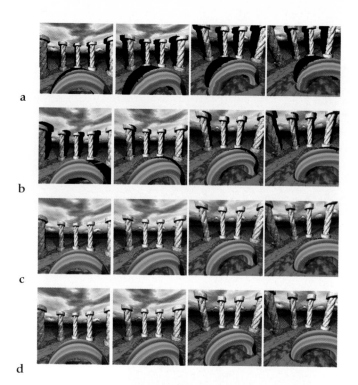

a

b

c

d

FIGURE 16.23

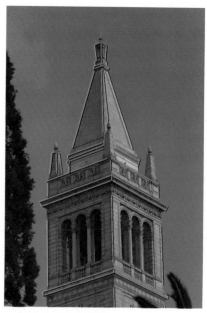

a

b

c

FIGURE 16.24

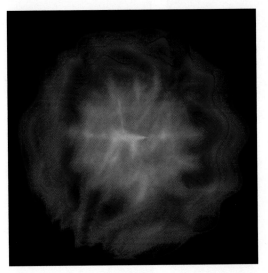
a
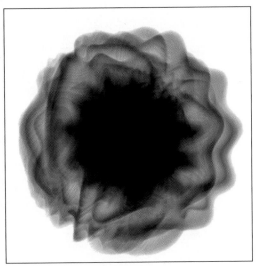
b

FIGURE 18.1

a

b

FIGURE 18.9

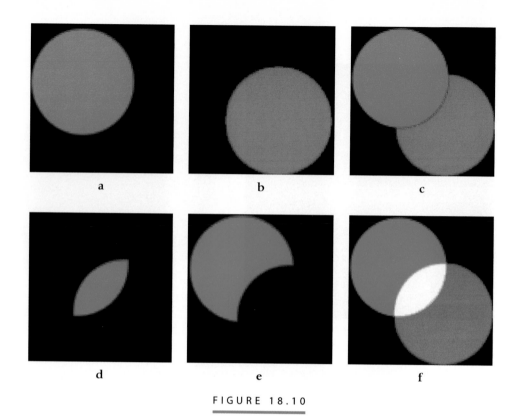

FIGURE 18.10

FIGURE 18.11

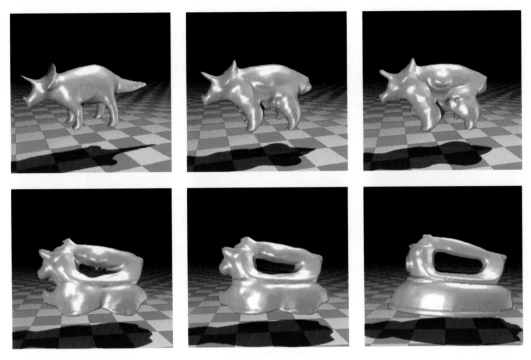

FIGURE 20.19

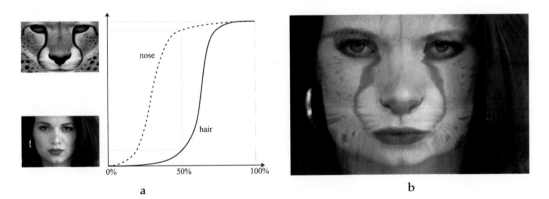

a

b

FIGURE 21.6

a   b

FIGURE 21.13

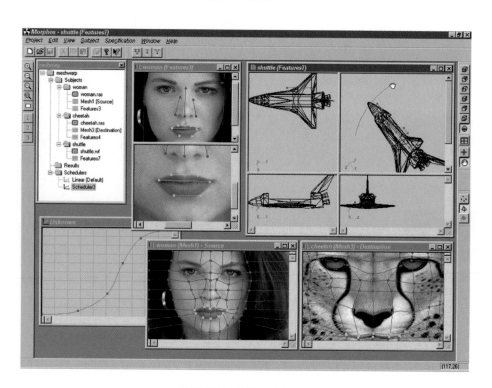

FIGURE CD-ROM.1

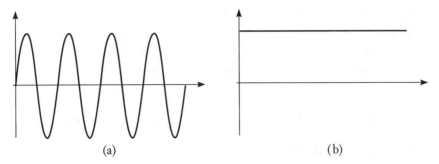

Figure 15.1 Time (a) and frequency (b) domain representations of a constant sound.

introduced in the book, warping and morphing of sounds is a problem of warping and morphing a 1D graphical object: a sound is defined in the time domain as a signal $f: [a, b] \to \mathbb{R}$, on a certain time interval $[a, b]$.

Nevertheless, our perception of sound is much more involved than the perception of the other graphical objects. While for curves, surfaces, images, and volumetric images the perception involves our vision system, the perception of sounds involves our auditory system.

Perception of sounds is solely a perception of frequencies. The natural domain to represent sounds is the frequency domain. Figure 15.1 is a convincing argument of this fact: a sound with constant frequency is heard as a constant sound, and this is clearly reflected on the time-frequency representation shown on (b). The time domain representation in (a) has no direct relation with the constant sound we hear.

When the frequency is not constant, the frequency representation of the sound has to be done in the time-frequency domain, which gives frequency information at a given instant of time. From this point of view, a sound is a 2D graphical object. Clearly, this is the sound representation that should be used to warp and morph sounds. This fact has been exploited to devise time warping techniques in [Goldenstein and Gomes, 1997].

Warping and morphing of sounds find many applications. Time warping of sounds can be applied to solve synchronization problems. Two of these problems are synchronization of sound and motion in animation systems, and synchronization of a given recorded sound with a video piece, for editing purposes.

Metamorphosis of sound is a very interesting tool for creating new voices from existing ones. This has been used in the movie and video industry, in spite of the fact that there does not exist a good working tool to cope with this problem.

We hope to include more material about sound warping and morphing at *www.visgraf.impa.br/morph/* in the near future.

15.3 Warping and Morphing Techniques and Representation

It is clear that the same warping techniques apply to different graphical objects. A simple example of this is to consider a global warping of the plane $\mathbb{R}^2$, which can be used to warp any graphical object embedded on the plane: plane curves, 2D solids, and images.

The possibility of using the same warping and morphing technique with different graphical objects and vice versa gives us a great flexibility in devising the best strategy to achieve a desired warping or morphing for some application. This fact is greatly enriched if the user has at his disposal a testbed morphing system that allows him to experiment with different warping and morphing techniques with different types of graphical objects. This is made possible with the *Morphos* system, which we discuss in Chapter 21.

Another important variable in the above scenario is the possibility of using different graphical object representations. We have already pointed out that one of the secrets for a good morphing is to use the right representation in the most suited domain. There is always a more suitable warping and morphing technique for each graphical object representation. This fact is illustrated in Figure 15.2.

Having morphing and warping techniques that can be used with different representations of a graphical object creates a very flexible environment for warping and morphing.

It is a well-known fact that changing between different graphical object representations is a very difficult problem. However, for many applications involving warping and morphing, the conversion between different representations can be computed only approximately.

As an example, consider the problem of plane curve morphing. Given a curve of the plane, rasterization gives an approximate conversion from the curve to the plane region bounded by it. On the other hand, when we have a rasterized region of the plane (2D volumetric-like solid), an approximate conversion to a boundary representation of it can be easily obtained. Once we

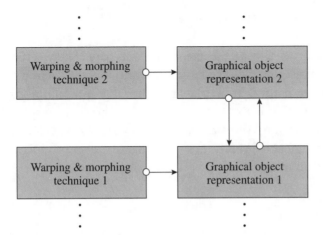

Figure 15.2 Warping, morphing, and graphical object representations.

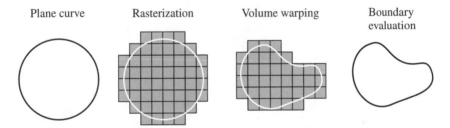

Figure 15.3 Curve warping using volumetric techniques.

have a 2D solid, we can apply volumetric warping and morphing techniques to it. In this way volumetric warping and morphing techniques can be used to compute warping and morphing of plane curves. This is illustrated in Figure 15.3, in which a rasterization is used as an approximate conversion from a boundary to a volumetric representation; a volumetric warping technique is applied to the 2D solid; and a boundary evaluation is used to compute a curve from the warped solid. A simple, approximated boundary evaluation here can be done by connecting the center of each volume element on the boundary (an 8-connected topology has to be used to compute the boundary).

This strategy has been exploited in the literature, and some of this work will be discussed in the chapters to follow.

15.4 Comments and References

There is no right order to read the chapters of this part. They were written to be as independent as possible. We have chosen to include them in the order that seems the most natural: from planar to spatial graphical objects.

A small history of the early use of metamorphosis as a special-effects tool can be found on the Web site *www.visgraf.impa.br/morph*. The site also contains a QuickTime movie of the first cross-dissolve ever produced to obtain transition effects on images.

References

Goldenstein, Siome, and Jonas Gomes. 1997. Time Warping of Audio Signals. *Preprint*, IMPA, Rio de Janeiro.

16

Image-Based Rendering

A RELATIVELY NEW APPLICATION OF WARPING AND MORPHING has been in the area of image-based rendering. Image-based renderers do not follow the traditional 3D rendering pipeline. They use prerendered images of the scene as the basic primitives to render a scene. This makes it possible to achieve much higher levels of realism. Also, there is a decoupling of the complexity of the models from the rendering frame rate, as basically just images of the models are used, which makes this approach potentially faster than traditional ones.

This chapter presents a conceptual discussion of the image-based rendering problem, its relation to the warping and morphing operations, and the description of some techniques. Also, several examples and applications will be studied.

16.1 Image-Based Rendering Pipeline

The traditional rendering pipeline is shown in Figure 16.1. It contains the basic tools used in the carpentry of image synthesis: shape modeling, illumination modeling, camera transformations, illumination computation, and sampling. In the rendering process the pixel values are computed by sampling the scene. A natural question can be posed: What function are we sampling when rendering a scene? This is the *plenoptic function*, to be described below.

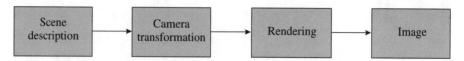

Figure 16.1   Rendering pipeline.

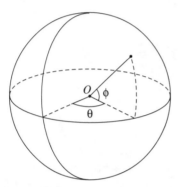

Figure 16.2   The plenoptic function.

16.1.1 The Plenoptic Function

A scene can be completely characterized by the *plenoptic function* (*plenoptic* comes from the Latin *plenus*, meaning full, and *optic*, meaning relating to the eye or vision) introduced by Adelson and Berger [Adelson and Berger, 1991]. The plenoptic function describes the complete flow of light on each direction of the space, from any point of view.

A parameterization of the plenoptic function is very easy to obtain: the viewpoint O is defined by euclidean coordinates $O = (x, y, z)$. To specify a direction vector from O, we use spherical coordinates with origin at O. In this case, the direction is defined by two parameters (θ, ϕ), longitude and latitude angles, on a sphere of radius 1 with center at O (see Figure 16.2). We have

$$p = p(\theta, \phi, x, y, z);$$

that is, p computes the radiant energy observed from the point O in the direction (θ, ϕ). The plenoptic function varies with time also, but we are mainly interested in snapshots of the function.

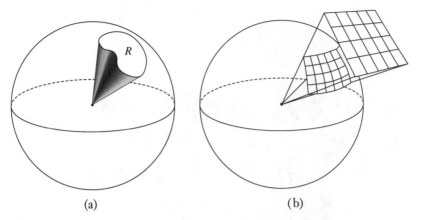

Figure 16.3 Solid angle (a), and image sample (b).

Consider a fixed position $O = (x_0, y_0, z_0)$ of the space, and a solid angle Ω with vertex at O. This angle determines a region R on the unit sphere with center O (see Figure 16.3(a)). By computing the plenoptic function on the points of R, we obtain a *partial sample*.

When the region R is determined by the radial projection of a rectangle Q (see Figure 16.3(b)), the partial sample is called an *image sample*, or simply an *image*. When the solid angle is 4π (the whole sphere), the sample of the plenoptic function is called an *environment map* centered at O. An environment map is also called a *complete sample* in the literature. This term is not appropriate because this is a particular sample of the plenoptic function where the viewpoint is fixed.

Besides the sphere, different surfaces can be used in the sampling process of the environment mapping. The only requirements are that the surface describes a solid angle of 4π, and that the radial projection from the surface into the surface of the sphere is a one-to-one mapping.

Certainly, computational issues must also be taken into account. A cube is a very natural choice. Cubic environment mapping have been used for a long time. Figure 16.4 shows an unfolded environment mapping on the cube.

16.1.2 Revisiting the Rendering Pipeline

Using the plenoptic function, the classical image rendering pipeline of Figure 16.1 can be restated as shown in Figure 16.5: From the scene description

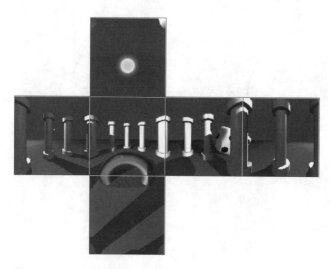

Figure 16.4 Cubic environment map unfolded.

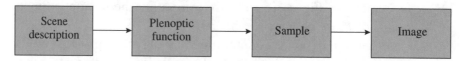

Figure 16.5 The rendering pipeline and the plenoptic function.

(shape and illumination) we compute the plenoptic function, and for a different specification of viewing parameters, we sample the plenoptic function to obtain the image.

The problems inherent in this traditional pipeline are well known: to compute the plenoptic function, we need to model the scene objects and the illumination, which is a difficult task. Also, the computation of the plenoptic function samples amounts to the computation of the illumination, which is a computer-intensive process. This makes it impossible in practice to compute the continuous plenoptic function for some scene descriptions. By imposing the additional requirement of producing photorealistic images in real time, we are faced with an even more difficult problem using the traditional rendering pipeline.

This is where image-based rendering enters the scene. The basic idea consists in changing the rendering pipeline of Figure 16.5, creating an image rendering pipeline into two steps:

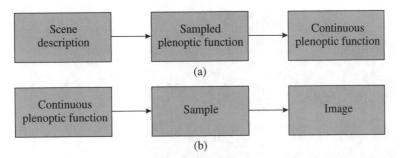

Figure 16.6   The image-based rendering pipeline: construction of the plenoptic function from the scene description (a) and image generation from the plenoptic function (b).

1. From the scene description, we sample the plenoptic function, and the samples are used to reconstruct a continuous plenoptic function (see Figure 16.6(a)).

2. The continuous plenoptic function is used to generate images by sampling it with the appropriate positioning and direction parameters (see Figure 16.6(b)).

A superficial analysis of the resampling process of this new rendering pipeline could lead us to believe that we are doing more work than before: we sample, reconstruct, and sample again. Nevertheless, the rationale behind this new pipeline is simple to understand:

- The sampling of the plenoptic function in the second part of the pipeline requires modest computational efforts.

- The samples of the plenoptic function in the first part of the pipeline can be obtained from a virtual environment or from real scenes (using camera, scanners, etc.).

- The cost of viewing the scene by sampling the reconstructed plenoptic function is independent of the scene complexity.

- The two parts of the pipeline can be decoupled; that is, the first part can be a preprocessing step, while just the second is executed in real time.

From all of the above, the new rendering pipeline should be able to provide interactive navigation of the scene with a high degree of realism.

Figure 16.7 Section of a panorama installation [from Comment, 1993]. See also color plate 16.7.

16.1.3 A New Paradigm in Image Rendering?

The use of samples of the plenoptic function to make observers believe they are seeing the real scene is not new. In fact, panoramas have been used since the 18th century.

A *panorama* is a sort of mural painting created on a circular space around a central platform where spectators can look in all directions and see a scene as if they were in the middle of it. It was patented by Robert Baker in 1787, and at that time it was a very popular way to represent landscapes and historical events. They were usually built in two or three floors so spectators could walk through different scenes. The drawing in Figure 16.7 shows a section of a three-floor panorama building from 1810 [Comment, 1993].

By the beginning of this century, several variations of panoramas had been created. One example is the Cinerama, in which cinematographic images were projected onto a circular surface covering 180 degrees. Although several projections were used, the image appeared to be only one.

The use of image samples of the plenoptic function in computer graphics is not new either. Geometry complexity has been traded for images since texture mapping was introduced in 1974 by Ed Catmull (see Chapter 6, Image Mapping). In fact, environment maps were used in [Blinn and Newell, 1976] for obtaining an approximation to ray tracing. The use of environment mapping as a sampling of the plenoptic function appeared some time ago in [Greene, 1986]. [Heckbert, 1989] used view-dependent texture mapping to obtain realistic renderings of scene details.

16.1.4 Extending the Plenoptic Function

It should be emphasized that a complete description of the plenoptic function contains indirectly the variation of light information along the rays. In fact, this information can be obtained by integrating the function along each ray.

Nonetheless, sometimes it is important to incorporate extra information in the plenoptic function. Depth information is a very interesting parameter to add. That is, for each point O, we consider the distance d along the ray as a parameter, and the wavelength λ depends on d, $\lambda = \lambda(d)$. Essentially, we have a volumetric function described in spherical coordinates.

Extra information such as material, opacity, and transparency could also be added. All of this information could be used to aid in the reconstruction phase of the image-based rendering pipeline.

16.2 Morphing and Image-Based Rendering

Warping and morphing constitute fundamental operations in the image-based rendering pipeline. We will clarify this assertion with a simple example. Consider two image samples I_1 and I_2 of the plenoptic function, one sample at position $O_1 = (x_1, y_1, z_1)$ and direction (θ_1, φ_1), and the other sample at a different position $O_2 = (x_2, y_2, z_2)$ and direction (θ_2, φ_2) (see Figure 16.8). Now we pose the following problem: From the two image samples I_1 and I_2, compute a new image sample I of the plenoptic function for a different position $O = (x, y, z)$ and direction (θ, φ).

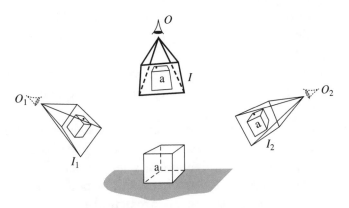

Figure 16.8 Reconstruction from two samples of the plenoptic function.

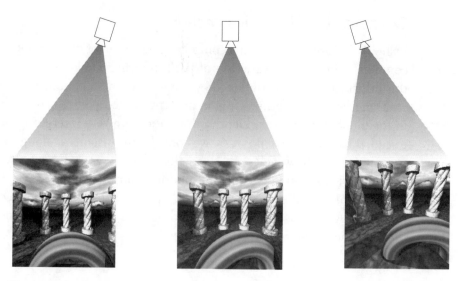

Figure 16.9 Projective warping and reconstruction.

From the point of view of the camera positioning, the fundamental theorem of projective geometry (see Chapter 3) guarantees that the viewing of the scene from O is obtained by using a 3D projective warping from the viewing of the scene in the positions O_1 or O_2.

It is interesting to observe that the 3D projective warping can be attained by applying a plane projective warping to the images taken from positions O_1 or O_2. On what concerns the illumination attributes, the pixel values of the image from O could be computed by blending the pixel values from these two images. In sum, a picture of the scene from position O could be obtained by using a projective morphing applied to the two images of the scene taken from two different positions O_1 and O_2. This is illustrated in Figure 16.9, where the intermediate image is reconstructed from the images on the left and on the right using a projective warping.

The above problem has appeared in the computer graphics literature in [Chen and Williams, 1993]. It constitutes the cornerstone of image-based rendering techniques.

The use of plane projective warping to compute the intermediate image I works fine except for the problem of visibility: some points of the scene visible at the position O of the observer might not be visible either from positions O_1 or O_2. Computing the illumination attributes of those points from the images I_1 and I_2, where they are not present, is an extremely ill-posed problem. This is

(a)   (b)

Figure 16.10 Visibility and projective warping: (b) shows a projective warping of the image in (a).

illustrated in Figure 16.10: in (b) we show a projective warping of the scene in (a). The black pixels indicate the regions that are not visible from the observer in the image sample in (a).

We will refer to this problem as the *parallax visibility problem*, or simply the *parallax problem*. We should remark that when the objects on the scene are too far away from the observer, these visibility problems are minimized. This fact is exploited in the problem we will study below.

16.3 Case Study: A Tour into the Picture

In this section we will look at a simple but illustrative example of image-based rendering. Consider the case where we have one image sample of the plenoptic function. From this image sample we wish to navigate in the scene of the image. That is, we need to compute image samples of the plenoptic function from different viewpoints starting from a single image sample. The problem was studied in [Horry et al., 1997]. This is a situation where the objects are considered too far away on the scene so as to avoid the parallax problem.

The goal of this technique is to navigate in existing pictures for which there is no projection or depth information. The first step is therefore to provide a mechanism for a user to deduce the projection parameters from the vanishing points of the image. Given these projection parameters, a very simple model of the scene is created, basically a box with handcut foreground objects.

It is then possible to move the observer around inside that box and reproject the image to the new viewpoint. For each side of the box and each foreground object, a projective warp is performed. Although the technique as presented required some degree of artistic input (hand-painting behind the foreground

(a)   (b)

Figure 16.11   Tour into the Picture: the original image (a) and a frame of the navigation (b) [from Horry et al., 1997]. See also color plate 16.11.

objects, for instance), the result of navigating in existing artwork is very effective, as shown in Figure 16.11. We have implemented this technique in the *Morphos* system included on the companion CD-ROM (see Chapter 21).

16.4   Scene Sampling

The image-based rendering problem would be solved if we had a complete sample of the plenoptic function for the scene. This would comprise the sampling of volumetric information of a high dimension, a formidable computational task.

In this section we will describe different types of strategies used to obtain different "partial samples" of the plenoptic function. There are many possibilities for computing partial samples, as different samples impose different restrictions and limitations depending on the techniques to be used on the reconstruction phase of the image-based rendering pipeline.

16.4.1   Image Sample and Image Array

This is a sample where the viewpoint and the sampling direction are fixed. In Section 16.3, we gave an example of navigating a scene from an image sample. An extension of an image sample consists in considering the depth as a parameter of the plenoptic function, and taking image samples using fixed viewpoints and directions but at different depth (see Figure 16.12). We obtain a volumetric sample of the scene, called a *volumetric image sample*, or simply an *image array* of the scene.

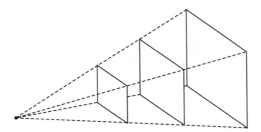

Figure 16.12 Image array.

16.4.2 Sampling with Variable Directions

In this case, we take samples of the plenoptic function in different directions, with the viewpoint fixed. A single representation for these samples consists in storing a collection of image samples. Another possible representation consists in taking enough samples to cover a solid angle of 4π, and stitching the samples together to create an environment map sample.

There are several possible representations for the environment map surface geometry. Although spherical maps are the most natural way to represent the environment information, they are not necessarily the most convenient or efficient. Other representations have been used, such as cubical maps [Greene, 1986] and cylindrical maps [Chen, 1995; McMillan and Bishop, 1995].

Spheres are difficult to represent digitally without too much variation in the information density. Cubes do not represent texture information homogeneously and have discontinuities at the edges, but the cube representation is the easiest to obtain for synthetic images and can be stored as six conventional rectangular images, which can be output by virtually any rendering software (see Figure 16.4). Cylinder-based techniques have the problem of limiting the field of view to avoid dealing with the caps, but have the advantage of representing the information homogeneously.

Certainly, these samples can include image arrays; therefore, a possible representation is a volumetric environment map, called a *depth environment map* in the literature.

16.4.3 Sampling with Variable Viewpoint and Direction

In this case, we sample the plenoptic function from different viewpoints $(x_0, y_0, z_0), \ldots, (x_n, y_n, z_n)$, and at different directions. This is represented by a collection of images for different camera positions. Certainly, these samples may include image arrays for different positions, or even a collection of depth

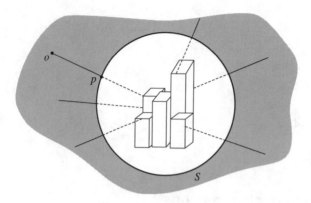

Figure 16.13   Computing the plenoptic function.

environment maps. Taking all of the possibilities of viewpoints and directions would result in a complete sample.

16.4.4   The Lumigraph or Light Field Samples

In this section we will describe another approach used to obtain a complete sample of the plenoptic function. We are interested in sampling different positions, in different directions. The work we will describe was introduced in the literature simultaneously and independently by [Gortler et al., 1996] and [Levoy and Hanrahan, 1996].

Suppose we are interested in computing the plenoptic function of some scenario (either real or virtual). We will suppose that there exists a surface S that contains all of the scene elements in its interior and separates these elements from the different viewpoints to be used in the sampling process (see Figure 16.13). Our purpose is to compute samples of the plenoptic function relative to the scenario for all points O on the exterior of S.

Notice that we are only interested in the rays that intersect the surface S, since the rays that do not intersect do not carry light information from the scene. In this case, any ray starting from a viewpoint O, exterior to S, and reaching an element of the scenario intersects the surface S. We will suppose that this intersection consists of only one point. Note that a convex surface S satisfies all of the above requirements. S could be the convex hull of the scenario objects.

From the above settings, our task consists in sampling the plenoptic function from different viewpoints outside the surface S. These samples are cast

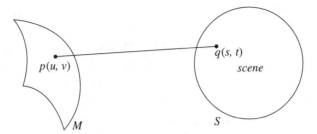

Figure 16.14   Four-parameter description of the plenoptic function.

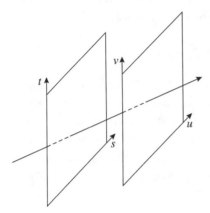

Figure 16.15   4D parameterization.

on another surface M as illustrated in Figure 16.14. Any sampling ray is completely defined by a point $p = p(u, v)$ on the surface M, and its hitting position on a point $q = q(s, t)$ on the surface S. Therefore, the sample is characterized by four parameters (u, v, s, t). This four-parameter description of the plenoptic function is called a *lumigraph* [Gortler et al., 1996] or a *light field* [Levoy and Hanrahan, 1996].

Computing the lumigraph amounts to computing a four-dimensional function, which is a simple task. In [Gortler et al., 1996] and [Levoy and Hanrahan, 1996], a simplification is done in order to compute the lumigraph. It is assumed that the scenario surface S is a cube, and another cube is used as the environment surface of the plenoptic function. This reduces to computing the lumigraph for two planes (the faces of the cubes), as shown in Figure 16.15.

We should notice that the lumigraph sampling of the plenoptic function accounts for the visibility problems mentioned before.

16.5 Reconstruction

In the previous sections, we discussed different approaches to sampling the plenoptic function for virtual or real environments. According to the image-based rendering pipeline (Figure 16.6), those samples should be used to reconstruct the plenoptic function. Certainly, each sampling strategy is directly related to some reconstruction technique.

All of the problems and concepts discussed previously related to sampling and reconstruction apply here to the reconstruction of the plenoptic function. Other new problems arise that are intrinsic to the sampling/reconstruction of the plenoptic function. One of these problems is posed by the view-dependent attributes (the parallax problem discussed before).

16.5.1 Reconstruction with a Fixed Camera

Given a fixed and known position (x, y, z), the use of an environment map sample gives all the information visible from that position. If the reconstruction phase is also limited to that position, the environment map sample solves the problem of sampling and reconstruction of the plenoptic function. In fact, if only the direction is allowed to change, the parallax problem disappears because no new areas within the scene can become visible (see Figure 16.16).

16.5.2 General Reconstruction

When we have a complete sample of the plenoptic function, or even a lumigraph, we can perform the reconstruction taking into account the parallax problem. But this is computationally a prohibitively expensive solution. As already remarked, in some applications it is possible to reconstruct the plenoptic function using partial samples of it. This is the main problem in image-based

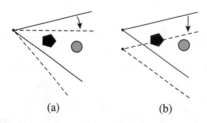

(a)   (b)

Figure 16.16   Visibility: rotation (a) and translation (b).

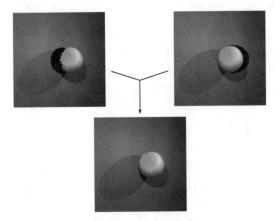

Figure 16.17 Reconstruction from two samples (visibility gaps in black). See also color plate 16.17.

rendering: *Devise good sampling-reconstruction strategies that produce an effective rendering of the scene and are computationally efficient.*

This combination is exemplified in Figure 16.17, which shows an image obtained from the combination of two samples. The top left was originally sampled from a top view of the sphere; the top right, as a side view. Notice how the visibility information that is missing from the top view is completely filled by the second sample. Similarly, the visibility gaps in the second sample are covered by the first. Given the depth value, it is possible to *warp* the image samples, reprojecting them to positions different from the ones where they were created.

Nevertheless, each sample provides limited information about the world, which is not sufficient to determine the view from arbitrary positions and directions in the resampling phase. If the sample is warped to different viewpoints, parallax is introduced and the restricted information provided by a single sample becomes evident; new areas not present in the original environment map can be revealed.

This problem can be overcome by combining the information from neighboring samples—through morphing—to create an image for any viewpoint and direction. The morphing here involves two projective warpings to register the information, followed by a complex blending, based on different parameters such as depth and camera parameters. The depth information and the visualization parameters allow the determination of the mapping functions between the original views and the new arbitrary view. After applying these mappings, the warped information can be combined with local control, used to determine the predominant information at each region.

In the next two sections we will study a successful use of reconstruction techniques in two different applications: virtual panoramas and image-based navigation of synthetic environments.

16.6 Virtual Panoramas

If fixed-position sampling is used to obtain an environment sampling of the plenoptic function, the reconstruction phase will allow just for rotations around fixed positions. The parallax problem disappears because we have a fixed position. This sampling-reconstruction scheme for the plenoptic function was first exploited in a commercial product in Apple QuickTimeVR [Chen, 1995], a system that simulates rotation within a scene, where cylindrical environment maps were available at specific positions.

The visualization of the scene using the environment map has been called *reprojection* in the literature because it constitutes a projecton from the (projected) environment map. In the reprojection phase, the viewing volume of the camera transformation intersects the environment map surface in a region R, as indicated in Figure 16.18. The region R is called the *visible region* of the environment map. In order to fully exploit the image-based rendering pipeline, the visualization of the visible region should be done using texture mapping techniques.

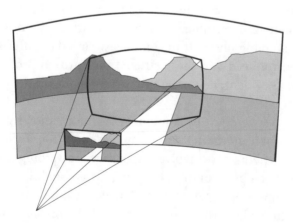

Figure 16.18   Viewing screen of a generic environment mapping.

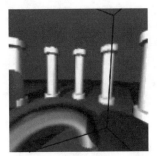

Figure 16.19 Cubical environment map reprojection.

The geometry of the environment map surface dictates the reprojection phase. In general, the visible region R has curved boundaries (see Figure 16.18); therefore, in order to map it to screen coordinates, it must be warped.

16.6.1 Cubical Environment Maps

In this case, the reprojection phase is very simple, consisting of projective transformation of the cube faces. This projective mapping of images is the basic operation of texture mapping, implemented in most graphics hardware. Even if performed in software, well-known incremental scanline algorithms can be used.

A reprojection of a cube texture-mapped by the environment of Figure 16.4 is shown for a particular viewing direction in Figure 16.19; the seams of the cube are highlighted to indicate the new viewing direction.

The reprojection of the cubical environment mapping is very simple. In this case the visible region consists of planar polygons on the faces of the cube. Therefore, we just have to display the visible regions of the six texture-mapped squares of the faces of the cube (see Figure 16.4).

16.6.2 Cylindrical Environment Maps

A unitary cylinder has a natural coordinate system

$$\varphi(u, v) = (\cos u, \sin u, v).$$

This coordinate system defines an intrinsic isometry between the cylinder and a region of the euclidean plane. Therefore, reconstructing an environment mapping on a cylinder by stitching image samples is a relatively simple task.

Figure 16.20 Warping to visualize a cylindrical environment mapping. See also color plate 16.20.

Also, panoramic photographies map naturally on the cylinder surface using the above coordinate system.

These properties make the cylinder a natural choice for the geometry of an environment map sample. Note that the sample is not a complete fixed-point sample because it misses the vertical direction.

As we remarked before, from the visualization point of view, the cylindrical sampling is more expensive than the cubic environment mapping. In fact, the visible region, obtained as the intersection of the viewing pyramid with the cylinder, has horizontal curved boundaries as shown by the upper image of Figure 16.20. A warping must be applied to correct the image and map it on the screen. This warping is shown in Figure 16.20.

16.7 Image–Based Navigation

In contrast with virtual panoramas, which did not allow arbitrary movement of the observer, the image-based navigation problem enables variable position and viewing direction of the observer. In this way, the scene samples will usually have a more complex structure and carry more information, which will be necessary to allow free navigation.

This section will describe a particular image-based rendering method to navigate an environment, from [Darsa et al., 1997], which is targeted at synthetic scenes. Synthetic scenes offer the advantage of having the depth information easily available when sampling the plenoptic function. The method we will describe uses texture-mapping hardware acceleration in the reconstruction process to achieve real-time performance.

First, we will give an overview of the method in order to correctly pose the problems involved, which will be discussed in the sections to follow.

16.7.1   An Overview of the Method

Cubical environment maps are used to sample the plenoptic function, and depth information is included in the samples for each face of the cube. Each of these samples is called an *environment node* because of its role in the navigation graph.

Using this kind of sample directly in the reconstruction phase is straightforward and yields results that are independent of scene complexity. Given an image I of resolution $m \times n$, we can reconstruct the scene from the original viewing position by reprojecting each pixel back onto object space. This results in a 3D triangle mesh M of resolution $(m + 1) \times (n + 1)$, which is texture mapped by the image I. Each vertex is projected back onto object space by using the depth component and the inverse of the original projection transformation. This 3D object, viewed from the original position, is exactly equal to the image I. This somewhat naïve scheme for reconstructing the scene has a complexity equal to the resolution of the image, and is independent of the complexity of the original 3D models.

If instead of using the original samples directly, they are simplified, the reconstruction phase can be accelerated.

In the sections that follow we will discuss the two problems: sample simplification and reconstruction.

16.7.2   Sample Simplification

The simplification is done in image space, using the depth information of the prerendered images. This simplification results in a far smaller number of triangles to be sent down the graphics pipeline. Note that this simplification step acts as a filter of the original samples and is done in a preprocessing step, still in the first part of the image-based rendering pipeline shown in Figure 16.6.

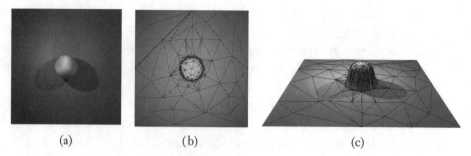

(a)	(b)	(c)

Figure 16.21   Range image triangulation: input image (a), 2D texture coordinates (b), and 3D triangulation textured by input image (c). See also color plate 16.21.

The goals of the simplification step are

- to match the object silhouettes, which correspond to depth discontinuities in the range images, as accurately as possible;
- to detect the areas in the depth information that are almost linear, and approximate them by triangles, which effectively corresponds to a view-dependent simplification of the object models; and
- to further refine the objects that are closer, where the parallax effect is more noticeable.

Since this must be done while minimizing the error in the scene representation, it is important to subdivide the nonlinear areas of the objects that are away from discontinuities as well, so that the geometry representation is more faithful, and the parallax effect *within* the objects can be simulated. Also, due to the perspective projection, the more distant an object is, the less relevant it is to the observer, and the less noticeable is its parallax effect. In this way, the mesh should approximate the object edges, and its sampling density should be inversely proportional to the depth.

This solution to the image-space-based rendering problem simplifies the environment, as seen from a given viewpoint, by linear polygons. This polygonal mesh is created by triangulating the depth information associated with the environment map, as shown in Figure 16.21. Each triangle in this mesh represents an object (or part of an object) at a certain depth.

16.7.3   Reconstruction

The reconstruction phase morphs the samples: the samples are warped to bring them to a registered position, and then are blended to produce the final image. Each of these steps is explained in the following sections.

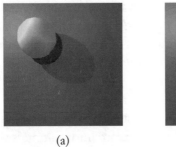

(a)   (b)

Figure 16.22   Visibility gaps: black (a) and filled by linear interpolation (b).

Warping the Samples

The parallax effect can be correctly simulated by warping each of the triangles that resulted from the simplification step appropriately. Since image warping can be efficiently performed with hardware assistance through texture mapping, we determine the appropriate projective transformation, which is then applied to this mesh textured by the environment map colors. The hardware z-buffer is used to resolve occlusions, or mesh *foldovers*.

The polygonal mesh derived from the depth information is in fact a 3D triangulation that, when viewed from the original viewpoint, will look exactly like the flat image. The triangulation can be reprojected to any other arbitrary viewpoint in space by using standard viewing transformations, such as in the side view shown in Figure 16.21(c).

When an observer moves, regions not visible from the original viewing parameters appear. These visibility gaps can be either shown in a background color or filled by a linear interpolation of the colors of their vertices. Both options are shown in Figure 16.22, where the observer has moved down and to the right from the original position, which was directly above the sphere. In an image-based navigation system, the visibility information from the original viewpoint is projected to a 2D plane and any obscured objects are "lost." Therefore, without a complete sample of the plenoptic function, the system does not have any information to fill uncovered areas, and an interpolation is just a crude approximation that is acceptable for very small gaps.

Morphing Between Warped Samples

Multiple samples are used to fill in the gaps resulting from mesh *tears* by combining z-buffered images from various samples using alpha blending and the stencil or the accumulation buffer [Neider et al., 1993]. This combination can be done based on the amount of texture each triangle carries. A measure for this information should be defined: the *triangle quality factor* is related to the angle that the normals of the original triangles make with the view ray, that is, how oblique is the triangle in relation to the image plane for a perspective projection. Triangles with greater angles are projected to proportionally smaller areas in 2D, and thus, less pixels will be texture mapped to them. When the angle is close to 0 degrees, the triangle is almost perpendicular to the observer, and its weight will be high, meaning that its texture information is well represented. For a large angle, closer to 90 degrees, the face is projected to a small area, and its quality will be low.

When the observer moves, this quality indicates how much a triangle can be warped without noticeable error. If the quality of a triangle is low, a modification in the observer position can cause it to become more visible, and the low quality of its texture would become apparent.

The information from the neighboring samples has to be merged to form a new view of the scene in real time, combining or replacing triangles based on their quality. In [Darsa et al., 1998], several ways to combine the warped images, based on different combinations of depth and triangle quality attributes, are presented.

The positional weighted blending technique, defined in that work, also takes into account the current position of the observer: the closer the observer is to the center of a node, the greater should be the influence of that sample on the resulting image. The morphing of two samples is achieved by warping the two original z-buffered images I_1^z and I_2^z to the current observer position, yielding $I_1^{z'}$ and $I_2^{z'}$. Let c_1 and c_2 be the colors of the warped images at pixel p, z_1 and z_2 be the corresponding depths, and q_1 and q_2 the qualities, that is, $(c_1, z_1, q_1) = I_1^{z'}(p)$ and $(c_2, z_2, q_2) = I_2^{z'}(p)$. The final color at position p is then obtained by multiplying the triangle qualities by a factor proportional to the distance d_i of the observer from the center of the node i:

$$c = \begin{cases} c_1, & \text{if } z_1 < z_2 - \delta \\ c_2, & \text{if } z_2 < z_1 - \delta \\ \frac{tq_1c_1+(1-t)q_2c_2}{tq_1+(1-t)q_2}, & t = \frac{d_2}{d_1+d_2}, \quad \text{otherwise.} \end{cases}$$

If the pixels are sufficiently different in depth according to an arbitrary constant δ, they are assumed to come from different objects, and thus, the pixel that is closer to the observer wins. Otherwise, a weighted average taking into

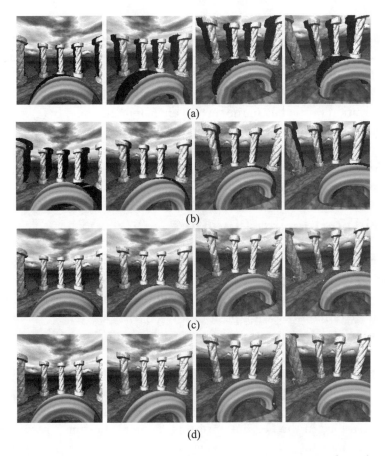

Figure 16.23 Navigation from the first node (a), navigation from the second node (b), blending of (a) and (b) parts (c), and ray-traced navigation (d). See also color plate 16.23.

account the distances to the observer and the relative qualities is used to compute the final pixel color.

This solution produces a smooth morphing between the samples: when the observer is exactly at the center, the resulting image is exact, and it becomes a combination of the two samples as the observer moves. Unfortunately, the blending computation cannot be efficiently implemented using the hardware with the current structure of OpenGL. The complex blending of the warped images based on depth/quality/position attributes has to be performed in software, by reading the warped images back from the frame buffer.

Figure 16.23 depicts a sequence of frames in a navigation using two environment nodes. The center of the first node is directly in front of the rainbow torus, and the second is to the left and front of the first center. In the navigation, the observer starts near the center of the first node, translates to the left, and then rotates to the right and to the bottom. In (a) we show four frames of the navigation warped from the first environment node (the gaps represent points with visibility problems causes by parallax). In (b) we show frames of the navigation warped from the second environment node. In (c) we show the blending of the two warped sequences in (a) and (b). For comparison purposes we have included in (d) an actual ray tracing of the navigation at the same viewpoints.

16.8 Hybrid Rendering Pipelines

The basic problem in image-based rendering consists in devising good techniques to represent and reconstruct the plenoptic function. The knowledge of the plenoptic function gives the correct perceptual reconstruction of the scene from different viewing positions.

A complete representation and reconstruction of the plenoptic function, as envisioned in lumigraph [Gortler et al., 1996] and in light field rendering [Levoy and Hanrahan, 1996], needs a huge computational effort. Certainly, additional research will be necessary in order to make these viable computational approaches.

As described in the beginning of this chapter, fine-tuned reconstructions of the plenoptic function can provide more efficient rendering pipelines than the traditional one. On the other hand, a different approach consists in reconstructing a complete scene model, both geometry and illumination, from samples of the plenoptic function (e.g., reconstruct the scene geometry from a finite number of depth images). This approach, strongly related to computer vision, is called *image-based modeling*. Obviously, from the scene geometry, coupled with illumination models and a traditional rendering algorithm, we can successfully evaluate the plenoptic function.

This duality between reconstructing the plenoptic function or the scene geometry can be greatly exploited in the rendering pipeline. Certainly, reconstructing the 3D scene geometry takes us back to the traditional rendering approach shown in Figure 16.1. Nevertheless, we should point out that the use of plenoptic function samples can help in automating the scene modeling, which is typically the most labor-intensive step of the image synthesis process.

In fact, there exists a whole spectrum of possibilities between reconstructing the plenoptic function, and reconstructing the 3D scene geometry and

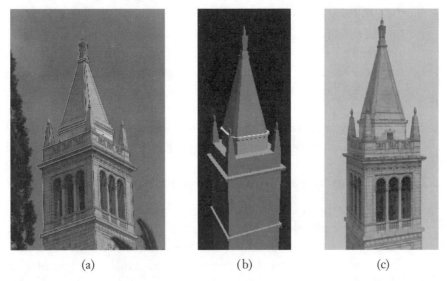

(a)   (b)   (c)

Figure 16.24 Photograph (a), reconstructed model (b), rendering (c) [from Debevec et al., 1996]. See also color plate 16.24.

illumination. In other words, different flavors of rendering pipelines can be obtained by combining image-based rendering with image-based modeling techniques. This strategy can be used to obtain hybrid rendering pipelines that are suitable for many different applications. Two examples of hybrid approaches will be given below.

16.8.1 A Hybrid Geometry and Image–Based Approach

Starting from samples of the plenoptic function (e.g., images), a simple geometry description of the scene can be created. The goal is to construct a perceptually good rendering of the scene from different viewpoints.

An example of one such hybrid approach has been given in [Debevec et al., 1996], where a simple geometric model is used along with different image samples.

The image samples are used with double purpose: to provide information to guide the construction of an approximate geometry of the model, and to provide view-dependent textures to give a good perceptual representation of the scene, completing the information missing from the simplified geometry.

Figure 16.24(a) shows a photograph with important features superimposed, (b) shows a model reconstructed from those features and the symmetry of the tower, and (c) shows a rendering with the photograph used as a texture map.

Rendering Using Projective Warping

Another interesting hybrid rendering pipeline when we have all of the scene information consists in avoiding the rendering of all frames. This can be achieved by combining rendered frames with image warping. Such an approach has been described in [Torborg and Kajiya, 1996], where a scene is navigated without rendering all of the frames: some key-frames are rendered and affine warps are used to compute new frames of the navigation. Certainly, better results are obtained by using projective warpings.

16.8.2   Image-Based Sampling and Reconstruction

Recovering the 3D geometry of the scene from samples of the plenoptic function is an example of an extremely ill-posed problem: for a given viewpoint, many different geometries provide the same images of the scene. This phenomenon of obtaining the same image from different geometries has been called *geometric metamerism*, analogous to a similar problem in color perception.

A very important question consists in developing a theoretical background for this sampling/reconstruction problem. In other words, it would be necessary to develop a Shannon theorem for the problem: devise sufficient conditions for a complete sampling and at the same time design robust reconstruction algorithms.

16.9   Comments and References

Image-based rendering is a very active area of research and has been used to navigate in environments modeled from real-world digitized images [Chen, 1995; Szeliski, 1996; McMillan and Bishop, 1995] and in synthetic scenes [Chen and Williams, 1993; Shade et al., 1996; Darsa et al., 1997; Mark et al., 1997].

The amount of data necessary for the lumigraph and light field rendering techniques somewhat restricts their use in current practical applications. Nevertheless, in [Sloan et al., 1997], the acceleration of the rendering process of these approaches is studied, regarding the time/quality trade-offs.

A combination of simple geometric building blocks with view-dependent textures derived from image-based rendering [Debevec et al., 1996] has resulted in a viable technique for navigation in environments that can be described by those simple blocks. Also, [Horry et al., 1997] derived simple 3D scene models from photographs that allowed navigation in a single image.

They use a *spidery mesh* graphical user interface, enabling the user to specify a vanishing point, background, and foreground objects in an existing picture easily.

There is extensive literature on reducing the geometric complexity of 3D models, including [Turk, 1992; Schroeder et al., 1992; Rossignac and Borrel, 1993; Cohen et al., 1996; Hoppe, 1996; DeRose et al., 1993; He et al., 1996]. A quite comprehensive overview of this area is found in the notes that Paul Heckbert organized for the SIGGRAPH '97 course entitled *Multiresolution Surface Modeling*.

More extensive information on the subject of visibility culling can be found in [Airey, 1990; Teller and Séquin, 1991; Greene and Kass, 1993; Luebke and Georges, 1995; Greene, 1996]. The use of frame-to-frame coherence to accelerate navigation can be found in [Bishop et al., 1994; Xia and Varshney, 1996].

References

Adelson, E. H., and J. R. Berger. 1991. "The Plenoptic Function and the Elements of Early Vision." Computational Models of Visual Processing, Chapter 1. M. Landy and J. A. Movshon (eds.), Cambridge, MA: MIT Press.

Airey, J. M. 1990. *Increasing Update Rates in the Building Walkthrough System with Automatic Model-Space Subdivision and Potentially Visible Set Calculations*. Ph.D. Thesis, University of North Carolina at Chapel Hill, Department of Computer Science.

Bishop, Gary, Henry Fuchs, Leonard McMillan, and Ellen Zagier. 1994. Frameless Rendering: Double Buffering Considered Harmful. *Computer Graphics (SIGGRAPH '94 Proceedings)*, 175–176.

Blinn, James F., and M. E. Newell. 1976. Texture and Reflection in Computer Generated Images. *Communications of the ACM,* **19**(10), 542–547.

Chen, Shenchang Eric. 1995. QuickTime VR—An Image-Based Approach to Virtual Environment Navigation. *Computer Graphics (SIGGRAPH '95 Proceedings)*, 29–38.

Chen, Shenchang Eric, and Lance Williams. 1993. View Interpolation for Image Synthesis. *Computer Graphics (SIGGRAPH '93 Proceedings)*, **27**(Aug.), 279–288.

Cohen, J., A. Varshney, D. Manocha, G. Turk, H. Weber, P. Agarwal, F. P. Brooks, Jr., and W. V. Wright. 1996. Simplification Envelopes. *Computer Graphics (SIGGRAPH '96)*, 119–128.

Comment, Bernard. 1993. *Le XIX Siecle des Panorama*. Paris: Adam Piro.

Darsa, Lucia, Bruno Costa, and Amitabh Varshney. 1997. Navigating Static Environments Using Image-Space Simplification and Morphing. *Proceedings of the 1997 Symposium on Interactive 3D Graphics*, 25–34.

Darsa, Lucia, Bruno Costa, and Amitabh Varshney. 1998. Walkthroughs of Complex Environments Using Image-Space Simplification. *Computers and Graphics*, Jan.

Debevec, Paul E., Camillo J. Taylor, and Jitendra Malik. 1996. Modeling and Rendering Architecture from Photographs: A Hybrid Geometry- and Image-Based Approach. *Computer Graphics (SIGGRAPH '96 Proceedings)*, 11–20.

DeRose, T. D., M. Lounsbery, and J. Warren. 1993. *Multiresolution Analysis for Surface of Arbitrary Topological Type*. Report 93-10-05. Department of Computer Science, University of Washington, Seattle.

Gortler, Steven J., Radek Grzeszczuk, Richard Szelinski, and Michael F. Cohen. 1996. The Lumigraph. *Computer Graphics (SIGGRAPH '96 Proceedings)*, 43–54. *Computer Graphics (SIGGRAPH '96 Proceedings)*, 65–74.

Greene, Ned. 1986. Environment Mapping and Other Applications of World Projections. *IEEE Computer Graphics and Applications*, **6**(11), 21–29.

Greene, N. 1996. Hierarchical Polygon Tiling with Coverage Masks. *Computer Graphics (SIGGRAPH '96 Proceedings)*, 65–74.

Greene, Ned, and M. Kass. 1993. Hierarchical Z-Buffer Visibility. *Computer Graphics (SIGGRAPH '93 Proceedings)*, 231–240.

He, T., L. Hong, A. Varshney, and S. Wang. 1996. Controlled Topology Simplification. *IEEE Transactions on Visualization and Computer Graphics*, **2**(2), 171–184.

Heckbert, P. 1989. "Fundamentals of Texture Mapping and Image Warping." Master's Thesis, (Technical Report No. UCB/CSD 89/516). University of California, Berkeley *(www.cs.cmu.edu/˜ph)*.

Hoppe, H. 1996. Progressive Meshes. *Computer Graphics (SIGGRAPH '96 Proceedings)*, 99–108.

Horry, Youichi, Ken Ichi Anjyo, and Kiyoshi Arai. 1997. Tour into the Picture: Using a Spidery Mesh Interface to Make Animation from a Single Image. *Computer Graphics (SIGGRAPH '97 Proceedings)*, 225–232.

Levoy, Marc, and Pat Hanrahan. 1996. Light Field Rendering. *Computer Graphics (SIGGRAPH '96 Proceedings)*, 31–42.

Luebke, D., and C. Georges. 1995. Portals and Mirrors: Simple, Fast Evaluation of Potentially Visible Sets. *Proceedings of the 1995 Symposium on Interactive 3D Graphics*, 105–106.

Mark, William R., Leonard McMillan, and Gary Bishop. 1997. Post-Rendering 3D Warping. *Proceedings of the 1997 Symposium on Interactive 3D Graphics*. ACM SIGGRAPH, 7–16.

McMillan, Leonard, and Gary Bishop. 1995. Plenoptic Modeling: An Image-Based Rendering System. *Computer Graphics (SIGGRAPH '95 Proceedings)*, 39–46.

Neider, Jackie, Tom Davis, and Mason Woo. 1993. *OpenGL Programming Guide: The Official Guide to Learning OpenGL, Release 1*. Reading, MA: Addison-Wesley.

Rossignac, J., and P. Borrel. 1993. Multi-Resolution 3D Approximations for Rendering Complex Scenes. *Modeling in Computer Graphics*. B. Falcidieno and T. L. Kunii (eds.), New York: Springer-Verlag, 455–465.

Schroeder, W. J., J. A. Zarge, and W. E. Lorensen. 1992. Decimation of Triangle Meshes. *Computer Graphics (SIGGRAPH '92 Proceedings)*, **26**(2), 65–70.

Shade, Jonathan, Dani Lischinski, David H. Salesin, Tony DeRose, and John Snyder. 1996. Hierarchical Image Caching for Accelerated Walkthroughs of Complex Environments. *Computer Graphics (SIGGRAPH '96 Proceedings)*, 75–82.

Sloan, Peter-Pike, Michael Cohen, and Steven J. Gortler. 1997. Time Critical Lumigraph Rendering. *Proceedings of the 1997 Symposium on Interactive 3D Graphics*. ACM SIGGRAPH, 17–23.

Szeliski, Richard. 1996. Video Mosaics for Virtual Environments. *IEEE Computer Graphics and Applications*, (Mar.), 22–30.

Teller, S., and C. H. Séquin. 1991. Visibility Preprocessing for Interactive Walkthroughs. *Computer Graphics (SIGGRAPH '91 Proceedings)*, **25**(4), 61–69.

Torborg, Jay, and James T. Kajiya. 1996. Talisman: Commodity Realtime 3D Graphics for the PC. *Computer Graphics (SIGGRAPH '96 Proceedings)*, 353–364.

Turk, Greg. 1992. Re-Tiling Polygonal Surfaces. *Computer Graphics (SIGGRAPH '92 Proceedings)*, **26**(2), 55–64.

Xia, J., and A. Varshney. 1996. Dynamic View-Dependent Simplification for Polygonal Models. *IEEE Visualization '96 Proceedings*. Los Alamitos, CA: IEEE Computer Society Press, 327–334, 498.

17

Warping and Morphing of Plane Curves

Mᴇᴛᴀᴍᴏʀᴘʜᴏsɪs ᴏғ ᴘʟᴀɴᴇ ᴄᴜʀᴠᴇs is very important in the areas of cartoon animation, digital publishing, and special 2D effects. In the area of image processing, a planar curve describes the boundary between two regions. Therefore, curve metamorphosis is closely related to the area of image metamorphosis as well.

17.1 Planar Curves and Regions

A planar or plane curve is a 1D subset of the plane. More precisely, a topological planar curve, or simply a *topological curve*, is a subset c of the euclidean plane $\mathbb{R}^2$, which is locally homeomorphic to an interval I of the real line $\mathbb{R}$: for each point $p \in c$, there exists a 2D ball $B^2 \subset \mathbb{R}^2$ of the plane, centered at p, and a homeomorphism $\varphi : I \to B^2 \cap c$ (see Figure 17.1).

It is important to note that a topological curve does not admit self-intersections (see Figure 17.2) because no neighborhood of the intersecting point is homeomorphic to an interval.

17.1.1 Plane Curve Description

There are two basic methods to describe a plane curve: parametric description and implicit description. In the *parametric description* the curve is defined by some application $\varphi : I = [a, b] \subset \mathbb{R} \to \mathbb{R}^2$, $\varphi(t) = (x(t), y(t))$. The curve itself is described by the image $\varphi([a, b])$ of the interval. As an example, the

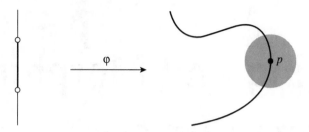

Figure 17.1   Definition of a planar curve.

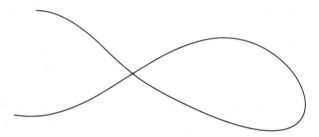

Figure 17.2   Curve with self-intersection.

equation $\varphi(t) = (t, t^2)$, $t \in \mathbb{R}$, describes a parabola. It should be noted that the parametric description in general does not describe a topological curve. Self-intersections might occur.

In the *implicit description*, the curve c is defined by the roots of some function $F \colon U \subset \mathbb{R}^2 \to \mathbb{R}$. More precisely,

$$c = \{(x, y); \quad F(x, y) = 0\}. \tag{17.1}$$

The set of roots that describes the curve is called the *inverse image* of 0 by the function F, and it is denoted by $F^{-1}(0)$. As in the case of parametric description, Equation (17.1) might not describe a topological curve. The equation $x^2 - y^2 = 0$, for instance, describes the pair of intersecting lines $y = x$ or $y = -x$.

The parabola described parametrically by $\varphi(t) = (t, t^2)$ is defined implicitly by the function $F(x, y) = x^2 - y$. Nevertheless, generally we do not have both descriptions for a given curve.

If the function F satisfies the condition grad $F(x, y) \neq 0$, for all $(x, y) \in c$, where

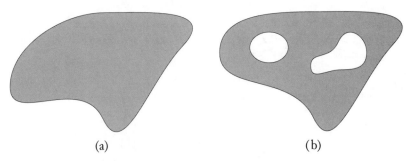

(a)   (b)

Figure 17.3 Simply connected region (a) and region with complex topology (b).

$$\text{grad } F = \left(\frac{\partial F}{\partial x}, \frac{\partial F}{\partial y} \right)$$

is the gradient of the function F, then c is a topological curve.

17.1.2 Planar Regions

A planar curve c is called a *Jordan curve* when it is homeomorphic to the circle

$$S^1 = \{(x, y) \in \mathbb{R}^2; \quad x^2 + y^2 = 1\}.$$

In other words, a Jordan curve is a planar closed curve that does not have self-intersections. A Jordan curve subdivides the plane into two regions; one is limited and the other is not (Jordan Curve theorem). The limited component defines a region of the plane that is *simply connected*. Simply connected regions of the plane are also called *Jordan regions* (see Figure 17.3(a)). Several disjoint Jordan curves define a region with a more complex topology, as shown in Figure 17.3(b).

17.2 Attributes of Plane Curves

The main attributes of a curve have a geometric nature. Among these attributes, we can mention the tangent vector field, the normal vector field, and the curvature.

17.2.1 Tangent and Normal Vector Fields

Given a parameterized curve $\varphi(t)$, its derivative $\varphi'(t)$ defines the *velocity vector* of the curve. For any point t_0 on the curve where $\varphi'(t_0) \neq 0$, this vector defines

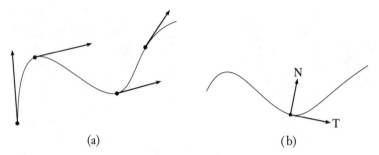

(a)   (b)

Figure 17.4   Velocity vector field (a) and normal and tangent vectors (b).

a line tangent to the curve at the point $\varphi(t_0)$, whose parametric equation is given by $r(s) = \varphi(t_0) + s\varphi'(t_0)$, $s \in \mathbb{R}$. The tangent vector field is illustrated in Figure 17.4(a).

If $\varphi(t) = (x(t), y(t))$, the velocity vector is computed by $\varphi'(t) = (x'(t), y'(t))$. If $\varphi'(t) \neq 0$, $\forall t$, the curve is called *regular*.

A curve φ is *parameterized by arc length* if its velocity vector field is unitary. This means geometrically that the parameterization function preserves the length of the interval where the parameter t is defined. When a curve $\varphi(t) = (x(t), y(t))$ is parameterized by arc length, the tangent vector $T = \varphi'(t) = (x'(t), y'(t))$ is unitary. The unit normal vector field of the curve c is defined by $N(t) = (-y'(t), x'(t))$. That is, N is obtained by a rotation of $90°$ of the tangent vector T in the counterclockwise direction (see Figure 17.4(b)).

Since the unit tangent vector T has constant length, it follows that $\langle T, T \rangle = 1$. Deriving this equation, we obtain $\langle T', T \rangle = 0$. That is, the derivative T' of the tangent vector is orthogonal to T. It follows that there exists a scalar $k(t)$ such that $T'(t) = k(t)N(t)$. The function k is called the *curvature* of the curve c.

Denote by $\theta(t)$ the angle of T with the x-axis (see Figure 17.5). We have

$$T(t) = (\cos \theta(t), \sin \theta(t)).$$

It is easy to prove that the curvature $k(t)$ is given by $k(t) = \theta'(t)$. Thus, intuitively, the curvature measures the rate of change of the direction of the curve.

The curvature $k(t)$ of a planar curve parameterized by $\varphi(t) = (x(t), y(t))$ can be computed by

$$k(t) = \frac{x'(t)y''(t) - x''(t)y'(t)}{((x'(t))^2 + (y'(t))^2)^{\frac{3}{2}}}, \tag{17.2}$$

where x', y', x'', and y'' denote first and second derivatives.

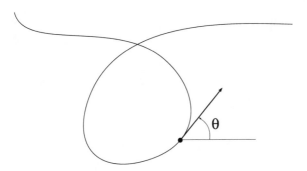

Figure 17.5   Curvature and curve variation.

Tangent and Normal Vectors to an Implicit Curve

Given a curve $c \in \mathbb{R}^2$, described implicitly by $F^{-1}(0)$, the gradient field of F

$$\mathrm{grad}\, F(x, y) = \left(\frac{\partial F(x, y)}{\partial x}, \frac{\partial F(x, y)}{\partial y} \right)$$

defines a normal vector field to the curve. For example, a circle of radius r, centered at the origin, is described implicitly by $C = \{(x, y);\ x^2 + y^2 - r^2 = 0\}$. The normal vector field is

$$N = \mathrm{grad}\, F(x, y) = \left(\frac{\partial F(x, y)}{\partial x}, \frac{\partial F(x, y)}{\partial y} \right) = (2x, 2y).$$

The tangent vector field T can be obtained from the gradient vector field of F

$$T(x, y) = \left(-\frac{\partial F}{\partial y}, \frac{\partial F}{\partial x} \right).$$

17.3   **Representation and Reconstruction**

The most common representation for planar curves is point sampling. The curve is represented by an ordered list $(p_1, p_2, \ldots, p_n)$ of n points. Figure 17.6(b) shows a sampling of the plane curve shown in (a).

Point sampling of a parametric curve $\varphi: [a, b] \to \mathbb{R}^2$, $\varphi(t) = (x(t), y(t))$, is a simple task. We take a partition

$$t_1 < t_2 < \cdots < t_n,$$

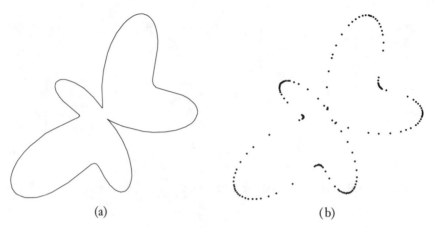

(a)   (b)

Figure 17.6   Point sampling (b) of the curve in (a) (Courtesy of L. H. de Figueiredo).

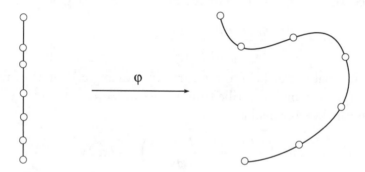

Figure 17.7   Sampling of a parametric curve.

of the interval $[a, b]$: the images of the partition points by the parametric equation, $p_i = \varphi(t_i)$, give the samples of the curve φ. This is illustrated in Figure 17.7. Sometimes it is more convenient to consider a partition as a subdivision into subintervals, and take the samples at the midpoints of each of these subintervals. Note that the partition induces a natural order on the samples that furnishes the necessary structuring to be used for curve reconstruction. Note also that this involves many of the sampling and reconstruction problems discussed in Part II.

If all intervals in the partition have the same length, the sampling is called *uniform*. When that is not the case, we call the sampling *adaptive*. There are many methods to compute the partition of the interval $[a, b]$ in an adaptive way. For a study of this subject, refer to [de Figueiredo, 1995].

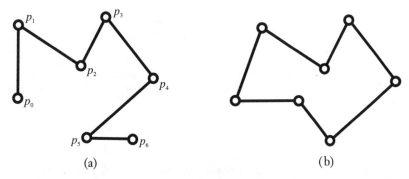

Figure 17.8 Polygonal curve (a) and Jordan polygonal curve—polygon (b).

The reconstruction of the curve from its samples is attained with the use of some interpolation technique. A large number of interpolation techniques exist in the literature, such as B-splines, Bézier, and so on. A very simple yet effective reconstruction technique is attained by using piecewise linear interpolation. Geometrically, two consecutive sample points p_i and p_{i+1} are connected by line segments. The resulting curve is called a *polygonal curve*. In this case, the reconstructed curve is a polygonal curve that approximates the original curve.

Polygonal curves play a very important role in the study of curves and will be examined in detail below.

17.3.1 Polygonal Curves

A polygonal curve is a sequence of line segments $p_0 p_1, p_1 p_2, \ldots, p_{n-1} p_n$ of the plane, as illustrated in Figure 17.8(a). Each element p_i is called a *vertex* of the curve, and each segment $p_i p_{i+1}$ is called an *edge*. If $p_0 = p_n$, we say that the polygonal curve is *closed* (Figure 17.8(b)). Closed polygonal curves that are also Jordan curves (i.e., do not self-intersect) are called *polygons*.

Polygonal curves have two important characteristics: they are simple to represent and encode on the computer; and there is a huge class of curves, called *rectifiable curves*, that are arbitrarily approximated by polygonal curves.

The above characteristics make the polygonal curves a ubiquitous representation for curves.

The process of sampling and piecewise linear reconstruction, which enables us to obtain a polygonal approximation to the curve, is called *polygonization*. As discussed before, polygonizations of parametric curves are easy to

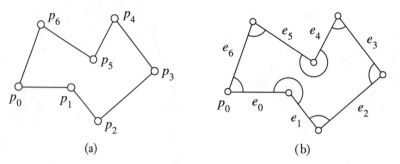

Figure 17.9   Vertex-edge representation (a) and edge-angle representation (b).

obtain. When the curve is described in an implicit form, the polygonization is more difficult to obtain. This problem is nicely addressed in [de Figueiredo, 1995].

17.3.2 Representation of Polygonal Curves

There are different representations for polygonal curves. The most-used ones are the vertex-edge and the edge-angle representations.

Vertex-Edge Representation

In the vertex-edge, the polygonal curve is determined by providing the ordered list of vertices

$$p_0, p_1, \ldots, p_{n-1}, p_n,$$

and the coordinates for each vertex. Figure 17.9(a) illustrates a vertex representation of a polygonal Jordan curve.

Edge-Angle Representation

In this case a polygonal curve with vertices $p_0, p_1, \ldots, p_n$ is represented by providing the following elements:

- a fixed vertex p_0 and edge $e_0 = p_0 p_1$
- the length $e_i = \|p_{i+1} - p_i\|$ of each of its edges
- the internal angle θ_i of each vertex p_i

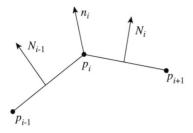

Figure 17.10   Normal vectors to the vertex (n_i) and to the edges (N_{i-1} and N_i).

Figure 17.9(b) illustrates this representation for a polygon. Except for the fixed vertex p_0 and edge $e_0 = p_0 p_1$, the angle representation is invariant by rigid motions of the plane. For this reason this representation is also called *intrinsic representation*.

17.3.3 Attribute Representation

Let $p = (p_0, p_1, \ldots, p_n)$, a polygonal representation of a plane curve c. An important problem consists in representing the attributes of c as attributes of the polygonal curve p. We will discuss this issue in this section. The Cartesian coordinates of the vertex p_i will be denoted by $p_i = (x_i, y_i)$, $i = 0, \ldots, n$.

Normal and Tangent Vector Field

The vector N_i, normal to an edge $p_i p_{i+1}$ of a curve c, can be computed by

$$N_i = (y_{i+1} - y_i, x_i - x_{i+1}).$$

Consider two adjacent edges $p_{i-1} p_i$ and $p_i p_{i+1}$. The vector n_i, normal to vertex p_i, can be computed by the average

$$n_i = \frac{1}{2}(N_{i-1} + N_i),$$

where N_{i-1} is the normal vector to the edge $p_{i-1} p_i$ and N_i is the normal vector to $p_i p_{i+1}$. Figure 17.10 shows normal vectors to the edges $p_{i-1} p_i$ and $p_i p_{i+1}$, and also to the vertex p_i. We can represent the tangent vector in an analogous way.

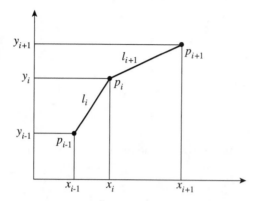

Figure 17.11   Computation of the curvature for a vertex.

Curvature

The curvature in each vertex p_i of the curve c is denoted by k_i. The computation of the discrete curvature k_i is based on the continuous curvature. Thus, to compute k_i, it is convenient that some expressions such as the first and second discrete derivatives are defined for each vertex $p_i = (x_i, y_i)$. Consider the vertices $p_{i-1} = (x_{i-1}, y_{i-1})$ and $p_{i+1} = (x_{i+1}, y_{i+1})$, which form the sequence of line segments $p_{i-1}p_i$, $p_i p_{i+1}$ (see Figure 17.11).

Define $l_{i-1} = \| p_i - p_{i-1} \|$ as the length of the edge $p_{i-1}p_i$ and $l_i = \| p_{i+1} - p_i \|$ as the length of the edge $p_i p_{i+1}$. The computation of the discrete derivatives x', in the direction x, and y', in the direction y, is given by

$$x_i' = \frac{x_{i+1} - x_{i-1}}{l_{i-1} + l_i}, \quad y_i' = \frac{y_{i+1} - y_{i-1}}{l_{i-1} + l_i}.$$

To compute the second discrete derivatives x'', in the direction x, and y'', in the direction y, it is convenient to define the discrete derivatives to the left and to the right, in both directions x and y. The derivative to the right, x_+', and to the left, x_-', in the direction x, are given by

$$x_+' = \frac{x_{i+1} - x_i}{l_i}, \quad x_-' = \frac{x_i - x_{i-1}}{l_{i-1}}.$$

Analogously, y_+' and y_-' are given by

$$y_+' = \frac{y_{i+1} - y_i}{l_i}, \quad y_-' = \frac{y_i - y_{i-1}}{l_{i-1}}.$$

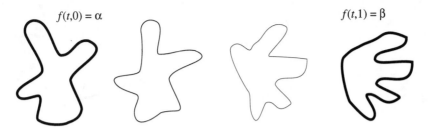

Figure 17.12 Morphing between two planar curves.

The second discrete derivatives x'', in the direction x, and y'', in the direction y, are given by

$$x_i'' = \frac{x_+' - x_-'}{l_{i-1} + l_i}, \quad y_i'' = \frac{y_+' - y_-'}{l_{i-1} + l_i}.$$

Once the expressions for the derivatives are defined, the curvature k_i, in each vertex p_i, is computed by Equation (17.2):

$$k_i = \frac{x_i' y_i'' - x_i'' y_i'}{((x_i')^2 + (y_i')^2)^{\frac{3}{2}}}.$$

17.4 Metamorphosis of Planar Curves

A metamorphosis between two planar curves α and β is defined by a k-parameter family of transformations

$$f : [0, 1] \times \mathbb{R}^k \to \mathbb{R}^2,$$

such that $f(t, v_0) = \alpha$, and $f(t, v_1) = \beta$, for some $v_0, v_1 \in \mathbb{R}^k$. By taking an animation path $\varphi : [0, 1] \to \mathbb{R}^k$, from v_0 to v_1 we obtain a one-parameter family of transformation

$$f : [0, 1] \times [0, 1] \to \mathbb{R}^2,$$

defined by $f(t, s) = f(t, \varphi(s))$.

For each $s \in [0, 1]$, $f(t, s)$ defines a planar curve, and as s varies from 0 to 1 this planar curve evolves from α to β (see Figure 17.12). The curve α is called the *source*, and the curve β is called the *target*. When the morphing is an isotopy, each intermediate curve is homeomorphic to the source.

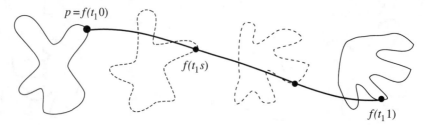

Figure 17.13   Animation path of a point in a metamorphosis operation.

In particular, for each point $p \in \alpha$, with $p = f(t_1 0)$, $f(t_1 s)$, $s \in [0, 1]$ defines a curve from the point $f(t_1 0) = p \in \alpha$, to the point $f(t_1 1) \in \beta$ (see Figure 17.13). This curve is called the *animation path* of the point p.

Notice that a metamorphosis from the curve α to β is completely determined if we know the trajectory of all points on α. In particular, if α and β are polygonal curves, we can define a metamorphosis by devising a correspondence between the vertices and defining an animation path connecting each pair of corresponding vertices. In this case, the animation path is called a *vertex path*.

17.4.1   Metamorphosis and Interpolation

According to the discussions in the previous section, obtaining a metamorphosis between two polygonal curves requires two steps. The first is to establish a correspondence between the vertices of the source curve and the vertices of the target curve. The second is to define a vertex path for each pair of corresponding vertices.

The vertex path is in fact an interpolation between the source and the target vertices. We have an infinite number of degrees of freedom to choose between different interpolation techniques. A simple choice is to use linear interpolation: Given the source and target vertices $v_0, v_1 \in \mathbb{R}^2$, the linear interpolation is defined by

$$p(t) = (1 - t)v_0 + tv_1, \quad t \in [0, 1].$$

Notice that $p(0) = v_0$ and $p(1) = v_1$.

It might occur that the two polygonal curves do not have the same number of vertices. In this case we have three options to proceed:

- Insert new vertices in one (or both) of the curves.

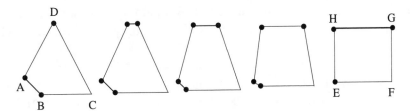

Figure 17.14 Multiple vertex correspondence in a morphing.

- Correspond one vertex of the source curve to more than one vertex of the target curve.
- Correspond more than one vertex of the source curve to one vertex of the target curve.

In the morphing sequence shown in Figure 17.14, the vertices A and B of the source curve correspond to the same vertex E of the target curve. Also, vertex D of the source curve corresponds to vertices H and G of the target curve.

The process of obtaining polygons with the same number of vertices in a one-to-one correspondence between them is called *combinatorial compatibility*. There are many different techniques for combinatorial compatibility in the literature.

Combinatorial Compatibility by Circle Mapping

This is a technique used by some morphing algorithms to achieve combinatorial compatibility. The vertices v_i^1, $i = 1, \ldots, m$ of the source curve α_1, and the vertices v_j^2, $j = 1, \ldots, n$ of the target curve α_2 are projected on circles of the same radius, and they are merged. The merged set of vertices are projected back onto each of the curves α_i. After these operations we obtain curves with the same number of vertices, and the vertices of source and target curves are in a pairwise correspondence.

Different mappings of each curve on the circle can be used. The most common ones are

1. polygon parameterization;
2. algorithmic based;
3. curve evolution; and
4. radial projection.

Polygon Parameterization. In polygon parameterization we parameterize the polygon by arc length and map the polygon vertices on the circle maintaining the distance relation between them.

Algorithmic Based. An algorithmic based technique that is physically inspired has been published in [Sederberg and Greenwood, 1992]. This technique described in Chapter 14 uses a minimization functional to determine where to insert vertices to produce a morphing.

Curve Evolution. Curve evolution techniques are based on the idea of the curve as a balloon that is inflated until it assumes a circular shape. We will discuss curve evolution techniques later in this chapter.

Radial Projection. Radial projection works for star-shaped polygons, that is, polygons that have an interior point with visibility for all vertices. The vertices or the polygons are mapped on a circle of radius R using a radial projection from the visibility point. Supposing that the visibility point is v_0, the radial projection on a circle of radius R, centered at v_0, is given by

$$T(v) = R \cdot \frac{v - v_0}{||v - v_0||}, \quad v \neq v_0.$$

Figure 17.15 illustrates the whole operation of combinatorial compatibility using radial projection for a star drawing and the drawing of a square. In Figure 17.15(a) the vertices of the star are radially projected onto the circle and then projected back onto the square. The same procedure is done in Figure 17.15(b), starting with the square and projecting the vertices back onto the star-shaped curve. After performing the operations above, the number of vertices on both curves is the same. Moreover, we have a one-to-one correspondence between the vertices.

17.4.2   Metamorphosis and Curve Representation

We have already mentioned in previous chapters that the blending interpolation of the morphing process is greatly influenced by the representation used for the graphical objects. In the case of polygonal curves, we have described the vertex-edge and the edge-angle representations. By using linear interpolation with these representations, we obtain different morphing techniques. This will be shown by the two examples below.

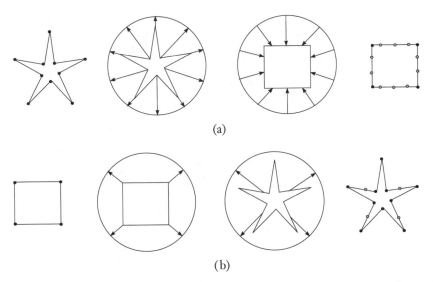

(a)

(b)

Figure 17.15 Combinatorial compatibility by radial projection: star vertices radially projected onto the circle then projected back onto the square (a) and the same procedure starting with the square and projecting back on the star (b).

Vertex-Edge Blending

This linear interpolation is applicable to polygonal curves using a vertex-edge representation. Given the source and target curves α and β, the interpolation is made between pairs of corresponding vertices (p_i, q_i), $p_i \in \alpha$ and $q_i \in \beta$: $(1 - t)p_i + tq_i$. The interpolation is done independently for each vertex without relating the vertex path with the shape and position of the source and target curves on the space (the vertex path is always a straight line segment). This fact, in general, may produce undesirable results in the morphing, as rotational features are not taken into account, and the technique is prone to foldovers, which manifest as self-intersections of the intermediate polygons. This is illustrated in Figure 17.16(a).

Edge-Angle Blending

This blending is applicable to polygonal curves given by an edge-angle (intrinsic) representation. The method uses linear interpolation on the elements of the representation, that is, linear interpolation of the edges and internal angles. In general, the linear interpolation of polygons using an edge-angle representation gives better results than the interpolation of vertex

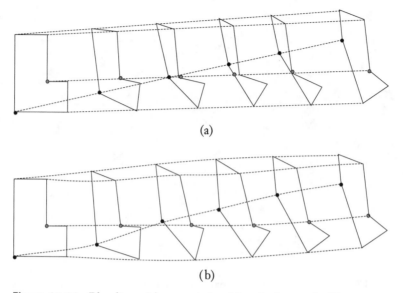

(a)

(b)

Figure 17.16   Blending with vertex-edge (a) and edge-angle (b) representations.

coordinates, especially in situations where the morph requires rotations. This is a consequence of the fact that the intrinsic representation is invariant by rigid plane motions. Figure 17.16(b) shows the linear interpolation between the two curves of Figure 17.16(a) using an edge-angle representation. Comparing the sequences in Figures 17.16(a) and (b), it is clear that the interpolation sequence that employs a representation using angles is superior.

17.5   Specification Techniques

Specifying the morphing is one of the important steps when performing a metamorphosis operation. This specification must be done in such a way to have a good user interface, and to allow for an efficient computation of the morphing transformation. A more complete account of specification techniques is found in Chapter 12.

17.5.1   Point-Based Specification

The user chooses a finite number of points $v_0, v_1, \ldots, v_n$ on the source curve and corresponding points $w_0, w_1, \ldots, w_n$ on the target curve (see Figure 17.17). The morphing transformation essentially has to perform two interpolations, as shown in the figure.

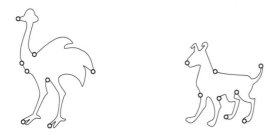

Figure 17.17   Point-based specification.

Figure 17.18   Vector-based representation.

Point specification is very effective for polygonal curves because those curves are defined by a finite number of vertices. In general, points are specified by the user in order to associate corresponding features of the target and source curves.

With respect to the user interface, the point specification can be implemented using a side-by-side interface: the user interacts with both the source and target curves using different windows to specify pairs of corresponding points.

17.5.2 Vector-Based Specification

In this specification, vectors are used to establish a correspondence between parts of the source and target curves. Figure 17.18 illustrates this technique.

17.5.3 Specification by Partition

This is a special case of specification by parts. The user defines a partition of the region described by the curve, and each partitioning set of the source region is associated with a partition set of the region defined by the target

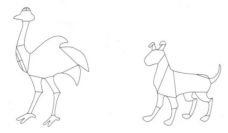

Figure 17.19   Partition specification.

curve. The metamorphosis between the two curves is attained by transforming each subset of the partition. This is illustrated in Figure 17.19.

17.6 Metamorphosis Techniques

In this section we will discuss some morphing techniques for plane curves that have appeared in the literature (see Chapter 14).

17.6.1 Metamorphosis by Circle Projection

These techniques use circle projection to attain a combinatorial compatibility, and devise some interpolation scheme to blend the two resulting polygonal curves.

An early description of curve metamorphosis using circle projection appeared in [Chen and Parent, 1989]. The method uses a convex projection strategy to attain a combinatorial compatibility and compute the interpolation path. Nevertheless, the paper does not provide details about the techniques used to compute the morph. The emphasis of the paper is on the use of metamorphosis as a modeling/design tool, as illustrated in Figure 17.20, where morphing is used as an aid in the design of glass frames.

In [Kent et al., 1992], combinatorial compatibility by spherical mapping is used to obtain metamorphosis for polyhedral surfaces. The techniques described apply as well to polygonal curves. The vertex path for the blending operation is obtained by using spline Hermite interpolation in such a way that the tangent to the spline at each vertex coincides with the vector of the vertex.

We should notice that morphing techniques based on circle projection generally give good results for curves where the correspondence of distinguished features is not important. When the curves have distinguished features, and

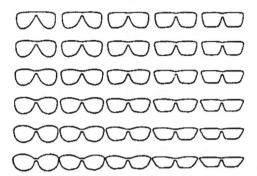

Figure 17.20 Metamorphosis and shape design [from Chen and Parent, 1989].

they should correspond in the morphing transformation, additional work, such as a warping phase, has to be done to obtain good results.

17.6.2 Algorithmic Morphing

Algorithmic morphing uses simulation techniques to obtain the warpings and the blending of the two curves. As we know, a morphing transformation is not uniquely defined from a user specification. One natural solution for an algorithmic morphing technique consists in determining the metamorphosis using optimization techniques.

An optimization technique inspired by methods from physics was introduced in [Sederberg and Greenwood, 1992]. The paper defines a stretching and bending work function, and the morphing between the polygons is computed in such a way as to minimize the work. Physically, the curves can be thought of as modeled by wires that can be stretched and bent during the morphing transformation.

The best morphing is considered to be the one that minimizes the stretching and bending work function. The source and target curves do not necessarily have the same number of vertices. In fact, new vertices are added during the process (automatically) based on the work minimization. The vertex insertion establishes a combinatorial compatibility that enables the use of some blending technique to compute the morph. Two different blending strategies have been used: vertex-edge blending and edge-angle blending.

Vertex-Edge Blending

In [Sederberg and Greenwood, 1992], after obtaining the combinatorial compatibility using minimization of the work functional, a linear interpolation is

Figure 17.21 Comparison of blendings using linear interpolation: linear interpolation of vertices (a) and linear interpolation of angles (b).

Figure 17.22 Horse trotting produced by a morphing operation [from Sederberg et al., 1992].

used to blend the two warped curves that are represented using a vertex-edge representation. As we have pointed out before, linear interpolation of vertices can introduce undesirable results, especially when the morph involves rotations. Figure 17.21(a) illustrates this problem: the arm of the dancer shrinks in the intermediate frames, due to the linear trajectories of its vertices.

Edge-Angle Blending

In [Sederberg et al., 1992], a morphing computation based on work minimization is used, but the blending phase of the morphing uses linear interpolation with the edge-angle representation. Therefore, internal angles and edge lengths are interpolated instead of vertices. The interpolation of angles and edge lengths is more effective than the interpolation of vertex coordinates, being very suitable for the animation of polygonal curves. Figure 17.21(b) shows the morphing of the dancer, using linear interpolation with an edge-angle representation. Note that the trajectory of the polygon vertices is not linear, which gives a better result for the rotating arm. Figure 17.22 shows the animation of a horse trotting. It uses angle interpolation to compute the intermediate frames.

Another optimization-based morphing algorithm, which uses a similarity function instead of a work function to obtain the vertex correspondence, is presented in [Zhang, 1996].

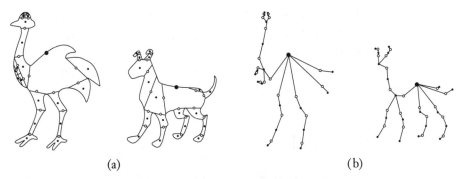

(a) (b)

Figure 17.23 Decomposition by star regions (a) and star skeletons (b).

17.6.3 Morphing Using the Star Skeleton

The specification should be planned so as to minimize the effort of giving all of the parameters that define the transformation. The general idea is that by transforming simpler shapes we will be able to reconstruct the transformation of the whole shape. This idea is exploited in its essence in the star skeleton technique introduced in [Shapira and Rappoport, 1995].

The morphing uses a specification by parts. Consider two curves α and β and the planar regions R_α, R_β that they define. First, we obtain a partition of these two regions:

$$R_\alpha = \bigcup_i R_i^\alpha, \qquad R_\beta = \bigcup_j R^\beta,$$

such that the partition sets R_i^α and R_j^β are star polygons. This is shown in Figure 17.23(a).

From the partition of the two regions, we create a skeleton for each of the regions called a *star skeleton*. This is a hierarchy of polygonal curves, as described below.

First, we take the midpoint of each edge in the region decomposition. In Figure 17.23(a) these midpoints are indicated by the small circles. For each star polygon of the decomposition, we take an interior point that has visibility for all vertices of the polygon. These points are called *star points*. In Figure 17.23(a) the star points are indicated by small black disks.

The star skeleton of the region is a dual graph of the region decomposition by star polygons. More precisely, it is the hierarchy of segments that is rooted at some star point, and connects the star points and the edge midpoints. Figure 17.23(b) shows the star skeleton for the curves in Figure 17.23(a).

The skeleton uses an edge-angle representation for each of the polygonal curves in the hierarchy. The metamorphosis is obtained in two steps. First, we compute a metamorphosis between the star skeletons. Second, for each morphed skeleton, we compute the transformed star polygons of the decomposition. From these polygons we obtain the morphed region.

17.7 Warping by Normal Evolution

This section will study the problem of warping by curve evolution. Later on, this technique will be used to obtain a mapping from the curve to a circle, which is useful in achieving combinatorial compatibility.

Let φ be a planar curve, defined parametrically by $\varphi(t) = (x(t), y(t))$. *Curve evolution* is just another name for a one-parameter warping family of curves. More precisely, an evolution of the curve φ is a family of curves $\varphi(t, s)$, $s \in [0, \infty)$, such that $\varphi(t, 0) = \varphi(t)$. Note that t is the curve parameter, while s is the evolution parameter. This is illustrated in Figure 17.24. For each value of the parameter s, there is a transformation $T_s : \varphi \to \mathbb{R}^2$, which defines a curve $\varphi(t, s)$.

For each point $p = \varphi(t_0)$ on the curve φ, $\varphi(t_0, s)$ defines the animation path of the point p along the evolution. The velocity vector $\partial \varphi(t_0, s)/\partial s$ of the curve is called the *evolution velocity vector.*

17.7.1 Normal Evolution

We are interested in studying the evolution of curves where the evolution velocity vector $\partial \varphi/\partial s$ is orthogonal to the curve. This is called a *normal evolution*. More precisely, if N is the unit normal vector field to the curve $\varphi(t)$, we have

$$\frac{\partial \varphi}{\partial s}(t, s) = F(\varphi(s))N(\varphi(t)),$$

where the scalar-valued function F is the *speed function* of the evolution. In general, F depends on different parameters associated with the curve geometry. When F is constant, the evolution produces offset curves, widely used in computer-aided design and manufacturing.

We should point out that the warping of a curve by normal evolution might present foldovers, which geometrically manifest as self-intersections of the evolving curves. Foldovers of offset curves are well known in computer-aided

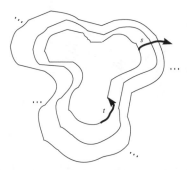

Figure 17.24 Family of curves defined by an evolution.

geometric design. The example below (from [Sethian, 1996]) illustrates this fact.

Example 17.1 (Evolution with Foldover) Consider the sine function defined by

$$\varphi(t, 0) = (-t, (1 + \cos 2\pi t)/2),$$

propagating with constant velocity $F(k) = 1$. The evolution $\varphi(t, s) = (x(t, s), y(t, s))$ of the curve is given by

$$x(t, s) = \frac{y_s(t, 0)}{(x_s^2(s, 0) + y_s^2(s, 0))^{\frac{1}{2}}} t + x(t, 0) \tag{17.3}$$

$$y(t, s) = \frac{-x_s(t, 0)}{(x_s^2(s, 0) + y_s^2(s, 0))^{\frac{1}{2}}} t + y(t, 0). \tag{17.4}$$

As indicated in Figure 17.25(a), this evolution creates a singularity, which develops into self-intersections. We are interested in evolution methods that do not produce foldover problems. That is, we would like to have an evolution of the sine function above, as depicted in Figure 17.25(b).

Foldover in the normal evolution can be avoided by modulating the speed of the evolution by the curvature. Intuitively, the curvature functions as the viscosity in a diffusion process, dampening the variations of the curve and avoiding the formation of the singularities that cause the foldover. The beautiful mathematics behind this fact is extensively discussed in [Sethian, 1996].

The equation for the normal evolution when the speed depends only on the curvature is given by

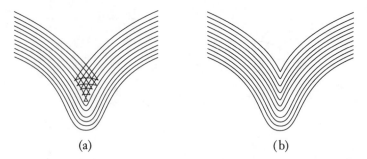

(a)   (b)

Figure 17.25 Evolution with foldover (a) and evolution without foldover (b) [from Sethian, 1996].

$$\frac{\partial \varphi}{\partial s}(t, s) = F(k(\varphi(t)))N(\varphi(t)). \tag{17.5}$$

If the curve φ is parameterized by $\varphi(t) = (x(t), y(t))$, we can easily compute the equations for normal evolution in coordinates.

In fact, $\varphi_s(t, s) = (x_s(t, s), y_s(t, s))$,

$$k(x, y) = \frac{y_{ss}x_s - x_{ss}y_s}{(x_s^2 + y_s^2)^{\frac{3}{2}}}, \qquad \text{and}$$

$$N(x, y) = \left(\frac{x_s}{(x_s^2 + y_s^2)^{\frac{1}{2}}}, \frac{y_s}{(x_s^2 + y_s^2)^{\frac{1}{2}}} \right),$$

hence

$$x_s(t, s) = F\left(\frac{y_{ss}x_s - x_{ss}y_s}{(x_s^2 + y_s^2)^{\frac{3}{2}}} \right) \frac{x_s}{(x_s^2 + y_s^2)^{\frac{1}{2}}},$$

$$y_s(t, s) = F\left(\frac{y_{ss}x_s - x_{ss}y_s}{(x_s^2 + y_s^2)^{\frac{3}{2}}} \right) \frac{y_s}{(x_s^2 + y_s^2)^{\frac{1}{2}}}.$$

The new curve results from $\varphi(t, s) + \varphi_s(t, s)$, as shown in Figure 17.26.

As an illustration of a normal evolution where the speed depends only on the curvature, consider the case where the speed of the evolution is proportional to the curvature, that is,

$$F(\varphi(t)) = ak(\varphi(t)), \qquad a = \text{constant}.$$

Figure 17.27 illustrates the evolution of a curve with $a < 0$. Notice that the inflection points ($k = 0$) remain fixed. Points with curvature $k > 0$ (convex

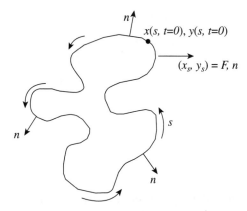

Figure 17.26 Normal evolution [from Sethian, 1996].

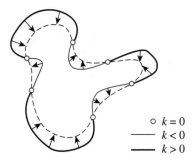

Figure 17.27 Convex evolution of a Jordan curve.

points) move inward, and points with curvature $k < 0$ (concave points) move outward.

It can be shown that in this case a smooth curve remains smooth during the evolution. Even more remarkable is the result below, proved in [Grayson, 1987]: *Any Jordan curve evolves to a convex curve regardless of its initial shape.* This shows that normal evolution can be used to define a circle mapping in order to achieve combinatorial compatibility.

17.8 Metamorphosis by Guided Warping

In the remainder of this chapter, we will describe a morphing technique introduced in [Carmel and Cohen-Or, 1997] that accomplishes a morphing

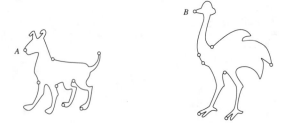

Figure 17.28   Source and target objects.

between two curves by using guided warping between the source and the target curves.

17.8.1   Steps for Guided Warping

The source and target curves are polygons and the morphing uses a point specification technique: the user chooses vertices on the source curves and their corresponding vertices on the target. The morphing transformation is accomplished in four steps:

1. user specification
2. approximate alignment
3. combinatorial compatibility
4. morphing computation

We will use the example of a morphing from a drawing of a dog and an ostrich (Figure 17.28) to give a brief explanation of the above steps. More details will be given in the sections to come.

User Specification

The user point specification in Figure 17.28 is shown by small circles. A side-by-side interface is used: point *A* corresponds to point *B*, and the other points correspond in an ordered way.

Approximate Alignment

From the specification, a warping operation is computed over the source polygon, so that an approximate alignment of the two curves is obtained. This alignment makes a correspondence between a set of features given by the user specification. The larger the number of points specified by the user, the

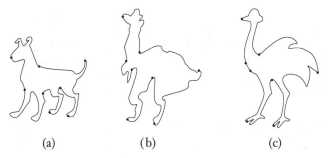

Figure 17.29   Source curve (a), approximate alignment (b), and target curve (c).

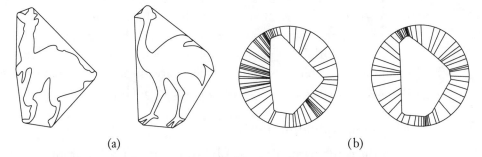

Figure 17.30   Convex evolution (a) and radial projection (b).

better will be the matching between the deformed source object and the target object. The illustration in the center of Figure 17.29 shows the approximate alignment of the dog with the ostrich after the warping.

Combinatorial Compatibility

After the initial alignment, it is necessary to make a combinatorial compatibility between the source and target curves, in such a way that they have the same number of vertices and there is a one-to-one correspondence among them. The method to accomplish this employs a normal evolution. Initially, both the source and target objects are warped using a normal evolution, until convex curves are obtained (see Figure 17.30(a)). After this evolution to a convex curve, a combinatorial compatibility between the two convex curves is made using radial projection, as illustrated in Figure 17.30(b).

The normal evolution defines a natural mapping between the vertices of the original curves and the vertices of the corresponding convex curves. Therefore, the combinatorial compatibility between the convex curves enables us

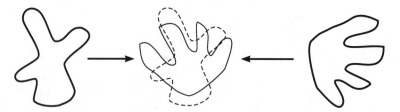

Figure 17.31   Morphing computation.

to attain a combinatorial compatibility between the original source and target curves.

Note that, because of the approximated initial alignment of the second step, the two convex curves obtained after the evolution stage are very close to each other. This fact guarantees the correspondence between their features during the combinatorial compatibilization process. In fact, vertices that represent common characteristics of both objects are automatically mapped in regions that are very close in each circle (Figure 17.30(b)).

Morphing Computation

After the combinatorial compatibility, we could use linear interpolation to do a *morphing computation* of the transformation (vertex path). Nevertheless, we know that linear interpolation is generally not a good choice. The morphing is computed in two steps: a rigid deformation, to bring the objects close together, followed by a linear interpolation of the vertices.

Denote by λ the morphing interpolation parameter. For each λ we compute the "best" rigid warping (rotation + translation) that brings the source curve close to the target curve, and the inverse rigid warping for the target curve. This results in two intermediate curves that are close together (see Figure 17.31). The vertices of these two objects are linearly interpolated to obtain the vertices of the morphed curve at time λ.

In the following sections we will give more details about the above steps.

17.8.2   Approximate Alignment

Given n specification points $s_1, s_2, \ldots, s_n$ of the source curve C_s, and their correspondents $t_1, t_2, \ldots, t_n$ in the target curve C_t, the warping alignment operation $W: C_s \to C_t$ satisfies $W(s_i) = t_i$, $1 \leq i \leq n$. The source curve C_s deformed in such a way that the specification points are mapped in the corresponding points in the target curve. The transformation W is computed over the curve C_s, in two steps: in the first step, a rigid alignment warping A is performed; in the second step, a nonlinear transformation E over the object $A(C_s)$ is performed. In that way, the warping over the source curve C_s is defined by a transformation $W: C_s \rightarrow \mathbb{R}^2$, $W(C_s) = E(A(C_s))$. The computation of the transformations A and E are explained below.

Rigid Warping

The rigid transformation $A: C_s \rightarrow \mathbb{R}^2$ is defined by $A = R_\theta + v$, where R_θ is a rotation of angle θ applied to the curve C_s, and v is a translation vector. The transformation A is used to rotate and translate the source curve in such a way that it is positioned in the best possible alignment with the target curve C_t. This problem is known in the literature as *rigid registration*.

Note that the specification points s_i do not coincide with the corresponding points t_i, after the transformation A is applied. The computation of the transformation A is done through the minimization of the sum of the distances between all pairs of points in the specification. In other words, we have to minimize

$$\sum_{i=1}^{n} ||A(s_i) - t_i||^2.$$

This least-square fitting problem is solved using *singular value decomposition* (see [Arun et al., 1987]).

Nonlinear Warping

The nonlinear transformation E deforms the transformed source curve $A(C_s)$ (i.e., the source curve, rotated and translated by A), such that the specification points of C_s coincide with the corresponding points in the target curve C_t. Let $p_i, i = 1, \ldots, n$, be the new positions of the specification points s_i ($p_i = A(s_i)$). The transformation E must be computed such that $E(p_i) = t_i$.

This problem of point interpolation can be solved using scattered data interpolation by *radial basis functions* (see Chapter 14, Warping and Morphing Techniques): the transformation $E: A(C_s) \rightarrow \mathbb{R}^2$ satisfies $E(p_i) = t_i$, $i = 1, \ldots, n$, and can be written in the form $E(p) = L(p) + Z(p)$, where $L(p) = Mp + b$ is an affine transformation (M is a real 2×2 matrix and b is a vector), and $Z(p)$ is a transformation defined by $Z(p) = (Z_1(P), Z_2(P))$, where the coordinate functions $Z_1(p)$ and $Z_2(p)$ are radial functions of the form

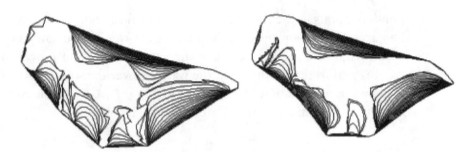

Figure 17.32   Normal evolution of two polygons.

$$F(p) = \sum_{i=1}^{n} a_i g(\| p - p_i \|).$$

17.8.3 Polygon Evolution

In this step we use a curve evolution technique to warp the transformed curve $E(A(s))$ and also the target curve C_t to a convex polygon. The evolution is computed using the discretization of Equation (17.5) of normal evolution, with the discrete expressions for the normal vector and curvature computed in Section 17.3.3. A comprehensive discussion of numerical methods to compute curve evolution can be found in [Sethian, 1996]. A simple finite difference technique can be implemented.

We observe that the purpose of computing the normal evolution is to obtain a convex polygon that projects radially on the circle. Therefore, an evolution into a star-shaped polygon would suffice.

At first sight, we could think of using the convex hull of the curve in the step above. This is not a good choice because we have to compute the mapping from the vertices of the original curve to the vertices of the convex hull curve. This mapping follows easily from the evolution method by tracking of the vertex path.

We could evolve the whole polygon to obtain a convex curve, according to the Grayson theorem described in Section 17.7.1. Nevertheless, the method used opts for an evolution technique that keeps the convex parts of the curve fixed (see Figure 17.32). This technique allows for better clustering properties of the convex vertices during the projection, which permits better feature matching during the metamorphosis.

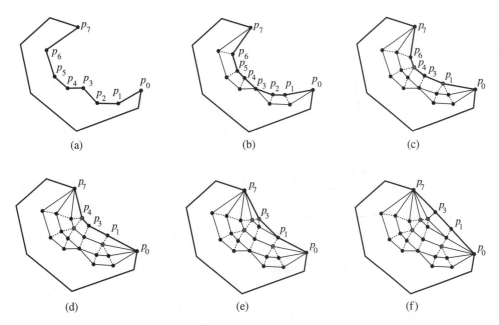

(a) (b) (c)

(d) (e) (f)

Figure 17.33 Convex evolution of a polygon: original polygon (a), same polygon with convex vertex p_3 (b), with collapsed p_1 and p_2 vertices (c), with collapsed p_4 and p_6 vertices (d), with collapsed p_3 and p_4 vertices (e), and the final convex polygon (f).

At each iteration of the evolution process, only the vertices of the concave parts of the curve must evolve. When an evolution is applied to concave vertices, they move in the normal direction. In that way, as the parameter s increases, the concave regions shrink, and the neighbor vertices in these regions get increasingly closer. When these vertices are too close, a *vertex collapsing* occurs (Figure 17.33). When this situation happens, the geometric configuration becomes numerically unstable. This means that the concave/convex relationship, the normal, and the curvature at these vertices become undefined, complicating the computation of the curve evolution. Thus, in the case of two vertices p_i and p_{i+1} collapsing, they must be treated as only one vertex p_i. Therefore, a single vertex of a convex curve in the end of the evolution process can represent several vertices of the initial curve. The evolution process of a polygon must be applied until the polygon becomes convex or, at least, a star polygon.

Figure 17.33 shows the convex evolution of a polygon. The polygon to be evolved is shown in Figure 17.33(a). In Figure 17.33(b), the vertex p_3 is convex, and therefore does not influence this iteration. In Figure 17.33(c), the

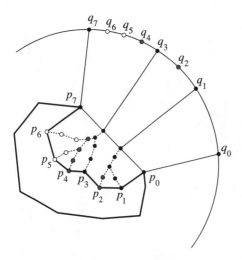

Figure 17.34   Projection of collapsed vertices.

vertices p_1 and p_2 collapse and, from that point on, p_1 represents both vertices. The same happens to vertices p_4 and p_5. In Figure 17.33(d), the vertices p_4 and p_6 also collapse, and p_4 represents p_4, p_5, and p_6. In Figure 17.33(e), due to the collapsing of p_3 and p_4, p_3 represents p_3, p_4, p_5, and p_6. Figure 17.33(f) shows the convex polygon at the end of the evolution process.

17.8.4   Projection to Circles

In this step the convex polygons produced by the evolution of the source and target polygons are projected in circles of the same radius.

It is important to remember that there are vertices in the convex polygon that may represent many vertices in the original polygon due to vertex collapsing during the evolution. Thus, the projection of the collapsed vertices must be reconstructed in the circle where the polygon was projected.

Figure 17.34 illustrates the projection of collapsed vertices. Vertex p_2 collapsed to p_1. The projection of p_2 must be reconstructed between q_1 (projection of p_1) and q_3 (projection of p_3). Vertices p_4, p_5, and p_6 have collapsed to p_3. The projections of these vertices must be reconstructed between q_3 and q_7. Figure 17.35 shows two polygons after convex evolution and projection to a circle of the same radius.

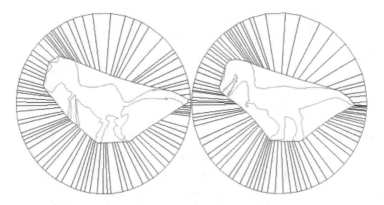

Figure 17.35 Convex polygons projected to circles.

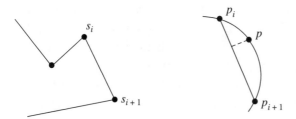

Figure 17.36 Mapping vertices on the original curve.

17.8.5 Combinatorial Compatibility

To obtain the combinatorial compatibility, the projected vertices on the circles from each of the curves are merged, resulting in a polygon inscribed on the circle containing all vertices from both convex curves. These vertices must be projected back onto each of the original source and target curves. The mapping is already defined for the vertices p_i, which correspond to vertices s_i of the original curve (see Figure 17.36). These vertices p_i are called *original vertices*. We will now describe how to map the new vertices. For each new vertex p, we find original vertices p_i and p_{i+1}, such that

- p_i and p_{i+1} are original vertices;
- there are no other original vertices on the arc from p_i to p_{i+1}; and
- the new vertex p is in the arc defined by p_i and p_{i+1}.

Now we project the vertex p orthogonally onto the segment $p_i p_{i+1}$, and we use the affine transformation L that maps the segment $p_i p_{i+1}$ onto the segment $s_i s_{i+1}$ of the original curve. The vertex p is mapped at $L(p)$. It should be noticed that the evolution process plays a fundamental role and greatly influences the quality of the morphing, especially on the concave parts of the curve.

17.8.6 Morphing Computation

Once we obtain polygons with the same combinatorial structure of vertices, we proceed with the computation of the morphing transformation. This computation is made in two parts: the interpolation of the rigid transformations, and the linear interpolation between the polygon vertices.

Interpolation with Rigid Transformation

Initially, we obtain a transformation A that gives an approximated alignment between the curve $A(C_s)$ and the target curve C_t. A is computed using the vertex correspondence. Note that the computation of A is similar in nature to the computation of the transformation used to obtain an approximated alignment in the beginning of the process (Section 17.8.2). But now we have the choice to use all of the corresponding vertices (or part of them). This rigid transformation A can be written as $A = R + v$, where R is a rotation and v is a translation vector.

Denoting the vertex path parameter by λ, for each $\lambda \in [0, 1]$, we interpolate linearly the rotation from the identity to R, and also the translation. This gives a one-parameter family of rigid transformations

$$A_\lambda = R_\lambda + \lambda v,$$

where $A_1 = A$ and A_0 is the identity mapping of the plane.

Each transformation A_λ, $\lambda \in [0, 1]$, applied to the source curve C_s, defines a curve $A_\lambda(C_s)$. We apply also the transformation $A_{1-\lambda}$ to the target curve C_t, obtaining the curve $A_{1-\lambda}(C_t)$, which is approximately aligned with the curve $A_\lambda(C_s)$. To compute the morphing transformation of the curve C_s in the time λ, we use a linear interpolation of the corresponding vertices in the two curves. Because the curves are, at this stage, close to each other, the linear interpolation gives good results and the chances of a foldover occurring are small.

17.8.7 One Example

Figure 17.37 shows the drawing of a lion and a duck. The lion polygon has 211 vertices, and the duck representation has 74 vertices. The specification

Figure 17.37 Morphing specification from a lion and a duck [from Carmel and Cohen-Or, 1997].

Figure 17.38 Morphing between a lion and a duck [from Carmel and Cohen-Or, 1997].

(shown by the black dots) uses 13 points. Figure 17.38 shows five frames of the morphing sequence.

17.9 Comments and References

In this chapter we have studied only morphing of planar curves. Metamorphosis of nonplanar curves is also a very important operation. An application is found in the area of motion warping. Motion trajectories are specified by the animation paths in 3D space; by warping these paths, we are warping the motion. By doing a metamorphosis between two different trajectories, we are interpolating between two different motions; that is, we are doing a motion morphing. We will not cover motion warping or morphing in this book. The interested reader should consult [Witkin and Popović, 1995].

We have opted to give a more detailed discussion and implement the technique of metamorphosis by guided warping for two reasons: the technique performs well, and it uses a rich arsenal of techniques encompassing the different elements that are generally found in a morphing computation. This technique was introduced in [Carmel and Cohen-Or, 1997]. It was implemented at IMPA by Adelailson da Silva as part of his master's thesis on curve metamorphosis [da Silva, 1997]. The illustrations of the method in this chapter were produced using this implementation. The examples and illustrations were inspired by the ones in [Carmel and Cohen-Or, 1997].

An interesting technique to compute a morphing between two planar regions is described in [Ranjan and Fournier, 1996]. The region is represented as a union of circles. This representation is used to define a distance between the two objects that is used to blend the objects.

In the beginning of this chapter we described the implicit and parametric methods for curve description. We have covered metamorphosis of parametric curves only (in fact, metamorphosis of polygonal curves). In general, metamorphosis techniques for implicitly defined objects do not depend on the dimensionality. For this reason, metamorphosis of curves defined implicitly will be covered as part of morphing with implicit functions, in Chapter 20, Warping and Morphing of Volumetric Objects.

The morphing technique using the star skeleton, described in Section 17.6.3, was published in [Shapira and Rappoport, 1995]. Details of the technique appeared in [Etzion and Rappoport, 1997].

For more information about the geometry of plane curves we recommend [do Carmo, 1976].

References

Arun, K. S., T. S. Huang, and S. D. Blostein. 1987. Least-Squares Fitting of Two 3D Point Sets. *IEEE Trans. on Pattern Analysis and Machine Intelligence, PAMI*, **9**, 698–700.

Carmel, Eyal, and Daniel Cohen-Or. 1997. Warp-Guided Object-Space Morphing. *The Visual Computer*, **13**, 465–478.

Chen, Shenchang Eric, and Richard E. Parent. 1989. Shape Averaging and Its Applications to Industrial Design. *IEEE Computer Graphics and Applications*, **9**(1), 47–54.

da Silva, Adelailson Peixoto. 1997. *Metamorphosis of Plane Curves Using Convex Evolution*. Master's Thesis. PUC-Rio (in Portuguese).

de Figueiredo, Luiz Henrique. 1995. Adaptive Sampling of Parametric Curves. In Paeth, Alan (ed.), *Graphics Gems V*. Boston: Academic Press, 173–178.

do Carmo, M. P. 1976. *Differential Geometry of Curves and Surfaces*. Englewood Cliffs, NJ: Prentice Hall.

Etzion, M., and A. Rappoport. 1997. On Compatible Star Decompositions of Simple Polygons. *IEEE Transactions on Visualization and Computer Graphics*, **3**(1), 87–95.

Grayson, M. 1987. The Heat Equation Shrinks Embedded Plane Curves to Round Points. *J. Diff. Geom.*, **26**, 285.

Kent, J. R., W. E. Carlson, and R. E. Parent. 1992. Shape Transformation for Polyhedral Objects. *Computer Graphics (SIGGRAPH '92 Proceedings)*, **26**(2), 47–54.

Ranjan, V., and A. Fournier. 1996. Matching and Interpolation of Shapes Using Unions of Circles. *Computer Graphics Forum (Eurographics '96 Proceedings)*, **15**(3), C-129–C-141.

Sederberg, Thomas W., and Eugene Greenwood. 1992. A Physically Based Approach to 2D Shape Blending. *Computer Graphics (SIGGRAPH '92 Proceedings)*, **26**, 25–34.

Sederberg, Thomas W., Peishing Gao, Guojin Wang, and Hong Mu. 1992. 2D Shape Blending: An Intrinsic Solution to the Vertex Path Problem. *Computer Graphics (SIGGRAPH '93 Proceedings)*, **27**, 15–18.

Sethian, J. A. 1996. *Level Set Methods: Evolving Interfaces in Geometry, Fluid Mechanics, Computer Vision and Materials Sciences*. New York: Cambridge University Press.

Shapira, M., and A. Rappoport. 1995. Shape Blending Using the Star Skeleton Representation. *IEEE Computer Graphics and Applications*, **15**, 44–50.

Witkin, Andrew, and Zoran Popović. 1995. Motion Warping. *Computer Graphics (SIGGRAPH '95 Proceedings)*, 105–108.

Zhang, Yuefeng. 1996. A Fuzzy Approach to Digital Image Warping. *IEEE Computer Graphics and Applications*, **16**(4), 34–41.

18

Warping and Morphing of Images

THE MAIN PROBLEM OF COMPUTER GRAPHICS is to convert data into images. On the other hand, images are used as input to generate other images, in texture-mapping or in image-based rendering, for instance. Thus, images are central graphical objects. This chapter studies in detail the image warping and morphing problem. The computational elements are reviewed specifically for images, including image representation and combination.

18.1 Images

An *image* is a 2D graphical object embedded in $\mathbb{R}^2$. More precisely, an image is a function $f: U \subset \mathbb{R}^2 \to \mathbb{R}^n$, where U is a subset of the plane, and $\mathbb{R}^n$ is the attribute space. The function f is the attribute function of the image that associates for each point $p \in U$ an attribute value $f(p)$. The set U, called the *support* of the image, is generally a rectangle, and the set $\mathbb{R}^n$ is commonly the 3D *RGB* color space where the color attributes are described.

18.1.1 Image Attributes

Other attributes besides color can be associated to the image function. This rich variety of image attributes is important in applications on different domains. These range from the typical color or grayscale values to *depth images*.

The nature of the attributes will influence the operations that are more appropriate for the blending step. The relation between the type of the attributes and the different forms of blending will be described in Section 18.5.

Luminance and Color

The perception of an image is primarily characterized by color. There are several ways to represent the color attribute, and the choice of the representation scheme significantly affects how this attribute can be manipulated in the computer.

Color is a perception of an electromagnetic signal and is strongly influenced by the response of the sensors in the human eye. A given color is a spectral distribution containing a mix of wavelengths—the range of frequencies that can be detected by the sensors is called the *visible spectrum*. The human eye has three types of receptors, whose sensitivity peaks at frequencies roughly corresponding to red, green, and blue.

These three colors can be used as a basis for representing colors in the computer. This very popular type of system, generically called *RGB* color space, has several problems, mainly because the computed intensities have a nonlinear relationship with the perceived colors. An *RGB* color image is therefore a function $f: U \subset \mathbb{R}^2 \to \mathbb{R}^3$. For a more complete description of the use of colors in digital images, with emphasis on the sampling and reconstruction paradigm, see [Gomes and Velho, 1997].

Experiments also show that the human perception of *luminance* and *chrominance* are different, with a greater importance placed on the luminance values. The luminance of a color is an average of the color spectral distribution weighted by a function dependent on the sensitivity of the human eye receptors. It is also natural to use as a compact color representation the luminance values.

Grayscale, or so-called *monochromatic,* images use this type of representation. A grayscale image is a function $f: U \subset \mathbb{R}^2 \to \mathbb{R}$. *Bilevel* or *binary* images—perhaps the simplest type of image representation—are quantizations of grayscale images to two levels, usually black and white.

Images and Two-Dimensional Solids

A binary image defines a 2D solid of the plane $\mathbb{R}^2$, that is, a region of the plane. This solid is comprised of all points where the image function assumes

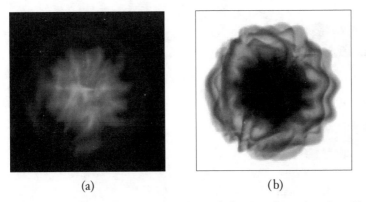

(a)   (b)

Figure 18.1   Image (a) and its α-channel (b). See also color plate 18.1.

value 1. Generally, image functions can be interpreted as density functions. In this case, an arbitrary image is considered a 2D solid with nonhomogeneous density function. This interpretation is very interesting because it extends to the 3D space in the study of volumetric objects (see Chapter 20).

Image Opacity

The concept of image opacity has very important applications in computer graphics. In the domain of graphic arts and publishing, opacity is used to cut out parts of images and to create composite images from a series of layers. In image synthesis, opacity is used as a representation of coverage of image samples.

The opacity measures the relative translucency of the image. It is a 1D attribute, usually ranging from 0 for completely transparent areas to 1 for opaque ones. The opacity attribute is a coordinate of the image function f and can be used as a separate image channel, which historically has been called *α-channel*. The α-channel is therefore a grayscale image function $f: U \subset \mathbb{R}^2 \to [0, 1] \subset \mathbb{R}$ (see Figure 18.1). A *mask* is a bilevel α-channel used to segment the domain of an image into fully opaque and fully transparent areas, although this term is also used as a synonym for α-channel.

A frequently used type of image is the so-called *RGBA*, or *RGBα* image, which contains both colors and opacity attributes. The image function is then $f: \mathbb{R}^2 \to \mathbb{R}^4$, and to each point p we associate the four values

Figure 18.2 Mask obtained through chroma-key.

$f(p) = (R, G, B, \alpha)$, of the image at the point p. Sometimes, a more convenient representation is to premultiply the α component, yielding $f(p) = (\alpha R, \alpha G, \alpha B, \alpha)$.

A popular way to obtain α-channels is to use a specific color or color range, called the *background color* or *chroma-key*, to indicate transparency. In this case, there is no need to have an explicit mask, as it is given implicitly by an *RGB* image and the chroma-key; that is, we can derive the mask f_α from f_{RGB}:

$$f_\alpha(p) = \begin{cases} 0, & f_{RGB}(p) \in K \\ 1, & \text{otherwise} \end{cases}$$

in such a way that the subset K of the color space determines the color key. Figure 18.2 shows an α-channel thus obtained from the image in Figure 18.1(a) using pure black as the color key.

When generating synthetic images, the α-channel is easily computed as part of the rendering process.

Depth Images

An image usually depicts a view of a scene. A very useful attribute, especially when combining images, is depth: the distance from the observer to each point in the scene that affects the image (this definition excludes translucent objects).

This information is natural and very easy to obtain for synthetic images, where it is the basis of the very important visibility algorithm of z-buffering. Images that have just this attribute are called *depth images* or *z-buffers*. Therefore, depth images with α-channel are functions $f: U \subset \mathbb{R}^2 \to \mathbb{R}^5$. As we will

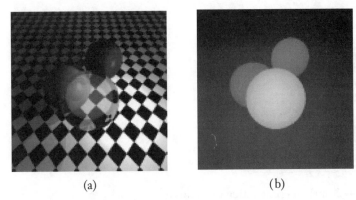

(a)　　　　　　　　　　　(b)

Figure 18.3 Ray-traced image (a) and its depth buffer (b).

see later on, depth images can be used for image combination. Depth images are also very important in the area of image-based rendering (see Chapter 16).

Figure 18.3 shows a ray-traced image and the depth buffer corresponding to the intersections of the primary rays. The depth attribute of an image can be very useful for generating certain postprocessed special effects. A linear fog or depth cueing can be generated by transforming the color as follows:

$$g_{RGB}(p) = \begin{cases} f_{RGB}(p), & f_z(p) < z_{near} \\ c_{fog}t + f_{RGB}(p)(1-t), & z_{near} \le f_z(p) \le z_{far} \\ c_{fog}, & z_{far} < f_z(p) \end{cases}$$

where c_{fog} is the color of the fog, z_{near} and z_{far} delimit the extent of the fog effect, and the linear fog factor is given by

$$t = \frac{f_z(p) - z_{near}}{z_{far} - z_{near}}.$$

Approximations to the depth-of-field effect caused by nonpinhole cameras can also be generated through postprocessing based on depth values [Potmesil and Chakravarty, 1982]. A variable amount of blur is applied to each point of the image based on the lens characteristics and the depth of the point.

18.2 Description and Representation

The manipulation of images is closely related to their representation. Certain transformations can be easier to implement, inherently more efficient, or of higher quality, according to the chosen representation.

Figure 18.4   Matrix representation of an image.

Representing an image involves sampling the 2D domain of the function, as well as discretizing its values. The problem of sampling and reconstruction of graphical objects has been studied in Part II. Here we will review the problem specifically for images.

18.2.1   Matrix Representation

A common representation of an image consists in subdividing its support using a uniform rectangular lattice, and taking samples of the image function in each cell of the lattice. If the support of the image is a rectangle, this representation is called a *matrix representation* (see Figure 18.4). The values of the image function f are also discretized to be manipulated in the computer, a process called *quantization*.

This traditional image representation gave rise to the raster display paradigm, making it especially efficient due to the tight relationship with typical hardware. On the other hand, as images must be regularly sampled, the transformation process will usually include a resampling phase.

18.2.2   Adaptive Sampling

A uniform sampling strategy does not match the image contents necessarily. If high precision is required, the global sampling resolution must be increased, often resulting in excessive sampling in some areas. Other schemes are possible that use nonuniform decompositions to match the details of the image function.

Quad-Trees

There are several ways to nonuniformly sample an image. One possible adaptive image representation scheme is the quad-tree–based image model

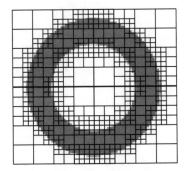

Figure 18.5 Quad-tree representation of an image.

[Samet, 1984]. This hierarchical subdivision scheme is based on a family of grids of variable resolution, each one with double the resolution of the preceding level. Areas of the image that have less detail information can be represented by elements of the low-resolution grids, whereas highly detailed areas are represented by finer elements (see Figure 18.5).

The name *quad-tree* comes from a treelike structure where each node can be a white leaf, a black leaf, or a gray node, with exactly four children. Although this scheme samples the image nonhomogeneously, it still uses a regular rectangular grid, which may cause aliasing artifacts.

Irregular Sampling

Irregular sampling strategies are less prone to aliasing, although they can introduce some noticeable noise. A possibility is to adaptively sample the images, with higher resolution over high-frequency areas, and to structure the samples with a Voronoi diagram [Darsa and Costa, 1996]. The dual Delaunay triangulation is then used as a basis to guide the reconstruction process.

Figure 18.6 shows an irregularly sampled image, with just 700 samples, reconstructed using Gouraud shading hardware; the Voronoi diagram used for structuring the samples is superimposed as a reference.

18.2.3 Multiresolution Representation

In this representation, the image function is represented in multiple levels of resolution f_i, $i = 0, 1, 2, \ldots$, and there are operators that change between the different levels (see Chapter 9).

Figure 18.6 Voronoi representation of an image.

Figure 18.7 Levels of a mip map representation.

Pyramidal Representation

This is the classical Gaussian pyramid multiresolution representation of an image, in which a sequence of images, each one half the resolution of the previous one, are stacked in a pyramidlike structure. Each lower-resolution level is a low-pass filtered version of the previous one. Therefore, each pyramid layer represents the image in a different scale. Figure 18.7 shows five levels of a pyramid representation of an image. Note that the information for all the lower-resolution levels fits in exactly one-third of the space of the base-level image.

Pyramidal representations of images have long been used in image processing and computer vision. Lance Williams [Williams, 1983] devised an interesting data structure to implement an image pyramid using a clever memory organization called *mip map* (Mip is an acronym for *multum in parvo*, meaning *much in little* in Latin). This structure uses a coordinate system (u, v, d) to access any information of the pyramid: (u, v) access the image pixels at each level, and d accesses different levels.

In this way, the mip map stores several prefiltered versions of the image, and when resampling, instead of filtering on-the-fly, it is enough to sample at the appropriate level in the pyramid, using the mip map structure. A careful reconstruction of the pyramid yields better quality samples:

- Simple box reconstruction yields the nearest sample.
- Bilinear interpolation results in a reasonable-quality intralevel reconstruction in (u, v) coordinates.
- Trilinear interpolation provides interlevel reconstruction by blending the results of two intralevel reconstructions using the d coordinate.

Wavelets

More compact pyramidal structures for multiresolution can be obtained using representation of images by wavelets. Also, by providing a space-frequency representation, the wavelets enable us to obtain localization of the frequency details on the spatial domain. This combination allows us to get representations with a good interplay between multiresolution and level of details of the image function. This fact can be greatly exploited in different operations with images, especially in image warping and morphing.

18.3   Image Warping and Morphing: A Brief Overview

Images are certainly the type of graphical objects that drove the applications of warping and morphing. In fact, analog image morphing by cross-dissolve (with no registration) was discovered by accident by French pioneer filmmaker Georges Méliés in the beginning of this century. A brief account of this is given in [Bordwell and Thompson, 1997]. Since then, image morphing by cross-dissolve has been used to obtain different transition effects in the movie and television industry (see Chapter 1).

We can identify five main areas that make use of warping and morphing techniques:

- computer vision and pattern recognition
- medical image analysis

- Remote sensing
- Special effects
- Visualization

In the area of *computer vision and pattern recognition*, warping is used as an aid to accomplish different tasks such as segmentation, shape reconstruction, and motion tracking.

In *medical image analysis*, image warping is used as an aid in computer-aided diagnosis for tasks such as tumor detection and other disease localization. Atlases of reference or template medical images are matched through deformation to identify diseases from measurement discrepancies or to assist surgical planning.

Remote sensing has many applications related to military, geological, and ecological problems. Image warping is used in remotely sensed data processing as a tool to correct distortions in captured images. These distortions are introduced by sensor errors or by external factors such as earth curvature or altitude effects.

In the area of *special effects*, morphing is commonly used in the movie and television industry to attain different kinds of transformations between objects on the scene. Less obviously, applications of warping and morphing for special effects include wire removal, replacement of bad frames, and glueing seamlessly long sequences that would be impossible to create otherwise. Examples of this last application include camera movements that go through closed windows and sequences with widely varying scale of detail, such as a fly-through that approaches a person, going from miles away into a close-up.

A very interesting and important application of warping and morphing in *visualization* is in the area of image-based rendering. We have dedicated Chapter 16 to this topic.

Early use of image warping in the area of remote sensing is found in [Markarian et al., 1971]. Several of the warping techniques described in this book have been used in this area. Interested readers can find information about early research in this field in the references [Bernstein, 1976; Goshtasby, 1986; and Goshtasby, 1987]. Also, in the area of medical images, the use of warping for registration dates far back. A comprehensive survey is found in [Brown, 1992].

The use of warping techniques to attain image registration in remote sensing and medical images developed very early and before their effective use in computer graphics. In graphics, image warping and morphing is mainly

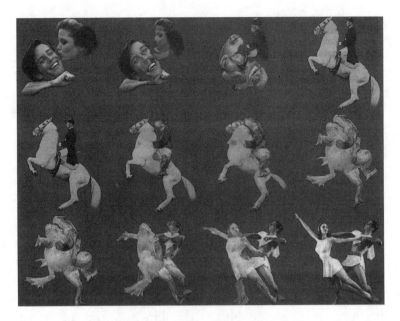

Figure 18.8   Image warping.

connected with applications in special effects and visualization. Early experiments with warping started at the New York Institute of Technology. A brief account of these activities is described in [Heckbert, 1994]: an image warping algorithm based on Coons patches was implemented and this algorithm was used by Tom Brigham to experiment with the technique. The beautiful warping sequence shown in Figure 18.8 dates from this period. The image warping technique using Coons patches is described in Part I of the book, and it is included on the companion CD-ROM as part of the *Morphos* system.

However, we should note that texture mapping, which, as we have seen, is intrinsically related to warping, was introduced in the literature by Ed Catmull in [Catmull, 1974]. In [Catmull and Smith, 1980] a clear connection was made between warping and texture. A good report on the subject of warping and texture mapping, including some warping applications related to image-based rendering, appeared in Paul Heckbert's master thesis [Heckbert, 1989]. George Wolberg's book [Wolberg, 1990] had a great influence on developments in the field of image warping and morphing.

For the reasons stated before, it is almost impossible to cover the many different applications and research articles in the area of image warping and morphing. But certainly the conceptual framework we have introduced in the book is very useful in understanding and classifying all of the techniques used in many different areas.

In this section we will make a brief survey of the work done, based on the different image warping and morphing techniques. We will focus on papers that have appeared in the computer graphics literature. Most of the techniques are described in Chapter 14. The use of image morphing in the area of image-based rendering is covered in Chapter 16.

18.4   Warping and Morphing Techniques

Many different techniques can be used to define the transformation of an image, including points, vectors, curves, and meshes. As images are 2D graphical objects, user interfaces to specify transformations can be easily implemented.

If the objective of the warping is to map image features, feature-based specifications are most suitable. As the dimensionality of the specification technique increases, the warping reconstruction becomes more restricted. Meshes, for instance, define very well the transformation of the whole support of an image, but are more cumbersome to manipulate.

Any technique presented in Chapter 14 that defines a 2D coordinate mapping is suitable for computing image warping. We review some of them here, taking into consideration the specification used.

It should be noted that a warping reconstruction technique can be used to obtain a function that will be applied to another specification, and this intermediate specification is then used to warp the image. Different hybrid techniques can be created in this way.

18.4.1   Affine Warping Computation

Warping using affine transformations was described in detail in Part I of the book. These warpings, especially rotations and scaling, are very important in image manipulation systems. The affine mappings are generally specified in a parametric form.

There are several computational techniques to compute warping using affine transformations. A good resampling scheme is described in [Fant, 1986]. A good description of the algorithm, including a pseudocode, is described in [Wolberg, 1990].

Specific algorithms to rotate and shear images appeared in [Braccini and Marino, 1980]. In [Weiman, 1980], an algorithm is described to rotate and scale images by decomposing them into 1D scale transformations and shear transformations. Another interesting algorithm for rotation is given in [Paeth, 1986] and [Tanaka et al., 1986]. These algorithms use decompositions of a rotation as three shear transformations. We have included the algorithm by [Paeth, 1986] in the *Morphos* system.

18.4.2   Point-Based

As we have seen in Chapter 14, if the warping is specified using a point specification, the extension of the function is a scattered data interpolation problem, and several warping reconstruction techniques can be used. For instance, piecewise linear mapping can be applied to a triangulation of the point set. Also, piecewise projective or piecewise bilinear reconstruction can be used. These techniques are described in Part I of the book.

Inverse-distance weighted interpolation can also be used, similarly to the 2D field-based warping technique described in Chapter 14 [Shepard, 1968]. Note that as we are using points instead of vectors, just the distance to the specification points must be used. As this scheme is global, taking into consideration all the points in the specification, it becomes more expensive as the number of points increase.

Another possibility is to use radial basis functions [Arad and Reisfeld, 1995]. The complexity of this technique also increases as we add more points to the specification. Some scheme taking into consideration just the points that affect a part of the domain can be used. Naturally, as discussed in Chapter 14, most scattered data interpolation techniques can be used (see [Ruprecht and Müller, 1995]). Radial basis functions and an inverse-distance weighted technique are included in the *Morphos* system.

18.4.3   Vector-Based

This specification uses oriented line segments instead of points. The advantage is that the specification is more expressive and compact: a source and a destination vector are enough to specify a local rotation, for instance. A careful reconstruction from the vector specification enables us to have a very flexible warping technique.

The pioneering work of vector-based morphing was done at Pacific Data Images (PDI) in the beginning of the '90s and was used to create Michael Jackson's classic video clip *Black or White*. The technique was described in [Beier and Neely, 1992], but it had been used at PDI's production environment two years before publication. Beier and Neely used a field-based reconstruction technique as described with details in Part III of the book. This technique is also implemented in the *Morphos* system.

It is possible to devise other reconstruction techniques such as a triangulation with restrictions, using affine interpolation inside each triangle. A piecewise affine transformation is obtained in this case.

Note that in both cases above, the warping reconstructions in the vector and point cases are very similar, which makes it possible to combine point and vector specifications in the same transformation.

Both point-based and vector-based techniques constitute examples of feature-based specification techniques. To corroborate the uncorrelated development of warping techniques in other areas, we should mention that a feature-based warping technique for images, in the area of medical images, was described in [Peli et al., 1987].

18.4.4 Curve-Based

It is straightforward to use a curve-based specification and convert it to a point or vector specification by carefully sampling the curve and using any of the above methods. An example is the use of curves and thin-plate spline interpolation [Litwinowicz and Williams, 1994]. Sometimes, working with the curve specification can be more convenient. Nevertheless, a converted specification will typically not result in the expected behavior, as the conversion can lose original constraints. We described in Part I the warping of an image using a Coons patch, and this technique is included in the *Morphos* system.

18.4.5 Two-Pass Computation

The matrix representation of an image is quite adequate to use two-pass computation techniques in the warping reconstruction, as described in Part III of the book (see also Part I). This technique consists in separating the transformation into a horizontal and vertical transformation, thus reducing the computation to 1D warps.

The use of this technique for images was pioneered by Ed Catmull and A. R. Smith in [Catmull and Smith, 1980], where it was used to apply a texture to a surface. In [Smith, 1987], the author shows how to use the technique to compute a wide class of image warping transformations. Also, the two-pass technique is very effective to compute warping using the free-form spline coordinate system.

18.4.6 Free-Form Coordinate Change

Although not easy to specify, this is an efficient technique for image warping. We use a free-form Cartesian coordinate system, and a change of coordinates is attained by warping the coordinate curves. For images, a very efficient implementation of these techniques can be done using a two-pass approach.

In fact, a two-pass spline mesh algorithm [Smithe, 1990; Wolberg, 1990] was the pioneering technique used to morph images using a warping alignment phase. In this technique, the warping reconstruction occurs as the image is traversed: the warping reconstruction was defined for scanlines (or scancolumns) of the image, because it coincides with the way the image is represented and traversed. This scheme enables very efficient implementations and is detailed in Chapter 14. This technique is included in the *Morphos* system.

18.4.7 Mesh–Based

The disadvantage of the use of free-form coordinates for images is that the coordinate curves are not necessarily aligned with distinguished image features. Adapted coordinate systems can be used, however. The representation of these coordinate systems can be done using meshes of different topology.

An interesting hybrid technique is the combination of active contour-seeking curves, or *snakes* [Kass et al., 1988], with free-form deformations [Lee et al., 1995]. The snakes lock on distinguished image edges and can track them during animations and aid the user specification. The use of multilevel deformations attempts to converge to the user-specified transformation, while avoiding foldovers.

18.5 Image Combination

We know that to obtain a good morph, we must devise good alignment warpings associated with good blending techniques. There are many different ways to blend images; for this reason we will refer to the blending operation as *image combination*.

We have seen some of the different attributes that an image can possess, and how they can vary in nature. This leads us naturally to define an image that takes values on an n-dimensional vector space: $f: U \subset \mathbb{R}^2 \to \mathbb{R}^n$, separating the different attributes into distinct components such as color, opacity, depth, and so forth. Consider a color, opacity, and depth image $f = (f_{RGB}, f_\alpha, f_z)$, and take a warping function $W: \mathbb{R}^2 \to \mathbb{R}^2$ that associates to each point p, a warped position $W(p)$. Recall that the warped image g is given by

$$g: \mathbb{R}^2 \to \mathbb{R}^n, \qquad g(p) = f(W(p)).$$

Therefore,

$$(g_{RGB}(p), g_\alpha(p), g_z(p)) = (f_{RGB}(W(p)), f_\alpha(W(p)), f_z(W(p))).$$

This means that each of the coordinate functions can be transformed, represented, reconstructed, and combined separately, as if they were three different images with simpler attributes. This may be highly advantageous; as the attribute combination step can be entirely different in those cases, it enables a more modular computation and potentially simplifies the interchange of attributes among images. However, more complex combinations may operate on the entire set of attributes, with correlations among the attributes, requiring the combination operation to be performed jointly. Some combination techniques will be studied in what follows.

18.5.1   Cross-Dissolve

Whenever we have functions f and g that take values on the euclidean space $\mathbb{R}^n$, we are able to blend them by using cross-dissolve:

$$h = (1 - t)f + tg. \tag{18.1}$$

This means that we can use cross-dissolve to blend different attributes of the image, other than color. We should remark that the vector space structure of $\mathbb{R}^n$ is of the utmost importance when we combine images using cross-dissolve. Figure 18.9 presents an example of linear interpolation taking place in two different color spaces. An interpolation between red and cyan, two colors that differ only in hue, is performed in both the *RGB* and the *HSB* (hue, saturation, and brightness) color spaces. While the saturation changes during the *RGB* interpolation, passing through a pure gray, the *HSB* interpolation visits a range of the spectrum, as it changes the hue value.

It should also be said that a perceptually linear color space may be desirable in certain color computations. Also, the image that reaches the observer is conveyed by a display device that has unique color responses. The relationship

(a)   (b)

Figure 18.9 Linear interpolation: *RGB* color space (a); *HSB* color space (b). See also color plate 18.9.

between the values that are fed to a display device I and the intensities it outputs O can be modeled by an exponential function:

$$O \propto I^{\gamma}.$$

It may be desirable to account for those color responses in the color combination computations, in such a way that linearity of the internally computed values is preserved in the output. This is typically done by applying a *gamma correction* that changes the internal values to compensate for the display response above. On the other hand, the computed images will be tied to this particular display device.

18.5.2 Adaptive Cross-Dissolve

The cross-dissolve equation (18.1) performs a uniform blending of the image attributes: as t varies from 0 to 1, f fades out and g fades in uniformly at all points of the domain. More interesting results are attained by constructing nonuniform fade-in and fade-out functions. This can be achieved by defining a one-parameter family of functions $w \colon [0, 1] \times U \to [0, 1]$, and using the blending equation

$$h_{\lambda}(p) = (1 - w(\lambda, p)) f(p) + w(\lambda, p) g(p).$$

Note that the weighting function depends on the position in the image.

18.5.3 Multiresolution Cross-Dissolve

When we have a multiresolution representation of an image, a good choice is to choose a progressive cross-dissolve using a schedule to blend different levels of detail at different rates.

In [Stein and Hitchner, 1988], a Gaussian pyramid multiresolution representation is used to compute a cross-dissolve by blending the images from

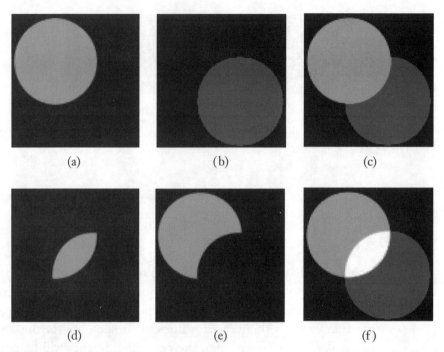

Figure 18.10 Some common composition operations: Image A (a), Image B (b), Operation A over B (c), Operation A in B (d), Operation A out B (e), and Operation A plus B (f). See also color plate 18.10.

coarser to finer resolutions. Better results are attained by using multiresolution representation based on wavelets, since we have information about the localization of the frequencies.

18.5.4 Alpha-Channel Combination

The α-channel can be used to combine two images. This operation is called *image compositing* in the literature. For premultiplied $RGB\alpha$ images, the compositing operations can be described by a single equation

$$c_f = w_a c_a + w_b c_b,$$

where c_f is the resulting $(\alpha R, \alpha G, \alpha B, \alpha)$ color, c_a and c_b are the input colors, and w_a and w_b are the weights that determine the operation to be performed. Some possible values for the weights are shown below (each operation is illustrated in Figure 18.10):

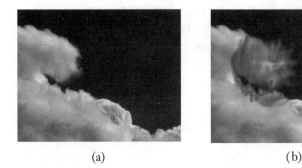

(a)   (b)

Figure 18.11 Combination using the *over* operator: background (a) and result (b). See also color plate 18.11. See also color plate 18.11.

Figure	Operation	w_a	w_b
(a)	A	1	0
(b)	B	0	1
(c)	A over B	1	$1 - \alpha_A$
(d)	A in B	α_B	$0 - \alpha_A$
(e)	A out B	$1 - \alpha_B$	0
(f)	A plus B	1	1

One of the most important operators is the *over* operator, which allows the placement of parts of one image on top of another. This is the basis of a layering scheme, very similar to that used in traditional cell animation. Each layer, analogous to a celluloid sheet, is represented by an image with an associated α-channel, indicating the painted and transparent areas. The layers are sorted, and the *over* operator is used to composite them into a final image.

Figure 18.11 shows a compositing *over* operation using the image and α-channel from Figure 18.1. Note how the α-channel controls the translucency of the blending locally, allowing the background to show through in some parts.

18.5.5 z-Buffering Combination

The idea of storing depth information across the image domain is a natural extension of the basic concept of layering. Layers have constant depth, related by a partial order defined by the way they are stacked. The result of a layering operation, however, cannot be represented in that way, as different areas of the images would have different depths.

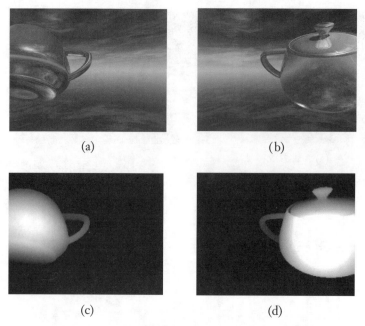

Figure 18.12   Original images (a),(b), and z-buffers (c),(d).

If the output of a layering operation includes depth information, this layered image can be further combined while maintaining a consistent depth ordering. The hidden-surface algorithm of z-buffering takes this idea a step beyond, determining the visibility at each point, by comparing the depths of the input elements and storing the dominant one. In other words, if h is the combination of f and g through z-buffering, we have

$$h(p) = \begin{cases} f(p), \, f_z(p) < g_z(p) \\ g(p), \text{ otherwise.} \end{cases}$$

Note that in this form of combination, one attribute, the depth, controls the outcome for all other attributes, and therefore the attribute combination should be performed in a single step. In Chapter 16 we describe another form of attribute combination that also takes depth into consideration.

Figure 18.12 shows two images and their respective z-buffers, represented by grayscale images, having lighter intensities for closer features. The z-buffered combination of these two images is shown in Figure 18.13. Note that the crossing handles cannot be represented by a simple layer representation.

Figure 18.13 Composition using z-buffers.

Note also that there is no reflection of one ray-traced teapot onto the other, a typical artifact when using compositing as a postproduction step.

18.6 Scheduled Image Morphs

We have seen in Chapter 13 that the flow of a transformation can be controlled by the use of scheduled transformations. Recall that an adaptive attribute combination between two images f and g is given by

$$h_\lambda(p) = (1 - w(\lambda, p))f(p) + w(\lambda, p)g(p),$$

where w is the weighting function, which depends on the position in the image. The function w will define the adaptiveness of the combination according to some criteria. One possibility is to let the user specify the values of this function at certain key positions and interpolate these values. The specification of this function is analogous to the problem of the specification of a transformation, discussed in Chapter 12.

In the case of image attributes, the weights that control the scheduled attribute combination can be defined just at the warp specification elements, effectively sharing those elements between the warp specification and the attribute combination specification. This is very convenient, as it provides a simplified user interface without loss of generality.

In this way, the specification of a scheduled attribute combination that will be used for morphing should be done in conjunction with the warping

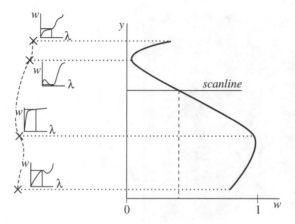

Figure 18.14   Weight interpolation using two-pass computation.

specification. In feature-based specification, for instance, the values would be associated with each of the marked features, emphasizing the idea that the specification will "move" as the features are transformed. In a spline mesh specification, the weighting values would be associated to each control point of the mesh.

Note that the weight can be a function of the family parameter, so that functions $w(\lambda)$ should be specified at each specification element. The techniques for interpolating the values, however, can be applied in the same way, as these functions are all evaluated for a particular value of λ when generating a transformation.

18.6.1   Two-Pass Interpolation

This form of interpolation is naturally associated with the two-pass spline mesh warping algorithm [Costa, 1994]. The major advantage of this form of interpolation is that the warping and the scheduled attribute combination weight can be computed in a combined and efficient way. As these computations are strongly connected, the description of two-pass spline mesh warping in Chapter 14 is worth reviewing.

Recall from the two-pass spline mesh warping discussion that in the horizontal pass, each column of control points is fitted with an interpolating spline. To create a scheduled transformation, an interpolation relating the weight and y-coordinates for each vertical spline of the intermediate mesh must also be created (see Figure 18.14, which matches the figures in Chapter 14). This interpolates weights for an entire column of the mesh (the selected spline) at each possible scanline. Note that the figure shows the weight function for each mesh vertex (on the left), which are all sampled at a given parameter λ.

This process is repeated for each column of the intermediate spline mesh, yielding the weight at each intersection of the scanline with the vertical splines. The x-coordinates of these intersections and the corresponding weight values are interpolated to obtain the weights for each pixel of the scanline.

Note that the output of each pass is in fact an α-channel, which is then used to control the blending of the other attributes of the image.

18.7   Real–Time Warping Using Texture Mapping

It is interesting to note that many of the image attributes and their transformations described here are present in most typical 3D rendering pipelines. Curiously, many of these same characteristics, such as alpha and space-variant filtering, are lacking from most 2D graphics systems. This seemingly paradoxical fact suggests an opportunity to use some of the capabilities of 3D pipelines to compute transformations that are essentially 2D.

The first important characteristic of 3D pipelines is their ability to compute piecewise linear reconstructions of different attributes. The application creates triangular meshes with attribute values defined at the vertices, and the pipeline can reconstruct the values using linear interpolation across the triangles. Some of the attributes supported include diffuse and specular color, α, and depth. Each of these attributes corresponds to one or more interpolants that have to be evaluated along the interior of a triangle.

Mapping an image onto these planar triangulations allows basic warping operations to be performed. The application can warp the vertices and let the 3D pipeline be responsible for the piecewise linear reconstruction of the warp, performed according to the triangular mesh. The pipeline can also apply good-quality filtering to the resampled images through the use of mip maps and bilinear or trilinear interpolation.

Naturally, the main advantage of this approach is that 3D pipelines are commonly available in hardware implementations, which makes this very attractive for high-performance image warping and morphing.

Figure 18.15 shows one frame of a real-time morph computed by a 3D pipeline. The mesh shown is the intermediate interpolated geometry. Each of the images is mapped onto this mesh using the appropriate relaxed meshes.

Figure 18.15 Morphing using texture-mapping hardware.

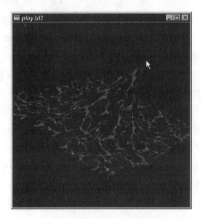

Figure 18.16 Interactive physically based warp.

The first image is drawn with an opacity α, and the second is composited with an opacity of $1 - \alpha$. An implementation using OpenGL is included on the companion CD-ROM.

An efficient implementation of warping is particularly important in interactive applications. In Figure 18.16 we show a screen shot of an interactive application that warps images in 3D space according to a physical model of a spring network. The user can freely apply arbitrary forces to the spring system using the mouse and get instant feedback. This software is also included on the companion CD-ROM.

18.8   Comments and References

A QuickTime movie of a morphing by cross-dissolve produced in the early part of this century by G. Méliés can be found on the Internet at *www.visgraf.impa.br/morph/*.

Chapter 7 of [Gomes and Velho, 1997] brings a comprehensive introduction to the problem of image combination and provides additional details about some of the techniques we discussed here.

The morphing transformations were initially studied for images, so there is a fair amount of literature specifically dedicated to these graphical objects. Most of the techniques, however, concentrate on the problem of warping reconstruction, which was covered in Chapter 14.

The z-buffer visibility algorithm was introduced in [Catmull, 1975]. Porter and Duff introduced the compositing operations using α-channels in [Porter and Duff, 1984]; the combined use of α and depth information for synthetic images is discussed in [Duff, 1985].

References

Arad, N., and D. Reisfeld. 1995. Image Warping Using Few Anchor Points and Radial Functions. *Computer Graphics Forum*, **14**(1), 35–46.

Beier, Thaddeus, and Shawn Neely. 1992. Feature-Based Image Metamorphosis. *Computer Graphics (SIGGRAPH '92 Proceedings)*, **26**, 35–42.

Bernstein, Ralph. 1976. Digital Image Processing of Earth Observation Sensor Data. *IBM J. Res. Development*, **20**, 40–57.

Bordwell, David, and Kristin Thompson. 1996. "The Power of Mise-en-Scene." In *Film Art, An Introduction*. New York: McGraw-Hill, 171–172.

Braccini, Carlo, and Giuseppe Marino. 1980. Fast Geometrical Manipulation of Digital Images. *Computer Graphics and Image Processing*, **13**, 127–141.

Brown, Lisa G. 1992. A Survey of Image Registration Techniques. *ACM Computing Surveys*, **24**(4), 325–376.

Catmull, E. 1974. *A Subdivision Algorithm for the Display of Curves and Surfaces*. Ph.D. Thesis, University of Utah.

Catmull, Edwin. 1975. Computer Display of Curved Surfaces. *Proceedings of the IEEE Conf. on Computer Graphics Pattern Recognition Data Structure*, May, 11.

Catmull, Edwin, and Alvy Ray Smith. 1980. 3D-Transformations of Images in Scanline Order. *Computer Graphics (SIGGRAPH '80 Proceedings)*, **14**(3), 279–285.

Costa, B. 1994. *Image Deformation and Metamorphosis.* Master's Thesis. Rio de Janeiro: Computer Science Department. PUC-Rio.

Darsa, Lucia, and Bruno Costa. 1996. Multi-Resolution Representation and Reconstruction of Adaptively Sampled Images. *(SIBGRAPI '96 Proceedings)*, 321–328.

Duff, T. 1985. Compositing 3D Rendered Images. *Computer Graphics (SIGGRAPH '85 Proceedings)*, **19**(3), 41–44.

Fant, Karl M. 1986. A Nonaliasing, Real-Time Spatial Transform Technique. *IEEE Computer Graphics and Applications*, **6**(1), 71–80.

Gomes, J., and L. Velho. 1997. *Image Processing for Computer Graphics.* New York: Springer-Verlag.

Goshtasby, A. 1986. Piecewise Linear Mapping Functions for Image Registration. *Pattern Recognition*, **19**(6), 459–466.

Goshtasby, A. 1987. Piecewise Cubic Mapping Functions for Image Registration. *Pattern Recognition*, **20**(5), 525–533.

Heckbert, P. 1989. *Fundamentals of Texture Mapping and Image Warping.* Master's Thesis (Technical Report No. UCB/CSD 89/516). University of California, Berkeley *(www.cs.cmu.edu/˜ph).*

Heckbert, P. 1994. Bilinear Coons Patch Image Warping. In Heckbert, Paul S. (ed.), *Graphics Gems IV.* Boston: Academic Press, 438–446.

Kass, Michael, Andrew Witkin, and Demetri Terzopoulos. 1988. Snakes: Active Contour Models. *International Journal of Computer Vision*, **1**(4), 321–331.

Lee, Seung-Yong, Kyung-Yong Chwa, Sung Yong Shin, and George Wolberg. 1995. Image Metamorphosis Using Snakes and Free-Form Deformations. *Computer Graphics (SIGGRAPH '95 Proceedings)*, 439–448.

Litwinowicz, Peter, and Lance Williams. 1994. Animating Images with Drawings. *Computer Graphics (SIGGRAPH '94 Proceedings)*, 409–412.

Markarian, H., R. Bernstein, D. G. Ferneyhough, L. E. Gregg, and F. S. Sharp. 1971. Implementation of Digital Techniques for Correcting High Resolution Images. *Proc. Amer. Inst. Aeronautics and Astronautics, 8th Annual Meeting*, 285–304.

Paeth, Alan W. 1986. A Fast Algorithm for General Raster Rotation. *Proceedings of Graphics Interface '86*, 77–81.

Peli, E., R. Aubliere, and G. T. Timberlake. 1987. Feature-Based Registration of Retinal Images. *IEEE Trans. Med. Im.*, **6**(3), 272–278.

Porter, T., and T. Duff. 1984. Compositing Digital Images. *Computer Graphics (SIGGRAPH '84 Proceedings)*, **18**(3), 253–259.

Potmesil, M., and I. Chakravarty. 1982. Synthetic Image Generation with a Lens and Aperture Camera Model. *ACM Transactions on Graphics*, **1**(2), 85–108.

Ruprecht, Detlef, and Heinrich Müller. 1995. Image Warping with Scattered Data Interpolation. *IEEE Computer Graphics & Applications*, March, 37–43.

Samet, H. 1984. The Quadtree and Related Hierarchical Data Structures. *ACM Computing Surveys*, **16**, 187–260.

Shepard, D. 1968. A Two-Dimensional Interpolation Function for Irregularly Spaced Data. *Proc. 23rd National Conference of the ACM*, 517–524.

Smith, Alvy Ray. 1987. Planar 2-Pass Texture Mapping and Warping. *Computer Graphics (SIGGRAPH '87 Proceedings)*, **21**(4), 263–272.

Smithe, D. B. 1990. *A Two-Pass Mesh Warping Algorithm for Object Transformation and Image Interpolation*. Technical Memo #1030. Industrial Light and Magic.

Stein, Charles S., and Lewis E. Hitchner. 1988. The Multiresolution Dissolve. *SMPTE Journal*, Dec., 977–984.

Tanaka, A., M. Kameyama, S. Kazama, and O. Watanabe. 1986. A Rotation Method for Raster Image Using Skew Transformation. *IEEE Conference on Computer Vision and Pattern Recognition Proceedings*, 272–277.

Weiman, Carl F. R. 1980. Continuous Anti-Aliased Rotation and Zoom of Raster Images. *Computer Graphics (SIGGRAPH '80 Proceedings)*, **14**(3), 286–293.

Williams, Lance. 1983. Pyramidal Parametrics. *Computer Graphics (SIGGRAPH '83 Proceedings)*, **17**, 1–11.

Wolberg, G. 1990. *Digital Image Warping*. Los Alamitos, CA: IEEE Computer Society Press.

19

Warping and Morphing of Surfaces

IN THIS CHAPTER WE WILL STUDY the problem of surface warping and morphing. These operations play a very important role in geometric modeling and animation. The greatest emphasis will be placed on surface warping. A surface defines both the shapes of 2D objects and the boundaries of solid objects.

19.1 Preliminary Definitions

A surface is a 2D subset S of the euclidean space $\mathbb{R}^3$, which is locally homeomorphic to the euclidean plane. More precisely, for each point $p \in S$, there exists a 3D ball $B^3 \subset \mathbb{R}^3$ centered at p, such that $B^3 \cap S$ is homeomorphic to the 2D ball

$$B^2 = \{(x, y) \in \mathbb{R}^2 \,;\, x^2 + y^2 < 1\} \tag{19.1}$$

of the euclidean plane (see Figure 19.1). Intuitively, this definition says that a surface is obtained by gluing together deformed pieces of the plane. By imposing different requirements on the homeomorphism, we obtain different classes of surfaces. A very common requirement is to demand that the homeomorphism between $B^3 \cap S$ and B^2 be a diffeomorphism. In this case we have a differentiable surface, which is characterized by having a tangent plane at every point.

We should observe that the above definition does not consider surfaces with boundaries. It can be easily modified to do so by considering not the

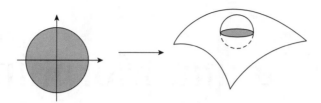

Figure 19.1   Definition of a surface.

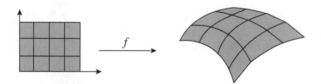

Figure 19.2   Parametric surface.

disk in (19.1), but a half disk of the closed half plane: $\{(x, y) \in \mathbb{R}^2;\ x^2 + y^2 < 1 \text{ and } y \geq 0\}$.

19.1.1 Surface Description

There are basically two methods to describe a surface: parametric description and implicit description.

Parametric Surfaces

A parametric surface is described by a transformation $f\colon U \subset \mathbb{R}^2 \to \mathbb{R}^3$, as shown in Figure 19.2. Geometrically, f defines a 2D coordinate system on the image set $f(U)$.

In order to avoid degeneracies, we must impose some conditions on the parameterization function f. A natural condition consists in imposing some differentiability class. Another important condition is that the Jacobian of f has rank 2. Geometrically, this means that the partial derivative vectors

$$\frac{\partial f}{\partial u} = \left(\frac{\partial f_1}{\partial u}, \frac{\partial f_2}{\partial u}, \frac{\partial f_3}{\partial u} \right),$$

and

$$\frac{\partial f}{\partial v} = \left(\frac{\partial f_1}{\partial v}, \frac{\partial f_2}{\partial v}, \frac{\partial f_3}{\partial v} \right),$$

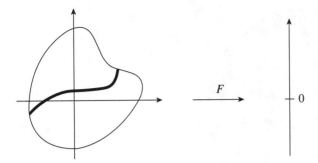

Figure 19.3 Implicit surface.

are linearly independent. This condition allows us to define a nondegenerate normal vector $\vec{n}$ to the surface, by the vector product

$$\vec{n} = \frac{\partial f}{\partial u} \times \frac{\partial f}{\partial v}.$$

This guarantees that we are able to define a tangent plane at each point of the surface. In brief, the Jacobian condition essentially guarantees the 2D character of the surface $f(U)$.

Implicit Surfaces

An implicit surface S is defined as the set of zeros of a function $F\colon U \subset \mathbb{R}^3 \to \mathbb{R}$, that is,

$$S = \{(x, y, z) \in \mathbb{R}^3 \, ; \ F(x, y, z) = 0\}.$$

This set is denoted by $F^{-1}(0)$, and it is called the *inverse image* of the set $\{0\} \subset \mathbb{R}$. A 2D illustration is shown in Figure 19.3.

As in the case of parametric surfaces, we must impose conditions on the function F in order to avoid degeneracies. A condition analogous to the Jacobian condition for parametric surfaces consists in imposing that the gradient vector

$$\operatorname{grad}(f) = \left(\frac{\partial F}{\partial x}, \frac{\partial F}{\partial y}, \frac{\partial F}{\partial z} \right)$$

is nonnull on the points of $F^{-1}(0)$. In fact, from this condition we conclude that the gradient vector defines a nonnull normal vector field to the surface.

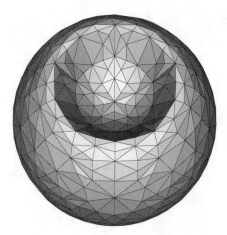

Figure 19.4 Piecewise linear representation of a surface.

19.1.2 Surface Representation

The area of surface representation is of great importance in geometric modeling. In fact, this was one of the first areas of computer graphics to deserve special attention for a formal conceptualization of representation [Requicha, 1980].

Point sampling of surfaces is a widely used representation in practice, and the associated use of piecewise linear reconstruction is also widely accepted. This combination of point sampling and piecewise linear reconstruction techniques turns out to consider a surface as being approximated by some 2D polyhedra (see Figure 19.4). Higher-order reconstruction is possible using piecewise polynomials of higher degree (splines).

More details and references about surface representation can be found in Chapter 9, Representation of Graphical Objects.

19.2 Warping Specification

In this section we will describe warping techniques for surfaces. When the surface is reconstructed using splines (B-spline, Bézier, etc.), we certainly obtain intrinsic warpings of it by moving the control points. These warpings are closely tied to the surface representation and reconstruction techniques. We are mostly interested in more generic warping techniques. In this section we will describe techniques for surface warping using three different specifications:

- **Parametric specification.** In the parametric specification we define a global transformation of the euclidean space by specifying the parameters for the transformation. The parameters enable us to obtain analytical equations of the transformations.

- **Change of coordinates.** In this case a global warping transformation is defined as a change of coordinates of the space. The coordinate change is specified by the user.

- **Point specification.** In this case the warping is computed as a solution to some scattered data problem: the user specifies the warping transformation at a finite number of points on the surface.

All of the three techniques above define global deformations of the space $\mathbb{R}^3$. Both the warping by changing of coordinates and the warping by point specification can be localized. Also, since these techniques deform the space, their 2D version is also a choice to warp plane curves, images, or other objects of the plane.

More details about these specification techniques can be found in Chapter 12.

19.3 Warping by Parametric Specification

Warping by parametric specification was introduced in the computer graphics literature in [Barr, 1984], where the transformations of taper, twist, and bending were defined. We will review the transformations of tapering and twist below.

19.3.1 Tapering

The operation of tapering along the z-axis consists in applying a variable scaling transformation on the coordinates (x, y). The mathematical description of the tapering transformation along the z-axis is given by $A(x, y, z, r) = (rx, ry, z)$, where the scaling factor r depends on the z-coordinate, $r = f(z)$. The function $f(z)$ is called the *tapering function*.

Each plane parallel to the XY-plane at height z is deformed by a different scaling transform that is determined by the value of the z-coordinate. In this

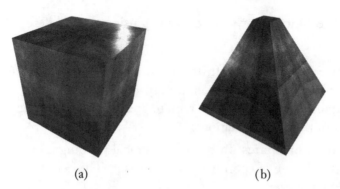

(a)   (b)

Figure 19.5   Tapering transformation: cube (a) and tapered cube (b).

way, the z-coordinate determines both the transformation region and the magnitude of the scaling transformation.

Observe that when the function $f(z) = 1$, the corresponding region of the object is not deformed. When the function $f(z) > 1$, the corresponding region is expanded, and conversely when $f(z) < 1$, the corresponding region is contracted. Figure 19.5(a) shows a cube; in (b) the cube is deformed with a linear tapering function.

19.3.2   Twist

A twist warping is defined by a family of rotations around an axis, using an angle that depends on the distance along the axis. By taking the z-axis as being the twist axis, the twist is computed by the equation

$$W(x, y, z) = (x \cos \theta - y \sin \theta, x \sin \theta + y \cos \theta, z),$$

where $\theta = f(z)$. The function $f(z)$ is called the *twist function*. As in the tapering operation, the z-coordinate determines the transformation function, as well as the region of space where this transformation will be applied. Figure 19.6 shows the twist of a prism around its vertical axis.

19.3.3   Combining Warpings

Combining warping operations constitutes a very powerful modeling tool. The operations of tapering, twisting, and bending can be combined in a hierarchical structure in order to create complex objects from simpler ones. This is one of the powerful applications of warping. Figure 19.7 illustrates the composition of a twist and a tapering applied to the prism of Figure 19.6.

Figure 19.6 Warping by torsion.

Figure 19.7 Twist and tapering of a prism.

19.4 Warping by Change of Coordinates

As discussed in Part III, the warping of a graphical object can be interpreted as a change of coordinate systems. The coordinate change between curvilinear systems allows a rich variety of possibilities for warping, as shown in Figure 19.8. Also, the change of coordinates defines a global transformation of the space, which means the resulting warping can be applied to different classes of graphical objects embedded in the space, independent of their description or representation.

19.4.1 Rectilinear and Curvilinear Coordinate Systems

A coordinate system is completely determined by its coordinate curves. A representation of a coordinate system is constructed by taking a finite number of coordinate curves for each spatial dimension. Figure 19.9(a) shows the representation of a rectilinear coordinate system. The representation of a rectilinear coordinate system corresponds to a lattice in the euclidean space.

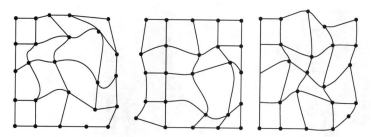

Figure 19.8   Spline coordinate systems.

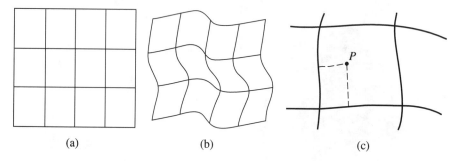

Figure 19.9   Rectilinear lattice (a), curvilinear lattice (b), and lattice cell (c).

When we have a curvilinear coordinate system, the coordinate curves used in the representation will be called a *curvilinear lattice*. A curvilinear lattice is shown in Figure 19.9(b). An element of the lattice (a lattice cell) is constructed from the intersection of coordinates in each dimension of the lattice, as shown in Figure 19.9(c).

Together with the representation of a coordinate system, we must devise a technique to compute the coordinates of an arbitrary point P in space from the coordinate curves of the representation (Figure 19.9(c)).

In the case of a rectilinear system, the coordinates of P are determined by the distance of P to the coordinate curves that define the representation, but the reconstruction of coordinates of a point can be very complex, involving interpolation methods. Such interpolation methods depend on the representation of the coordinate curves.

19.4.2   Methodology for Warping Using Coordinate Change

The process of warping a graphical object using change of coordinates can be attained in four steps (see Figure 19.10):

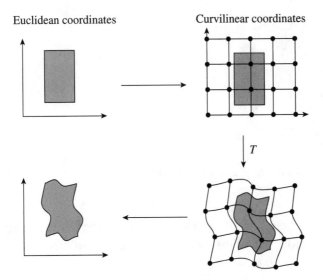

Figure 19.10 Warping by coordinate deformation.

1. A new coordinate system is defined on the space where the object is embedded. Some representation of the coordinate system is used to define it.

2. We represent the coordinates of the object shape on this new coordinate system.

3. The representation curves of the coordinate system are warped, which causes a deformation of the space.

4. We compute the new object coordinates to Cartesian coordinates in order to reconstruct the deformed object.

19.4.3 Free-Form Coordinate Change

In order to achieve good flexibility in warping using change of coordinates, we must require two properties from the coordinate systems. The first is the use of curvilinear coordinate systems, and the second is that the coordinate systems used should provide to the user a flexible interface to specify different warpings.

These two goals are attained using *free-form coordinate systems*. These coordinate systems are represented by free-form coordinate curves, with control points, which enable the user to specify the change of coordinates by moving them.

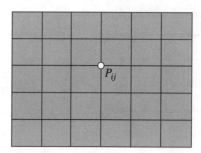

Figure 19.11   Representation of a Cartesian system.

We will discuss below the Bézier and B-spline free-form coordinate systems. We will consider in this discussion the 2D case, but extensions to spatial coordinates are immediate.

Bézier Free-Form Coordinate System

Consider a rectangular region R of the plane and define on R a representation of the Cartesian coordinate system using a lattice of $(m+1)(n+1)$ points P_{ij}, $0 \le i \le m, 0 \le j \le n$ (see Figure 19.11).

A point p of the representation lattice will have coordinates $(i/m, j/n)$, with $i = 0, \ldots, m, j = 0, \ldots, n$. We now define a free-form coordinate system on the region R by using the points P_{ij} as control points of Bézier curves.

The Bézier curve $b(t)$ determined by $n+1$ control points $p_0, \ldots, p_n$ is defined by

$$b(t) = \sum_{i=0}^{n} p_i B_i^n(t), \tag{19.2}$$

where $B_i^n(t)$ is the Bernstein polynomial of degree n:

$$B_i^n(t) = \frac{n!}{i!(n-i)!} t^i (1-t)^{n-i}, \quad i = 0, \ldots, n.$$

Extension of the Bézier reconstruction equation (19.2) to higher dimensions is attained using tensor product. In this way, the free-form coordinates (s, t) introduced on the region R are related with the Cartesian coordinates by

$$p = (x, y) = W(s, t) = \sum_{i=0}^{m} \sum_{j=0}^{n} P_{ij} B_i^m(s) B_j^n(t).$$

Generalization of the above equation to dimension 3 is immediate:

$$p = (x, y, z) = W(s, t, u) = \sum_{i=0}^{m} \sum_{j=0}^{n} \sum_{k=0}^{q} P_{ijk} B_i^m(s) B_j^n(t) B_k^q(u). \qquad (19.3)$$

Notice that initially the coordinate curves of the Bézier and the Cartesian coordinate systems coincide, but the Bézier coordinates are normalized to the interval $[0, 1]$.

The warping is specified by moving the lattice points P_{ijk}, so as to obtain new points P'_{ijk}. These new points substitute for the old ones in Equation (19.3), which is used to compute the new deformed coordinates.

The use of Bernstein polynomials makes this warping transformation global; that is, the modification of a single control point influences the whole domain. To get the effect of a local deformation, it is necessary to position the lattice just over the area of interest, limiting the part of the object that lies inside the lattice. To have precise deformations, it is necessary to position the control points accordingly, which is not very easy.

B-Spline Free-Form Coordinate System

The Bézier free-form coordinate system does not have good localization properties. Also, the degree of the reconstruction basis (Bernstein basis) increases with the number of points in the representation lattice. These two problems are solved using B-splines instead of Bézier.

The cubic B-spline curves [Bartels et al., 1987] are obtained from the sum of four polynomial functions, and these functions are given by

$$b_0(t) = \frac{1}{6}t^3$$

$$b_1(t) = \frac{1}{6}(1 + 3t + 3t^2 - 3t^3)$$

$$b_2(t) = \frac{1}{6}(4 - 6t^2 + 3t^3)$$

$$b_3(t) = \frac{1}{6}(1 - 3t + 3t^2 - t^3)$$

Given $n + 1$ control points $p_0, \ldots, p_n$, each pair of four points defines a spline segment of the reconstructed curve, by the equation

$$b_{jr}(t) = \sum_{i=0}^{3} P_{r+i} b_i(t),$$

with $r = 0, \ldots, n - 3$. If the representation lattice has $(m + 1)(n + 1)$ points $P_{i,j}$, $i = 0, \ldots, m$, $j = 0, \ldots, n$, the reconstruction equation for the B-spline coordinate system is

$$P = (x_1, x_2) = W_2(y_1, y_2) = \sum_{i=0}^{3} \sum_{j=0}^{3} b_i(y_1) b_j(y_2) P_{i+r,j+p}, \qquad (19.4)$$

where $r = 0, 1, \ldots, m - 3$, $p = 0, 1, \ldots, n - 3$, and $m - 1$ and $n - 1$ are the number of control points in each of the directions. The extension of this scheme for three dimensions is done by adding coordinate curves in a third orthogonal direction. In this way the transformation of coordinates is given by

$$P = (x_1, x_2, x_3) = W_3(y_1, y_2, y_3) = \sum_{i=0}^{3} \sum_{j=0}^{3} \sum_{k=0}^{3} b_i(y_1) b_j(y_2) b_k(y_3) P_{i+r,j+p,k+q}$$

$$(19.5)$$

The above equations compute the change from coordinates y_i to coordinates x_i. The inverse change of coordinates is done by using the inverse transformation. In general, it is difficult to obtain the equation of the inverse. An alternative is to solve the equation $f(y_1, y_2, y_3) = (x, y, z)$, using numerical methods.

If the coordinate curves are described by B-spline functions, it is necessary to add control points to the grid, because the B-spline curves do not interpolate the first and last control points of the coordinate curves. It is possible to add these control points using the technique of *ghost vertices*. The coordinates of these vertices are computed such that the B-spline curve interpolates the first and last control points. Figure 19.12 shows the grid with the ghost vertices.

19.4.4 Free-Form Surface Warping

The free-form coordinate systems introduced in the previous sections allow us to obtain a warping technique. The user specifies a free-form coordinate system and deforms the coordinate curves that represent the coordinate system.

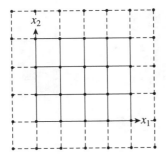

Figure 19.12 Ghost vertices of a grid.

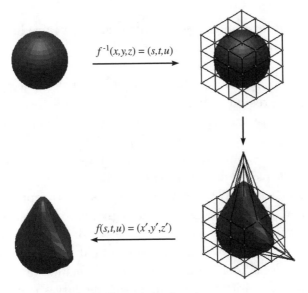

$f^{-1}(x,y,z) = (s,t,u)$

$f(s,t,u) = (x',y',z')$

Figure 19.13 Deformation of a sphere.

The deformation technique for the geometric support of a graphical object using a change of coordinates consists in creating a base coordinate system, usually rectilinear, and mapping it into a free-form coordinate system. In this way, it is possible to deform the object by moving the control points of the free-form coordinate system. The change of coordinates of the free-form coordinate system deforms the geometric support of the graphical object. Then, a change of coordinates is applied to map points of the spline coordinate system back to the base coordinate system of the objects. Figure 19.13 shows the deformation of a sphere using this technique.

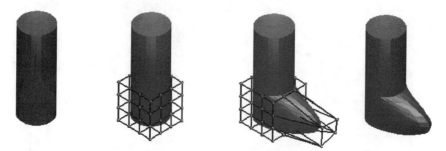

Figure 19.14   Partial deformation of a cylinder.

The use of this deformation technique for surfaces was introduced in the computer graphics literature by [Sederberg and Parry, 1986], and is known as *free-form deformation*.

It is also possible to obtain a partial deformation of the object, that is, to deform only a given region of the geometric support of the object. This is done by embedding just the region of interest into the deformation grid. The transformation of coordinate change is applied only to the points that lie inside the grid, that is, points with coordinate values in the interval [0, 1]. Figure 19.14 shows the partial deformation of a cylinder.

In [Sederberg and Parry, 1986], a rectilinear system is represented by taking the coordinate curves uniformly spaced in each of the coordinate axes. Very often the user needs to deform some regions of the grid more than other regions. A solution for this problem would be to employ more coordinate curves to give a finer control over the deformation in those areas of interest. However, if a large number of coordinate curves is included in the representation, the computational complexity will increase, and the user interface will become cluttered.

The work of [Forsey and Bartels, 1988] solves the above problem by adaptively increasing the number of coordinate curves only in the regions that are subject to larger deformations. This technique starts with a coarse uniform rectilinear coordinate system that is incrementally refined in certain regions of the grid. Figure 19.15(a) shows the base mesh and (b) shows the refined mesh.

The coordinate curves are described by B-spline curves of degree n. The grid refinement is performed by inserting control points in these coordinate

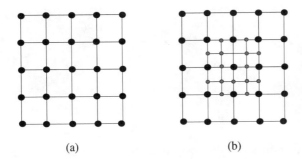

Figure 19.15   Grid refinement: base mesh (a) and refined mesh (b).

curves. The process relies on the fact that it is possible to add new control points without altering the shape of the curve.

In [Chadwick et al., 1989], the free-form warping technique is used as a tool in a 3D cartoon animation.

19.4.5 Deformation Using Arbitrary Lattices

An extension of the work of [Sederberg and Parry, 1986] was developed by [Coquillart, 1990]. The basic idea of this extension consists in allowing lattices with different topology and geometry, other than the parallelepipedal lattices used in [Sederberg and Parry, 1986]. The use of more generic lattices allows the production of "shaped" warps to the surface, which is a very useful modeling tool.

An important problem also addressed in this extension consists in devising tools for constructing different lattices. Beginning with a small set of primitive lattices such as parallelepipedal and cylindrical lattices, new lattices are created. A tool for editing lattices is described, as well as some combination operations to construct new lattices from the basic ones.

This work employs Bézier curves of degree 3 to define the coordinate curves. The coordinate change transformation, mapping points of the spline system to points of the euclidean space, is obtained using a tensor product of Bézier curves. Certainly B-splines can be used as well. Figure 19.16 shows a deformation of a plane surface using an "eight"-shaped lattice: (a) shows the lattice over the plane, (b) shows the deformation of the lattice, and (c) shows the final deformed plane with a texture applied.

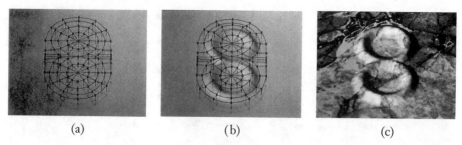

(a)   (b)   (c)

Figure 19.16 Warping using an "eight"-shaped lattice: the lattice over the plane (a), the deformation of the lattice (b), and the final deformed plane with a texture applied (c) [from Coquillart, 1990].

The fact that we have lattices of arbitrary topology leads naturally to the problem of using these lattices for morphing: a source lattice and a target lattice are used, and a lattice morphing operation between them is defined. The lattice resulting from the morphing of the two lattices is used to deform the surface, which results in a morphing of the surface itself. This strategy for lattice morphing has been exploited in [Coquillart and Jancene, 1991]. This is a morphing using feature specification, where the features are defined by the lattice geometry.

Another work that enables free-form deformations between lattices of arbitrary topology appeared in [Maccracken and Joy, 1996]. It is based on the subdivision surface scheme of Catmull-Clark. In this scheme, the lattice possesses a well-defined topological structure, with faces, edges, and vertices. In addition to the mesh construction operations developed in [Coquillart, 1990], this structure allows the construction of lattices using union of faces.

19.5 Warping Using Point Specification

So far in this chapter, we have seen parametric and free-form specifications for warps of surfaces. In parametric specification, the whole embedding space is deformed based on parameters given by the user. In general, this type of parametric warping is global and does not allow a local control of the deformation.

The warping techniques based on free-form deformation allow the use of localized transformations using B-splines or Bézier coordinate systems.

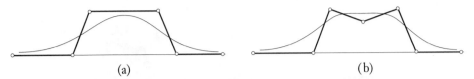

Figure 19.17 Nonintuitive specification of deformation: control lights aligned with plane (a) and control points positioned to obtain the desired flat bump deformation (b).

However, these techniques present several problems in terms of user interface. In fact, the specification of the initial lattice by the user, as well as the deformation of the coordinate curves, is a tedious and complicated task, especially in the 3D case. Also, in order to deform the coordinates, the user needs to anticipate how the surface will be deformed.

This problem of an indirect specification highlighted above is really difficult to solve. This can be exemplified in the case where we need to deform a surface to produce a flat bump. The user probably would position the control points aligned with the plane, as shown in Figure 19.17(a). However, to obtain the desired flat bump deformation, the control points should be positioned as shown in Figure 19.17(b).

In this section we are interested in warping techniques for surfaces that use point specification. The user chooses n points $p_1, \ldots, p_n$ of a surface $S \subset \mathbb{R}^3$ and specifies the values of the warping transformation $T(p_i)$ at each of the points. From these n values we must find a reconstruction technique that enables us to compute the values of T for any point of the surface S. This technique is illustrated in Figure 19.18: on the left, we show a sphere with a point P; in the center, we show the specification value of the transformation at P (the point P_1); on the right, we show the deformed sphere.

In the technique of warping using coordinate change, the user specifies the transformation points on the vertices of the lattice. In the point specification technique, the user specifies the transformation directly on points of the surface. For this reason, surface warping by point specification has been called *warping by direct specification* in the literature.

19.5.1 Warping Specification

As was mentioned in the previous chapter, when a specification by points is used, the deformation is computed from the coordinate values of n points of

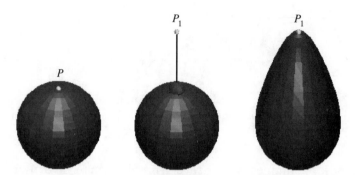

Figure 19.18   Warping by direct specification [from Pinheiro, 1997].

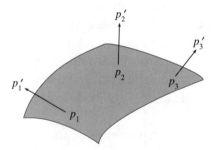

Figure 19.19   Point specification.

the surface. In this way, we know n points $p_1, p_2, p_3, \ldots, p_n$, and displacement vectors associated with these points

$$\overrightarrow{p_1 p_1'}, \overrightarrow{p_2 p_2'}, \overrightarrow{p_3 p_3'}, \ldots, \overrightarrow{p_n p_n'}$$

(Figure 19.19), or equivalently, the points $p_1', \ldots, p_n'$.

19.5.2   User Interface

In the deformation by direct specification, the user should select points $p_1, p_2, p_3, \ldots, p_n$ on the surface, as well as their displacement vectors.

The interface must provide the user with a mechanism to allow the specification of a vector $v = \overrightarrow{p_i p_i'}$. This specification is commonly done with 2D locators, such as mice or tablets. This can be accomplished using a specifica-

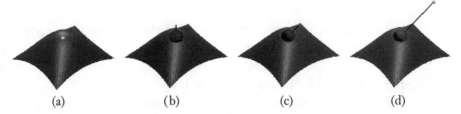

(a)   (b)   (c)   (d)

Figure 19.20 Displacement vector specification using arcball: the surface with the point to be moved (a), the arcball sphere centered on that point and the default displacement direction (b), change of direction using arcball (c), and the displacement vector (d).

tion in two stages. The user chooses the direction of the displacement vector; after choosing the direction, the user specifies the length of the displacement.

In the specification of the displacement direction we suggest the use of the technique of arcball with constraints [Shoemake, 1994]. Figure 19.20 shows the specification process: in (a) we show the surface with the point to be moved; in (b) we show the arcball sphere centered on that point and the default displacement direction (normal to the surface); in (c) we have used arcball to change the direction; and finally, in (d) we show the displacement vector obtained after a new direction was specified.

19.5.3 Warping Reconstruction

To obtain the deformation of the surface, it is necessary to reconstruct the warping transformation from the displacement vectors specified. The problem of reconstructing the transformation reduces to that of obtaining a function $T : \mathbb{R}^3 \to \mathbb{R}^3$ such that, given a set of points $p_1, p_2, p_3, \ldots, p_n$ on the geometric support of the object, and their new positions $p'_1, p'_2, p'_3, \ldots, p'_n$, we have

$$T(p_1) = p'_1, T(p_2) = p'_2, T(p_3) = p'_3, \ldots, T(p_n) = p'_n.$$

In other words, from a set of samples of the function T, we want to reconstruct T for all points in space.

We have seen in Chapter 14, Warping and Morphing Techniques, that this reconstruction scheme is a problem of scattered data interpolation.

Radial Splines

In [Borrel and Rappoport, 1995], a system using interpolation based on *radial functions* was used. The radial functions are constructed using B-splines to solve the problem of scattered data interpolation. The technique enables the use of a localized warping transformation with a good control of the morphing transformation. The technique is quite effective for some localized warping operations used for interactive modeling.

In the next section we will describe a solution to compute the transformation from a point specification, using change of coordinates.

Change of Coordinates

In [Hsu et al., 1992], the warping strategy discussed above has been described, using change of coordinates to solve the scattered data interpolation problem: the user specifies displacement vectors on points of the surface, and the program chooses a coordinate transformation that reconstructs the warping on the specified points.

By using Bézier or B-spline coordinate systems, we obtain local warpings of the space. It is important to emphasize that the user does not interact with the coordinate system, but only with the points at which the transformation is specified.

The coordinate system is represented by a lattice of the space. It is necessary to find the displacement values for each control point of the lattice that would produce the desired surface deformation.

We have seen in Section 19.4.3 that if the coordinate curves of the lattice are described by B-splines, then the change of coordinates from this B-spline coordinate system to Cartesian coordinates is given by

$$(x, y, z) = W(s, t, u) = \sum_{l,m,n=0}^{3} P_{i+l,j+m,k+n} B_l(s) B_m(t) B_n(u), \qquad (19.6)$$

here $P_{i,j,k}$ is the control point in position i, j, k, of the spline system, (s, t, u) are the coordinates of a generic point relative to the spline system, and (x, y, z) are the coordinates of this point expressed in the euclidean coordinate system.

Certainly the reconstruction of the warping function using change of coordinates does not have a unique solution: different coordinate changes would give the same result. A natural coordinate change is the one that moves the lattice control points the least in the sense of least squares. Equation (19.6) represents a weighted average of the control points where the spline basis is the weights. The closer the control point is to the target point, the greater will be the influence of that control point.

Equation (19.6) can be written in matrix form as $q = BP$, where B is a matrix 1×64 that contains the product of the spline functions and P is a matrix 64×3 that contains the coordinate of the control points. Given a point $Q = (x, y, z)$, of a surface, and its new location $Q' = (x', y', z')$, determined by a displacement vector, then Q' is given by $q' = B(P + \Delta P)$. From that, we have

$$\Delta q = B \Delta P, \tag{19.7}$$

where ΔP is the displacement of the control points and Δq is the displacement of the object points, that is, the difference between points q and q'. To solve Equation (19.7), it is necessary to find the values ΔP, and this can be done using a *pseudoinverse* (or *generalized inverse*) B^+ of B. In that way, the values ΔP are given by

$$\Delta P = B^+ \Delta q.$$

The result obtained by using this pseudoinverse scheme satisfies the requirement above that the most natural solution to our problem is to use a lattice transformation that minimizes the amount of transformation of each lattice vertex.

Some Examples

Before giving an example, we should note that in general, when we use a point-based specification, two possibilities arise concerning the user interface. The first is that the system computes the warping for a unique displacement vector. The second is that the system computes the warping for a finite number of specified displacement vectors.

The first interface option is convenient for obtaining a deformation interactively by successive transformations. Figure 19.21 shows a sequence of three deformations of a torus.

The second option allows the user to specify the final position of n points of the deformed surface, producing a set of displacement vectors that is used to transform the surface. Figure 19.22 shows this interface option with a specification in three points.

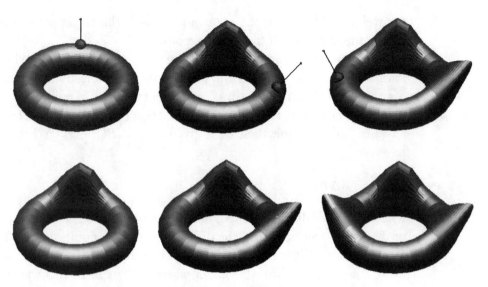

Figure 19.21   Successive deformations of a torus [from Pinheiro, 1997].

Figure 19.22   Deformation using a set of points [from Pinheiro, 1997].

19.6   Surface Metamorphosis

In this section we will describe some techniques for surface morphing. The literature in this area is not as rich as the literature on warping.

19.6.1   Morphing by Linear Interpolation

If the surfaces S_1 and S_2 have a point sampling representation (e.g., a polyhedral surface), it is possible to use linear interpolation to compute a morphing operation between them:

1. Take the set of sample points $p_1, p_2, \ldots, p_m$ that represent S_1, and associate to sample points $q_1, q_2, \ldots, q_m$ of S_2.

2. For each pair p_i, q_i of sample points, compute the interpolated point $r_i = \text{lerp}(p_i, q_i) = (1 - t)p_i + tq_i$.

3. Each intermediate morphed surface is reconstructed from the interpolated samples r_i, using the same structuring of the original surface.

This is certainly the oldest technique for surface morphing. The linear interpolation along with reconstruction from the interpolated samples put together in a very simple scheme the forward warpings of the source object, the inverse warping of the target object, and the blending. The use of linear interpolation for surface blending has appeared in the literature in [Hong et al., 1988] to compute morphing of polyhedral surfaces.

We have already discussed the problems presented by using linear interpolation for morphing in different parts of this book. The correspondence between the samples p_i and q_i of the source and target surfaces has a great influence on the morphing result. Therefore, we must devise techniques to attain a good correspondence.

It is always possible to use a one-to-many or a many-to-one correspondence, but better results are achieved when we have a one-to-one correspondence between the samples. We have discussed this problem for polyhedral surfaces before (combinatorial compatibility problem).

19.6.2 Curve and Surface Morphing

Many of the techniques for curve metamorphosis extend to surfaces, although generally the computational framework for surfaces is much more involved.

We have described in Chapter 17 a morphing technique for polygonal curves that solves the combinatorial compatibility problem by merging the vertices using a projection on a circle. This technique was introduced in [Kent et al., 1992] to compute metamorphosis of polyhedral surfaces. The merging of the vertices is attained by projecting them on a sphere. Different spherical projection techniques are discussed in this reference.

The morphing technique from [Sederberg et al., 1992] that computes a morphing using linear interpolation and an intrinsic angle/length representation of the polygonal curve has been extended to polyhedral surfaces in [Sun et al., 1995]. The polyhedral surface is represented using intrinsic shape parameters such as dihedral angles and lengths.

In the chapter about curve metamorphosis, we studied the technique of morphing by guided warping described in [Carmel and Cohen-Or, 1997]. It computes the morphing in four steps:

1. point specification by the user
2. approximate alignment
3. combinatorial compatibility
4. morphing computation

In [Cohen-Or et al., 1998], the authors also discuss the extension of the technique to work with polyhedral surfaces.

19.6.3 Morphing Using Set Operations

The technique of morphing using linear interpolation to blend the surfaces is based on vector space operations of the euclidean space: vector addition and product by some real number. Whenever the graphical objects are represented by elements of some vector space, we always have linear interpolation at our disposal as an option to compute the metamorphosis between two objects.

The above remark can be easily generalized. Suppose we are able to define two operations on a set Ω of graphical objects:

1. Product $\lambda \otimes \mathcal{O}$ of a real number λ by a graphical object $\mathcal{O} \in \Omega$.
2. Sum $\mathcal{O}_1 \oplus \mathcal{O}_2$ of two graphical objects $\mathcal{O}_1, \mathcal{O}_2 \in \Omega$.

Then we can compute a metamorphosis between two graphical objects by doing linear interpolation on the space Ω. More precisely, for any two graphical objects $\mathcal{O}_1$ and $\mathcal{O}_2$, we define the one-parameter morphing family

$$\mathcal{O}_\lambda = (1 - \lambda) \otimes \mathcal{O}_1 \oplus \lambda \otimes \mathcal{O}_2, \quad 0 \leq \lambda \leq 1.$$

The product $(1 - \lambda) \otimes \mathcal{O}_1$ is the forward warping of the source object. The product $\lambda \otimes \mathcal{O}_2$ is the inverse warping of the target object, and the blending of the warped objects is performed by the sum operation $\oplus$.

The product $\otimes$ of an object shape by some real number has a natural solution as the scaling operation of the shape. For the sum operation $\oplus$, we have several possibilities such as

- union of sets
- Minkowski sum
- Fourier descriptor algebra

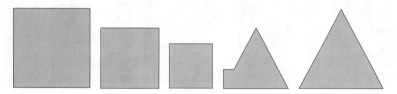

Figure 19.23 Linear interpolation using union [from Kaul and Rossignac, 1991].

Figure 19.24 Linear interpolation using Minkowski sum [from Kaul and Rossignac, 1991].

We will describe these possibilities briefly in what follows.

Union of Sets

An immediate possibility arises to use the union of sets (or the regularized union) as the sum operation. In this case the morphing by linear interpolation is given by

$$\mathcal{O}_\lambda = (1 - \lambda)\mathcal{O}_1 \bigcup \lambda\mathcal{O}_2.$$

A morphing sequence between a square and a triangle using the above equation is shown in Figure 19.23.

Minkowski Sum

Another possibility for the sum operation between graphical object shapes has been nicely exploited in [Kaul and Rossignac, 1991]: morphing of polyhedral surfaces using Minkowski sum and the scaling operation of a subset of the euclidean space. The Minkowski sum of two sets $A, B \subset \mathbb{R}^3$ is defined by

$$A \oplus B = \{a + b \,;\, a \in A, b \in B\}.$$

They constitute the basic operation in the area of mathematical morphology [Serra, 1982], and it has been used in geometric modeling [Rossignac and Requicha, 1986]. Figure 19.24 shows the metamorphosis sequence between the triangle and the square using Minkowski sum for blending. The result is

Figure 19.25 Morphing with topological type change [from DeCarlo and Gallier, 1996].

much more pleasing than the morphing shown in Figure 19.23 using union of sets to blend.

In [Kaul and Rossignac, 1991], the authors also discuss the computation of the Minkowski sum of two polyhedral surfaces and describe the algorithm to compute the linear interpolation morphing using Minkowski sum. The paper is very well written and includes several details. We should remind the reader interested in this technique that new results about the computation of the Minkowski sum of polyhedrals have appeared in the literature since the paper was published.

Fourier Descriptor Algebra

In [Ghosh and Jain, 1993] the authors describe an algebra of geometric shapes for planar regions, using a Fourier series representation scheme (Fourier descriptors). The operation of sum in this algebra is used to interpolate shapes as described above.

19.6.4 Surface Morphing with Topology Change

In general we have not been concerned with topology change in a metamorphosis. In image morphing there is no topological change, and in plane curves morphing we have supposed that both the source and target objects are Jordan curves. When we come to surfaces, we have a great variety of different topology types, and the problem of morphing surfaces with different topologies becomes important.

This problem has been nicely addressed in [DeCarlo and Gallier, 1996]. The paper has a precise description of the topological surgeries necessary to perform a topology type change during the morphing. Figure 19.25, which was also used in Chapter 4, shows a morphing sequence with topological type change during the morphing. The morphing technique described in the paper uses surface subdivision in the specification, with a side-by-side user interface. This is illustrated in Figure 19.26.

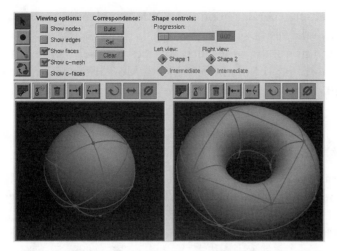

Figure 19.26 Side-by-side user interface [from DeCarlo and Gallier, 1996].

Topology changes also are easier to deal with when computing metamorphosis using a volumetric approach. For surfaces we could use the change of representation scheme that we discussed in the introductory chapter of this part, in order to compute a morphing between two surfaces: compute the associated solid, use a volumetric morphing technique, and compute a boundary evaluation to obtain the associated surface for each intermediate morphed volume.

19.6.5 Warping and Morphing of Implicit Surfaces

This is a special class of surfaces for which we can develop specific warping and morphing techniques. It should be noted that the global warping techniques perform a change of coordinates of the space; therefore, they can be used to warp implicit surfaces as well. These techniques in fact are independent of the surface description or representation.

The naïve solution to obtaining a morphing between two implicit surfaces $F^{-1}(0)$ and $G^{-1}(0)$ is to use linear interpolation between F and G

$$H_t = (1 - t)F + tG,$$

to compute a one-parameter family of functions $H_t \colon \mathbb{R}^3 \to \mathbb{R}$, and define the one-parameter morphing sequence by $H_t^{-1}(0)$. Note that the resulting surface is an approximation of the union of the two implicit surfaces defined by $(1 - t)F$ and tG, and, as we have seen before in Section 19.6.3, the resulting morphing is not, in general, a good one. Different blending equations can be used to improve the result.

Warping and morphing of implicit surfaces is closely connected with the warping and morphing of volumetric objects. More information can be found in Chapter 20, Warping and Morphing of Volumetric Objects.

19.7 Comments and References

For theoretical study of surfaces from the point of view of differential geometry, we recommend [do Carmo, 1976]. Implicit surfaces are well covered in [Bloomenthal et al., 1997]. A detailed study of parametric free-form surfaces is found in [Bartels et al., 1987] for splines and [Farin, 1988] for Bézier.

The literature of surface warping and morphing is vast and widespread. One of the reasons is the many useful applications of warping and morphing as a modeling tool and also as an effective animation technique.

Direct warping of surfaces has appeared in the literature in different articles. In [Parent, 1977], a system for direct manipulation of surfaces defined by polygonal meshes is described. A technique that allows for direct manipulation of B-spline surfaces has been described as a CMU technical report in [Welch et al., 1991].

Sergio Pinheiro implemented several warping techniques using direct specification as well as change of coordinates as part of his master's thesis [Pinheiro, 1997], and some of this code is included on the companion CD.

A good review of surface warping using change of coordinates is [Bechmann, 1994]. It contains an extensive bibliography of the subject.

References

Barr, A. H. 1984. Global and Local Deformation of Solid Primitives. *Computer Graphics (SIGGRAPH '84 Proceedings)*, **18**, 21–30.

Bartels, Richard H., John C. Beatty, and Brian Barsky. 1987. *An Introduction to Splines for Use in Computer Graphics and Geometric Modeling*. San Mateo, CA: Morgan Kaufmann.

Bechmann, Dominique. 1994. Space Deformation Models Survey. *Computers & Graphics*, **18**, 571–586.

Bloomenthal, Jules, Chandrajit Bajaj, Jim Blinn, Marie-Paule Cani-Gascuel, Alyn Rockwood, Brian Wyvill, and Geoff Wyvill. 1997. *Introduction to Implicit Surfaces*. San Francisco: Morgan Kaufmann.

Borrel, P., and A. Rappoport. 1995. Simple Constrained Deformations for Geometric Modeling and Interactive Design. *ACM Transactions on Graphics*, **13**(2), 137–155.

Carmel, Eyal, and Daniel Cohen-Or. 1997. Warp-Guided Object-Space Morphing. *The Visual Computer*, **13**, 465–478.

Chadwick, J. E., D. R. Haumann, and R. E. Parent. 1989. Layered Construction for Deformable Animated Characters. *Computer Graphics (SIGGRAPH '89 Proceedings)*, **23**(July), 243–252.

Cohen-Or, D., D. Levin, and A. Solomovici. 1998. Three-Dimensional Distance Field Metamorphosis. To appear in *ACM Transactions on Graphics*.

Coquillart, Sabine. 1990. Extended Free-Form Deformation: A Sculpturing Tool for 3D Geometric Modeling. *Computer Graphics (SIGGRAPH '90 Proceedings)*, **24**(Aug.), 187–196.

Coquillart, S., and P. Jancene. 1991. Animated Free-Form Derformation: An Interactive Animated Technique. *Computer Graphics (SIGGRAPH '91 Proceedings)*, **25**(July), 23–26.

DeCarlo, Douglas, and Jean Gallier. 1996. Topological Evolution of Surfaces. *Proceedings of Graphics Interface '96*, 194–203.

do Carmo, M. P. 1976. *Differential Geometry of Curves and Surfaces.* Englewood Cliffs, NJ: Prentice Hall.

Farin, Gerald. 1988. *Curves and Surfaces for Computer Aided Geometric Design.* San Diego: Academic Press.

Forsey, D., and R. Bartels. 1988. Hierarchical B-Spline Refinement. *Computer Graphics (SIGGRAPH '88 Proceedings)*, **22**, 205–212.

Ghosh, P. K., and P. K. Jain. 1993. An Algebra of Geometric Shapes. *IEEE Computer Graphics and Applications*, Sep., 50–58.

Hong, M. T., N. M. Thalmann, and D. Thalmann. 1988. A General Algorithm for 3D-Shape Interpolation in a Facet-Based Representation. *Proceedings of Graphics Interface*, 229–235.

Hsu, William M., John F. Hughes, and Henry Kaufmann. 1992. Direct Manipulation of Free-Form Deformations. *Computer Graphics (SIGGRAPH '92 Proceedings)*, **26**(2), 177–184.

Kaul, A., and J. Rossignac. 1991. Solid-Interpolating Deformations: Construction and Animation of PIPs. *Proceedings of Eurographics '91.* Amsterdam: Elsevier Science Publishers, 493–505.

Kent, J. R., W. E. Carlson, and R. E. Parent. 1992. Shape Transformation for Polyhedral Objects. *Computer Graphics (SIGGRAPH '92 Proceedings)*, **26**(2), 47–54.

Maccracken, Ron, and Kenneth I. Joy. 1996. Free-Form Deformation with Lattices of Arbitrary Topology. *Computer Graphics (SIGGRAPH '96 Proceedings)*, **30**, 181–188.

Parent, Richard E. 1977. A System for Sculpting 3D Data. *Computer Graphics (SIGGRAPH '77 Proceedings)*, **11**(2), 138–147.

Pinheiro, Sergio E. M. L. 1997. *Interactive Deformations Using Direct Specification*. Master's Thesis. PUC-Rio (in Portuguese).

Requicha, A. A. G. 1980. Representation for Rigid Solids: Theory, Methods, and Systems. *ACM Computing Surveys*, **12**(Dec.), 437–464.

Rossignac, J., and A. Requicha. 1986. Offset Operations in Solid Modeling. *Computer Aided Geometric Design*, **3**, 129–148.

Sederberg, T., and S. Parry. 1986. Free-Form Deformation of Solid Geometric Models. *Computer Graphics (SIGGRAPH '86 Proceedings)*, **20**(4), 151–160.

Sederberg, Thomas W., Peishing Gao, Guojin Wang, and Hong Mu. 1992. 2D Shape Blending: An Intrinsic Solution to the Vertex Path Problem. *Computer Graphics (SIGGRAPH '93 Proceedings)*, **27**, 15–18.

Serra, J. 1982. *Image Analysis and Mathematical Morphology*. San Diego: Academic Press.

Shoemake, Ken. 1994. Arcball Rotation Control. In *Graphics Gems IV*, 175–192. San Diego: Academic Press.

Sun, Y. M., W. Wang, and F. Y. L. Chin. 1995. Interpolating Polyhedral Models Using Intrinsic Shape Parameters. *Proceedings of the Third Pacific Conference on Computer Graphics and Applications, Pacific Graphics '95*. World Scientific, 133–147.

Welch, W., M. Gleicher, and A. Witkin. 1991. *Manipulating Surfaces Differentially*. Technical Report. CMU.

20
Warping and Morphing of Volumetric Objects

V OLUMETRIC OBJECTS ARE USEFUL IN MANY AREAS, especially in the manipulation and visualization of sampled volumetric data provenient from acquisition devices, such as computerized tomography (CT) or magnetic resonance (MR). Also, these objects are present in many scientific simulations. In the area of medical images, volumetric objects play an important role. Warping and morphing are particularly applicable in this area related to nonrigid registration problems.

With respect to modeling, there exists a close relationship between volumetric objects and implicit defined models. For this reason, warping and morphing of implicit models will be covered here.

20.1 Volumetric Objects

A *volumetric object* is a 3D graphical object embedded in $\mathbb{R}^3$ or, more generally, an n-dimensional graphical object in $\mathbb{R}^n$, for $n \geq 3$. A volumetric object is also called a *solid object*. A volumetric object is described by its density function: a constant density function describes solids used in the area of solid modeling that are completely characterized by their boundary surface (hence the name *boundary representation*); a variable density function describes volumetric objects with variable opacities, such as those used in the area of medical images.

An image can be considered a 2D volumetric object with a variable density function. In fact, an image is a 2D graphical object embedded in $\mathbb{R}^2$, and its function can be interpreted as a density function. Nevertheless, there is a characteristic distinction between images and volumetric objects: the attribute function of a volumetric object dictates shape features of the object, allowing for a significant overlap between the study of volumetric objects and the area of solid modeling.

20.1.1   Description and Representation

In this section we will discuss different ways to describe a volumetric object. We will also present different representations used for these objects. In general, for each description we will have a most suitable corresponding representation.

Boundary Description

A 2D compact surface in $\mathbb{R}^3$ is the boundary of a solid (the interior of the surface). Therefore, a representation of the boundary surface gives a representation of the solid. This is called a *boundary representation* of the volumetric object. Boundary representation is not an effective method to represent a volumetric object, for two reasons. First, we have to solve the point membership classification problem in order to decide whether or not a point belongs to the solid. Second, boundary representation is not capable of describing solids constituted by nonhomogeneous matter.

Solids with nonhomogeneous matter are very common in medical images because the tissue density varies for different parts of the body (skin, bones, muscles, etc.). Solids represented by their boundaries are extensively used in the area of computer-aided design and manufacturing.

Constructive Solid Geometry—CSG

This is a widely used representation of volumetric objects in the area of solid modeling and computer-aided manufacturing. It is the preferred representation for volumetric objects that possess a well-defined geometry and topology. CSG comprises both a description and a representation of a solid. The CSG description is easily extended to include different set operations other than the Boolean operators.

It is difficult to describe nonhomogeneous volumetric objects using the CSG representation. Also, objects with irregular shape are not easy to handle; this class includes volumetric objects from parts of the human body.

Implicit Function Description

Implicit functions are a very effective method to describe volumetric objects. In fact, if $f: U \subset \mathbb{R}^3 \to \mathbb{R}$ is a function and the set

$$\mathcal{O} = \{(x, y, z) \in \mathbb{R}^3 ; \ f(x, y, z) \leq 0\}$$

is bounded, than $\mathcal{O}$ defines a volumetric object. The function f can be interpreted as the density function of the object. Certainly, this description can be used for nonhomogeneous volumetric objects: the variation of the density function is encapsulated into the function f.

On the other hand, when the object $\mathcal{O}$ has a variable density function f, it defines naturally an implicit description of $\mathcal{O}$. In fact, different parts of $\mathcal{O}$ can be characterized as implicit volumes $\{p \in \mathbb{R}^3; \ f(p) \leq c\}$, that is, the set of points in the space with a density below a certain threshold.

When a volumetric object $\mathcal{O}$ has a constant density function, it can be described implicitly by

$$\mathcal{O} = \{(x, y, z) \in \mathbb{R}^3 ; \ \chi_\mathcal{O}(x, y, z) = 1\}$$

where $\chi_\mathcal{O}$ is the *characteristic function* of its shape. That is,

$$\chi_\mathcal{O}(p) = \begin{cases} 1, & \text{if } p \in \mathcal{O}; \\ 0, & \text{if } p \notin \mathcal{O}. \end{cases} \tag{20.1}$$

We have shown that volumetric objects and implicit functions are closely interrelated. Implicit function description of volumetric objects constitutes a very powerful tool to synthesize volumetric objects with complex shape geometry (for examples, see Chapter 8, Description of Graphical Objects).

Level Sets Description

Level sets are closely related to the implicit description of a volumetric object. Suppose a volumetric object $\mathcal{O}$ is described by some implicit function f. For each $c \in \mathbb{R}$, the inverse image $f^{-1}(c)$ describes a level set of the object. If f describes the density of the object, the level set $f^{-1}(c)$ contains all points of the space with constant density c. Level sets are also called *isosurfaces*.

Level sets constitute a very useful tool as an aid in visualizing, manipulating, and analyzing volumetric objects.

Description by Slices

Suppose $\mathcal{O}$ is a volumetric object, ℓ is a straight line, and Λ is a family of planes orthogonal to ℓ. The object $\mathcal{O}$ can be described by the family

$$\mathcal{O}_\lambda = \Pi_\lambda \cap \mathcal{O}, \Pi_\lambda \in \Lambda;$$

that is, the object is described by a set of intersections between each of the planes orthogonal to ℓ and the original object. The family of planes slices the object into 2D volumetric objects. These 2D objects are either images or 2D solids, that is, regions of the plane defined by their boundary curves. In both cases, robust reconstruction techniques are necessary to obtain the volumetric object from the slices.

Point Sampling Description

A very common description of a volumetric object is done by explicitly defining a point sampling of the density function. This is the description of choice used by acquisition devices.

From the samples of the density function, we should be able to use some reconstruction method to compute the density function at any point of the space. An important representation related to point sampling is the matrix representation discussed below.

Matrix Representation

For variable density solids, a widely used representation is given by the matrix representation studied in Part II. Each matrix cell (called a *voxel*) carries density information besides the other object attributes. A volumetric graphical object given by some matrix representation is the 3D analogue of an image, where the voxels play the role of the pixels. For this reason, volumetric objects represented in matrix form are also called *3D-images*. The matrix representation of a volumetric object is also called *voxel representation*. Figure 20.1 shows a voxel representation of a solid torus.

The matrix representation is widely used with volumetric objects; for this reason it is very common to consider a volumetric object as being a solid given by its matrix representation. We have broadened this view in this section: voxels are just another representation of a volumetric object, which can be described and represented in many different ways.

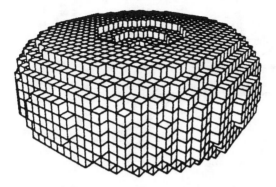

Figure 20.1 Matrix representation of a solid torus.

Unstructured and Adaptive Representations

Voxel representations of volumetric objects are largely used for two main reasons. First, many techniques from image analysis and processing can be extended to them (see [Kaufman, 1991]). Second, visualization of the voxel representation is easier because of its simple structuring.

Apart from this, there is no reason to have a preference for this representation. (This will change as voxel display devices start appearing on the market.) More flexible and robust representations using decomposition of volumetric objects can be used. In particular we could mention adaptive representation by voxels of different sizes (using the octree data structure), or unstructured decomposition such as spatial simplicial decomposition. Another choice is to use binary space partition trees to represent the volumetric object as a hierarchy of intersecting half-spaces.

For each application, the user should look for the most adequate description and representation of the volumetric object. Unstructured representations generally allow better adaptation to the data, but are more complex to manipulate.

20.1.2 Conversion Between Representations

Representation conversion is a very difficult problem in geometric modeling. In this section we will describe some techniques that can be used for obtaining approximate conversions between different descriptions of volumetric objects.

In the previous section we have seen the equivalence between implicit and volumetric objects. An important related problem is the conversion between a boundary description of a solid, and a description based on the solid density

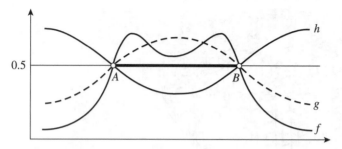

Figure 20.2   Different implicit descriptions of the same solid AB.

function. Note that this problem greatly resembles the classical problem of implicit-parametric conversion.

We should remark that conversion techniques between a boundary and a voxel representation enable us to use volumetric warping and morphing techniques for surfaces, and vice versa, as we described in Chapter 15.

Boundary to Voxel Conversion

A complete boundary representation of a solid must have attached to it a solution to the point-membership classification problem for the solid. Mathematically, this means that we must provide a method to compute the characteristic function of the solid defined by Equation (20.1). Using this computation scheme along with a 3D scan conversion algorithm (see [Kaufman, 1991]), we are able to compute a voxel representation of the solid.

One approach to solving the point membership classification problem for a solid $\mathcal{O}$ consists in describing it by an implicit function. If S is the boundary surface, we must find f such that $S = f^{-1}(c)$, and $p \in \mathcal{O} \Leftrightarrow f(p) \leq c$. There are many choices for the function f, as illustrated in Figure 20.2: The segment AB is defined by $f \geq 0.5$, $g \geq 0.5$, or $h \leq 0.5$.

Distance Field

The oriented distance function has been used in the literature as a choice for the function f: for each $p \in \mathbb{R}^3$, $f(p)$ is the oriented euclidean distance from p to the surface on the boundary of the solid. This distance function has been called *distance field* in the literature; it is discussed in [Payne and Toga, 1992], along with an algorithm to compute it when the boundary surface is described using a polygonal mesh representation.

Distance fields have been used as an effective tool to describe implicit surfaces (see [Bloomenthal et al., 1997]).

Approximate Conversions

We have seen that conversion between volumetric and boundary descriptions is related with the parametric-implicit conversion. We know that the conversion problem between parametric and implicit is very difficult: in most cases it has no solution, and when an analytic solution exists, it is usually very expensive to compute it.

A more practical question is how to devise techniques to obtain approximate conversions between implicit and piecewise parametric descriptions. The polygonization of implicit surfaces is a solution in this direction: an implicit surface is approximated by a piecewise linear surface. Each polygon is trivially parameterized by using, for instance, affine coordinates. There are many polygonization algorithms in the literature; they all started with the classical *marching cubes* [Lorensen and Cline, 1987]. A general overview of these methods, with abundant references, is found in [Bloomenthal et al., 1997].

Resampling

Resampling is an effective computational strategy for different conversion problems. Given a finite set $\{f(p_i)\}$, $i = 1, \ldots, n$, of samples of a function f, the technique of resampling f consists of three steps:

1. Reconstruct the function f from the samples $f(p_i)$.

2. Filter the reconstructed function to remove high frequencies.

3. Sample the reconstructed function on another set of points.

The resampling operation, or the reconstruction operation alone, is very useful when we need to convert from a sampled volumetric object to some other representation. As an example, to obtain a voxel representation from sampled data, we resample the function on the vertices of the voxel grid.

20.1.3 Visualization of Volumetric Objects

For user interface purposes, and in particular for some warping specification techniques, the visualization of volumetric objects constitutes a very important issue. Several visualization techniques can be used as an aid in warping specification. Here we will discuss three of these techniques.

- **Cloud of points.** This is a very inexpensive visualization method that consists of visualizing a distribution of points belonging to the volumetric object. When the object is given by a voxel representation, we can use the barycenter of the voxels as the elements of the cloud (see Figure 20.3).

- **Isosurfaces.** Rendering specific isosurfaces gives a very good interface for interacting with the volumetric object. The pioneering marching cubes algorithm, and the huge number of polygonization algorithms existing in the literature of implicit surfaces, makes this a very attractive visualization option.

- **Volume rendering.** By visualizing the volume directly using some volume rendering technique, low-resolution versions of the dataset can be used for interactive previews. Volume rendering techniques allow us to introduce translucency index to the volumetric elements, which gives us a very flexible visualization for positioning warping feature elements. Volume rendering is a vast subject, with a proportionally large literature. There are two basic ways to render the volumetric data: ray tracing [Levoy, 1988] and splatting [Westover, 1992]. A good introduction to the subject is [Kaufman, 1991].

20.2 Warping Techniques

A volumetric object has the same dimension as the ambient space; therefore, global warping techniques of the space constitute the most natural choice to transform them. In particular, we can use global warping techniques by changing spatial coordinates, as described in Chapter 14.

20.2.1 Warping Using Change of Coordinates

This is a natural choice to specify a global warping technique. We have two possibilities: free-form coordinates or mesh specification.

Free-Form Technique

This technique uses a free-form coordinate system. The user specifies the coordinate system by a representation lattice, where the lattice vertices are control points of spline curves. A warping is obtained by moving the lattice vertices. Details about this technique have been extensively discussed in Chapters 14 and 19.

Computationally, there are many different choices to use, such as Bézier and B-spline coordinate systems. The use of splines localizes the warp, which results in a better control for the user. When the volumetric object uses a matrix representation, it is possible to use a computational strategy based on a three-pass method. The three-pass method, described in Chapter 13, is very effective because it reduces the warp to three 1D warps.

The problem with this technique is that the coordinate curves and surfaces in general are not aligned with the object features. Improved techniques could be devised by using adapted coordinate systems. We will explain some of them below.

Mesh-Based Technique

This technique consists of using coordinate systems represented by nonrectangular lattices. These coordinate systems are adapted to the features of the volumetric object. This adaptiveness is a great advantage over the free-form technique.

This technique is quite suitable for obtaining semiautomatic interface for morphing between two volumetric objects. In fact, the automatic or semiautomatic construction of well-adapted lattices can be attained using techniques from the area of numerical grid generation. Once we have the two lattices associated to the source and target objects, the transformation reduces to specifying a lattice transformation.

From the user point of view, warping or morphing using coordinates is cumbersome. Even if we automate the lattice generating phase, the specification of the warping on the lattice elements is not an easy task when dealing with lattices in the 3D space.

20.2.2 Field-Based Technique

This technique extends the field-based technique for images. The use of the field-based technique, as described in Part III, provides the user easy matching and control over the transformation. This technique uses vectors (oriented line segments) as the specification handles for the transformation. A family $v_i, i = 0, \ldots, n$ of vectors on the source object is given, and for each vector v_i, the image vector w_i under the transformation is given. The transformation is reconstructed from this information.

The family of segments constitutes a *skeleton* of the specification. For this reason, each of the vectors used in the specification is also called a *bone*.

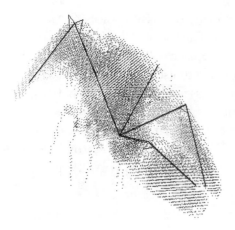

Figure 20.3   Skeleton of a field-based specification.

Figure 20.3 shows a skeleton composed of 3D vector features, where the volumetric object (a lobster) is rendered using a cloud of points. This figure also appears in Section 14.2.3, where the 3D field-based technique is covered in depth.

Semiautomatic warping specification might be possible with this method, using the medial axis transform to compute the skeleton.

20.2.3   Feature-Based Technique

This technique extends the field-based technique described above, allowing the specification of warping handlers with a more complex geometry than that of oriented line segments. These specification features include oriented cylinders, oriented rectangles, and boxes. This is illustrated in Figure 20.4, which shows an example of a specification using a side-by-side interface.

The use of a richer set of specification features allows a better matching between them and the object features. This gives more flexibility in devising good warpings that satisfy the feature matching property.

20.2.4   Point-Based Technique

This is a particular case of the feature-based technique, where we have points, or zero-dimensional features. More precisely, we have n points $p_1, \ldots, p_n$ of the volumetric object, and we know the value of the transformation at these points.

From the user point of view, this method uses no coordinate system, mesh, or feature for the specification. It allows the user to interact directly with

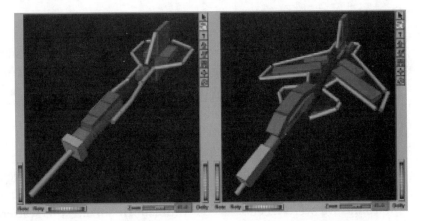

Figure 20.4 Feature-based specification [from Lerios et al., 1995].

points in the volumetric object specifying the transformation on them. This specification technique is very effective if associated with a visualization technique that allows the user easy access to points of the volumetric object and provides the direction to move them. The reconstruction of the transformation from the specification reduces to a classical problem in scattered data interpolation (see Chapter 14).

It is worth mentioning that this specification technique can be used for warping associated with trackers, where the points and their transformations are captured.

20.2.5 Algorithmic-Based Techniques

This class of warping and morphing techniques constitutes the best choice for performing warping of volumetric objects connected with simulation. A good example is simulating twisters on the computer, where the density of the air is modeled as a volumetric object.

Sometimes physical methods are used as a motivation to tackle some warping and morphing problems, but we do not have a real physical simulation. That is, the warping methods themselves are not related to the physics of the objects being warped. As an example, fluid dynamics and energy-based techniques have been largely used as a motivation to obtain warping techniques for images and volumetric objects in the area of medical images. Because of the normal gradient vector fields, the technique of morphing by normal evolution (studied in Chapter 17) is a natural fit for use with implicit objects.

20.3 Warping Computation

All of the information about the volumetric object is concentrated in the density function, as in the case of images, which turns out to be the most important attribute. Because of this, there are some similarities in the computational aspects of warping and morphing of volumetric objects and images. To mention one example, the same problems and solutions for computing the inverse and forward mappings of images extend to volumetric data:

- The matrix cells of the image are defined by rectangles that are approximated by quadrilaterals under the warping. When computing image warping, we were faced with the problem of solving the scattered data interpolation for a rectangle: reconstruct a transformation on a rectangle when we know its values on the vertices of the rectangle. Several methods were mentioned to solve this problem, including affine, projective, and bilinear interpolation.

- In volumetric objects, the geometry of the matrix cells is defined by parallelepipeds. The scattered data problem on images extends to a similar problem: we know the values of the transformation on the eight vertices of the parallelepiped, and we must reconstruct the transformation on the whole parallelepiped.

Some of the solutions we have devised for image warping extend naturally to volume warping. Piecewise affine interpolation extends to this case by subdividing the parallelepiped into a finite number of 3D simplexes. Also, it is easy to see that bilinear interpolation extends to *trilinear interpolation* (see Part I). Projective interpolation does not extend to this case. In fact, the fundamental theorem of projective geometry needs only five points to completely determine a transformation of the space (see Part I). Certainly, piecewise projective reconstruction can also be used.

As in the case of images, it is possible to work with irregular unstructured grids, to represent and warp the graphical object, and to render the volumetric object directly from this representation, using splatting [Westover, 1992], for instance.

20.3.1 Computing Isosurfaces

Another problem that arises when warping volumetric objects is the use of reconstruction techniques for isosurfaces. The usual techniques work very well for solid volumes where the opacity values are the focus of interest. For

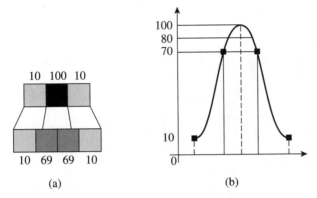

Figure 20.5 Magnification: scaling of a three-voxel volume (a) and aliasing problem (b).

isosurfaces, however, there are additional reconstruction problems that are not necessarily improved by filtering.

Figure 20.5(a) shows a warping by expansion from three voxels to four, and the resulting reconstructed values using a simple weighted average. Suppose the isosurface value of interest is 80: in the top row, we have two exterior voxels and one interior, whereas in the magnified version in the bottom row all the voxels are exterior (density < 80). This is an aliasing problem, illustrated in the graph in Figure 20.5(b). The original three samples are reconstructed using a high-quality filter, resulting in the curve shown. The new samples, marked with squares, are a good representation of the overall shape of the curve, but are inadequate for representing the isosurface, as they all fall below the threshold.

20.3.2 Computation Acceleration

The problem of warping volumes of density $n \times n \times n$ has a complexity of $O(n^3)$, as with the majority of volumetric objects manipulation problems. The use of spatial subdivision techniques, such as octrees, is a natural way to accelerate the process, restricting the computations to branches where there is data; that is, the volumetric object is not transparent.

20.4 Blending Techniques

We have stated before that one of the rules for a good morphing consists in transforming features from one object into features of the other object. This feature mapping is attained by warping of the object shape, without taking

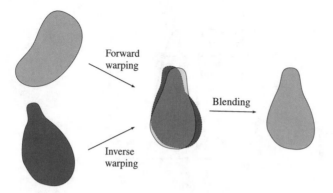

Figure 20.6   Usual morphing steps: two geometric warps + attribute blending.

into consideration the attribute changes. After we obtain the right geometry alignment, we must blend both the shape and the attributes. This is illustrated in Figure 20.6, which was also used in Chapter 4: The source and target shapes are aligned using two warpings, and the two aligned objects are blended.

In general we have to blend both shape and attributes, but in the case of volumetric objects, as in images, shape is not relevant because it is completely dictated by the attribute function.

20.4.1   Blending by Weighted Average

This is a simple and generic approach to blend two functions. In particular, it can be used to blend attributes of volumetric objects. It performs a weighted interpolation of the function values. Given two functions f and g, we blend them obtaining a function h by

$$h(p, t) = w(p, t)f(p) + (1 - w(p, t))g(p), \quad p \in \mathbb{R}^3, t \in [0, 1] \qquad (20.2)$$

where

$$w(p, 0) = 1, \quad \text{and} \quad w(p, 1) = 0, \quad \forall p.$$

The function $w(p, t)$ is the weight function that controls the time parameter. Note that it performs an adaptive blending, where the blending weight varies from point to point of the graphical objects.

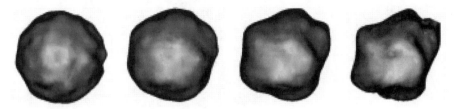

Figure 20.7 Cross-dissolve combination of volumetric objects.

Cross-Dissolve

The simplest case of the above blending technique is the linear interpolation blending, known in the literature as *cross-dissolve*. In this case we have $w(p, t) = 1 - t$, and the blending equation is

$$h(p, t) = (1 - t)f(p) + tg(p), \quad p \in \mathbb{R}^3, t \in [0, 1].$$

Notice that the attributes are blended with the same weight for every point p. Figure 20.7 shows some frames of a cross-dissolve sequence between two volumetric objects (noisy spheres).

We should remark that when using cross-dissolve with implicit volumes, the boundary surfaces should be defined implicitly by $f^{-1}(c)$ and $g^{-1}(c)$, with $c \neq 0$. In fact, for $c = 0$ and $t \neq 1$, the function $(1 - t)f = 0$ defines the same surface as the equation $f = 0$, and the same happens with the equation tg, for $t \neq 0$. Also, better results are attained if the functions f and g are normalized to vary on the same interval. A natural choice consists in normalizing f and g to the interval $[0, 1]$ and take $c = 0.5$.

Scheduled Blending

A very interesting weighted blending technique is the *scheduled blending* that was described in Chapter 13, Computation of Transformations. This technique uses a scheduling function that produces a preprogrammed blending of the attribute properties. Using the function

$$w(t, \lambda) = \begin{cases} 0 & \text{if } 0 < t < -2\lambda + 1 \\ t - (2\lambda - 1) & \text{if } -2\lambda + 1 < t < -2\lambda + 2 \\ 1 & \text{if } -2\lambda + 2 < t < 1 \end{cases} \quad (20.3)$$

we obtain the scheduled cross-dissolve shown in Chapter 13, repeated here as Figure 20.8 between two sinusoidal signals.

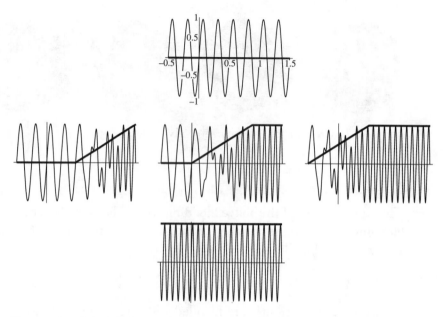

Figure 20.8   Scheduled cross-dissolve [from Goldenstein, 1997].

20.5 Warping, Morphing, and Cross-Dissolve

We should analyze the blending equation (20.2) with respect to the morphing strategy in Figure 20.6. In fact, the blending equation is a complete morphing equation: the forward warping of the object defined by the function f is computed by equation $w(p, t)f(p)$, and the inverse warping of g is given by $(1 - w(p, t))g(p)$.

These two warpings apply an adaptive scaling to each object: one of them scales down the object f and the other scales up the object g. The blending is done by the sum

$$h(p, t) = w(p, t)f(p) + (1 - w(p, t))g(p). \tag{20.4}$$

What does the blending in Equation (20.4) mean geometrically?

When we have two implicit volumes $f^{-1}(0)$ and $g^{-1}(0)$, the implicit object $(f + g)^{-1}(0)$ gives an approximation of the union $f^{-1}(0) \cup g^{-1}(0)$. Indeed, the union is given by the implicit function

$$h = \max\{f, g\}.$$

On the other hand, it is easy to see that

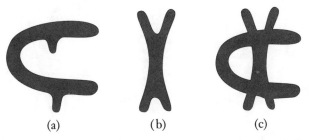

(a) (b) (c)

Figure 20.9 Source object (a), target object (b), and blending of source and target objects (c).

$$h = \lim_{p \to \infty} (f^p + g^p)^{1/p}.$$

This converges very fast as p increases. For $p = 1$, we get the desired approximation $h \approx f + g$.

From the previous remarks, geometrically the blending equation (20.4) performs the following operations:

1. scales up the object f;
2. scales down the object g; and
3. takes the union of the two scaled objects.

With the above interpretation, the limitations of morphing by cross-dissolve are clear: No effort is made to align features of the two object attributes f and g. When there is a natural alignment, the morphing by cross-dissolve technique works nicely, especially if we use some scheduled blending. This is well illustrated by the example of Figure 20.7 between two noisy spheres.

Nevertheless, using cross-dissolve to compute a morphing sequence between the 2D solids of Figure 20.9(a) and (b), we would obtain an intermediate solid like the one shown in (c): there is a drastic change of topology, and the morphing is quite unnatural.

Better morphing techniques could be attained by using warpings that perform a registration of the objects' features instead of just scaling them up and down. A possible morphing sequence between the two solids in Figure 20.9(a) and (b) using this technique is illustrated in Figure 20.10.

Several of the morphing techniques described in this chapter perform better registration warpings before blending. A particularly robust one will be described in Section 20.7.4.

Figure 20.10   Union blending with nonlinear warping.

20.5.1 Blending with Other Set Operations

Now we have seen that the operation of sum in the blending equation is geometrically the operation of set union. This fact motivates the creation of different morphing techniques substituting the union operation by some other set operation.

A possible choice is to use Minkowski sum between two sets. We have discussed this topic with examples in Chapter 19.

20.6 Jump Discontinuity and Regularization

When blending surfaces described by an implicit function, we have to be very careful with the values of the implicit functions outside the level sets. The blending operation is greatly influenced by the behavior of the function on a neighborhood of the level sets. This is nicely exemplified by the example in Figure 20.11: In (a) we show a ring-shaped region, in (b) we show a disk, and in (c) we show a cross-section of the graph of the functions f and g that describes these two objects (this cross-section is representative because the objects have axial symmetry). The morphing by cross-dissolve is computed by

$$h(x, y) = (1 - t)f(x, y) + tg(x, y). \tag{20.5}$$

If the values of f in the interval AB that correspond to the ring hole are too small, the values of the blended function h in Equation (20.5) are smaller than 0.5 for any value of t. This means that the hole will not disappear during the

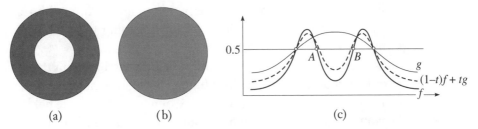

Figure 20.11 Ring-shaped region (source) (a) disk (target) (b), and cross-section of the graph of functions f and g that describes these two objects (c).

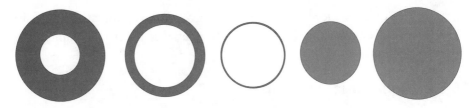

Figure 20.12 Jump discontinuity problem.

morphing. As illustrated in Figure 20.12, as the morphing progresses, the ring will get thinner until it disappears and suddenly a small disk will appear. The morphing continues with a scaling of the disk until it matches the target disk.

This morphing artifact that causes the sudden appearance of intermediate objects in the morphing sequence is called *jump discontinuity*. This phenomenon is also called *unsmooth transformation of isosurfaces* in the literature.

In order to avoid, or at least alleviate, the problem of jump discontinuity, we must devise techniques to control the behavior of the implicit functions on a neighborhood of the level sets. In the above example of the morphing from the ring to the disk, the jump discontinuity would disappear by changing the function f on the open interval (A, B) so that it does not assume small values.

Some techniques to avoid or minimize jump discontinuities will be discussed below.

20.6.1 Unsharpening Filtering

One technique to alleviate the jump discontinuity problem is to filter the volume data using a mask so as not to change the data in a tubular neighborhood of the isosurface. This can be done by extending traditional linear image filtering techniques such as those used for obtaining the *unsharp masking* (see [Gomes and Velho, 1997]).

Another technique is to use nonlinear filtering based on the distance field described in Section 20.1.2. In [Hughes, 1992], it is suggested to process the data using a filter f defined as follows: Compute the distance field associated to the volumetric object, and define a function of $\lambda(d)$ that is 1 in a neighborhood of the origin and approaches 0 as d increases. If the isosurface is defined by $f^{-1}(d)$, define a new volumetric object g from f, by

$$g(p) = \lambda(d)f(p) + (1 - \lambda(d))\frac{d}{2}.$$

A highly successful generic operation to overcome the jump discontinuity problem is obtained using the exponential transform, as explained in the next section.

20.6.2 Exponential Transform

The exponential transform is another technique used as a global solution to the problem of neighborhood regularization.

The exponential function $\exp: \mathbb{R} \to \mathbb{R}^+$ is defined by $\exp(t) = e^t$. Its inverse is the natural logarithm $\exp^{-1}(s) = \log_e(s)$. The exponential transform acts on the space of real-valued functions by the compositing operation $\circ$:

$$\exp(f) = \exp \circ f = \exp(f(t)).$$

It should be noted that isosurfaces of level 0 are transformed by the exponential into isosurfaces of level 1. More precisely, if $g = \exp(f)$, the isosurface $f^{-1}(0)$ is the same as the isosurface $g^{-1}(1)$. More generally, an isosurface of level c is transformed into the isosurface of level 1 using the shifted exponential $\exp(t - c)$ to transform the function f.

The effect of the exponential transform is to perform a regularization on the values of the function f: it maps the unbounded interval $(-\infty, L]$ of the real line into the bounded interval $(0, \exp(L)]$.

Example 20.1 (Normalizing a Quadratic Function)   Consider the functions $f(t) = -(t + 2.5)^2 + 5$ and $f(t) = -(t - 2.5)^2 + 5$ whose graphs are shown in Figure 20.13(a). Taking the exponential results in the functions whose graphs are shown in Figure 20.13(b) (not to scale).

Instead of performing the blending in the attribute domain directly, it is possible to transform the original values by an exponential function, perform

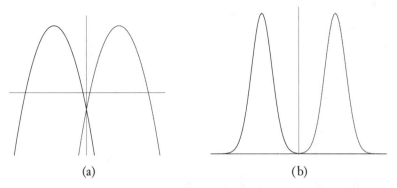

Figure 20.13 Regularization: two parabolas (a) and their exponential regularization (b).

the combination in this transformed space, and then transform back to the original domain. This kind of exponential blend produces improved results and is defined, for an isosurface density value d and for two input objects f and g, as

$$\mathrm{E}(x) = e^{x-d}$$
$$\mathrm{E}^{-1}(x) = d + \log_e(x)$$
$$h(f, g) = \mathrm{E}^{-1}(w(t)\mathrm{E}(f) + (1 - w(t))\mathrm{E}(g)).$$

When blending two functions f and g using linear interpolation

$$(1 - t)f + tg,$$

for $t = 0$, tg reduces to the null function. In general, for t close to 0, tg is not uniformly closed to the null function (this happens in the parabola example given above). Using the exponential transform to blend, we have

$$\mathrm{E}^{-1}\left((1 - t)\mathrm{E}f + t\mathrm{E}g\right)$$

It is easy to see that $t\mathrm{E}g$ uniformly approximates the null function as t approaches 0. This regularization attained with the exponential in general gives better results in the computations.

Figure 20.14(a) shows a linear blend between the two parabolas from Figure 20.13(b). Notice how the 0-level set disappears during the transformation. Figure 20.14(b) shows a linear blend using the exponential transform, which gradually transforms from one object into the other.

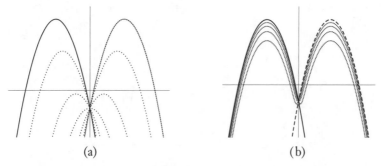

(a)   (b)

Figure 20.14   Blends: linear (a) and exponential (b).

20.7 A Brief Survey of Volumetric Morphing

In this section we will give a brief survey of the computer graphics literature about warping and morphing of volumetric objects.

20.7.1 Scheduled Fourier Morphing

Scheduled Fourier volume morphing was introduced in the literature in [Hughes, 1992]. This technique uses a scheduled cross-dissolve technique in the frequency domain. The idea is to program a schedule blending of the frequencies in such a way that we blend the low frequencies first and add high frequencies progressively as the animation morphing parameter changes.

Consider two attribute functions f and g of the volumetric object. Their combination is defined as follows. Compute the Fourier transform $\hat{f}$ and $\hat{g}$ of the attributes. Define a partition of the frequency domain of $\hat{f}$ and $\hat{g}$ into frequency bands obtaining two families of n functions $f_1, \ldots, f_n$ and $g_1, \ldots, g_n$ defined on the frequency domain. Use the adaptive cross-dissolve technique described previously to combine the frequency bands f_i and g_i, pairwisely, for $k = 1, \ldots, n$:

$$c(f_i, g_i)(t, \omega) = s(t, \omega)f_i(\omega) + (1 - s(t, \omega))g_i(\omega).$$

The combination in the spatial domain is obtained by using the inverse Fourier transform: $F^{-1}(c(f_i, g_i))$.

This technique is performed in the frequency domain, in a scheduled fashion. First the details, or the low-frequency component, of the objects are combined, next the higher frequency bands is interpolated, and so on, until the

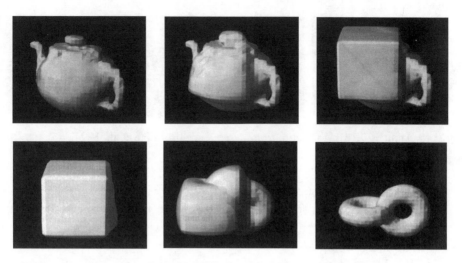

Figure 20.15   Morphing using Fourier scheduling [from Hughes, 1992].

high frequency components of the destination object are blended. In [Hughes, 1992] a wiping scheduling, similar to the one described by Equation (20.3) was used. Figure 20.15 shows some frames of a morphing sequence from a volumetric teapot to a cube, and then to a volumetric two-holed torus.

While this is a clever procedure to automatically obtain a morphing with matching features, it presents two problems: first, how to obtain the frequency band partition; second, how to obtain the correct blending for the frequencies. The second problem in particular poses a very interesting question: what are the constraints to obtaining perceptually good blendings in the frequency domain?

Also, it is very difficult to solve the problem of jump discontinuities using the scheduled Fourier blending because the Fourier transform has no information about the localization of the frequencies. In [Hughes, 1992], this problem is minimized using a regularization of the implicit function along the lines described in Section 20.6.

20.7.2   Morphing Using Wavelets

One strategy to overcome the problem of jump discontinuities when combining attribute functions of volumetric objects consists of obtaining a *space* × *frequency* description of the attribute functions by using an adequate

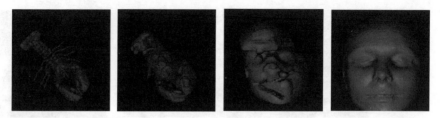

Figure 20.16 Wavelet morphing sequence [from He et al., 1994].

transform. In fact, from this description we are able to localize high frequencies and devise a scheduled transform that takes into account the frequency locations in the transformation. This achieves a feature matching transformation.

The first attempt to obtain this morphing appeared in the literature in [He et al., 1994]. Figure 20.16 shows some frames of a morphing sequence from this article. This article provides a scheduled transform between the voxel scanlines of one object into the voxel scanlines of the other. Each voxel scanline is properly segmented so that the high-frequency boundaries are properly mapped within each scanline.

The problem with the above technique is that it is too much correlated with the voxel representation of the volumetric object. Much better results should be obtained using a wavelet that can compute a good spatial distribution of the high frequencies and reconstruct the object prior to doing the morphing transformation.

20.7.3   Field-Based and Feature-Based Techniques

Both scheduled Fourier morphing and the wavelet basis morphing described above are semiautomatic morphing techniques. The reduced user input, however, results in less control over the transformations. We should point out that the above techniques perform semiautomatic morphings without requiring a warping to perform geometric alignment.

To overcome the jump discontinuity problem, we have to warp the source and target volumetric objects in order to obtain an alignment of their features. The morphing is done in such a way as to compute the geometric warp and the attribute combination simultaneously. Two techniques using this approach have appeared in the literature.

In [Darsa, 1994], the technique of field-based morphing for images is extended to volumetric objects. The user specifies the transformation on pairs

Figure 20.17 Volumetric lobster, warped to raise its claws.

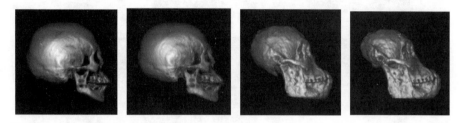

Figure 20.18 Morphing sequence between two volumetric objects [from Lerios et al., 1995].

of vectors from the source and target image. By carefully choosing the vectors, a good geometric alignment is attained. The interface is shown in Figure 20.3. Figure 20.17 (reprinted from Chapter 14) shows a warping sequence of a lobster raising its claws.

Other techniques also solve the alignment problem by providing a warping phase, using a feature-based specification. A nice example of this approach was introduced in the literature in [Lerios et al., 1995]. Figure 20.18, also shown in Chapter 4, shows a morphing sequence between a human skull and a monkey skull.

Feature-based techniques also can be used as a modeling tool, in the sense that they allow the creation of new volumetric objects by warping a single volumetric object.

20.7.4 Metamorphosis by Guided Warping

The registration warping can also be computed from a point-based specification. In fact, the technique of guided warping used in [Carmel and Cohen-Or, 1997] has been used in [Cohen-Or et al., 1998] to obtain a morphing technique that works for volumetric objects.

The method uses guided warps and interpolates the distance field of the graphical object shape. The use of the distance field forces the method to use volumetric information about the solid bounded by the surface. We could

Figure 20.19   Morphing with topology change [from Cohen-Or et al., 1998]. See also color plate 20.19.

consider it as being a volumetric morphing technique for surfaces. The use of volumetric information on the distance field makes the method very robust with respect to changes in the topology during the morphing. This is illustrated in Figure 20.19 between a triceratops and an iron. In this example, the triceratops and the iron are polygonal boundary models that are transformed into volumetric models by using scan conversion.

20.8 Comments and References

Chapter 8 of [Bloomenthal et al., 1997] brings abundant material with additional references to the problem of morphing implicitly defined objects. It also describes in detail some methods for conversion between implicit and boundary descriptions. A multiresolution approach to the problem of approximate conversion between volumetric and piecewise parametric boundary description, using wavelets, has been given in [Velho and Gomes, 1996].

An algorithm that uses Minkowski sum to compute a morphing between blob objects is described in [Galin and Akkouche, 1996]. The method describes implicit surfaces using skeletons and uses Minkowski sum as the blending operation for skeletons.

The field of volumetric warping and morphing is a very active area of research especially because of the huge number of applications in medical images. Warping of images and volumetric objects have been used as a means to define a metric on the space of these objects. This metric can be used to solve different problems related with proximity between two objects, such as character recognition in digital publishing and automatic diagnosis in medical imaging.

References

Bloomenthal, Jules, Chandrajit Bajaj, Jim Blinn, Marie-Paule Cani-Gascuel, Alyn Rockwood, Brian Wyvill, and Geoff Wyvill. 1997. *Introduction to Implicit Surfaces*. San Francisco: Morgan Kaufmann.

Carmel, Eyal, and Daniel Cohen-Or. 1997. Warp-Guided Object-Space Morphing. *The Visual Computer*, **13**, 465–478.

Cohen-Or, D., D. Levin, and A. Solomovici. 1998. Three-Dimensional Distance Field Metamorphosis. To appear in *ACM Transactions on Graphics*.

Darsa, L. 1994. *Graphical Objects Metamorphosis*. Master's Thesis. Rio de Janeiro: Computer Science Department. PUC-Rio.

Galin, E., and S. Akkouche. 1996. Blob Metamorphosis Based on Minkowski Sums. *Computer Graphics Forum (Eurographics '96 Proceedings)*, **15**(3), C-143–C-153.

Goldenstein, Siome K. 1997. *Sound Metamorphosis*. Master's Thesis. PUC-Rio (in Portuguese).

Gomes, J., and L. Velho. 1997. *Image Processing for Computer Graphics*. New York: Springer-Verlag.

He, Taosong, Sidney Wang, and Arie Kaufman. 1994. Wavelet-Based Volume Morphing. *Proceedings of Visualization '94*, 85–91.

Hughes, John F. 1992. Scheduled Fourier Volume Morphing. *Computer Graphics (SIGGRAPH '92 Proceedings)*, **26**(2), 43–46.

Kaufman, Arie. 1991. *Volume Visualization*. Los Alamitos, CA: IEEE Computer Society Press Tutorial.

Lerios, Apostolos, Chase D. Garfinkle, and Marc Levoy. 1995. Feature-Based Volume Metamorphosis. *Computer Graphics (SIGGRAPH '95 Proceedings)*, **29**, 449–456.

Levoy, Mark. 1988. Display of Surfaces from Volume Data. *IEEE Computer Graphics and Applications*, **8**(3), 29–37.

Lorensen, W. E., and H. E. Cline. 1987. Marching Cubes: A High Resolution 3D Surface Construction Algorithm. *Computer Graphics (SIGGRAPH '87 Proceedings)*, (7), 163–169.

Payne, B. A., and A. W. Toga. 1992. Distance Field Manipulation of Surface Models. *IEEE Computer Graphics and Applications*, **12**(1), 65–71.

Velho, Luiz, and Jonas Gomes. 1996. Approximate Conversion of Parametric to Implicit Surfaces. *Computer Graphics Forum*, **15**(5), 327–338.

Westover, L. 1992. *Splatting: A Parallel, Feed-Forward Volume Rendering Algorithm*. Ph.D. Thesis, University of North Carolina at Chapel Hill.

21

The Morphos System

In this chapter we will give a description of the architecture we used in the implementation of the *Morphos* system included on the companion CD-ROM. This architecture will make it easier for the user to navigate through the code, modify it, or introduce new modules into the system.

The *Morphos* system is an intrinsic part of the book for those interested in implementation issues, as well as for experimenting with several morphing and warping techniques.

We have decided not to include pseudocodes for the algorithms in the book. The source code of the *Morphos* system, the documentation about it included on the companion CD ROM, and the material in this chapter certainly provide a very complete complement to the discussion of implementation.

21.1 System's Characteristics

Our intention was to make the *Morphos* system a testbed morphing system. To attain this, the system should be portable and extensible, providing well-defined entry points to make the addition of new characteristics an easy task. More precisely, we describe a software architecture we have developed that attempts to

- allow for warping and morphing of different graphical objects such as images, surfaces, plane curves, and volume data;

- allow the development of plug-ins using different warping and morphing techniques, that can be shared among various types of graphical objects;

- allow the inclusion of new graphical objects in the system; and

- provide a uniform and coherent interface across different graphical objects and techniques.

Accomplishing all these goals is a very difficult task because of the rich diversity of existing graphical objects (sound, image, curves, surfaces, volumetric objects, etc.), and the different nature and user interface issues of warping and morphing techniques.

21.1.1   Computational Elements

We have seen that a morphing transformation consists of two warps (of the source and target objects) and a blending operation. Based on this conceptual view of the morphing operation, the design of a computational framework for the warping and morphing system should comprise six fundamental elements:

- graphical object creation/representation
- transformation specification/representation
- warping reconstruction
- mapped object computation
- shape blending
- attribute blending

Graphical Object Creation/Representation

In the implementation of a graphical object we associate a data structure to a discretization of the object, encapsulating the description of its shape and attributes. A typical application may handle only a specific type of graphical object—for example, an image represented by a matrix of pixel values—whereas a more generic one should be able to handle a variety of them. The representation is closely related with the specification: the user generally specifies a representation of the object.

Transformation Specification/Representation

The specification of the transformation consists of a discrete representation of the transformation, usually obtained from user input. In a typical situation, the user specifies values of the warp at a discrete set of positions at initial and final states. In some key-frame systems, these values are specified at different intermediate key states.

Warping Reconstruction

The warping reconstruction uses the discrete representation of the transformation to compute the transformation values at any point of the spatial and time domains of interest. This includes interpolating the key states in time and extending the transformation values to all points of the object shape.

Mapped Object Computation

This step of the technique enumerates the elements of the representation of the graphical object, traversing its structure. This is necessary in order to apply the warping to the object. The computation of the mapped object is closely related to the reconstruction of the transformation, and in some cases both elements are intermixed in actual implementations.

Shape Blending

This operation is necessary because we do not have a perfect alignment between the geometry of the two objects. When computing an image metamorphosis, the shape combination usually is not present because we have perfect alignment of the image boundaries. Nevertheless, shape combination is of fundamental importance when computing morphing of other graphical objects such as curves and surfaces.

Attribute Blending

The operation of blending attributes is used in the morphing transformation to compute the resulting attribute function from the attributes of the source and target graphical objects. The method of combination will vary according to the attribute nature.

A *morphing technique* is a combination of the above six elements, but the essence of the methods is contained in the specification and reconstruction of the transformation and the graphical objects, and the blending operations.

21.2 System's Architecture

We will now give a description of an architecture of a generic morphing system that addresses the problems stated in the previous section.

A morphing system has to manage the computational elements of warping and morphing, and orchestrate their interactions. Although these elements are not necessarily clearly identified and isolated in a given implementation, this separation can bring several benefits to the design and functionality of a system. As an example, the separation of the elements in a system makes it easy to experiment with hybrid techniques. Nevertheless, not all combinations are possible, and the set of specification techniques that suits a particular warping reconstruction technique has to be limited by the system.

21.2.1   System Components

The architecture of the system is based on a separation into three different levels: *platform*, *kernel*, and *support* levels, as shown in the diagram in Figure 21.1.

Platform Level

This module is responsible for the entire interface with the operating system. This includes in particular user interface and memory management. This is the level where all the platform dependencies are concentrated.

Kernel Level

This constitutes the core of the warping and morphing system. It is responsible for managing all the computational elements. Each type of element will be implemented in several different ways, corresponding to different techniques for performing the computation relative to that element. This level should be independent of the platform level.

Support Level

This module is responsible for the utility libraries, such as container classes, safe object-sharing mechanisms, and geometry and math libraries. It is also responsible for the input and output of graphical objects, supporting various standard and custom file formats for each type of graphical object. Portability of this level is one of the goals in the implementation of the system.

Figure 21.1 also shows the internal structure of each level of the system architecture. Each of these levels will ultimately correspond to classes. In the following sections, we will give more details about each of the system levels and their components.

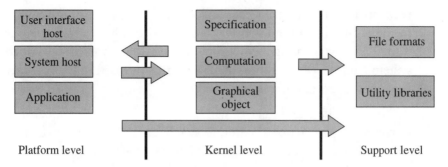

Figure 21.1 Morphing system architecture.

21.3 Kernel Level

The kernel level performs the operations necessary to compute warpings and morphings of graphical objects. In this level, the implementation notably benefits from the warping and morphing concepts introduced in Part III.

The kernel level is divided into three parts, which encompass all the computational elements:

- **graphical objects:** graphical object representation
- **specification of transformations:** transformation specification and representation
- **computation of transformations:** warping reconstruction, mapped object computation, shape, and attribute blending

Each of these parts will be controlled by a *manager,* which is responsible for keeping track of all the available computational element implementations, or *techniques.* It also defines the basic interface for each element, which provides all the operations and information needed for using those elements in computations, so that they are managed independently of their implementation.

Example 21.1 (Reusing Techniques)   Suppose the system contains a widget on its interface allowing for vector specification techniques. Assume we have implemented a 2D field-based warping technique as described in Chapter 14. This technique uses a vector specification and reconstructs the warping using a weighted interpolation. Implementing a second warping method that also uses vector specification amounts to actually implementing just the warping reconstruction part: given a set of corresponding vectors, the transformation to the entire domain must be reconstructed using an appropriate interpolation. This new warping reconstruction technique should be dropped into the system, and the computation manager will automatically make it available to the other layers and use it when requested.

Note that no user interface will have to be implemented, because the new warping reconstruction technique shares an existing form of specification. This makes the experimentation with new warping and morphing techniques very enticing, once some basic specification techniques are implemented.

21.3.1 Graphical Objects

The implementation of graphical objects naturally follows object-oriented concepts, with each type of graphical object being derived from a generic graphical object. The object interface will have to adapt to the graphical object class, and to the dimension of the space in which the graphical object is embedded.

The graphical objects classes are organized in a hierarchy of abstract data types, starting from a very generic root level. A simplified example of such a hierarchy is represented in Figure 21.2. Each technique that manipulates graphical objects will attempt to plug into this hierarchy at the highest level possible, so that it encompasses the largest group of graphical object types. For instance, the inverse mapping object computation technique can be applied to any implicit discrete graphical object, so this technique should be implemented at this level and not for some specific class of graphical objects, such as images.

21.3.2 Specification of Transformations

The specification of a warping or morphing has a strong relationship with the user interface, as the transformations are usually specified graphically through the use of geometric primitives, resulting in a discrete representation of the transformation.

Manipulators

All the specification techniques in our system are built upon basic interface building blocks, which we call *manipulators*. They are high-level geometric and interactive entities, similar in essence to *widgets* [Conner et al., 1992]. Ma-

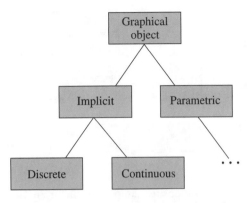

Figure 21.2 Simplified graphical object hierarchy.

nipulators provide both the semantics and the appearance of the components that allow the handling and modification of the specification of a transformation. Manipulators can be either 2D or 3D, depending on the dimension of the space where the graphical object is embedded. The implementation of the manipulators is portable, using the high-level input and output graphics primitives from the platform level.

Manipulators can be of two types: basic and composite. Basic manipulators are very simple geometric primitives, including points, squares, lines, and so on, with some basic interaction capabilities, such as hit testing and dragging. The composite manipulators are more complex and are constructed from basic manipulators. The composite manipulators are container classes that have to process messages and appropriately propagate them to their children. Examples of messages include drawing, dragging, selection, and deselection.

There are several types of composite manipulators, including basic and composite groups, which are ordered collections of basic and composite manipulators, respectively. Figure 21.3 shows partial class hierarchies for basic and composite manipulators. As composite manipulators are collections of other manipulators, manipulators have a hierarchical instantiation structure.

Example 21.2 (Curve Set Manipulator) Take the curve set composite manipulator, whose structure is shown in Figure 21.4: the curve set manipulator is a composite group, constituted by curve manipulators. The curve manipulators derive from the basic group manipulators and contain a number of square manipulators. The curves are manipulated via these square handles. The curve manipulator simply overrides the rendering routine of the basic

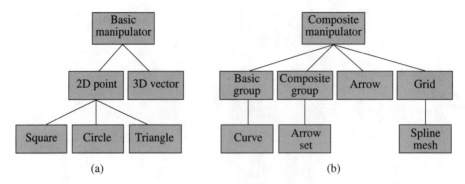

Figure 21.3   Basic manipulator (a) and composite manipulator hierarchy (b).

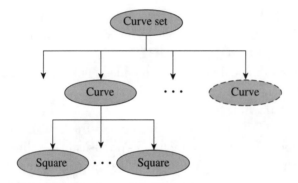

Figure 21.4   Structure of a curve set manipulator instance.

group manipulator to draw the spline connecting its control points. All the other operations of the composite manipulator are performed by the basic group and square manipulator base classes.

Specification Techniques

The specification manager offers a set of manipulators to the specification techniques. The specification techniques can choose manipulators from this set or can derive even more complex manipulators from the existing ones, with modified appearance, or imposing technique-specific constraints, priorities, and relationships among manipulators. In this way, the specification techniques can share and reutilize the provided graphical elements.

Object traversal	Warping reconstruction
Inverse mapping Direct mapping . . .	Field-based Radial functions . . .
Attribute combination	**Shape combinations**
Cross-dissolve z-buffering . . .	Exponential blend Linear interpolation . . .

Figure 21.5 Computation modules.

The specification manager defines the interface of a generic specification technique, that is, the operations that a given specification technique will have to perform. It also requires that the specification techniques provide methods to extract the geometric and topological parameters from the manipulators that will be needed by the warping reconstruction techniques.

The specification manager defines the syntax of the specification, and the implementation of the technique defines its semantics. In this way, the addition of a new specification technique does not involve tracking of user state or any system-dependent graphics, just the implementation of the meaning of the graphical manipulators.

21.3.3 Computation of Transformations

The separation between the computation manager and the computation techniques makes the process of adding a new computation technique straightforward. The parts that are common to any computation technique, such as the generation of a series of frames of a transformation by varying the time parameter, are factored out to the computation manager level. The computation manager is also able to handle families of transformations and generate animations from them. The implementations of the computation techniques have to deal with just the computation, at a given point in time, of the specific operation: mapping object computation, warping reconstruction, attribute combination, or shape combination. Examples of computation modules are shown in Figure 21.5.

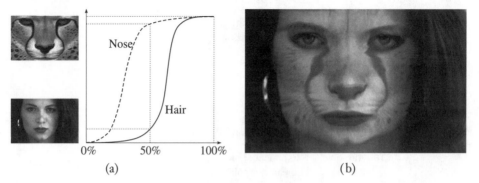

Figure 21.6   Two schedulers (a) for a scheduled morph in (b). See also color plate 21.6.

Transformations Schedulers

The computation manager is also responsible for controlling the flow of the transformations, that is, controlling the rate of change for different parts and attributes of the graphical objects. This control is offered by the *schedulers*, which determine the schedule according to which different parts of the graphical object will be transformed, as seen in Chapter 13. The schedulers can be interpreted as unidimensional functions that warp the time parameter and have the identity transformation as their default state.

Schedulers can be applied to modify the effect of a transformation globally, or modify some elements of the morphing technique (warping reconstruction, attribute, or shape combination). The use of different functions for different parts of the domain of the graphical object undergoing the transformation has the effect of localizing the transformation. As an example, consider the image in Figure 21.6(b). The attribute combination schedulers for the nose and hair specification elements are shown in Figure 21.6(a). The warping is controlled simply by a global scheduler with ease-in and ease-out. It is interesting to note that the schedulers themselves are specified using a derivation of the curve composite manipulator, constrained to be a function in the domain of interest.

21.4 Support Level

This module of the system (Figure 21.1) manages input and output of graphical objects, and provides several utility libraries.

Input and output of graphical objects is performed by filters managed by an external object format manager, in much the same way as the warping techniques are managed by the computation manager. The addition of new filters is also a well-defined process, limited to implementing a module that performs the operations defined by the file format manager, and adding the new module into the system. The file format manager provides mechanisms for the user to select preferred formats (according to the graphical object type), configure format-specific options, and to automatically identify the format of input files so that the appropriate graphical objects can be created and loaded.

The support level is also responsible for providing all the functionality of commonly used classes, such as vectors, matrices, hash tables, lists, and so on, which will facilitate the sharing of code throughout the system.

21.5 Platform Level

The main goal of the platform level (Figure 21.1) is to concentrate all the information related to the operating system and user interface. Besides allowing an easier port of the morphing system, the separation between the platform level and the rest of the software allows the implementation of different front ends for the same kernel level, on the same platform. For instance, it is possible to have two different applications, one using a graphical interface and the other using a command line or scripting interface, using the same kernel and support levels.

21.5.1 User Interface Host

The simple mapping of calls to the operating system does not solve completely the problem of portability of the morphing system. The *user interface host*, besides providing this "driver" functionality, is responsible for making the morphing application seem native to the system it is being ported to. This obviously implies that the semantics of the graphical user interface of the operating system has to leak into the morphing system at some stage. The goal here is to confine that leak to the system-dependent part of the code, so that it can be properly adjusted when porting the system.

In this way, the user interface host provides both event-handling and output-drawing methods at a high level, which are used in the implementation of the manipulators. If the interface functionality were designed at a lower level, this could imply in code redundancy: for example, both point and line manipulators would receive mouse events, and might have to duplicate the implementation of rubber banding.

The color and pattern management is an integrated part of the user interface host. Rather than directly requesting a particular color or pattern to be used in a drawing operation, the manipulators select *representation types* according to the idea conveyed and to their states. Examples include hot-spot and selected manipulator representation. These can be mapped to monochrome patterns or to the user's color scheme.

21.5.2 System Host

The system host manages the platform-dependent resources used by the application, such as memory, interprocess communication, and error handling. As the usage of the standard libraries is recommended to maximize portability, the importance of the system host tends to be reduced. For instance, the use of the C/C++ standard I/O library is usually enough to process file I/O.

The system host is also responsible for providing simple user interfaces for asking questions and notifying the user of errors, and also for exceptional situation handling to be used in the kernel and support levels. It also provides services for saving and retrieving persistent configuration options in the system that can be implemented, for instance, through environment variables.

21.5.3 Application

Given the kernel level, the support level, and the core modules of the platform level, an application can be built by making use of the parts of the system that are of interest.

In a command-line application, the specification of the warping or morphing transformation would not be given interactively, but by files. These specification files could be generated by using a separate specification-only software. This kind of separation would enable the user to compute transformations previously specified in an offline fashion, to split up the work in a farm of workstations. This kind of application can be made portable by providing appropriate user interface and system hosts.

More commonly, the application will use system-dependent features and graphical interfaces. The use of application frameworks to automate the construction of most of the user interface of the software is a relatively simple approach.

21.6 The System

The *Morphos* warping and morphing system has been implemented in C++. The kernel and platform levels are currently implemented for the Windows

Figure 21.7 Morphos plug-ins.

family of operating systems, using OpenGL for the 3D interface and for real-time previews of image warpings.

As stated before, the fundamental operations of the system are concentrated in the kernel level. A user-friendly interface, project management, intelligent file format usage, and configurability are important aspects of an actual system that must be taken into consideration when designing the architecture. We have concentrated most of the system development effort in designing the kernel level, the support level, and the relation of these parts with the user interface.

21.6.1 Objects and Transformations

Morphos currently supports three types of graphical objects: images, polygonal curves, and surfaces. It has several techniques implemented, including mesh, features, and point specifications; linear and exponential dissolve attribute combination; field-based, radial-basis functions; two-pass spline mesh warping; projective mapping; and so on.

A snapshot of the plug-in modules linked to the system is shown in Figure 21.7. Note that, as the managers are responsible for keeping track of the techniques and graphical objects under their control, none of the dialogs showing plug-ins has to be modified when adding new modules. Also, all the plug-ins can be configured regardless of their type.

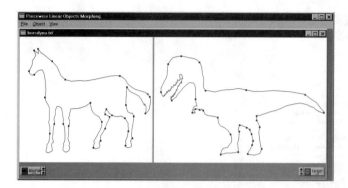

Figure 21.8   Curve metamorphosis using side-by-side interface.

21.6.2 User Interface

We have seen in Part III that there are two basic strategies to construct a user interface for a warping and morphing system: side-by-side interface and single-window interface.

The *side-by-side interface* is a natural choice for metamorphosis: the user interacts with the source and the target objects into two different windows in order to specify the animation path for corresponding features. The transformation is specified by giving elements of the specification on the source and target objects. This is the interface that the Morphos system uses. Figure 21.8 illustrates the side-by-side interface for curve metamorphosis. As our system allows the use of different specification types, several different specifications can be placed over the same graphical object, as illustrated in Figure 21.9 for images.

Side-by-side interfaces can also be used for specifying warping operations, especially for graphical objects embedded on the plane (curves and images). This interface is useful when we need to specify precisely the handlers constraints, referencing them to the graphical object shape. This is a common requirement when we need to warp two images to bring them into registration.

For interactive use, the *single-window interface* is the best choice for warping: the user specifies the transformation on constrained handlers on the window where the object is displayed. An example is the point-based specification, where the user specifies the displacement vectors of each point.

Morphos has an interface for displacement vectors using a single-window interface. Also, the system has an interface to specify displacement vectors in 3D space, using constrained arcball (see Figure 21.10). This interface is very

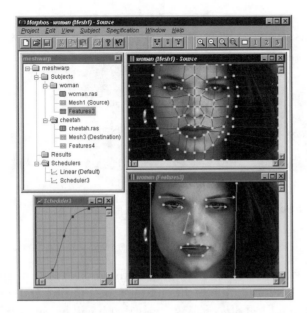

Figure 21.9 Two specifications for a subject.

Figure 21.10 3D displacement vector interface for warping [from Pinheiro, 1997].

effective for interactive warping of graphical objects embedded on the 3D space such as surfaces and volumes (see Chapter 19, Warping and Morphing of Surfaces).

21.7 Examples

In this section we give some examples that demonstrate the extensibility and flexibility of our unified architecture for warping and morphing systems.

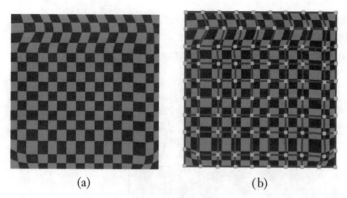

(a)   (b)

Figure 21.11   Scanning deformation (a) and correction grid (b).

These examples illustrate situations that require the ability to use many different specification and computation techniques for the warping and morphing
of distinct types of graphical objects. We stress that it will be very difficult, or
even impossible, to deal with these situations in the current warping and morphing systems, because they don't implement techniques and representations
in an integrated way.

21.7.1   Adapted Image Warping Specification

This example reveals the importance of having several specification techniques for the same type of graphical object and computation method. This
makes it possible to use a specification that best adapts to the problem at
hand. Take the specification of a warping for two different purposes: the first
for correcting distortions, and the second for real-time registration.

In Figure 21.11(a), we show the image of a grid that was obtained through
a scanning process. The grid is distorted in this image due to problems in
the acquisition process. For this reason, we want to determine a morphing
specification that will correct the distortion of the input device. The best specification technique for the above problem is a grid-based specification, shown
in Figure 21.11(b). The one-to-one correspondence between the specification
primitives and the image makes the task very simple.

In Figure 21.12(a) we show the image of a texture that needs to be aligned
with features of the geometric model shown in Figure 21.12(b). The best
specification technique, in this case, is a feature-based technique. The tech-

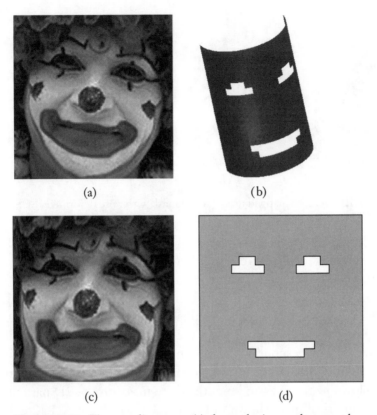

(a)

(b)

(c)

(d)

Figure 21.12 Texture alignment: (a) shows the image that must be mapped on the mask shown in (b), and (c) shows the image warped according to the mask features on the parameter space of the mask shown in (d).

nique allows the direct indication of features in the image of correspondence with the geometry.

The above examples clearly demonstrate that the effectiveness of a specification technique depends on its adequacy to the task at hand. Therefore, a warping and morphing system should provide a variety of specification techniques, as well as the possibility of adding new ones to the system.

21.7.2 Integration of Warping and Morphing

The example of this section illustrates the importance of integrated warping and morphing operation for different types of graphical objects. Such a system

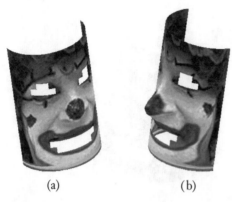

(a)   (b)

Figure 21.13   Texture mapped mask (a) and mask with nose deformed (b). See also color plate 21.13.

is well suited to deal with the problem of registering a texture to a warped surface, as described in [Litwinowicz and Miller, 1994].

As an example, consider the problem of applying the clown texture from Figure 21.12(a) onto the cylindrical mask shown in Figure 21.12(b). In order to get good results, we must align the features of the clown face (eyes and mouth) to the corresponding features of the mask. This alignment is attained with a warping operation of the clown image to align the eyes and mouth of the clown to the eyes and mouth of the mask on the 2D parameter space of the cylindrical mask shown in Figure 21.12(d). Figure 21.12(c) shows the warped clown. The mask with the clown texture mapped on it is shown in Figure 21.13(a).

Now we have the second task: create a nose on the 3D mask. For this, we have to deform the geometry of the cylindrical mask in order to create the nose. Figure 21.13(c) shows the warping of the mask, where the texture is deformed with the mesh. It is clear that when one operation is performed, the object representation should remain consistent. In particular, the correspondence of the texture image with the mesh geometry should be maintained at all times. Also, the user should be able to intermix these two operations in any order using the system.

The system could be able to handle even more complicated versions of the problem above. For instance, consider the case of a morphing between two textured parametric surfaces, in which both the textures and the meshes are being warped and the correspondence needs to be maintained so that the representations can be combined. Complex transformations involving the various aspects of several graphical objects, such as the case described above, can be handled by the integrated architecture of our system.

Figure 21.14 Spidery mesh interface and results.

21.7.3 Incorporating New Techniques

This example illustrates the usefulness of an extensible architecture that allows incorporating new techniques into the system, showing how an image-based rendering method can be easily added to the system. In [Horry et al., 1997], a technique called *Tour into the Picture* (TIP) is described. This technique uses a spidery mesh interface to specify a projective warping of some image. In that way, the 3D scene depicted in the image can be approximately reconstructed, and rerendered from different points of view.

Since our system already has a projective warping reconstruction technique, the only component that needed to be added to incorporate the TIP method is the spidery mesh specification technique. Figure 21.14 shows the interface that we developed for the spidery mesh. The specification consists of a composite manipulator based on two elements. The first is a rectangle indicating the back plane, where the rectangle is derived from the quadrilateral manipulator, with an added constraint. The second is a square, derived from the punctual manipulator and used to indicate the vanishing point.

The drawing of the composite manipulator is augmented to draw the perspective lines converging to the vanishing point and passing through the rectangle.

Figure 21.15   Original image (a), two-pass spline mesh warp (b), piecewise linear warp (c), and RMS difference (d).

This specification implicitly defines five regions that will be warped using a projective transformation corresponding to the planes of a cube, with the back plane indicated by the rectangle. The implementation of this specification technique was done in a few hours, and all of the functionality of the TIP technique was made available to the system.

21.7.4   Comparison of Computational Methods

When we have a system that enables us to compute warping and morphing of different graphical objects using different techniques, it is natural to use it as a warping and morphing testbed system with the ability to compare different methods and techniques, and the possibility of experimenting with various comparison schemes and metrics.

In this example we illustrate the comparison of two different warping computation methods: two-pass warping and piecewise affine warping. In order to compare these two methods, we are going to measure the RMS error of warped images using each method with a reference warped image using exact computation.

Figure 21.15(a) shows the original image and the warping specification. Figure 21.15(b) depicts the warped image using the two-pass spline mesh warping, and Figure 21.15(c) shows the warped image using piecewise linear computation technique. Figure 21.15(d) shows the RMS error between the two warped images.

21.8   Comments and References

This chapter described an architecture for a warping and morphing system. The architecture is based on the fundamental unifying concepts of graphical objects and transformations of graphical objects, presented throughout the book. These two concepts allow us to create an integrated framework that encompasses all warping and morphing techniques, as well as all types of graphical objects, such as curves, images, surfaces, and volumes.

The framework clearly separates the representation from the computational aspects, allowing almost any transformation to be applied to any object in the system. Also, a warping/morphing scheme can be decomposed into several computational elements. This decomposition is very important because it greatly enhances the expressive power of the system and allows the definition of customized warping and morphing schemes that best match the problem at hand.

We should point out that not all of the details of the architecture have necessarily been fully implemented. The *Morphos* system is a work in progress, and we intend to continue using it as a basis for future development and experimentation. Possible extensions to the system include addition of volumetric data into the system, with the development of efficient methods for visualization and feedback; surface morphing; automatic feature detection techniques as an alternative form of warping specification; hierarchical correspondence schemes for schedule control of the transformations; and capability to handle time-varying graphical objects (motion, video and audio warping, and morphing). For more information on future versions of *Morphos*, visit the Web site *www.visgraf.impa.br/morph/*.

The code on the companion CD-ROM is organized according to this architecture, and specific information about the modules, including a step-by-step description of how to add new specification and computation techniques to the system, can be found through navigation on the CD-ROM.

A useful reference for portability concerns is [Jaeschke, 1989]. The object-oriented programming languages field is vast; the user should consult [Stroustrup, 1997] and [Ellis and Stroustrup, 1990] for the traditional references on the C++ programming language. Also, [Cline and Lomow, 1995] illustrates various interesting topics about the language with a straightforward style.

References

Cline, Marshall P., and Greg A. Lomow. 1995. *C++ FAQs*. Reading, MA: Addison-Wesley.

Conner, D. B., S. S. Snibbe, K. P. Herndon, D. C. Robbins, R. C. Zeleznik, and A. van Dam. 1992. Three-Dimensional Widgets. *Computer Graphics (1992 Symposium on Interactive 3D Graphics)*, **25**(2), 183–188.

Ellis, Margaret, and Bjare Stroustrup. 1990. *The Annotated C++ Reference Manual*. Reading, MA: Addison-Wesley.

Horry, Youichi, Ken Ichi Anjyo, and Kiyoshi Arai. 1997. Tour into the Picture: Using a Spidery Mesh Interface to Make Animation from a Single Image. *Computer Graphics (SIGGRAPH '97 Proceedings)*, 225–232.

Jaeschke, Rex. 1989. *Portability and the C Language*. Indianapolis, IN: Macmillan Computer Publishing, Hayden Books.

Litwinowicz, Peter, and Gavin Miller. 1994. Efficient Techniques for Interactive Texture Placement. *Computer Graphics (SIGGRAPH '94 Proceedings)*, 119–122.

Pinheiro, Sergio E. M. L. 1997. *Interactive Deformations Using Direct Specification*. Master's Thesis. PUC-Rio (in Portugese).

Stroustrup, Bjarne. 1997. *The C++ Programming Language, Third Edition*. Reading, MA: Addison-Wesley.

Bibliography

Adelson, E. H., and J. R. Berger. 1991. "The Plenoptic Function and the Elements of Early Vision." Computational Models of Visual Processing, Chapter 1. M. Landy and J. A. Movshon (eds.), Cambridge, MA: MIT Press.

Airey, J. M. 1990. *Increasing Update Rates in the Building Walkthrough System with Automatic Model-Space Subdivision and Potentially Visible Set Calculations*. Ph.D. Thesis, University of North Carolina at Chapel Hill, Department of Computer Science.

Arad, N., and D. Reisfeld. 1995. Image Warping Using Few Anchor Points and Radial Functions. *Computer Graphics Forum*, **14**(1), 35–46.

Arun, K. S., T. S. Huang, and S. D. Blostein. 1987. Least-Squares Fitting of Two 3D Point Sets. *IEEE Trans. on Pattern Analysis and Machine Intelligence, PAMI*, **9**, 698–700.

Aubert, Fabrice, and Dominique Bechmann. 1997. Animation by Deformation of Space-Time Objects. *Computer Graphics Forum (Eurographics '97 Proceedings)*, **16**(3), 57–66.

Bajcsy, R., and S. Kovacic. 1989. Multiresolution Elastic Matching. *Computer Vision, Graphics and Image Processing*, **46**, 1–21.

Barr, A. H. 1984. Global and Local Deformations of Solid Primitives. *Computer Graphics (SIGGRAPH '84 Proceedings)*, **18**, 21–30.

Bartels, Richard H., John C. Beatty, and Brian Barsky. 1987. *An Introduction to Splines for Use in Computer Graphics and Geometric Modeling*. San Mateo, CA: Morgan Kaufmann.

Bechmann, Dominique. 1994. Space Deformation Models Survey. *Computers & Graphics*, **18**(4), 571–586.

Becker, Barry G., and Nelson L. Max. 1993. Smooth Transitions Between Bump Rendering Algorithms. *Computer Graphics (SIGGRAPH '93 Proceedings)*, **27**, 183–189.

Beier, Thaddeus, and Shawn Neely. 1992. Feature-Based Image Metamorphosis. *Computer Graphics (SIGGRAPH '92 Proceedings)*, **26**(2), 35–42.

Berger, M. 1987. *Geometry I*. New York: Springer-Verlag.

Bernstein, Ralph. 1976. Digital Image Processing of Earth Observation Sensor Data. *IBM J. Res. Development*, **20**, 40–57.

Bézier, P. 1978. General Distortion of an Ensemble of Biparametric Patches. *Computer Aided Design*, **10**(2), 116–120.

Bier, E., and K. Sloan. 1986. Two Part Texture Mapping. *IEEE Computer Graphics and Applications*, **6**(9), 40–53.

Bishop, Gary, Henry Fuchs, Leonard McMillan, and Ellen Zagier. 1994. Frameless Rendering: Double Buffering Considered Harmful. *Computer Graphics (SIGGRAPH '94 Proceedings)*, 175–176.

Blinn, James F. 1978. Simulation of Wrinkled Surfaces. *Computer Graphics (SIGGRAPH '78 Proceedings)*, **12**(3), 286–292.

Blinn, James F. 1982. A Generalization of Algebraic Surface Drawing. *ACM Transactions on Graphics*, **1**(3), 235–256.

Blinn, James F., and M. E. Newell. 1976. Texture and Reflection in Computer Generated Images. *Communications of the ACM*, **19**(10), 542–547.

Bloomenthal, Jules, Chandrajit Bajaj, Jim Blinn, Marie-Paule Cani-Gascuel, Alyn Rockwood, Brian Wyvill, and Geoff Wyvill. 1997. *Introduction to Implicit Surfaces*. San Francisco: Morgan Kaufmann.

Blum, Lenore. 1991. *Lectures on a Theory of Computation over the Reals*. Rio de Janeiro: Instituto de Matemática Pura e Aplicada (IMPA).

Bookstein, F. L. 1989. Principal Warps: Thin-Plate Splines and the Decomposition of Deformations. *IEEE Transactions of Pattern Analysis and Machine Intelligence*, **11**, 567–585.

Bordwell, David, and Kristin Thompson. 1996. "The Power of Mise-en-Scene." In *Film Art, An Introduction*. New York: McGraw-Hill, 171–172.

Borrel, P., and A. Rappoport. 1995. Simple Constrained Deformations for Geometric Modeling and Interactive Design. *ACM Transactions on Graphics*, **13**(2), 137–155.

Braccini, Carlo, and Giuseppe Marino. 1980. Fast Geometrical Manipulation of Digital Images. *Computer Graphics and Image Processing*, **13**, 127–141.

Bregler, Christoph, Michelle Covell, and Malcom Slaney. 1997. Video Rewrite: Driving Visual Speech with Audio. In *Computer Graphics (SIGGRAPH '97 Proceedings)*, 353–360.

Brown, Lisa G. 1992. A Survey of Image Registration Techniques. *ACM Computing Surveys*, **24**(4), 325–376.

Burtnik, N., and M. Wein. 1971. Computer Generated Key-Frame Animation. *SMPTE Journal*, **80**, 149–153.

Carmel, Eyal, and Daniel Cohen-Or. 1997. Warp-Guided Object-Space Morphing. *The Visual Computer*, **13**, 465–478.

Catmull, E. 1974. *A Subdivision Algorithm for the Display of Curves and Surfaces*. Ph.D. Thesis. University of Utah.

Catmull, Edwin. 1975. Computer Display of Curved Surfaces. *Proceedings of the IEEE Conf. on Computer Graphics Pattern Recognition Data Structure*, May, 11.

Catmull, Edwin, and Alvy Ray Smith. 1980. 3D-Transformations of Images in Scanline Order. *Computer Graphics (SIGGRAPH '80 Proceedings)*, **14**(3), 279–285.

Chadwick, J. E., D. R. Haumann, and R. E. Parent. 1989. Layered Construction for Deformable Animated Characters. *Computer Graphics (SIGGRAPH '89 Proceedings)*, **23**(July), 243–252.

Chen, Shenchang Eric. 1995. QuickTime VR—An Image-Based Approach to Virtual Environment Navigation. *Computer Graphics (SIGGRAPH '95 Proceedings)*, 29–38.

Chen, Shenchang Eric, and Richard E. Parent. 1989. Shape Averaging and Its Applications to Industrial Design. *IEEE Computer Graphics and Applications*, **9**(1), 47–54.

Chen, Shenchang Eric, and Lance Williams. 1993. View Interpolation for Image Synthesis. *Computer Graphics (SIGGRAPH '93 Proceedings)*, **27**(Aug.), 279–288.

Christensen, G. E. 1994. *Deformable Shape Models for Anatomy*. Ph.D. Thesis. Washington University.

Cline, Marshall P., and Greg A. Lomow. 1995. *C++ FAQs*. Reading, MA: Addison-Wesley.

Cohen, J., A. Varshney, D. Manocha, G. Turk, H. Weber, P. Agarwal, F. P. Brooks, Jr., and W. V. Wright. 1996. Simplification Envelopes. *Computer Graphics (SIGGRAPH '96)*, 119–128.

Cohen-Or, D., D. Levin, and A. Solomovici. 1998. Three-Dimensional Distance Field Metamorphosis. To appear in *ACM Transactions on Graphics*.

Comment, Bernard. 1993. *Le XIX Siecle des Panorama*. Paris: Adam Piro.

Conner, D. B., S. S. Snibbe, K. P. Herndon, D. C. Robbins, R. C. Zeleznik, and A. van Dam. 1992. Three-Dimensional Widgets. *Computer Graphics (1992 Symposium on Interactive 3D Graphics)*, **25**(2), 183–188.

Cook, Robert L. 1984. Shade Trees. *Computer Graphics (SIGGRAPH '84 Proceedings)*, **18**, 223–231.

Coons, S. 1974. Surface Patches and B-Spline Curves. In Barnhill, R., and R. Riesenfeld (eds.), *Computer Aided Geometric Design*. San Diego: Academic Press.

Coquillart, Sabine. 1990. Extended Free-Form Deformations: A Sculpturing Tool for 3D Geometric Modeling. *Computer Graphics (SIGGRAPH '90 Proceedings)*, **24**(Aug.), 187–196.

Coquillart, S., and P. Jancene. 1991. Animated Free-Form Derformation: An Interactive Animated Technique. *Computer Graphics (SIGGRAPH '91 Proceedings)*, **25**(July), 23–26.

Costa, B. 1994. *Image Deformation and Metamorphosis*. Master's Thesis. Rio de Janeiro: Computer Science Department. PUC-Rio.

Costa, B., L. Darsa, and J. Gomes. 1992. Image Metamorphosis. In Gomes, J., and G. Câmara (eds.), *SIBGRAPI '92 Proceedings*, 19–27.

Darsa, Lucia, and Bruno Costa. 1996. Multi-Resolution Representation and Reconstruction of Adaptively Sampled Images. *(SIBGRAPI '96 Proceedings)*, 321–328.

Darsa, Lucia, Bruno Costa, and Amitabh Varshney. 1997. Navigating Static Environments Using Image-Space Simplification and Morphing. *Proceedings of the 1997 Symposium on Interactive 3D Graphics*, 25–34.

Darsa, Lucia, Bruno Costa, and Amitabh Varshney. 1998. Walkthroughs of Complex Environments Using Image-Space Simplification. *Computers and Graphics*, Jan.

Darsa, L. 1994. *Graphical Objects Metamorphosis*. Master's Thesis. Rio de Janeiro: Computer Science Department. PUC-Rio.

da Silva, Adelailson Peixoto. 1997. *Metamorphosis of Plane Curves Using Convex Evolution*. Master's Thesis. PUC-Rio (in Portuguese).

Daubechies, I. 1992. *Ten Lectures on Wavelets*. Philadelphia: SIAM Books.

Debevec, Paul E., Camillo J. Taylor, and Jitendra Malik. 1996. Modeling and Rendering Architecture from Photographs: A Hybrid Geometry- and Image-Based Approach. *Computer Graphics (SIGGRAPH '96 Proceedings)*, 11–20.

DeCarlo, Douglas, and Jean Gallier. 1996. Topological Evolution of Surfaces. *Proceedings of Graphics Interface '96*, 194–203.

de Figueiredo, Luiz Henrique. 1995. Adaptive Sampling of Parametric Curves. In Paeth, Alan (ed.), *Graphics Gems V*. Boston: Academic Press, 173–178.

de Reffye, Phillippe, Claude Edelin, Jean Francon, Marc Jaeger, and Claude Puech. 1988. Plant Models Faithful to Botanical Structure and Development. *Computer Graphics (SIGGRAPH '88 Proceedings)*, **22**, 151–158.

DeRose, T. D., M. Lounsbery, and J. Warren. 1993. *Multiresolution Analysis for Surface of Arbitrary Topological Type*. Report 93-10-05. Department of Computer Science, University of Washington, Seattle.

do Carmo, M. P. 1976. *Differential Geometry of Curves and Surfaces*. Englewood Cliffs, NJ: Prentice Hall.

Duff, T. 1985. Compositing 3D Rendered Images. *Computer Graphics (SIGGRAPH '85 Proceedings)*, **19**(3), 41–44.

Ebert, David S., F. Kenton Musgrave, Darwyn Peachey, Ken Perlin, and Steven Worley. 1994. *Texturing and Modeling: A Procedural Approach*. San Diego: Academic Press.

Ellis, Margaret, and Bjare Stroustrup. 1990. *The Annotated C++ Reference Manual*. Reading, MA: Addison-Wesley.

Encyclopedia Brittanica. 1973. Chicago: Encyclopedia Brittanica Educational Corporation. Vol. 15, p. 259.

Etzion, M., and A. Rappoport. 1997. On Compatible Star Decompositions of Simple Polygons. *IEEE Transactions on Visualization and Computer Graphics*, **3**(1), 87–95.

Fant, Karl M. 1986. A Nonaliasing, Real-Time Spatial Transform Technique. *IEEE Computer Graphics and Applications*, **6**(1), 71–80.

Farin, Gerald. 1988. *Curves and Surfaces for Computer Aided Geometric Design.* San Diego: Academic Press.

Fiume, E. 1989. *The Mathematical Structure of Raster Graphics*. Boston: Academic Press.

Fiume, E., A. Fournier, and V. Canale. 1987. Conformal Texture Mapping. *Proceedings of Eurographics '87*. Amsterdam: Elsevier Science Publishers, 53–64.

Forsey, D., and R. Bartels. 1988. Hierarchical B-Spline Refinement. *Computer Graphics (SIGGRAPH '88 Proceedings)*, **22**, 205–212.

Franke, R., and G. Nielson. 1980. Smooth Interpolation of Large Sets of Scattered Data. *Int'l J. for Numerical Methods in Engineering*, **15**, 1691–1704.

Frederick, Carl, and Eric L. Schwartz. 1990. Conformal Image Warping. *IEEE Computer Graphics and Applications*, **10**(3), 54–61.

Galin, E., and S. Akkouche. 1996. Blob Metamorphosis Based on Minkowski Sums. *Computer Graphics Forum (Eurographics '96 Proceedings)*, **15**(3), C-143–C-153.

Ghosh, P. K., and P. K. Jain. 1993. An Algebra of Geometric Shapes. *IEEE Computer Graphics and Applications*, Sep., 50–58.

Gitlin, C., J. O'Rourke, and V. Subramanian. 1996. On Reconstruction of Polyhedra from Slices. *Int. J. Computational Geometry and Applications*, **6**(1), 103–112.

Glassner, A. 1995. *Principles of Digital Image Synthesis*. San Francisco: Morgan Kaufmann.

Goldenstein, Siome K. 1997. *Sound Metamorphosis*. Master's Thesis. PUC-Rio (in Portuguese).

Goldenstein, Siome, and Jonas Gomes. 1997. Time Warping of Audio Signals. *Preprint*, IMPA, Rio de Janeiro.

Gomes, Jonas, Bruno Costa, Lucia Darsa, and Luiz Velho. 1996. Graphical Objects. *The Visual Computer,* **12**, 269–282.

Gomes, J., and L. Velho. 1992. *Implicit Objects in Computer Graphics*. Rio de Janeiro, Brazil: Instituto de Matemática Pura e Aplicada (IMPA).

Gomes, Jonas, and Luiz Velho. 1995. Abstraction Paradigms for Computer Graphics. *The Visual Computer,* **11**, 227–239.

Gomes, J., and L. Velho. 1997. *Image Processing for Computer Graphics.* New York: Springer-Verlag.

Gortler, Steven J., Radek Grzeszczuk, Richard Szelinski, and Michael F. Cohen. 1996. The Lumigraph. *Computer Graphics (SIGGRAPH '96 Proceedings),* 43–54.

Goshtasby, A. 1986. Piecewise Linear Mapping Functions for Image Registration. *Pattern Recognition,* **19**(6), 459–466.

Goshtasby, A. 1987. Piecewise Cubic Mapping Functions for Image Registration. *Pattern Recognition,* **20**(5), 525–533.

Grayson, M. 1987. The Heat Equation Shrinks Embedded Plane Curves to Round Points. *J. Diff. Geom.,* **26**, 285.

Greene, Ned. 1986. Environment Mapping and Other Applications of World Projections. *IEEE Computer Graphics and Applications,* **6**(11), 21–29.

Greene, Ned. 1989. Voxel Space Automata: Modeling with Stochastic Growth Processes in Voxel Space. *Computer Graphics (SIGGRAPH '89 Proceedings),* **23**, 175–184.

Greene, N. 1996. Hierarchical Polygon Tiling with Coverage Masks. *Computer Graphics (SIGGRAPH '96 Proceedings),* 65–74.

Greene, Ned, and M. Kass. 1993. Hierarchical Z-Buffer Visibility. *Computer Graphics (SIGGRAPH '93 Proceedings),* 231–240.

Hardy, R. L. 1971. Multi Quadratic Equations of Topography and Other Irregular Surfaces. *Journal of Geophysical Research,* **76**(8), 1905–1915.

He, Taosong, Sidney Wang, and Arie Kaufman. 1994. Wavelet-Based Volume Morphing. *Proceedings of Visualization '94,* 85–91.

He, T., L. Hong, A. Varshney, and S. Wang. 1996. Controlled Topology Simplification. *IEEE Transactions on Visualization and Computer Graphics,* **2**(2), 171–184.

Heckbert, Paul S. 1986. Survey of Texture Mapping. *IEEE Computer Graphics and Applications*, **6**(11), 56–67.

Heckbert, P. 1989. *Fundamentals of Texture Mapping and Image Warping*. Master's Thesis (Technical Report No. UCB/CSD 89/516). University of California, Berkeley (*www.cs.cmu.edu/~ph*).

Heckbert, P. 1994. Bilinear Coons Patch Image Warping. In Heckbert, Paul S. (ed.), *Graphics Gems IV*. Boston: Academic Press, 438–446.

Henrici, P. 1986. *Applied and Computational Complex Analysis*. New York: John Wiley.

Hoffmann, Chris. 1989. *Geometric and Solid Modeling: An Introduction*. San Mateo, CA: Morgan Kaufmann.

Hong, M. T., N. M. Thalmann, and D. Thalmann. 1988. A General Algorithm for 3D-Shape Interpolation in a Facet-Based Representation. *Proceedings of Graphics Interface '88*, 229–235.

Hoppe, H. 1996. Progressive Meshes. *Computer Graphics (SIGGRAPH '96 Proceedings)*, 99–108.

Horry, Youichi, Ken Ichi Anjyo, and Kiyoshi Arai. 1997. Tour into the Picture: Using a Spidery Mesh Interface to Make Animation from a Single Image. *Computer Graphics (SIGGRAPH '97 Proceedings)*, 225–232.

Hsu, William M., John F. Hughes, and Henry Kaufmann. 1992. Direct Manipulation of Free-Form Deformations. *Computer Graphics (SIGGRAPH '92 Proceedings)*, **26**(2), 177–184.

Hughes, John F. 1992. Scheduled Fourier Volume Morphing. *Computer Graphics (SIGGRAPH '92 Proceedings)*, **26**(2), 43–46.

Jaeschke, Rex. 1989. *Portability and the C Language*. Indianapolis, IN: Macmillan Computer Publishing, Hayden Books.

Kajiya, James T., and Timothy L. Kay. 1989. Rendering Fur with Three Dimensional Textures. *Computer Graphics (SIGGRAPH '89 Proceedings)*, **23**(3), 271–280.

Kalra P., A. Mangili, N. M. Thalmann, and D. Thalmann. 1992. Simulation of Facial Muscle Actions Based on Rational Free-Form Deformation. In *Eurographics '92 (Computer Graphics Forum)*, **2**, 56–69.

Kass, Michael, Andrew Witkin, and Demetri Terzopoulos. 1988. Snakes: Active Contour Models. *International Journal of Computer Vision*, **1**(4), 321–331.

Kaufman, Arie. 1991. *Volume Visualization*. Los Alamitos, CA: IEEE Computer Society Press Tutorial.

Kaufman, Arie. 1994. Voxels as a Computational Representation of Geometry. In *The Computational Representation of Geometry*. SIGGRAPH '94 Course Notes.

Kaul, A., and J. Rossignac. 1991. Solid-Interpolating Deformations: Construction and Animation of PIPs. *Proceedings of Eurographics '91*. Amsterdam: Elsevier Science Publishers, 493–505.

Kawaguchi, Yoichiro. 1982. A Morphological Study of the Form of Nature. *Computer Graphics (SIGGRAPH '82 Proceedings)*, **16**(3), 223–232.

Kent, J. R., W. E. Carlson, and R. E. Parent. 1992. Shape Transformation for Polyhedral Objects. *Computer Graphics (SIGGRAPH '92 Proceedings)*, **26**(2), 47–54.

Koenderink, Jan J. 1990. *Solid Shape*. Cambridge, MA: MIT Press.

Kolomijec, William. 1976. The Appeal of Computer Graphics. In *Artist and Computer*. New York: Crown Publishers Inc., Harmony Books.

Lasseter, John. 1987. Principles of Traditional Animation Applied to 3D Computer Animation. *Computer Graphics (SIGGRAPH '87 Proceedings)*, **21**(4), 35–44.

Lee, Seung-Yong, Kyung-Yong Chwa, Sung Yong Shin, and George Wolberg. 1995. Image Metamorphosis Using Snakes and Free-Form Deformations. *Computer Graphics (SIGGRAPH '95 Proceedings)*, 439–448.

Lerios, Apostolos, Chase D. Garfinkle, and Marc Levoy. 1995. Feature-Based Volume Metamorphosis. *Computer Graphics (SIGGRAPH '95 Proceedings)*, **29**, 449–456.

Levoy, Mark. 1988. Display of Surfaces from Volume Data. *IEEE Computer Graphics and Applications*, **8**(3), 29–37.

Levoy, Marc, and Pat Hanrahan. 1996. Light Field Rendering. *Computer Graphics (SIGGRAPH '96 Proceedings)*, 31–42.

Lischinski, Dani. 1994. Incremental Delaunay Triangulation. In Heckbert, Paul S. (ed.), *Graphics Gems IV*. Boston: Academic Press, 47–59.

Litwinowicz, Peter, and Gavin Miller. 1994. Efficient Techniques for Interactive Texture Placement. *Computer Graphics (SIGGRAPH '94 Proceedings)*, 119–122.

Litwinowicz, Peter, and Lance Williams. 1994. Animating Images with Drawings. *Computer Graphics (SIGGRAPH '94 Proceedings)*, 409–412.

Loop, Charles, and Tony DeRose. 1990. Generalized B-Spline Surfaces and Arbitrary Topology. *Computer Graphics (SIGGRAPH '90 Proceedings)*, **24**(4), 347–356.

Lorensen, W. E., and H. E. Cline. 1987. Marching Cubes: A High Resolution 3D Surface Construction Algorithm. *Computer Graphics (SIGGRAPH '87 Proceedings)*, (7), 163–169.

Luebke, D., and C. Georges. 1995. Portals and Mirrors: Simple, Fast Evaluation of Potentially Visible Sets. *Proceedings of the 1995 Symposium on Interactive 3D Graphics*, 105–106.

Maccracken, Ron, and Kenneth I. Joy. 1996. Free-Form Deformation with Lattices of Arbitrary Topology. *Computer Graphics (SIGGRAPH '96 Proceedings)*, **30**, 181–188.

Mark, William R., Leonard McMillan, and Gary Bishop. 1997. Post-Rendering 3D Warping. *Proceedings of the 1997 Symposium on Interactive 3D Graphics*. ACM SIGGRAPH, 7–16.

Markarian, H., R. Bernstein, D. G. Ferneyhough, L. E. Gregg, and F. S. Sharp. 1971. Implementation of Digital Techniques for Correcting High Resolution Images. *Proc. Amer. Inst. Aeronautics and Astronautics, 8th Annual Meeting*, 285–304.

McMillan, Leonard, and Gary Bishop. 1995. Plenoptic Modeling: An Image-Based Rendering System. *Computer Graphics (SIGGRAPH '95 Proceedings)*, 39–46.

Milnor, J. 1965. *Topology from the Differentiable Viewpoint*. Charlottesville, VA: University of Virginia Press.

Munkres, J. M. 1984. *Elements of Algebraic Topology*. Menlo Park, CA: Addison-Wesley.

Neider, Jackie, Tom Davis, and Mason Woo. 1993. *OpenGL Programming Guide: The Official Guide to Learning OpenGL, Release 1*. Reading, MA: Addison-Wesley.

Paeth, Alan W. 1986. A Fast Algorithm for General Raster Rotation. *Proceedings of Graphics Interface '86*, 77–81.

Parent, Richard E. 1977. A System for Sculpting 3D Data. *Computer Graphics (SIGGRAPH '77 Proceedings)*, **11**(2), 138–147.

Payne, B. A., and A. W. Toga. 1992. Distance Field Manipulation of Surface Models. *IEEE Computer Graphics and Applications*, **12**(1), 65–71.

Peli, E., R. Aubliere, and G. T. Timberlake. 1987. Feature-Based Registration of Retinal Images. *IEEE Trans. Med. Im.*, **6**(3), 272–278.

Penna, Michael A., and Richard R. Patterson. 1986. *Projective Geometry and Its Applications to Computer Graphics*. Englewood Cliffs, NJ: Prentice Hall.

Perlin, Ken, and E. M. Hoffert. 1989. Hypertexture. *Computer Graphics (SIGGRAPH '89 Proceedings)*, **23**(3), 253–262.

Pinheiro, Sergio E. M. L. 1997. *Interactive Deformations Using Direct Specification*. Master's Thesis. PUC-Rio (in Portugese).

Porter, T., and T. Duff. 1984. Compositing Digital Images. *Computer Graphics (SIGGRAPH '84 Proceedings)*, **18**(3), 253–259.

Potmesil, M., and I. Chakravarty. 1982. Synthetic Image Generation with a Lens and Aperture Camera Model. *ACM Transactions on Graphics*, **1**(2), 85–108.

Preparata, F. P., and M. I. Shamos. 1985. *Computational Geometry: An Introduction*. New York: Springer-Verlag.

Prusinkiewicz, Przemyslaw, Mark S. Hammel, and Eric Mjolsness. 1993. Animation of Plant Development. *Computer Graphics (SIGGRAPH '93 Proceedings)*, **27**(Aug.), 351–360.

Prusinkiewicz, P., A. Lindenmayer, and J. Hanan. 1988. Developmental Models of Herbaceous Plants for Computer Imagery Purposes. *Computer Graphics (SIGGRAPH '88 Proceedings)*, **22**(4), 141–150.

Ranjan, V., and A. Fournier. 1996. Matching and Interpolation of Shapes Using Unions of Circles. *Computer Graphics Forum (Eurographics '96 Proceedings)*, **15**(3), C-129–C-141.

Reeves, W. R. 1983. Particle Systems: A Technique for Modeling a Class of Fuzzy Objects. *Computer Graphics (SIGGRAPH '83 Proceedings)*, **17**(3), 359–376.

Requicha, A. A. G. 1980. Representation for Rigid Solids: Theory, Methods, and Systems. *ACM Computing Surveys*, **12**(Dec.), 437–464.

Rose, Charles, Brian Guenter, Bobby Bodenheimer, and Michael F. Cohen. 1996. Efficient Generation of Motion Transitions using Spacetime Constraints. *Computer Graphics (SIGGRAPH '96 Proceedings)*, 147–154.

Rosenfeld, A. 1969. *Picture Processing by Computer*. New York: Academic Press.

Rossignac, J., and P. Borrel. 1993. Multi-Resolution 3D Approximations for Rendering Complex Scenes. *Modeling in Computer Graphics*. B. Falcidieno and T. L. Kunii (eds.), New York: Springer-Verlag, 455–465.

Rossignac, J., and A. Requicha. 1986. Offset Operations in Solid Modeling. *Computer Aided Geometric Design*, **3**, 129–148.

Ruprecht, Detlef, and Heinrich Müller. 1995. Image Warping with Scattered Data Interpolation. *IEEE Computer Graphics & Applications*, March, 37–43.

Samet, H. 1984. The Quadtree and Related Hierarchical Data Structures. *ACM Computing Surveys*, **16**, 187–260.

Schroeder, W. J., J. A. Zarge, and W. E. Lorensen. 1992. Decimation of Triangle Meshes. *Computer Graphics (SIGGRAPH '92 Proceedings)*, **26**(2), 65–70.

Schumaker, L. L. 1976. Fitting Surfaces to Scattered Data. In Lorentz G. G., C. K. Lui, and L. L. Schumaker (eds.), *Approximation Theory II*. San Diego: Academic Press, 203–268.

Sclaroff, S., and A. Pentland. 1994. Object Recognition and Categorization Using Modal Matching. *Proceedings of 2nd IEEE CAD-Based Vision Workshop*, 258–265.

Sederberg, Thomas W., Peishing Gao, Guojin Wang, and Hong Mu. 1992. 2D Shape Blending: An Intrinsic Solution to the Vertex Path Problem. *Computer Graphics (SIGGRAPH '93 Proceedings)*, **27**, 15–18.

Sederberg, Thomas W., and Eugene Greenwood. 1992. A Physically Based Approach to 2-D Shape Blending. *Computer Graphics (SIGGRAPH '92 Proceedings)*, **26**, 25–34.

Sederberg, T., and S. Parry. 1986. Free-Form Deformation of Solid Geometric Models. *Computer Graphics (SIGGRAPH '86 Proceedings)*, **20**(4), 151–160.

Serra, J. 1982. *Image Analysis and Mathematical Morphology*. San Diego: Academic Press.

Sethian, J. A. 1996. *Level Set Methods: Evolving Interfaces in Geometry, Fluid Mechanics, Computer Vision and Materials Sciences*. New York: Cambridge University Press.

Shade, Jonathan, Dani Lischinski, David H. Salesin, Tony DeRose, and John Snyder. 1996. Hierarchical Image Caching for Accelerated Walkthroughs of Complex Environments. *Computer Graphics (SIGGRAPH '96 Proceedings)*, 75–82.

Shannon, C. E. 1949. *The Mathematical Theory of Communication*. Urbana, IL: University of Illinois Press.

Shapira, M., and A. Rappoport. 1995. Shape Blending Using the Star Skeleton Representation. *IEEE Computer Graphics and Applications*, **15**, 44–50.

Shepard, D. 1968. A Two-Dimensional Interpolation Function for Irregularly Spaced Data. *Proc. 23rd National Conference of the ACM*, 517–524.

Shoemake, K. 1985. Animating Rotation with Quaternion Curves. *Computer Graphics (SIGGRAPH '85 Proceedings)*, **19**, 245–254.

Shoemake, Ken. 1994. Arcball Rotation Control. In *Graphics Gems IV*, 175–192. San Diego: Academic Press.

Sims, Karl. 1990. Particle Animation and Rendering Using Data Parallel Computation. *Computer Graphics (SIGGRAPH '90 Proceedings)*, **24**, 405–413.

Sims, Karl. 1991. Artificial Evolution for Computer Graphics. *Computer Graphics (SIGGRAPH '91 Proceedings)*, **25**(4), 319–328.

Sloan, Peter-Pike, Michael Cohen, and Steven J. Gortler. 1997. Time Critical Lumigraph Rendering. *Proceedings of the 1997 Symposium on Interactive 3D Graphics*. ACM SIGGRAPH, 17–23.

Smith, Alvy Ray. 1984a. *Graftal Formalism Notes*. Technical memo 4. Pixar, Richmond, CA.

Smith, Alvy Ray. 1984b. Plants, Fractals and Formal Languages. *Computer Graphics (SIGGRAPH '84 Proceedings)*, **18**(3), 1–10.

Smith, Alvy Ray. 1987. Planar 2-Pass Texture Mapping and Warping. *Computer Graphics (SIGGRAPH '87 Proceedings)*, **21**(4), 263–272.

Smith, M. 1974. Computers and the Art of Animation. In Halas, John (ed.), *Computer Animation*. New York: Hastings House, 149–155.

Smithe, D. B. 1990. *A Two-Pass Mesh Warping Algorithm for Object Transformation and Image Interpolation*. Technical Memo #1030. Industrial Light and Magic.

Stein, Charles S., and Lewis E. Hitchner. 1988. The Multiresolution Dissolve. *SMPTE Journal*, (Dec.), 977–984.

Stollnitz, E. J., T. D. DeRose, and D. H. Salesin. 1996. *Wavelets for Computer Graphics*. San Francisco: Morgan Kaufmann.

Stroustrup, Bjarne. 1997. *The C++ Programming Language, Third Edition*. Reading, MA: Addison-Wesley.

Sun, Y. M., W. Wang, and F. Y. L. Chin. 1995. Interpolating Polyhedral Models Using Intrinsic Shape Parameters. *Proceedings of the Third Pacific Conference on Computer Graphics and Applications, Pacific Graphics '95*. World Scientific, 133–147.

Sutherland, Ivan E. 1963. Sketchpad: A Man-Machine Graphical Communication System. In *SJCC*. New York: Crown Publishers, Inc., Spartan Books.

Szeliski, Richard. 1996. Video Mosaics for Virtual Environments. *IEEE Computer Graphics and Applications*, (Mar.), 22–30.

Tanaka, A., M. Kameyama, S. Kazama, and O. Watanabe. 1986. A Rotation Method for Raster Image Using Skew Transformation. *IEEE Conference on Computer Vision and Pattern Recognition Proceedings*, 272–277.

Teller, S., and C. H. Séquin. 1991. Visibility Preprocessing for Interactive Walkthroughs. *Computer Graphics (SIGGRAPH '91 Proceedings)*, **25**(4), 61–69.

Terzopoulos, Demetri, and Kurt Fleischer. 1988. Modeling Inelastic Deformation: Viscoelasticity, Plasticity, Fracture. *Computer Graphics (SIGGRAPH '88 Proceedings)*, **22**, 269–278.

Thompson, D. W. 1961. *On Growth and Form*. New York: Cambridge University Press.

Torborg, Jay, and James T. Kajiya. 1996. Talisman: Commodity Realtime 3D Graphics for the PC. *Computer Graphics (SIGGRAPH '96 Proceedings)*, 353–364.

Turk, Greg. 1992. Re-Tiling Polygonal Surfaces. *Computer Graphics (SIGGRAPH '92 Proceedings)*, **26**(2), 55–64.

Unuma, M., K. Anjyo, and R. Takeuchi. 1995. Fourier Principles for Emotion-Based Human Figure Animation. *Computer Graphics (SIGGRAPH '95 Proceedings)*.

Velho, Luiz, and Jonas Gomes. 1996. Approximate Conversion of Parametric to Implicit Surfaces. *Computer Graphics Forum*, **15**(5), 327–338.

Watson, Benjamin A., and Larry F. Hodges. 1995. Using Texture Maps to Correct for Optical Distortion in Head-Mounted Displays. In Bryson, Steven, and Steven Feiner (eds.), *Proceedings of IEEE Virtual Reality Annual International Symposium '95*, 172–178.

Weaver, J. 1989. *Theory of Discrete and Continuous Fourier Transform*. New York: John Wiley and Sons.

Webster. 1989. *Webster's Encyclopedic Unabridged Dictionary of the English Language*. New York: Random House.

Weiman, Carl F. R. 1980. Continuous Anti-Aliased Rotation and Zoom of Raster Images. *Computer Graphics (SIGGRAPH '80 Proceedings)*, **14**(3), 286–293.

Welch, W., M. Gleicher, and A. Witkin. 1991. *Manipulating Surfaces Differentially*. Technical Report. CMU.

Wesley, E. Bethel, and S. P. Uselton. 1989. Shape Distortion in Computer-Assisted Keyframe Animation. In Thalmann, N. M., and D. Thalmann (eds.), *State-of-the-Art in Computer Animation*, 215–224. New York: Springer-Verlag.

Westover, L. 1992. *Splatting: A Parallel, Feed-Forward Volume Rendering Algorithm*. Ph.D. Thesis, University of North Carolina at Chapel Hill.

Williams, Lance. 1983. Pyramidal Parametrics. *Computer Graphics (SIGGRAPH '83 Proceedings)*, **17**, 1–11.

Witkin, Andrew, and Zoran Popović. 1995. Motion Warping. *Computer Graphics (SIGGRAPH '95 Proceedings)*, 105–108.

Wolberg, George. 1989. Skeleton-Based Image Warping. *The Visual Computer*, **5**(1/2), 95–108.

Wolberg, G. 1990. *Digital Image Warping*. Los Alamitos, CA: IEEE Computer Society Press.

Wyvill, Brian. 1994. *Building and Animating Implicit Surface Models*. In SIGGRAPH '93 Course Notes.

Xia, J., and A. Varshney. 1996. Dynamic View-Dependent Simplification for Polygonal Models. *IEEE Visualization '96 Proceedings*. Los Alamitos, CA: IEEE Computer Society Press, 327–334, 498.

Zhang, Yuefeng. 1996. A Fuzzy Approach to Digital Image Warping. *IEEE Computer Graphics and Applications*, **16**(4), 34–41.

Zonenschein, Ruben, Jonas Gomes, Luiz Velho, and Luiz Henrique de Figueiredo. 1997. Texturing Implicit Surfaces with Particle Systems. *Computer Graphics (SIGGRAPH '97 Visual Proceedings)*, 172.

Index

About the Authors

Jonas Gomes is a professor at the Institute of Pure and Applied Mathematics (IMPA) in Rio de Janeiro. He received a Ph.D. in mathematics in 1984 at IMPA and has worked with computer graphics since then. He is a member of the Brazilian Academy of Sciences. He was the R&D manager of the graphics team at Globo Television Network from 1984 to 1988. He started the computer graphics research project at IMPA in 1990. This project is involved with research and development in graphics and also supports a graduate program in computer graphics.

He has published several books and research papers in graphics. He has organized four SIGGRAPH courses: "Modeling in Graphics" in SIGGRAPH '93, "Warping and Morphing of Graphical Objects" in SIGGRAPH '94 and '97, and "From Fourier Analysis to Wavelets" in SIGGRAPH '98.

His current research interests include the mathematical foundations of graphics, modeling, visualization, image processing and multimedia. He is the chief editor of the *Série de Computação e Matemática*, which publishes books in the Portuguese language on both the use of computers in mathematics and the use of mathematical models in computer science.

Lucia Darsa obtained M.Sc. degrees in computer science from SUNY at Stony Brook and from Pontificia Universidade Catolica (PUC) in Rio de Janiero. She has been involved with computer graphics research and development since 1990, having started at the VisGraf project at IMPA. She has worked with implicit surfaces rendering and modeling, motion control hardware, and image processing. Her current interests include real-time graphics and integrated environments for warping and morphing and their applications, specifically image-based rendering. She works at Equator Technologies, developing platform technology for digital convergence.

Bruno Costa works at Microsoft, creating and applying graphics technology to computer games. Games inspired him to start working with computer graphics in 1989, going from realistic rendering and image processing to real-time graphics and animation. His current interests involve image-based rendering, character motion, and real-time image processing. He has coauthored *Visionaire*, warping and morphing software published in 1992, as a by-product of his Master's research. He has an M.Sc. degree in computer graphics from SUNY at Stony Brook, and an M.Sc. degree in computer engineering from PUC in Rio de Janiero.

Luiz Velho is an associate researcher at IMPA. He received a B.E. in industrial design from Universidade do Rio de Janeiro (ESDI) in 1979; an M.S. in computer graphics from the Massachusetts Institute of Technology, Media Laboratory, in 1985; and a Ph.D. in computer science from the University of Toronto in 1994.

His experience in computer graphics spans the fields of modeling, rendering, imaging, and animation. In 1982 he was a visiting researcher at the National Film Board of Canada. From 1985 to 1987 he was a systems engineer at the Fantastic Animation Machine in New York, where he developed the company's 3D visualization system. From 1987 to 1991 he was a principal engineer at Globo TV Network in Brazil, where he created special-effects and visual simulation systems. In 1994 he was a visiting professor at the Courant Institute of Mathematical Sciences, New York University. His current research interests include theoretical foundations of computer graphics, physically based methods, wavelets, modeling with implicit objects, and volume visualization. He also organized the SIGGRAPH '98 course "From Fourier Analysis to Wavelets."

About the CD-ROM

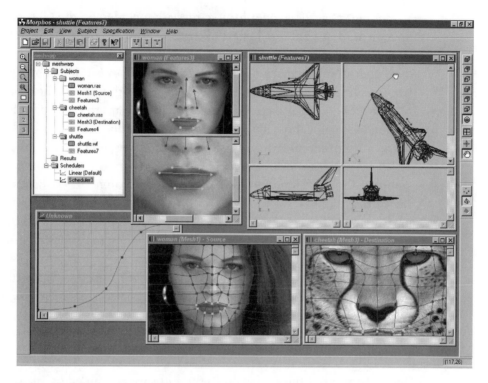

Figure CD-ROM.1 2D and 3D graphical objects with different interfaces and specification techniques in a *Morphos* project. See also color plate CD-ROM.1.

The conceptual framework introduced in this book allows a unified presentation of the different problems in the area of warping and morphing. We have brought this framework to the implementation level, developing a warping and morphing system called *Morphos* included on the companion CD-ROM. A detailed description of *Morphos'* architecture is found in Chapter 21.

Morphos is a fully featured warping and morphing package that works with diverse types of graphical objects, allowing the use of multiple specification and related computational techniques. It currently supports images, drawings, and 3D polygonal objects, being able to specify transformations using points, vectors, curves, spline meshes, and so forth. The entire package is provided, with full source code, exclusively on the companion CD-ROM. The

C++ source code contains about 40,000 lines of code and supports plug-ins, allowing full extension of the software for experimentation and learning. We also provide executables to run *Morphos* in the Windows 95/NT platforms directly.

Both user and developer html guides are included on the CD-ROM. This documentation contains hyperlinks to the source code to facilitate understanding and browsing. It is of a great value both to academic users and developers. No installation is necessary to run *Morphos*. It can be run directly from the html pages of the CD-ROM, or as stand-alone applications.

The CD-ROM also contains additional software that helps in the manipulation of graphical objects. Additional multimedia material is also included, in the form of samples, results, slide presentations, and references.

To be able to modify *Morphos* and the other software, you will need a complete C++ development system for your environment. We have developed the software under Windows NT using Microsoft Visual C++ 5.0, and we have included the corresponding workspace and project files. Although most of the software is portable, we do not provide any makefiles or instructions on porting the software to other environments.

Supplemental material to the CD-ROM and future versions of *Morphos* will be published on the warping and morphing Web site *www.visgraf.impa.br/ morph/*.

Copyright Note